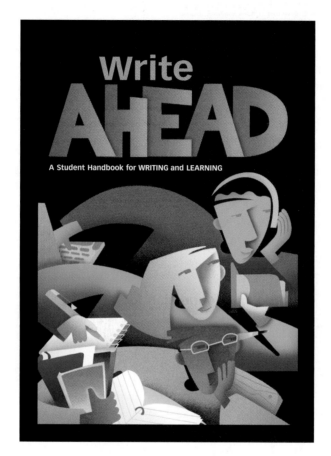

Write AHEAD

A Student Handbook for WRITING and LEARNING

Written and Compiled by
**Dave Kemper, Patrick Sebranek,
and Verne Meyer**

Illustrated by
Chris Krenzke

WRITE SOURCE®

GREAT SOURCE EDUCATION GROUP
a division of Houghton Mifflin Company
Wilmington, Massachusetts

Acknowledgements

We're grateful to many people who helped bring *Write Ahead* to life. First, we must thank all the teachers and students from across the country who contributed writing models and ideas. Also, thanks to the following consultants who helped make this book a reality.

Kitty Okano	**Patricia Payne**
Judith O'Loughlin	**Regina Peña**

In addition, we want to thank our Write Source/Great Source team for all their help: Laura Bachman, Ron Bachman, Colleen Belmont, Sherry Gordon, Kathy Henning, Kathy Kahnle, Rob King, Sonya Jongsma Knauss, Lois Krenzke, Ellen Leitheusser, Randy Rehberg, Lester Smith, Ken Taylor, Jean Varley, Sandy Wagner, and Claire Ziffer.

Technology Connection for *Write Ahead*

Visit our Web site for additional student models, writing prompts, updates for citing sources, multimedia reports, information about submitting your writing, and more.

The Write Source Web site . . . . . . <thewritesource.com>

Printed in the United States of America

International Standard Book Number: 0-669-50787-5 (hardcover)

1 2 3 4 5 6 7 8 9 10 -QWT- 11 10 09 08 07 06 05 04 03

International Standard Book Number: 0-669-50786-3 (softcover)

1 2 3 4 5 6 7 8 9 10 -QWT- 11 10 09 08 07 06 05 04 03

Using the Handbook

The *Write Ahead* handbook contains guidelines, samples, and strategies to help you improve your writing skills. It also contains information that will help you with your other learning skills, including reading textbooks, taking tests, and giving speeches. You will be able to find everything quickly and easily using the guides explained below.

The **Table of Contents** (starting on the next page) lists the five major sections in the handbook and the chapters found in each section. Use the table of contents when you are interested in a general topic.

The **Index** in the back of the handbook (starting on page 538) lists, in alphabetical order, all of the specific topics discussed in *Write Ahead*. Use the index when you are interested in a specific topic.

The **Color Coding** used for the "Proofreader's Guide" (yellow pages) makes this important section easy to find. These pages contain rules for spelling, grammar, usage, mechanics, and much more.

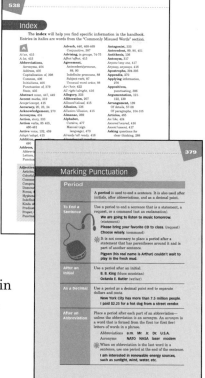

The **Special Page References** in the book itself tell you where to turn in the handbook for additional information about a specific topic. Example:

(See page 402.)

※ If, at first, you're not sure how to find something in the handbook, ask your teacher for help. With a little practice, you will find everything quickly and easily.

Table of
Contents

The Process of Writing

The Forms of Writing

The Tools of Learning

Proofreader's Guide

Student Almanac

Why Write?

Why write? The following story might answer this question:

> **In Africa, a little boy asked his father if the lion is the king of the jungle. His father replied, "Yes, son, the lion is the king of the jungle." The little boy said to his father, "Then why, when I read a story about a lion and a warrior, does the warrior always win?" The father answered, "When the lion learns to write, the ending will then, and only then, be different."**

Writing requires the ability to reason, or think things out. While you and all of your classmates have this ability, lions and other four-legged creatures do not. Thinking and writing give each of you special powers—the ability to explain, describe, analyze, persuade, and, of course, tell a story.

Write Ahead and You

The *Write Ahead* student handbook will help you develop your writing, thinking, and learning skills. Once you get to know this handbook, it will become your most valuable school resource:

Writing Skills Writing is covered in a variety of ways, including how to write paragraphs, essays, and narratives.

Study-Reading Skills The reading strategies included in your handbook will help you read with more purpose.

Learning Skills Thinking clearly, speaking and listening, and taking notes are some of the skills covered in *Write Ahead.*

Editing and Language Skills The "Proofreader's Guide" covers all of the rules for language and grammar.

There's More!

The "Student Almanac" in the back of the handbook includes charts and maps that cover everything from science and math to geography and history. This section truly makes *Write Ahead* an all-school handbook—and your personal learning guide.

Learning
About the
Writing Process

All About Writing

Experienced basketball players know exactly how to react to every situation during a game: A lane is clear, and they drive to the basket. A shot goes up, and they automatically get in position for a rebound. An opponent dribbles into a corner, and they immediately double-team the player.

In the same way, experienced writers know how to react to every situation during a writing project: An assignment is made, and they start listing possible writing ideas. A first draft sounds dull, so they improve the personal voice. A revised draft needs editing, so they check the words and sentences for style and correctness.

Writer James L. Collins says, "Control is at the heart of writing development." And control comes from learning the fundamentals and practicing them. (Ask any writing teacher, or basketball coach.) Every chapter in this section will help you learn the fundamentals of writing.

What's Ahead

This chapter reviews the five steps in the writing process, provides tips for building good writing habits, and much more.

- Building Good Writing Habits
- The Steps in the Writing Process
- The Writing Process in Action
- A Basic Writing Guide

"Young writers **need to know** what can be done with **language**."

—Ralph Fletcher

Building Good Writing Habits

To become a good writer, you should act like one, which means that you should follow the tips listed on this page.

- **Make reading an important part of your life.** Read anything and everything—books, magazines, and newspapers. Reading helps you see how effective stories and essays are put together.

- **Make writing an important part of your life.** Write every day. When writing becomes something that you want to do, rather than something that you have to do, you will begin to see improvement. (Do your personal writing in a journal. See pages 145-148 for guidelines and tips.)

- **Write about topics that really matter to you.** In your personal writing, explore your thoughts, feelings, and experiences. In your assignments, write about topics that have special meaning to you. You can learn a lot about writing when you deal with topics that truly interest you.

- **Set high standards.** If a first draft does not seem inviting, add more detail or voice to the writing. If the verbs in your writing are too general, replace them with more specific ones. Writer William Zinsser says, "Quality is its own reward." In other words, you will feel good about your writing if it is the result of your best efforts.

- **Try different forms.** Write stories, poems, essays, or letters. They all can teach you something about writing.

- **Become a student of writing.** Learn about the traits of effective writing (see pages 19-24), and build your writing vocabulary. You should, for example, know what is meant by *main ideas, specific details,* and *linking words.* You should also know the difference between *narrative, descriptive, expository,* and *persuasive* writing.

(**Think process.** Think of writing as a process in which you explore and shape your thoughts. (See the next page.))

The Steps in the Writing Process

A famous Supreme Court justice once said, "There is no such thing as good writing, only good rewriting." He knew from experience that writing must go through a series of steps before it is ready to share. That is why writing is called a process. (*Process* means "the steps or actions it takes to do something.") To do your best work, you should think of writing as a process. The steps described below cover the process from start to finish.

Prewriting At the start of the process, a writer explores possible topics before selecting one to write about. A topic can be a person, a place, a thing, an event, or an idea. Then a writer collects details about the topic and plans how to use them.

Writing Next, a writer does the actual writing, connecting his or her ideas about the topic. This writing is called the *first* draft because it is not a finished piece.

Revising During revising, a writer reviews the first draft and changes any parts that are not clear or complete. He or she may also ask a partner to review the draft.

Editing A writer then edits the revised writing for style and correctness and prepares a neat final copy. The final copy is proofread for errors before it is shared.

Publishing This is the final step in the writing process. Publishing simply means "sharing a finished piece of writing." There are many forms of publishing.

Points to Remember . . .

- **Writers may move back and forth between the steps in the process.** For example, after starting a first draft, a writer may decide to learn more about the topic before going any further.
- **Each writer's process is different.** Some writers do a lot of their early work in their heads, while others need to put everything on paper. In addition, some writers find it helpful to talk about their work throughout the process.
- **No two writing assignments develop in the same way.** A writer may do a lot of prewriting and planning for one assignment, and go immediately to the first draft for another.

"One of the best things about writing is that you can **keep working** on it **until you get it right**, until the words say what you want them to say."

—Andrea Estepa

The Writing Process in Action

Writing is the process of exploring your thoughts, feelings, and experiences. The next two pages show you the writing process in action. Use this information as a general guide whenever you write. *Remember:* If you follow the steps in the writing process, you will do your best work.

Prewriting / Choosing a Topic

1. Explore possible topics to write about. If you need help, try one of the selecting strategies on pages 42-48.
2. Choose a specific topic that really interests you and meets the requirements of the assignment.

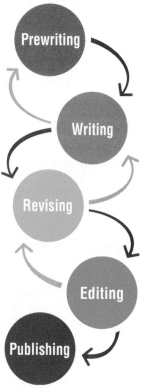

Gathering Details

1. Learn as much as you can about your topic using the strategies listed on pages 50-54. If you already know a lot about your topic, you may not need to do much collecting.
2. Collect details by reading or talking about your subject.
3. Think of a focus for your writing. (A *focus* is an interesting part of the topic that you want to write about.)
4. Decide which details you will include in your writing. (Select details that support your focus.) Also decide on the best way to organize these details. (See pages 57-58 for help.)

Writing — Writing the First Draft

1. Complete your first draft while your prewriting is still fresh in your mind. Keep your writing as neat as possible, but don't worry if you cross out a few words.
2. Use your planning as a guide, but feel free to add new ideas that come to mind. (See pages 59-64.)
3. Keep your audience and purpose in mind as you write.
4. Write until you get all of your ideas on paper. (Remember that your writing should have a beginning, a middle, and an ending.)

Revising — Improving Your Writing

1. Review your first draft, but only after setting it aside for a while. If possible, have another person review your work as well.
2. Decide which parts need to be changed. Look for ideas that are out of order or confusing.
3. Improve your writing by adding, cutting, rewriting, or reordering different parts. (See pages 65-72.)

Editing — Checking for Style and Correctness

1. Edit your revised writing for style by checking for effective word choice and smooth-reading sentences.
2. Then check for capitalization, punctuation, spelling, and grammar errors. (See pages 378-471 for help.) Also ask a trusted friend to check for errors.
3. Prepare a neat final copy of your writing. Proofread this copy for errors.

Publishing — Sharing Your Writing

1. Share your final copy with your classmates, teacher, friends, and family members.
2. Decide if you will include the writing in your portfolio. (See pages 29-34 for help.)
3. Think about submitting your writing for publication outside of your classroom. (See pages 35-39 for ideas.)

"The best advice I've ever received was 'Rewrite it!' A lot of editors said that. They were all right. **Writing is really rewriting**."

—Robert Lipsyte

A Basic Writing Guide

On the next three pages, you can find answers to seven important questions about the writing process.

1. How should I get started

First make sure that you understand everything about the assignment—including the purpose, audience, and due date. Then select a topic that you find personally meaningful. Doing otherwise makes about as much sense as joining the track team when softball is your first love.

Remember: You won't be able to do your best work unless you have strong feelings about a topic.

See pages 41-48 for selecting strategies to use.

2. Do I have to gather a lot of details before I write

That depends on the assignment. If you are writing about one of your personal experiences, you already know the important facts and details. So you may be able to start the first draft right away.

But let's say you are writing an essay about a specific health-related issue. You may have quite a bit of gathering to do before you are ready to write.

Start your collecting by talking about your topic with someone you know. Also record your thoughts about it. Then try one or two of the gathering activities listed in the handbook.

Remember: You can never know too much about a topic.

See pages 49-54 for gathering strategies to use.

3. Should I use all of the information that I have gathered ❓

No, you should decide on a focus for your writing. A focus is an interesting part of the topic that you want to emphasize or a special feeling you have about the topic. In an essay or a report, the focus is usually expressed in a thesis statement. Then, when you write, include only those details that support or explain your focus.

Remember: Writing that lacks focus is hard to follow.

See page 56 for information about finding a focus.

4. How should I write my first draft ❓

When you write your first draft, follow any plan or outline that you may have put together, but also feel free to add new ideas as they come to mind. Keep going until you get all of your ideas on paper.

Remember: A first draft is your first look at a developing writing idea; you will make changes as you go along.

See pages 59-64 for more tips on writing first drafts.

5. How do I know what changes or revisions to make in my first draft ❓

When you revise, concentrate on the ideas, organization, and voice in your writing: *Are your ideas clear and complete? Are they in the best order? Do you sound truly interested in the topic? Does the language seem right for your audience?* After answering these questions, add to, cross out, rewrite, and reorder the ideas in your first draft.

Make changes until all of the parts—the beginning, middle, and ending—say exactly what you want them to say.

Remember: You are the best judge of your own writing, but it also helps to have one or two other people review your work.

See pages 65-72 for more information about revising.

6. Do I have to find all of the spelling and grammar errors in my writing ?

No one expects you to be an expert speller or a master of all the grammar rules. But *everyone* expects you to correct as many errors as you can before you share a finished piece of writing.

First find as many errors as you can on your own. Then ask a trusted classmate to check your work for errors. Since professional writers have editors who help them edit and proofread their work, so should you.

Remember: Don't be too concerned about finding the errors in your writing until you have made the important revisions in your first draft.

See pages 77-81 for information about editing and proofreading.

7. How do I know if my writing is good ?

Here is a quick way to evaluate your writing. If you can answer *yes* to at least three of these questions, you should feel good about your writing.

_____ Did I select a topic that really interests me?

_____ Did I find a focus—a special way to write about this topic?

_____ Did I make changes in the writing so that all of my ideas are clearly stated?

_____ Did I ask others to review my writing?

Remember: Writing that works best includes stimulating ideas, engaging voice, original word choice, and so on. (See page 24.)

Refer to your handbook for other checklists and rubrics that can be used as assessment guides.

One Writer's Process

Some people complain about "writer's block"—staring at a blank piece of paper and not being able to write a single word. Writer's block results from the fear of taking risks or making mistakes in the writing. All of your favorite writers are risk takers. Even when their "risks" don't turn out so well, they still have the opportunity to change and improve their ideas. It's all part of the writing process.

Well-known editor Maxwell Perkins gives this advice about writing: "Just get it down on paper, and then we'll see what to do with it." That's the point of the writing process. Your writing must go through a series of changes before it is ready to share. You collect your thoughts, write a first draft, make revisions, and so on. Each change that you make gets you closer to the finish—an effective story or essay.

What's Ahead

This chapter shows how student writer Latrisha Jones used the writing process to produce an effective personal story. As you will see, she did a lot of planning, writing, and revising.

- Prewriting: Selecting and Gathering
- Writing: Writing the First Draft
- Revising: Improving Your Writing
- Editing: Checking for Style and Correctness
- Publishing: Sharing Your Writing

Prewriting / Selecting a Topic

Latrisha Jones was asked to share a personal adventure. To get started, she considered a number of possible topics.

Listing: Latrisha listed a few recent experiences. After a quick review, she circled the one she wanted to write about.

Adventurous Experiences
tobogganing at the Dunes
monster fest at the theater
(feast at the Islamic Center)
swimming at the Dells

Gathering Details

To gather details, Latrisha first answered the 5 W's and H.

Who? — *Helah and me*
What? — *ate Persian food and listened to Pakistani music*
When? — *about three months ago, during Ramadan*
Where? — *at the Islamic Center*
Why? — *to learn about Helah's religion and celebrate Ramadan with her*
How? — *by attending the annual Ramadan feast*

Time Line: Since personal stories are arranged chronologically (by time), Latrisha used a time line to help with her planning. Above the time line, she listed the actions related to the event; below the line, she listed thoughts and details related to each action.

Feast at Islamic Center

met Helah at the Islamic Center	learned about Ramadan	watched the praying	joined in the feast
nervous about what to expect	reason for fasting, eating a date	women and men pray separately	dancing, kabobs great

Writing | Writing the First Draft

Latrisha freely wrote her first draft using her 5 W's and H chart and timeline as basic guides. Here is the first part of her first draft.

The sun was setting behind me. I walked into the Islamic Center. I was going to a feast to celebrate the holiest month of the Islamic year: Ramadan

Latrisha"! called a voice. I turned to see my friend Helah coming toward me. She wore a pretty hooded robe that reached to her ankles, and she was smiling.

"Helah! I said. I took her hands. "I'm so nervous!" I touched the kente hat I'd worn.

Helah smiled. "I like the hat, but you didn't have to cover your head. We know you're not Muslim. We just want you to celebrate with us."

I wondered what to expect? Would I see stuff from old movies? No. Instead, I saw floors, painted cinder blocks, ceiling tiles, and lights. This could almost have been Grover Cleveland high.

Latrisha sets the scene for the experience.

She uses dialogue to move the story along.

After a short break, Latrisha reviewed her first draft. Her review prompted the following revisions or changes.

Details are added to help explain the action.

The sun was setting behind me. I walked into

I'd never been in a mosk. Now

the Islamic Center. I was going to a feast to celebrate

the holiest month of the Islamic year: Ramadan

Latrisha"! called a voice. I turned to see my

friend Helah coming toward me. She wore a pretty

hooded robe that reached to her ankles, and she was

smiling.

"Helah! I said. I took her hands. "I'm so

Girls were supposed to cover their heads.

nervous!" I touched the kente hat I'd worn.

Helah smiled. "I like the hat, but you didn't have

to cover your head. We know you're not Muslim. We

just want you to celebrate with us."

A paragraph is moved.

I wondered what to expect? Would I see stuff

from old movies? No. Instead, I saw floors, painted

cinder blocks, ceiling tiles, and lights. This could

almost have been Grover Cleveland high.

Revising / Using Peer Responses

Latrisha also had her friend Helah react to the first draft. Helah's comments (see side notes) prompted more changes.

The sun was setting behind me. I walked into the Islamic Center. I'd never been in a mosk. Now I was going to a feast to celebrate the holiest month of the Islamic year: Ramadan

What kind of "stuff" from old movies?

I wondered what to expect? Would I see ~~stuff from~~ *big pillows and tapestries, like in the* old movies? No. Instead, I saw floors, painted cinder

What details were similar to GCH?

blocks, ceiling tiles, and lights. This could almost have been Grover Cleveland high. *Kid's drawings celebrating Ramadan. Essays about being Muslim in America.*

Latrisha"! called a voice. I turned to see my friend Helah coming toward me. She wore a pretty hooded *caftan, a silk* robe that reached to her ankles, and she was smiling.

The robe is silk and is called a "caftan."

"Helah! I said. I took her hands. "I'm so nervous!" I touched the kente hat I'd worn. Girls were supposed to cover their heads.

Helah smiled. "I like the hat, but you didn't have to cover your head. We know you're not Muslim. We just want you to celebrate with us."

Editing Checking for Style

After Latrisha had made all of her revisions, she was ready to edit her revised writing for style. She paid special attention to word choice and sentence structure.

Choppy sentences are combined.	The sun was setting behind me, ^as^ I walked into the Islamic Center. I'd never been in a mosk. ^but^ Now I was going to a feast to celebrate the holiest month of the Islamic year: Ramadan
Word choice is improved.	I wondered what to expect? Would I see ~~big~~ *puffy* pillows and *fancy* tapestries, like in the old movies? No. Instead, I saw *lynolium* floors, painted cinder blocks, ceiling tiles, and *floresint* lights. This could almost have been Grover Cleveland high. *On the walls hung* Kid's drawings celebrating Ramadan, *and* ~~Essays about being Muslim in America.~~
Sentence fragments are corrected.	
A more specific verb is used.	Latrisha"! called a voice. I turned to see my friend Helah ~~coming~~ *hurrying* toward me. She wore a pretty hooded caftan, a silk robe that reached to her ankles, and she was *beaming* ~~smiling.~~

"Helah! I said. I took her hands. "I'm so nervous!" I touched the kente hat I'd worn. Girls were supposed to cover their heads.

Editing ▸ Checking for Correctness

Next, Latrisha checked her writing for errors. She had a trusted editor, her mother, check her writing for errors, too. (See the inside back-cover of the handbook for the common editing and proofreading symbols.)

Spelling errors are corrected.

End punctuation is added and corrected.

Other punctuation is corrected.

A proper adjective is capitalized.

The sun was setting behind me as I walked into the Islamic Center. I'd never been in a *mosk* **mosque** but now I was going to a feast to celebrate the holiest month of the Islamic year: Ramadan⊙

I wondered what to expect? Would I see puffy pillows and fancy tapestries, like in the old movies? No. Instead, I saw *lynolium* **linoleum** floors, painted cinder blocks, ceiling tiles, and *floresint* **fluorescent** lights. This could almost have been Grover Cleveland **H**igh. On the walls, hung kid's drawings celebrating Ramadan and essays about being Muslim in America.

"Latrisha!" called a voice. I turned to see my friend Helah hurrying toward me. She wore a pretty hooded caftan, a silk robe that reached to her ankles, and she was beaming.

"Helah!" I said as I took her hands. "I'm so nervous!" I touched the **K**ente hat I'd worn. Girls were

Publishing / Sharing Your Writing

Publishing means "making public," and Latrisha made sure her narrative was clean and correct before she shared it with classmates and teachers. Here is a portion of Latrisha's first page. (See pages 26-27 for design tips for final copies.)

Latrisha Jones
Ms. Stinebrink
Language Arts
January 27, 2004

Ramadan Feast

The sun was setting behind me as I walked into

the Islamic Center. I'd never been in a mosque, but

now I was going to a feast to celebrate the holiest

month of the Islamic year: Ramadan.

I wondered what to expect. Would I see puffy

pillows and fancy tapestries, like in the old movies?

No. Instead, I saw linoleum floors, painted cinder

Points to Remember . . .

- **Prewriting makes writing easier.** It helped Latrisha get ready to write. She listed ideas, answered the 5 W's and H, and used a time line to decide what to say and when to say it.
- **Let the first draft flow.** Once Latrisha was ready to write, she worked quickly, not fussing over every word. She got the story on paper, where she could work with it.
- **Revising makes writing better.** Latrisha put her work aside and came back to it later when she could see ways to improve it. She then revised and refined her ideas until her story said what she wanted it to say.

Traits of Effective Writing

At times, jazz musicians stay with the beat, playing within a specific rhythm or pattern; at other times, they improvise, suddenly breaking out of the basic structure to create a whole new sound. Good writers often work in a similar way. They start with a basic plan, but as they go along, new ideas may come to mind, taking them in more interesting directions. As writer Ken Macrorie says, "Good writing is formed partly through plan *and* partly through accident."

You will do your best writing if you keep an open mind, always expecting to take a few side trips that reveal new ways of thinking about your topic. Writing that isn't forced, that is formed "partly through accident," will likely display the traits found in all good writing—stimulating ideas, engaging voice, original word choice, and so on.

What's Ahead

The next page in this chapter reviews the traits of effective writing. The pages that follow give writing samples that show these traits in action. Think of this chapter as your guide to good writing.

- Traits of Effective Writing
- Writing Traits in Action
- Evaluating Your Writing

> "Don't take yourself too seriously. **Good writing can't be forced**." —Donald Murray

Traits of Effective Writing

There are six main traits found in the best essays, stories, and reports. (A *trait* is a quality or feature.) Write with these traits in mind, and you and your readers will be pleased with the results.

STIMULATING IDEAS

Effective writing presents plenty of interesting information. It holds a reader's attention from start to finish and shows that the writer knows a lot about his or her topic.

LOGICAL ORGANIZATION

Good writing has a clearly developed beginning, middle, and ending. The overall organization effectively holds the writing together and makes it easy to follow.

ENGAGING VOICE

In the best writing, you can hear the writer's personal voice. Voice is the special way a writer expresses his or her ideas. Writing that has voice shows that a writer really cares about his or her topic.

ORIGINAL WORD CHOICE

Good writing contains all the right words in all the right places. It includes vivid action verbs (*sizzle, stumble, chop*), specific nouns (*stopwatch, chili, laptop*) and colorful modifiers (*earsplitting, shocking, steamy*).

EFFECTIVE SENTENCE STYLE

Effective writing flows from sentence to sentence, but it isn't predictable. Sentences vary in length and begin in different ways. Smooth-reading sentences give writing a pleasing rhythm.

CORRECT, ACCURATE COPY

Good writing follows the rules for punctuation, mechanics, usage, and spelling. It is carefully edited to make sure that it is accurate and easy to follow.

Writing Traits in Action

On the next three pages, a writing sample is provided for each of the six traits of effective writing.

STIMULATING IDEAS

In the following passage from *Catfish and Mandala* by Andrew X. Pham, the writer describes a low point in his life.

Four months ago, I emerged from Mexico and returned to the Bay Area, jobless and homeless. I did something unthinkable in America: I moved home to my parents. It was the perfect Vietnamese thing to do, fall back into the folds of the clan. Free food, free shelter while you lick your wounds and plot your resurrection. My non-Asian friends pitied me. My Vietnamese-American friends wondered why I hadn't lived at home in the first place; a good son doesn't leave home until he is married. . . .

No one, not my brothers or my best friends, know about my plan to bicycle to Vietnam.

Pham discusses his difficult return home and gives interesting information about Vietnamese culture. The passage makes a reader want to find out what happens next in Pham's life.

LOGICAL ORGANIZATION

In this passage from *The Short Sweet Dream of Eduardo Gutiérrez,* Jimmy Breslin captures the drama of an attempted border crossing into Texas from Mexico.

At dawn, the group stopped while the guide looked at his watch and muttered. A truck was supposed to be here, he said. They waited for two hours. Then in the first heat of morning, Silvia walked into a town with her uncle and Moises, Eduardo's cousin, to buy food. Suddenly a white Border Patrol van came onto the street. The three crouched behind bushes—big bushes that could hide them all day, Silvia thought. Some moments later, she heard a sound alongside her. Next to her now was the polished boot of an immigration agent. Several Border Patrol cops with guns in their hands stood over them. They put Silvia, her uncle, and Moises into the van and . . .

Breslin organizes this scene chronologically (by time), using the following linking words and phrases—"at dawn," "then in the first heat of morning," "suddenly," and "some moments later."

ENGAGING VOICE

In the following sample from "What's Wrong with Black English?" Rachel L. Jones discusses her troubles with language.

I'm a 21-year-old black born to a family that would probably be considered lower-middle class—which in my mind is a polite way of describing a condition only slightly better than poverty. Let's just say we rarely if ever did the winter vacation thing in the Caribbean. I've often had to defend my humble beginnings to a most unlikely group of people for an even less likely reason. Because of the way I talk, some of my black peers look at me sideways and ask, "Why do you talk like you're white?"

The first time it happened to me I was nine years old. Cornered in the school bathroom by the class bully and her sidekick, I was offered the opportunity to swallow a few of my teeth unless I satisfactorily explained why I always got good grades, why I talked "proper" or "white." I had no ready answer for her, save the fact that my mother had from the time I was old enough to talk stressed the importance of reading and learning . . .

Note how Jones's personal voice comes through in her writing. Ideas like ". . . we rarely if ever did the winter vacation thing in the Caribbean" and "I was offered the opportunity to swallow a few of my teeth" reveal her clever sense of humor.

ORIGINAL WORD CHOICE

In the following excerpt from A Beautiful Mind, the biography of mathematician John Nash, author Sylvia Nasar describes Nash's hometown during World War II.

The war came thundering through Bluefield, West Virginia, in the roaring, rattling shapes of freight car after freight car heaped high with coal from the great Pocahontas coalfield in the mountains to the west . . . and troop trains crowded with sailors and soldiers, round-faced farm boys from Iowa and Indiana and edgy factory hands from Pittsburgh and Chicago. The war shook and rattled the city out of its Depression slumber, filling its warehouses and streets, making overnight fortunes for scrap speculators and wheeler-dealers of all kinds.

See how Nasar uses descriptive expressions like "thundering through Bluefield, West Virginia," "roaring, rattling shapes," "round-faced farm boys," and "edgy factory hands" to capture the war fever in the town. Also note the specific action verbs "heaped," "shook," and "rattled."

EFFECTIVE SENTENCE STYLE

In this excerpt from *An American Story*, Debra J. Dickerson talks about young women, like herself, who have enlisted in the military.

Most of the other young enlisteds were either working class, like myself, or rural. Also like me, most were diamonds in the rough. While I'd only just begun to see it in myself, I was saddened by how many of these bright, inquisitive young people had no idea how smart they were. One woman on my squad was breezing through Serbo-Croatian during the day and teaching herself Polish at night with my roommate's materials, just for the joy of it. When I complimented her, her eyes went round. Then she burst into tears. No one had ever told her she was talented. I was surrounded by gifted, hardworking, self-sacrificing kids whom society was prepared to squander, but for the services.

> Notice how smoothly this passage reads from sentence to sentence. This shows that the writer paid special attention to the sound, length, and flow of each idea. No two sentences start in the same way, and the sentences vary in length from 5 to 29 words.

CORRECT, ACCURATE COPY

In the following passage from *A Personal Odyssey*, writer Thomas Sowell re-creates a heated phone conversation that he had as a young man with a magistrate (court official).

"I've decided not to come in for any meetings," I told the magistrate.
"It's not up to you!" he said angrily. "The law requires you to come in."
"I'm not coming in."
"We can go get you."
"You can't find me."
"We know where you live!"
"I've moved."
"We know where you work!"
"I've quit."
"We can still find you! You're in violation of the law!"
"There are eight million people in New York," I said. "You'll never find me."
There was a long pause on the other end of the line. When the magistrate came back on again, he had a wholly different tone and a quieter voice.

> Sowell starts a new paragraph each time a different person speaks; he is also careful to set the words of each speaker within quotation marks. The result is a conversation that is easy to follow.

Evaluating Your Writing

Use the following checklist to decide if something you or your classmate has written includes the traits of effective writing.

Assessment Rubric

____ **STIMULATING IDEAS**

The writing . . .

- presents important and interesting information.
- has a clear focus or purpose.
- holds the reader's attention.

____ **LOGICAL ORGANIZATION**

- includes a clear beginning, middle, and ending.
- uses specific details to support main ideas.

____ **ENGAGING VOICE**

- shows enthusiasm for the topic.
- speaks in a pleasing and sincere way.

____ **ORIGINAL WORD CHOICE**

- contains specific and colorful words.
- uses a level of language that the audience can relate to.

____ **EFFECTIVE SENTENCE STYLE**

- flows smoothly from sentence to sentence.
- uses varied sentence beginnings and lengths.

____ **CORRECT, ACCURATE COPY**

- follows the basic rules of grammar, punctuation, and spelling.
- observes the established format.

Writing with a Computer

Writer William Zinsser calls the computer his "perfect new writing toy" because it allows him to write, and rewrite, more easily. A computer can be the perfect writing tool for you, too, but only if you know how to keyboard. (To hunt and peck actually slows down the process.)

The computer is especially useful for revising and editing. When revising, you can easily rewrite, rearrange, or cut parts of your first draft right on the screen—or on a clean printed copy. When editing, you can use the spell and grammar checkers to help you edit your revised writing for errors. (Just remember that these checkers won't catch everything.)

What's Ahead

Most software programs include many design and format options to help you create effective page layouts for essays and reports. This chapter includes guidelines for effective design, plus a few general reminders about writing with a computer.

- Designing Your Writing
- Elements of Design in Action
- Computer Tips

Designing Your Writing

Good page design makes your writing clear and easy to follow. Remember to focus on content and ideas first, and then consider the design tips below. Also check with your teacher for design and layout requirements.

Typography

- **Use an easy-to-read serif font**. Serif type—the type used in this sentence—has tails at the tops and bottoms of the letters. For most kinds of writing, use a 10- or 12-point serif font.

- **Keep titles and headings short**. Follow the rules for capitalizing titles and headings. (See page 401.) Headings are like mini-titles and are used to introduce different sections in writing. Write all headings in the same way; for example, use all *-ing* words, all short phrases, or so on.

- **Consider using a sans serif font for the title and headings**. Sans serif type—like this type—does not have tails. Use **boldface** for headings if they seem to get lost on the page. Use larger type, perhaps 18-point, for your title and 14-point type for any headings.

> By varying the size and style of your type, you help readers follow your ideas. But avoid fancy, hard-to-read typefaces.

Spacing and Margins

- **Keep one-inch margins on all four sides of each page.**

- **Indent the first line of each paragraph.** Set the tabs at five spaces.

- **Leave only one space after a period** for easier reading.

- **Avoid placing headings, hyphenated words, and new paragraphs** at the bottom of a page. Also avoid *widows* (single words, or a part of a word at the bottom of a page or column) and *orphans* (single words or a part of a word at the top of a page).

Graphic Devices

- **Create bulleted lists**. Most computer programs allow you to do this quite easily. (See page 27.) Be careful, though, not to use too many lists in your writing.

- **Include charts or other graphics** to add visual appeal. You can also put graphics on a separate sheet.

Elements of Design in Action

This sample page from a student essay includes several effective design elements.

Kaylee Barkley
Ms. Stephens
English 10
March 13, 2004

The Gift of Life

The procedure for donating bone marrow is fairly simple and very interesting. When a person who is interested in becoming a donor enters an approved donor center, this is what happens:

A bulleted list is used.

- A small amount of blood is taken from the volunteer.
- The sample is typed for antigens (immunity factors).
- The results are entered on a computer registry.

If all six of the donor's antigens match a patient's, the donor is counseled about the donation process and given a physical examination. After the exam, potential donors are advised about the risks of the procedure during a thorough information session. If all goes well, the donor makes the decision to donate and signs an "intent to donate" form.

A graphic adds visual appeal.

Becoming a Donor

Any person between the ages of 18 and 60 who is in generally good health may become a bone marrow donor. All that person has to do is go to a National Marrow Donor Program center, get a blood test, and enter the tissue type in the National Registry. Then it's time to wait until a match is found.

National Marrow Donor Registry

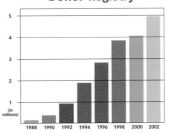

The headings are 14-point sans serif.

Extracting Bone Marrow

Marrow is extracted from the donor in a simple surgical procedure under general or spinal anesthesia. Two to five percent of the donor's marrow is extracted from the back of the pelvis through a special needle and syringe. The extraction is fairly simple—only a few tiny incisions are made. They are so small, in fact, they require no stitches.

Computer Tips

■ **Understand the computer's role when writing.** Like pen and paper, the computer is only a tool. You still must supply the words. A computer simply allows you to get more ideas on paper—in less time. It also allows you to gather your thoughts without worrying about sloppy handwriting. Using a computer may help you stay with a piece of writing longer and develop it more completely.

■ **Become keyboard fluent.** Until you know how to keyboard, you may want to use pen and paper for your freewriting and drafting to ensure a free flow of ideas. In the meantime, keep practicing your keyboarding skills. Then you will be able to make full use of the computer as a writing tool.

■ **Discover your own computer style.** Some writers do all of their writing on a computer. Others like to write their drafts by hand and then enter their work on a computer. Still others like to do their revising and editing on printouts. Your own style will evolve over time.

> Do your final editing and proofreading on a printed copy of your writing. It is easier to find errors and missing words on paper than on the screen.

■ **Save your work.** When using a computer, remember to save your work at regular intervals. Also print out backup copies of every piece of writing. Work that you don't save or print out will be lost forever if your computer suddenly crashes.

■ **Learn the language of computers.** Writing with a computer involves a special vocabulary—*cursor, hard drive, hard copy,* etc. Learning the language of computers will help you become a better computer user. (See pages 497-500.)

■ **Watch for eyestrain.** Staring at a monitor screen can cause eyestrain. When your eyes begin to ache, save your text, turn off your machine, and come back to your work at a later time. If eyestrain is a recurring problem, adjust the contrast and brightness on your monitor and check the lighting in the room.

Developing a Portfolio

A collection of writing that you complete during a semester can show your progress as a writer. This type of collection is often called a *writing portfolio*. Think of a portfolio as a form of publishing, but instead of sharing just one piece, you are sharing a "writing album" that presents a complete picture of you as a writer.

Developing a portfolio gives you ownership of your writing in three important ways: (1) You decide, for the most part, what writing to include. (2) You evaluate your strengths and weaknesses. (3) You make sure that your collection shows you at your best. A portfolio does, after all, present the story of *your own writing*. It says, "This is who I am; this is what I can do."

What's Ahead

This chapter will help you better understand how to develop a writing portfolio. It includes helpful background information, guidelines, and explanations as well as sample portfolio reflections by student and professional writers.

- Types of Portfolios
- Creating a Portfolio
- Planning Ideas
- Sample Portfolio Reflections

Types of Portfolios

Showcase Portfolio

A showcase portfolio presents the best of your writing in school. It will include a sampling of different writing assignments. It might also show certain skills: researching, organizing, revising, editing, and so on. This type of portfolio is usually presented for evaluation at the end of a grading period. (See the sample parts below from Marissa Faerber's portfolio and the guidelines on page 32.)

Sample Showcase Portfolio

Portfolio Folder

Essay Cover Sheet

Dear Ms. Seigel,

I selected the "Path Essay" for my portfolio because I think it accurately shows a path that I have taken. I remember turning in this essay and not being one hundred percent satisfied with its content. I later received the piece back with a grade that reflected a different opinion. The grade made me realize that perhaps I am too critical of my own work and that I need to have more confidence in my writing. I revised my writing a number of times, yet it still has room for improvement. I enjoyed using metaphors to give the essay an overall theme, and I know I could expand more on the topics covered. I think the "Path Essay" is an important piece to highlight in my portfolio because it helped me understand the importance of being confident in my work while still realizing that my work can always be improved.

Sincerely,
Marissa Faerber

Growth Portfolio

A growth portfolio shows your progress as a writer. It might include examples of writing assignments completed during the grading period. Comparing the examples will show how your writing skills, like the ones listed here, are developing:

- writing beginnings and endings,
- supporting thesis statements,
- writing with voice,
- including specific details,
- creating effective dialogue, and so on.

Personal Portfolio

Keeping a personal portfolio is a way of saving writing that is important to you, writing you want to keep and share with others. Many professional people, including writers, artists, musicians, and designers, keep personal portfolios. You can arrange this type of portfolio according to different types of writing, different themes, and so on.

Electronic Portfolio

An electronic portfolio is any type of portfolio (personal, showcase, or growth) that is available on the World Wide Web. With this type of portfolio, you can include text, graphics, video, and sound. Your audience obviously expands when you go on-line. An electronic portfolio makes your writing available to friends, family members, and members of your community.

Why Compile a Portfolio . . .

Developing a portfolio helps you think and act like a true writer. As you compile a portfolio, you will . . .

- preserve important thoughts, feelings, and experiences;
- display your best, or favorite, pieces of writing; and
- reflect upon your own process of writing.

Creating a Portfolio

A showcase portfolio may include the parts listed below, but check with your teacher for the specific requirements. (A growth portfolio will not include as many parts.)

- A **table of contents** lists the samples and other material included in your portfolio.

- **An opening letter or essay** introduces your portfolio—telling how you put it together, what you discovered about your writing, and what it means to you.

- **A collection of writing samples** presents your best work. Your teacher will ask you to include a certain number of pieces; he or she may also ask you to include all of your planning, drafting, and revising for one of these pieces.

- **A best "other" piece** shows your writing ability from another class.

- **A cover sheet** for each piece of writing explains the reason for its selection.

- **Reflective sheets or checklists** discuss the basic skills you have mastered and those skills that you still need to work on.

Developing a **portfolio makes** the **writing process** more meaningful to you.

Compiling Tips

- **Keep track of all of your work,** including prewriting notes, rough drafts, and revisions, during each writing project. Then, when you are ready to compile your portfolio, you'll have everything that you need.

- **Know the specific guidelines** for the type of portfolio you are putting together. (Ask questions if you are not sure about something.)

- **Store all of your writing in a pocket folder** to avoid dog-eared and ripped pages.

- **Set a schedule for working on your portfolio.** You can't wait until the last minute to put together an effective portfolio.

- **Take pride in your work.** Make sure it shows you at your best.

"A **portfolio** is **a window** into your learning."

—Barry Lane

Planning Ideas

The following tips will help you plan an effective portfolio.

Be patient.

Don't make hasty decisions about which pieces of writing to include in your portfolio. Just keep compiling everything until you are ready to review your writing assignments.

 Never, ever lose any of the drafts for a piece of writing that you may want to include in your portfolio.

2 Make thoughtful selections.

When it's time to choose writing for your portfolio, lay out your work in front of you. Review each piece. Recall the feelings you had as you completed each assignment. Which one satisfies you the most? Which one did your readers like the best? Which one taught you the most about writing?

3 Reflect on your choices.

Your teacher may have evaluation or reflection sheets for you to complete. Otherwise, try to answer the following questions (see page 34 for sample reflections):

- Why did I choose this piece for my portfolio?
- How did I write it? (What was my writing process?)
- What does it say about my writing abilities?
- What would I do differently next time?
- What have I learned that will make me a better writer?

4 Set writing goals.

After reflecting on your portfolio, set some goals for future writing. Here are some of the goals that other students have set:

I will write about subjects that really interest me.
I will try to explain or support every main point.
I will spend more time on my beginnings and endings.
I will make sure that my sentences are clear and interesting.

Sample Portfolio Reflections

When you reflect on your writing, consider the process that you used to develop the piece, or decide what you might do differently next time. The following reflections will show you some of the things writers think about.

Student Reflections

I consider this story of my best friend my best piece of writing because it expresses my true feelings. It shows, instead of tells, my happiness when Santeena was here and my sadness when I found out she was leaving. Descriptive words were needed to do this. For example, instead of saying, "We linked our arms," I said, "We linked our mahogany arms." This provided a picture in the mind of the reader and made the piece seem more real.

—Mabel Chandy

I don't remember ever writing about a secret or special place before. I wonder if I avoided writing about this special subject before. Even in this writing, especially in the early stages, I really wasn't sure what I should say about my subject. But, as I went along, I became more confident that I could honestly express my thoughts and feelings, and I am happy with the finished piece.

—Juan Mendoza

Professional Reflections

As my final piece for New Youth Connections, I decided to write a personal narrative about being a recent immigrant in New York. I wrote about my first weeks in school, how lost and lonely I felt, how overwhelming the whole experience had seemed.

—Novelist Edwidge Danticat

I knew that in [The Chocolate Wars] the climax had to be a confrontation between the good guys and the bad guys, Jerry Reynold and Archie Costello. I didn't know what it would be at that time, but I knew there was a strong element of boxing in the story. So, before I began, I knew the climax would be physical and probably include some kind of boxing match.

—Novelist Robert Cormier

Publishing Your Writing

Student writer Marshall Williams states: "The thing I like best about writing is the satisfaction of viewing my finished products." Marshall knows from experience that if he puts enough effort into his writing, he will feel good about it when he is finished. You should have the same feelings about your own writing. Your finished pieces should reflect your best efforts, whether you are writing an essay, a letter, or a report.

Once your writing meets your personal approval, it is ready to publish. Sharing your finished work with your classmates is the most helpful form of publishing. As writer Tom Liner states, "You learn ways to improve your writing by seeing its effect on others." Other forms of publishing include selecting a piece for your portfolio, submitting your work to your school newspaper, posting your writing on a Web site, and so on.

What's Ahead

This chapter gives you tips on where to publish your writing, how to prepare it, and even how to design your own Web site for your writing.

- **Publishing Ideas**
- **Sending Your Writing Out**
- **Publishing On-Line**
- **Designing Your Own Web Page**

"No author dislikes to be **edited** as much as he or she dislikes **not** to **be published**."

—Russell Lynes

Publishing Ideas

As you will see below, there are many ways to publish your writing. Some of the ways are easy to carry out, like sharing your writing with your classmates. Others take more time and effort, like submitting your writing to a magazine. With each publishing experience, you will learn something new about the writing process.

Performing

Sharing with Classmates
Reading to Other Audiences
Recording for a Class Project
Producing a Video
Performing on Stage

Publishing In School

School Newspaper
Literary Magazine
Classroom Collection
Writing Portfolio
(See pages 29-34.)

Posting

Classroom Bulletin Boards
Hallway Display Cases
Library Reading Area
Business Waiting Rooms

Publishing Outside of School

Local Newspapers
Church Publications
Writers' Conferences
Magazines and Contests
On-Line Publications
(See page 38.)

Self-Publishing

Family Newsletters
Booklets (Hand-Bound)
Cards for Special Occasions
Personal Web Site

Sending Your Writing Out

The information that follows will help you learn how to submit your writing to publishers. (*Submitting* in this case means "to send in a piece of writing for possible publication.")

1. What types of writing can I try to publish

You can submit essays, articles, stories, plays, poems, and children's books. Newspapers are most interested in essays, articles, and editorials. Some magazines publish most types of writing; others publish only certain types.

> Check the *Writer's Market* (Writer's Digest Books) or the *Writer's Market: The Electronic Edition* (CD-ROM) to find out who publishes what. If your school library doesn't have either of these resources, your city library will.

2. Where should I send my writing

It's usually best to stick close to home, so consider area newspapers and publications put out by local organizations. If you're interested in submitting something to a national publication, check the *Writer's Market* for ideas.

3. How should I submit my work

Most publications expect you to include these things:

- a **brief cover letter** identifying the title and form of your writing (story, essay, article) and the word count,
- a **neat copy of your work** with your name on each page, and
- a **SASE** (*self-addressed stamped envelope*) large enough for your writing so it can be returned to you after it has been read.

> Check the masthead in the publication for more specific guidelines. (The *masthead* is the small print on one of the opening pages that lists key people, addresses, subscription rates, and so on.)

4. What should I expect ?

Expect a long wait for a reply. Also don't be surprised if your writing is not accepted for publication, especially by national publications. Consider it a learning experience and keep trying.

Publishing On-Line

The Internet offers a variety of publishing ideas. There are on-line magazines, writing contests, and other special sites that accept writing from students. The information below will help you submit your writing on the Net.

1. How should I get started ?

Check with your teachers to see if your school has its own Internet site where you can post your work. Also ask your teachers about other Web sites. They may know about on-line magazines and contests that accept student writing.

2. How do I search for possible sites ?

Use a search engine to find places to publish. Before you begin your search, study the search engine's home page. Some search engines offer their own student links.

3. How should I submit my work ?

Before you do anything, make sure that you have a clear understanding of the publishing guidelines related to each site, and share this information with your parents. Then follow these steps:

- Explain why you are contacting the site.
- Send your work in the correct form. (Some sites have on-line forms into which you can paste text. Others list the formats they prefer to receive.)
- Give the publisher information for contacting you. (However, don't give your home address or other personal information unless your parents approve.)

4. Does Write Source have a Web site ?

Yes. You can visit our Web site at <thewritesource.com>. Follow the "Publish It" link for a list of Web sites that accept student submissions.

5. What should I expect ?

Within a week or so after you submit your writing, the site should contact you, noting that your work has been received. However, it may take many weeks for the site to consider your work for publication.

Designing Your Own Web Page

To create a Web site on your home computer, check with your Internet service provider for help. If you are using a school computer, speak with your teacher. Then use the information below as a guide to start your designing.

1. How do I plan my site

Consider the number of pages you want on your Web site. Should you put everything on one page, or would you like to have many pages (a home page, pages for stories or essays, a page of favorite links)?

Check out other student sites for ideas. Then plan your pages by sketching them out. Decide how the pages will be linked and mark the hot spots on your sketches.

2. How do I make the pages

Start each page as a separate file. Many word-processing programs let you save a file as a Web page. If yours doesn't, you will have to add HTML (hypertext markup language) codes to format the text and make links. Your teacher may be able to explain how to do this. Otherwise, you can find instructions about HTML on the Net. (Also see our Web site at <thewritesource.com> for help.)

3. How do I know whether my pages work

Always test your pages. Using your browser, open your first page. Then follow the links to make sure they work correctly and that all the pages look right.

4. How do I get my pages on the Net

Upload your pages to your Internet provider's server. Ask your provider how to do this. (If you're working on your home computer, make sure to get your parents' approval first. If you're using the school's equipment, work with your teacher.) Your provider will also tell you how to access the pages later in case you want to make changes. After you upload a page, visit your site to make sure it still works.

Once your site is up and working, announce it to your friends and family members and mention it in chat rooms and on electronic bulletin boards. Also ask your provider for tips on how to advertise your page to the rest of the Net.

Using
the Writing Process

Selecting a Topic

Gathering Details

Writing the First Draft

Revising Your Writing

Peer Responding

Editing and Proofreading

Selecting a Topic

Repeat the following statement until you have it memorized: "Writing is a process of discovery." Then write it at the top of your paper before you start each new writing assignment. This idea will remind you that writing is more than putting words on paper. Real writing is discovering how you think and feel about a specific topic.

Your first step in any writing assignment—selecting a topic—may also be the most important one. In order to do your best work, you must write about a topic that truly interests you, a topic you have strong feelings about. Student writer Christina Sung's best piece of writing is a letter she recently composed—all because of her feelings about her topic. As she states, "I was writing to my mother, thanking her for the ways she inspires me. I worked very hard on that letter because I wanted everything to be just right."

What's Ahead

This chapter will help you select meaningful topics for your writing assignments. It includes selecting strategies, suggestions for building a file of writing ideas, and much more.

- Selecting Strategies
- Building a File of Writing Ideas
- Starting Points for Writing
- Forms of Writing

Selecting Strategies

Teachers usually base their writing assignments on the general subjects that you are studying. For example, if in English class you are reading stories and articles that deal with community life, your teacher may ask you to write an essay about this theme. Your job would be to select a specific topic for the essay.

General Subject Area: **Community Life**
Specific Writing Topic: **A New Citizen Watchdog Group**

The following strategies—clustering, freewriting, listing, using a checklist, and completing sentences—will help you select worthy topics for your writing.

Clustering

Begin a cluster, or web, with a nucleus word or phrase. (*Nucleus* means "in the center or middle.") Use the general subject as the nucleus word. Then cluster related words around it, as you see in this model:

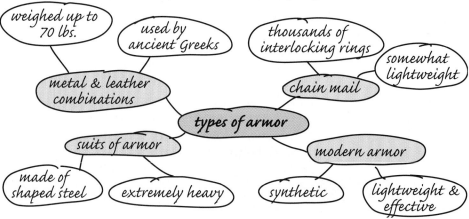

✳ After you are finished, review your cluster for an idea that interests you. Write for 3 to 5 minutes about this idea. A few specific topics will probably come to mind as you write.

Freewriting

With a general subject in mind, write quickly for 5 to 8 minutes. Do not stop and think during this time; just keep writing. You will probably discover one or two specific topics during this time.

Listing

While thinking about your assignment, freely list ideas as they come to mind. Keep your list going for as long as you can. Then look through your list for a few good writing topics.

Using the Basics of Life Checklist

This checklist names the categories or groups of things that we need to live a full life.

acceptance	faith	money
agriculture	family	music
animals	food	nationality
art	freedom	natural resources
books	friends	neighborhood
choices	health/medicine	plants
clothing	housing	rules
community	justice	safety
culture	language	science/technology
education	laws	tools
energy	lifestyle	trade
environment	love	values
exercise	machines	work/play

Here's how this checklist can help you think of writing topics:

- Choose one of the categories: **agriculture**
- Decide how it relates to your assignment: **Write about farming in today's world.**
- List possible topics: **the use of chemical fertilizers; farm life today vs. yesterday; raising buffalo; organic farming**

Completing Sentences

To think of writing ideas, complete open-ended sentences in as many ways as you can. Word these sentence so that they relate to your writing assignment. Here are some samples:

I hope our school . . .	**Television is . . .**
I just learned . . .	**Music can be . . .**
One place I like . . .	**A friend will . . .**

"The **hardest part** for me is actually **coming up with an idea**." —Barry Lane

Building a File of Writing Ideas

You can create a file of writing ideas—just like experienced writers do—by following the guidelines on these two pages.

Pay attention to your world.

Keep your eyes and ears open for interesting sights and sounds. On the way to school, you might notice a tree that has been badly damaged by a storm. During school, you might hear two students sharing their first thoughts about a new classmate. Write about these sights and sounds in a notebook. These "scenes" can lead to good ideas for stories, poems, and essays.

Keep a record of your life.

Start a list of the important people, places, and events in your life—and keep adding to it during the school year. You may want to organize your personal record in the following ways:

- Important people
- Favorite books, movies, music
- Strengths and weaknesses
- Dreams and wishes
- Major accomplishments
- Big mistakes
- Strong beliefs
- Key news events

Write in a personal journal.

Explore your thoughts, feelings, and experiences in a journal. For the best results, write in it every day. As you write, you will discover many possible ideas for writing assignments. (See pages 145-148 for help.)

Read like a writer.

Read anything and everything—books, magazines, newspapers, billboards, bumper stickers, etc. Take note of interesting names, details, and descriptions. These notes may give you ideas for your writing.

Get involved in your community.

Visit museums, businesses, and libraries; volunteer your services for worthwhile causes. As you expand the scope of your world, you will discover many things to write about.

Search sources of information.

Review print resources in your classroom and school library, and surf the Net. There are countless ideas for writing available to you—but you must look for them.

Draw a life map.

To create a life map, draw pictures that represent important events in your life. Add numbers or dates to indicate your age or the year. Start with your birth and work up to the present. As you develop your map, you will think of many ideas for narratives. Kathy Kahnle created the life map below.

Sample Life Map

Starting Points for Writing

The general subjects listed below and the prompts on the next page offer many starting points for writing.

Sample Subjects

Review the following subjects and see what specific writing ideas come to mind. They are organized according to four basic reasons to write.

Describing (telling what a subject looks like, sounds like, does . . .)

People: a new friend, a teacher, a classmate, a neighbor, a public official, a tough opponent, a family member, someone you admire

Places: a kitchen, a rooftop, an alley, the gym, the library, a river, a park, a church, a store, a place to avoid, a place to hang out

Objects or things: a poster, a video game, a book, a photograph, a hat, a letter, a stuffed animal, a collection, a piece of clothing, a billboard, a backpack, a key chain, a toy

Narrating (telling about something that happened)

attending a first game or concert, staying with a relative, fearing for your safety, moving to a new place, getting hurt, doing something funny, learning a lesson, losing something (or someone) important

Explaining (giving the steps, the causes, or the kinds of something)

How to . . . make macaroni and cheese, study for a test, help a friend, carry out an experiment, play a game, dress in style, fix something, get in shape, care for a pet

The causes of . . . the Civil War, prejudice, migraine headaches, work strikes, earthquakes, heart attacks, hiccups, weight loss, lung cancer, success/failure in school (or anywhere), computer viruses

Kinds of . . . dances, running backs, bus drivers, television shows, kindness, cliques, weight trainers, pasta or rice, after-school jobs, lawyers, snacks, compliments

Definition of . . . friendship, a neighborhood, faith, endurance, school, survival, love, charity, advice, determination, beauty, freedom, a grandparent, responsibility, a teacher, wisdom, willpower, success

Persuading (proving your belief or feeling about something)

graduation tests, study halls, year-round school, cell phones, security officers in schools, curfews, something that needs improving, something that seems unfair, something everyone should see or do

Writing Prompts

These common everyday thoughts make excellent writing prompts. As you write about one of these prompts, a number of specific topics will come to mind.

Best and Worst

My most memorable day in school

My best hour

My first encounter with a bully

It could only happen to me!

A narrow escape from trouble

I was so shocked when . . .

My life began in this way.

My strangest phone conversation

If only I had done that differently

Whatever happened to my . . .

Quotations

"Someone who makes no mistakes does not usually make anything."

"When people are free to do as they please, they usually imitate each other."

"Democracy means 'I am as good as you are,' and 'You are as good as I am.' "

"More is not always better."

"It is easier to forgive an enemy than a friend."

"Never give advice unless asked."

"Honesty is the best policy."

"Know thyself."

"Like mother, like daughter."

"Like father, like son."

I was thinking.

Everyone should know . . .

Where do I draw the line?

Is it better to laugh or cry?

Why do people like to go fast?

I don't understand why . . .

First and Last

My first game or performance

My last day of _____

My last visit with _____

School, Then and Now

The pressure of tryouts

Grades—are they the most important part of school?

Finally, a good assembly

What my school really needs is . . .

A teacher I respect

I'm in favor of more . . .

People and Places

Who knows me best? What does he or she know?

Getting along with my boss

A person I admire

My grandparents' house

The emergency room

A guided tour of my neighborhood

Forms of Writing

Thinking about the forms listed below should give you ideas for writing. (Many of these forms are covered in the handbook.)

Anecdotes ■ Brief stories that make a point

Autobiographies ■ Writing about yourself

Biographies ■ Writing about other people

Book Reviews ■ Brief essays expressing your opinion about the books you read

Character Sketches ■ Writing that examines the important qualities of characters

Dialogues ■ Written conversations

Editorials ■ Newspaper letters or articles giving an opinion

E-Mail (electronic mail) ■ Messages sent on a computer

Essays ■ Factual writing that explains, describes, or persuades

Family Parables ■ Family stories that teach something

Journals ■ Writing that records your thoughts, feelings, and experiences

Myths ■ Stories trying to explain natural events

Oral Histories ■ Accounts based on recorded or taped conversations

Parodies ■ Funny versions of serious writing

Photo Essays ■ Essays using pictures and captions to share information

Play Scripts ■ The text of plays

Poems ■ Brief creative writing that gives special attention to every word and phrase

Profiles ■ Detailed reports about individuals

Research Reports ■ Lengthy essays requiring careful researching, planning, and writing

Short Stories ■ Fictional writing that can be read in one sitting

Tall Tales ■ Unbelievable stories with characters like Paul Bunyan

Travelogues ■ Writing that describes places you visit

Web Sites ■ Theme pages on the Internet

Gathering Details

When you put pen to paper, or fingers to the keyboard, you are forming your thoughts about a topic. In order to form meaningful thoughts, you must have plenty of background information to draw from. That is why it is so important to gather details about a topic before you begin your writing.

For some of your writing assignments, you may know a lot about a topic without having to do much collecting. This is usually true when you are writing about an event in your life. But when your personal knowledge of a topic is limited, you must learn as much as you can about it before you write a first draft. Professional writers are well aware of the importance of this step. Author Richard Rhodes put it best when he said, "Everyone does research to prepare for writing."

What's Ahead

The first part of this chapter includes strategies and graphic organizers for gathering details. The second part will help you find a focus and organize your details for writing.

- Gathering Strategies
- Using Graphic Organizers
- Using Collection Sheets
- Checking Your Progress
- Planning Your Writing
- Organizing the Details

Gathering Strategies

These two pages list strategies that you can use to collect ideas and details about a topic. Use two or three strategies if you have a lot to learn.

Gathering Your Own Thoughts

Freewriting Write freely about your topic for 5 to 8 minutes, recording whatever thoughts come to mind. If you have trouble getting started, write this idea at the top of your paper—*Here's what I know about my topic*—and go from there.

Listing List things that you know about the topic and questions you have about it. Keep your list going as long as you can.

Clustering Use your writing topic as the nucleus or key word and cluster ideas and details around it. (See page 42 for an example.)

Analyzing Think carefully about your topic by answering two or three of the following questions:

- What do I see or hear when I think of my topic? (*Describe it.*)
- What is it similar to? What is it different from? (*Compare it.*)
- What parts does the topic have? (*Break it down.*)
- What are its strengths and weaknesses? (*Evaluate it.*)
- How can the topic be used? (*Apply it.*)

Answering Offbeat Questions Answer offbeat or unusual questions about your topic. This strategy will help you think about your topic in new ways. Sample questions are listed below.

Writing About a Person
   What type of music is this person like?
   What type of food is he or she like?

Writing About an Experience
   What colors does this experience make you think of?
   What book or movie is this experience like?

Writing About an Important Issue or Idea
   What famous person does this issue make you think of?
   What would you say about this issue to a parent? a friend?

Answering the 5 W's Answer the 5 W's—*Who? What? Where? When?* and *Why?*—to collect basic details about your topic. Add *How?* to the list for even better coverage. (See page 52 for a graphic organizer.)

Researching

Reading To learn more about your topic, refer to nonfiction books, encyclopedias, and magazines. Take notes as you read. (See pages 344 and 346 for help.)

Viewing and Listening Watch television programs and videos; also listen to CD's about your topic. (See pages 337-342 for help.)

Surfing Search the Internet for ideas and details. (See page 261 for help.) List Web sites that you may want to visit, or revisit.

Experiencing Watch your subject in action, or participate in an activity that involves your topic.

Talking to Others

Interviewing Interview an expert about your topic. (In an interview, you ask someone questions about a topic.) You can meet the expert in person, talk by phone, or send questions (either by letter or e-mail) to be answered in writing. (See page 176 for help.)

Discussing Talk with your classmates or family members to see what they know about the topic. Take notes to help you remember the important things they say.

Using Graphic Organizers

Graphic organizers help you gather and organize details for writing. This page lists sample organizers included in your handbook.

Line Diagram

To collect and organize details for informational essays.

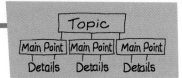

5 W's Chart

To collect the important details (*who? what? when? where?* and *why?*) for narratives, expository essays, and news stories.

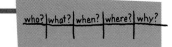

Sensory Details

To collect ideas for descriptions and observation reports.

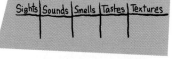

Venn Diagram

To collect details for two subjects you are comparing.

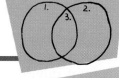

Process List (Cycle Diagram)

To collect details for science reports explaining a process.

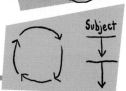

Cause/Effect Organizer

To collect details for essays showing causes and effects, such as the effects of secondhand smoke.

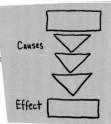

Time Line

To collect details or events chronologically (*according to time*) for essays and reports.

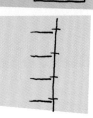

Using Collection Sheets

You can use a collection sheet for gathering and organizing ideas. The sample on this page can be used as a guide for research reports and essays. The sample on the next page is better suited to fictional forms of writing. (You may also create your own collection sheet.)

Gathering Grid

The collection sheet below is called a gathering grid. (A *grid* is a type of chart.) Use a gathering grid when you are reading and learning facts about a topic.

The questions you list down the side of the grid help you decide what to learn about a topic.

Sample Gathering Grid

Subject → Sources of Information

Bruce Springsteen	Encyclopedia and Books	Magazines	Internet
How did he get started?		Signed with Columbia Records	
What makes him different?	Does not sell souvenirs at concerts		Your Answers
How has he maintained his popularity?			Writes songs to people his age
How did he become a star?		Columbia Records used positive review	

Questions About Your Subject

Story Map

A story map can help you plan a fictional (made-up) story. All stories need a setting, characters, and a problem or conflict that results in the action of the story. As you fill in different parts, your story will begin to take shape. But it's not necessary to fill in every blank before you start writing. Just complete enough of the map to get a good idea of what's going to happen in your story.

Sample Story Map

Title: _____

Setting:
```
┌──────────────────────────────────────┐
│                                        │
│                                        │
└──────────────────────────────────────┘
```

Characters: _____ _____

_____ _____

_____ _____

Problem:
```
┌──────────────────────────────────────┐
│                                        │
│                                        │
│                                        │
└──────────────────────────────────────┘
```

Event 1: _____

Event 2: _____

Event 3: _____

Event 4: _____

Solution:
```
┌──────────────────────────────────────┐
│                                        │
│                                        │
│                                        │
└──────────────────────────────────────┘
```

Checking Your Progress

After gathering details about your topic, it may help to evaluate your prewriting up to this point. Use the following questions to check your progress.

Purpose

- Does my topic meet the guidelines for the assignment?
- Am I writing to explain, describe, persuade, or retell?

Self

- Do I still have a strong interest in my topic?
- Do I have enough time to work with it?

Topic

- Do I know enough about my topic?
- Can I think of an interesting way to write about it?

Audience

- Who are my readers?
- How much do they already know about this topic?
- How can I get them interested in my ideas?

Form

- What form of writing am I expected to use—essay, report, narrative, description?
- Do I know the basic parts of this form?

Traits Check

To check your prewriting progress, consider two traits of good writing—*stimulating ideas* and *logical organization*.

For Ideas Development: Make a list of questions that your readers might ask about your topic. Then review your collecting notes to see if you have gathered enough information to answer these questions.

For Organization: Think of ways to group your facts and details so that your main points will be clear. (Use a graphic organizer to help you put information in the best order.)

Planning Your Writing

Follow these steps when you are ready to plan your writing:

1. Review all of your collecting.

2. Think of an interesting focus—the special way you will write about a topic. (See below.)

3. Underline or mark the details that support your focus.

4. Organize these details in the best order for your writing.

Creating a Focus

Your focus may be based either on your main feelings about a topic, or on a special part of the topic you wish to emphasize. Suppose you are writing an essay about childhood malnutrition. You could focus on any one of the following ideas:

- the causes of malnutrition
- the outlook for children suffering from it
- the story of one child's experience with malnutrition
- solutions to the problem

Remember: Your writing would go on and on and be hard to follow if you tried to cover all of these ideas. Instead, you should focus on one main part of your topic.

Samples

A focus gives you a starting point and directs your writing. Take note of the following examples.

Writing Assignment: Essay on Personal Growth
Topic: Values
Focus: Personal values that guide me

Writing Assignment: Essay on Community Life
Topic: New citizen watchdog group
Focus: The founders of the group

A focus statement is similar to a topic sentence (the controlling idea in a paragraph). It is also similar to a thesis statement (the controlling idea in an essay or a report).

Organizing the Details

For most types of writing—especially essays and reports—you need to organize your details carefully.

You can organize information in a list or an outline. (See the next page for help with outlining.) Or you can use a cluster or another type of graphic organizer. A sample cluster follows. (The numbers in the cluster show the order in which the information will be used.)

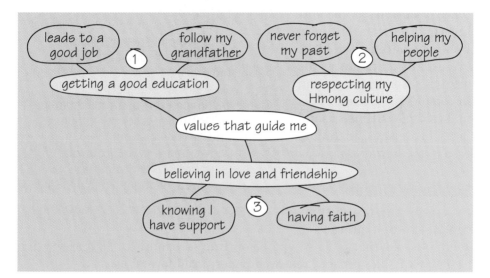

Methods of Organization

This list explains different ways to organize information.

- **Chronological (Time) Order** Arrange details in the order in which they happened. (Use words like *first, second,* and *third.* See page 106 for more time words.)

- **Order of Location** Arrange details by location, or spatially. (Use words like *above, below,* and *beneath.* See page 106 for more location words.)

- **Order of Importance** Arrange details from the most important to the least—or the other way around.

- **Cause and Effect** Begin by stating the cause of a problem and then identify the effects. (The problem-and-solution method is similar. First state the problem and then explore the solutions.)

- **Comparison** Organize details to show how two subjects are alike and different.

Using an Outline

An outline is an organized list of the details you plan to use in your writing. The details are listed from general to specific. In an outline, if you have a I., you must have at least a II. If you have an A., you must have at least a B., and so on.

Topic Outline

There are two basic types of outlines: topic outlines and sentence outlines. In a topic outline, the ideas are usually stated in words and phrases rather than in complete sentences. This makes topic outlines useful for short essays, including essay-test answers.

Sentence Outline

In a sentence outline, the ideas are expressed in complete sentences. This type of outline is useful for longer writing assignments like reports, research papers, and formal essays.

Focus statement: Africa can help itself solve its hunger problem.

I. Natural resources
   A. Great area of unused resources
   B. Capable of feeding Africa
   C. Planning necessary
II. India
   A. A similar hunger problem
   B. Planned for food production
   C. Controlled a serious problem
III. "Harare Declaration"
   A. A promise of self-control
   B. Unites African countries
   C. Already working in some areas

Focus statement: Africa can help itself solve its hunger problem.

I. Africa is a land of many valuable resources.
   A. It contains great areas of unused land, water, and minerals.
   B. There are enough resources to feed all of Africa.
   C. Developing these resources will take time and cooperation.
II. India should give African countries hope.
   A. They experienced a similar hunger problem.
   B. The government began producing enough food for its people.
   C. India is in much better shape than it was 25 years ago.
III. A group of agricultural officials produced the "Harare Declaration."
   A. The declaration promises self-control in Africa.
   B. The declaration also unifies many African countries.
   C. It is already helping starving refugees in parts of Africa.

Writing the First Draft

All of your prewriting leads up to the second step in the writing process—writing the first draft. Use your planning notes as a general guide as you write, but keep an open mind. Important new ideas may occur to you once you begin your writing. Also keep your purpose and audience in mind. Always know *why* you are writing, and *who* you are writing for.

Think of a first draft as your first look at a developing writing idea. Your writing will go through many changes before it becomes a finished product. Experienced writers think of the first draft as a "discovery draft" because they are never sure how it will turn out, even if they have done a lot of planning.

What's Ahead

This chapter will help you write effective first drafts. It includes a useful graphic that explains the three basic parts of a writing assignment—the beginning, middle, and ending. It also gives guidelines and samples for developing each part.

- **The Basic Shape of Writing**
- **Writing the Beginning Paragraph**
- **Developing the Middle Part**
- **Writing the Ending**

The Basic Shape of Writing

As you develop your first draft, keep in mind that a complete paper includes three main parts—the beginning, middle, and ending. The graphic below identifies the type of information usually covered in each part of an essay or report.

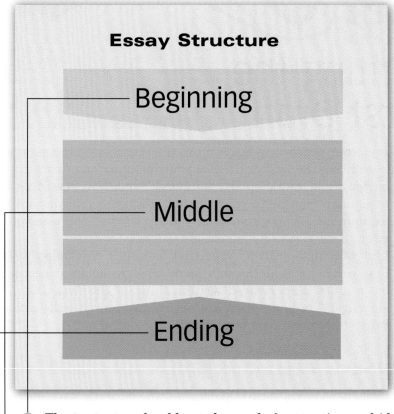

Essay Structure

Beginning

Middle

Ending

- The **beginning** should get the reader's attention and identify the topic or focus of your paper. It should also smoothly lead into the middle part of your writing.

- The **middle** should present the main points and details that support your focus. Usually, each main point is covered in a separate paragraph.

- The **ending** should review your main points or stress the importance of one of them. It may also present an idea that keeps readers thinking about the topic.

Writing the Beginning Paragraph

When writing a first draft, pay special attention to your beginning. Remember that this part should get your reader's attention and identify the topic or focus of your paper. Here are six different ways to get the reader's attention:

- **Explain some interesting details about your topic.**
- **Make a surprising statement about it.**
- **Create an effective image.**
  (An *image* is a mental picture of something.)
- **Ask a question.**
- **Start with a quotation.**
  (A *quotation* repeats someone else's words.)
- **Share a brief story about the topic.**

> If your first opening doesn't turn out, keep trying. You'll know when you get it right because it will lead smoothly into the middle part of your draft.

Sample Beginning Paragraph

The sample that follows comes from a student essay discussing the benefits of drinking water. Notice how the writer creates an image to get the reader's attention. He uses this image to introduce the focus of his essay—that water, not sports drinks, is the most healthful beverage.

Creating an image

Stating the focus

When you stop at a convenience store, you see bottles of sports drinks lining the shelves. The candy-colored drinks catch your eye—bright blue, orange, neon green, and ruby red. The labels promise you all kinds of benefits, especially extra energy. However, if you look at the main ingredient, you'll see that it is water. So are the sports drinks really effective? In truth, if you want a healthful, pure beverage, you should drink water instead of sports drinks.

> When drafting with pen and paper, write on every other line, and use only one side of the paper. When using a computer, double-space throughout. This will make revising your first draft much easier.

Developing the Middle Part

Types of Support

The middle part of your draft should include the main points and related details that support your focus. Here are five different ways to provide support:

Explain Give facts, details, and examples:

A lot of sports drinks and energy drinks have all kinds of chemicals in them that can actually harm you.

Narrate Tell a brief story:

At my last checkup, my dentist asked if I was drinking a lot of soda. I said that I drank more bottled water than sports drinks. "Good thing," he said. "Those sports drinks are loaded with sugar."

Prove Use convincing information to make a point:

Doctors at the University of Texas Southwestern Medical Center say only superathletes and marathon runners lose significant amounts of [salts and electrolytes].

Compare or Contrast Show how two things are alike or different:

Water is pure and natural; sports drinks are candy-colored, sugar-and-salt water.

Analyze Break down the topic into parts:

Water doesn't contain sugar. And sugar is one of the substances that you can get too much of if you are not careful.

Levels of Detail

Usually, each main point is developed in a separate paragraph. A well-written paragraph may contain three different levels of detail:

Level 1: A controlling sentence (topic sentence) names the main point of a supporting paragraph.
First of all, water is natural and essential to life.

Level 2: Clarifying sentences make the main point clearer.
It's all around you in rivers and lakes, and, of course, inside of you, too. A large percentage of the human body is water.

Level 3: Completing sentences add more detail.
It's true that there are other essential things in the human body, like minerals and salts, but . . .

Sample Middle Paragraphs

In each of the sample middle paragraphs below, the writer uses a different type of support. He provides facts and details in the first paragraph.

Providing facts and details

> First of all, water is natural and essential to life. It's all around you in rivers and lakes, and, of course, inside of you, too. A large percentage of the human body is water. It's true that there are other essential things in the human body, like minerals and salts, but you can actually get enough of these from a balanced diet and plenty of water. Sports drinks may contain essential minerals, but they also have chemicals that can harm you. . . .

In this paragraph, the writer refers to authorities on the subject (university doctors).

Referring to authorities

> Water is what the body needs during workouts and heat waves. If you work out or spend time outdoors when it's hot, your body sweats and loses a lot of water. That's why you need to drink water before and after any exercise, especially in the heat. Sports drinks claim to have salts and electrolytes that get lost when you sweat. But doctors at the University of Texas Southwestern Medical Center say only superathletes and marathon runners lose significant amounts of those things. . . .

Finally, the writer compares water and sports drinks in terms of their sugar content.

Making a comparison

> Water doesn't contain sugar. And sugar is one of the substances that you can get too much of if you are not careful. Consuming too much sugar can make you gain weight and may also damage your teeth. Sports drinks are loaded with sugar. That's where the energy boost comes from. However, that boost doesn't last long, and it may leave you more tired than you were before. Water will never give you cavities, and it will never make you tired.

Writing the Ending

After covering all of the main points, you're ready to bring your writing to a close. An ending or closing paragraph should do one or more of these things:

- Remind the readers about the focus of your writing.
- Review the main points.
- Emphasize the importance of one of the main points.
- Say something that will keep readers thinking about the topic.

Sample Ending Paragraph

In this sample closing, the writer reviews some of his main points and then adds an idea that will make his readers think.

Reviewing the main points

Connecting with the readers

Drinking enough water is one of the best things that you can do for yourself and your body. It's natural and life giving. For the most part, it contains no unnecessary substances. In addition, it is free, unless you are drinking bottled water. So the next time you are tempted to buy a sports drink, remember that it is candy-colored, sugar-and-salt water. Save your money for something really great—like that new CD you've been wanting—and drink water instead. Your wallet and your body will thank you for being so smart.

Special Drafting Tips

If you have trouble . . .

- **getting started,** try "telling your story" or "talking about your topic" as if you were surrounded by a group of friends, and go from there.
- **continuing with your writing,** try timing yourself. Write in a series of short bursts (3 minutes), and see what happens. If your problem is not having enough to say, you may need to learn more about the topic.
- **sounding natural and sincere,** relax. Think about what you've already said, and let that help you decide what to say next.
- **ending your writing,** wait awhile. An effective ending may come to mind later on when you revise.

Revising Your Writing

Student writer Nicki Allen has this to say about her process of writing: "I try to write so that I won't have to change things later on. But I change things anyway." Nicki has learned from experience a very valuable lesson about writing—that no matter how hard you try, writing never turns out the way you want it to after just one draft. Writing that shows you at your best, and attracts your readers, must go through a series of revisions.

When you revise, you improve the ideas, organization, and voice in your first draft. You may add new details, cross out unnecessary ideas, rewrite unclear parts, and reorder out-of-place ideas. However, don't pay undue attention to spelling, grammar, punctuation, and usage. Doing so may cause you to overlook ways to improve the most important part of your writing—its message.

What's Ahead

This chapter will help you revise your first draft. You'll find guidelines, tips, and strategies to help you make the best changes in your writing.

- ● Keys to Effective Revision
- ● Using a Basic Guide to Revising
- ● A Link to the Traits
- ● Revising in Action
- ● Revising Checklist

Keys to Effective Revision

1 **Pace yourself.** Step away from your writing for awhile before you attempt to make any improvements. Doing this will help you to see more clearly the parts that need to be changed. When you are ready to revise, work carefully, focusing on the ideas in one part at a time.

2 **Share your writing.** Have at least one classmate review your first draft before you revise it, and later on, after you've started making changes. (See pages 73-76 for help.)

3 **Remember your purpose.** Remember your reason for writing—to explain, to persuade, to describe, to tell a story. You will find it much easier to know what changes you need to make with your purpose clearly in mind.

4 **Keep your audience in mind.** As you revise, ask yourself the following types of questions: *Who are my readers? How much do they know about my topic? What do they need to know? Is this the right voice for my audience? Does my beginning get their attention?*

5 **Take some risks.** Don't be afraid to experiment in your writing. For example, you might begin an essay with a personal story, or organize a report around a series of questions and answers, or change the order of events in a personal narrative. If one experiment doesn't turn out, try something else.

Special Revising Tips

- **Put a star (*) next to parts of your draft that you like and a check (✓) next to the parts that need work.** Focus all of your attention on the parts that you checked.

- **Keep your changes as neat as possible** so you can follow them later on. If you're working on a computer, make your changes on a printout of your draft. Then key them in.

- **Save all of your drafts** so that you have a record of the changes you have made.

"**Revising helps** you **turn** your early **drafts into** more **complete pieces** of writing."

—Josie Penna

Using a Basic Guide to Revising

Use the information that follows to help you make the best revising moves. *Remember:* Revising is the process of improving the ideas that carry the message of your writing.

- **First, review your first draft**. Read it straight through to get an overall feeling about your writing.

- **Then, look at the big picture**. Have you stated a focus, or thesis, in the beginning part and effectively supported it in the rest of your writing? If you can't find the focus, write one. If your thinking on your topic has changed, write a new focus statement. (See page 56 for help.)

- **Next, check specific parts**. Rewrite any parts that aren't as clear as you would like them to be. Cut ideas that don't relate to your focus, and add ideas if your readers need more information. Also reorder any parts that could be arranged more effectively.

- **Finally, evaluate your beginning and ending paragraphs**. Make sure that they effectively introduce and conclude your writing. (See pages 61 and 64 for help.)

If you need more ideas for your writing, complete one or more of the prewriting activities in the handbook. (See pages 50-51 for ideas.)

Revising for Timed Writings

If you are working on an in-class timed writing (like a writing test), you may have little time for revising. When your time is limited, writer Peter Elbow recommends that you use the strategy that follows:

1. Don't add any new information.
2. Cut unnecessary facts and details.
3. Put the pieces in the best possible order.
4. Do what rewriting is necessary.

A Link to the Traits

When revising, focus your attention on these traits of writing: *ideas, organization,* and *voice.* Any improvements that you make in these three areas will greatly improve your writing.

Revising for Ideas

Make sure that all of your ideas are clear and complete. If there is a problem with the content, it's usually because your writing is not focused, or it lacks supporting details.

Keep your writing focused.

Your writing should focus on one important part or feature of your topic or on a main feeling you have about it.

Before: This sample opening is unfocused because it includes too many different types of information.

Whales are the largest mammals. You can go on whale-watching charters to see them. The blue whale is the largest type of whale. All whales have a streamlined body. Many types of whales migrate.

After: This sample opening is focused because it deals with one main point—mass whale suicides or "strandings."

Picture a New England beach in autumn. The sky is clear, the sun warms your face, and the green sea has washed ashore almost 100 magnificent creatures to die. Mass whale suicides, or "strandings," as they are called, occur year after year, and scientists are not sure why.

Include enough facts and details.

Support each of your main points with enough facts and details to give readers a complete picture of your topic.

Before: This sample only gives brief, general information.

Mass whale suicides have gone on for a long time. These suicides have interested many people.

After: This sample names a specific person and his theory.

Mass whale suicides occur year after year. Many people have tried to understand these bizarre suicides. Even Aristotle, the ancient Greek philosopher, thought about the whale deaths. Although he decided the suicides may happen "without any apparent reason," modern biologists are not so sure about that.

Revising for Organization

Your writing must have a clearly developed beginning, middle, and ending; otherwise, readers will have a hard time following it.

Check the beginning.

The opening paragraph should identify your focus and get readers interested in your writing. (See page 61.)

Before: This beginning doesn't capture the readers' interest.
> "The Lottery" is a story about people in a village. There is not a single main character, just a lot of villagers.

After: This beginning makes readers want to know more.
> **"The Lottery" is a scary story with monsters. But these monsters are found within a group of small-town people, people much like you and me.**

Use linking words and phrases.

Make sure that you have used linking words and phrases to connect the details within each paragraph. (See page 106 for a list of these words.)

Before: This paragraph lacks linking words.
> The lottery works in this way. Names of families are placed in a black box. The heads of the families draw a slip from the box. The "winner" is the family drawing the slip with a black dot. . . .

After: This paragraph connects ideas with linking words (in italics).
> **The lottery works in this way. *First*, names of families are placed in a black box. *Then*, the heads of the families draw a slip from the box. The "winner" is the family drawing the slip . . .**

Check the ending.

A closing paragraph should summarize your main points and make a connection with your readers.

Before: This ending gives a very general review.
> "The Lottery" is a scary story about a group of villagers. They join in a lottery that leads to the death of one of their neighbors.

After: This ending makes the readers think about the story.
> **Because of the shocking actions in this story, violence seems to be a basic part of village life. But there is much more going on. "The Lottery" raises questions about human actions. It focuses our attention on the evil hidden beneath the surface of life.**

Revising for Voice

Writer John Jakes states, "Above all, let who you are . . . shine through every sentence you write, every piece you finish." In other words, make sure that your voice comes through in all of your writing. Writing has voice when it reveals your special personality.

Check your purpose.

When you revise, keep your purpose in mind. If, for example, you are developing a personal narrative, your purpose may be to entertain. In order to be entertaining, your personal voice must come through in your thoughts and ideas.

Before: These lines lack personality.

Storms and spiders scared me. Really bad storms frightened me, especially ones with tornado warnings. The spiders that scared me were in the basement.

After: These lines contain more personality.

I was generally a brave little kid, but two things really scared me: storms and spiders. The storms that scared me were the ones with tornado warnings that sent everyone to the basement. I'd always have to go to the bathroom because I was so nervous. Two experiences show my deep fear of spiders. First, my brother and sister . . .

Check your energy and enthusiasm.

If your first draft lacks voice, it may be because it doesn't express strong feelings. The cure is to express your ideas with more sincerity and honesty.

Before: These lines lack feeling and energy.

She turned to me. My grandmother was 86 years old. Her skin was wrinkled, but she had youthful blue eyes. She placed her gnarled hand on mine and squeezed it.

After: These lines are energized with real feelings.

She turned to me. My grandmother was 86 years old, and she was beautiful. Her wrinkled skin was a detailed map of wisdom and hard times, but the sparkle in her eyes was youthful and energetic. In a sign of genuine tenderness, she placed her gnarled hand on mine and squeezed it.

Revising in Action

In the following sample, the writer makes a number of important revisions. Each revision improves the content, organization, or voice in the writing.

An unnecessary ideas is cut.

An idea is made clearer.

An interesting idea is added.

A sentence is reordered.

The average cost of a Hollywood film runs between $30 and $50 million. There are many reasons for this great expense. ~~These reasons won't surprise you.~~ Current action productions are filled with special effects that cost huge amounts of money. In addition, *in terms of blockbuster films.* most producers think big. Instead of making a number of smaller, less-expensive films, they focus on spectacular productions that could be smash hits. Of course, blockbuster films require big stars, which adds *A star's salary can add millions to the cost of a major film.* significantly to the production costs. ∧ Then the advertising of a film adds another huge expense. Anyone who has bought a movie ticket recently knows that the consumer pays for these big productions. All of these factors have contributed to the high costs of making and watching movies.

Revising Checklist

Use this checklist as a guide when you revise a first draft. **Remember:** When you revise, you improve the *ideas* in your writing. Don't spend a lot of time worrying about mechanics or grammar at this point. You can deal with these issues later in the writing process.

✔ **Did I create a strong focus ?**

_____ Did I narrow the topic enough to cover it properly?

_____ Did I focus on an interesting part of my topic or on a certain feeling I have about it? (See page 56.)

✔ **Did I use clear organization ?**

_____ Did I use an effective method of organization? (See page 57.)

✔ **Did I use my natural voice ?**

_____ Did I show true interest in the topic? (See pages 20 and 22.)

✔ **Did I add necessary information ?**

_____ Did I use enough details to make my beginning clear and interesting?

_____ Did I include enough ideas in the middle part to support my focus?

_____ Did I include a meaningful ending?

✔ **Did I cut unnecessary information ?**

_____ Did I include only the necessary details, without getting off the topic?

_____ Did I avoid writing too much about any one idea?

✔ **Did I rewrite unclear parts ?**

_____ Did I make my ideas understandable?

_____ Did I write clear explanations?

✔ **Did I reorder out-of-place ideas ?**

_____ Did I put all ideas or details in the right place?

_____ Did I place the most important point near the beginning or near the end?

Peer Responding

Sharing your writing with your classmates is important through-out a writing project, but it is especially important during the revising process. Peer responders can tell you what does and doesn't work for them in your writing. Their suggestions can help you make your writing clearer and more interesting. Thoughtful responders will offer you many valuable revising ideas.

When you and your classmates respond to each other's writing, a community spirit will develop, a spirit that makes writing an exciting learning experience. The give-and-take of ideas will encourage you to put more effort into your writing and produce finished products that you can truly be proud of.

What's Ahead

During peer-responding sessions, you are either the person sharing a piece of writing, or you are a responder reacting to someone else's work. The information in this chapter will assist you in making helpful responses to your fellow writers.

- Writing-Group Guidelines
- Using a Response Sheet

Writing-Group Guidelines

Some of you might already work in writing groups, so you know how helpful this process can be. If you're just starting out, however, you may want to work with only one person: a teacher or a trusted classmate. After awhile, you may feel comfortable working with a small group of two or three classmates.

With experience, you will find that talking to others about writing is much easier than you thought it would be. You will come to rely on the input you receive in peer-responding sessions. Use the guidelines that follow to help you get started.

The Author's Role

Come prepared with a piece of writing (first draft, revision, final draft) and, if possible, make a copy of it for each member of the group.

GUIDELINES	SAMPLE RESPONSES
● **Introduce your writing,** but don't say too much. Briefly explain the background of your paper.	**This paper is about the Jones Act of 1917. I got interested in this topic when we studied the Spanish-American War.**
● **Read your writing out loud.** Or ask group members to read it silently.	**March 2, 1917, is an important day in the lives of all Puerto Ricans. . . .**
● **Invite group members to comment.** Listen carefully.	**OK, please give me your input. I'm listening.**
● **Take notes** so you will remember what was said and be able to ask questions.	**Did I make it clear what rights the act granted to Puerto Ricans?**
● **Answer all questions as best you can.** Be open and polite. Don't try to defend your writing; just explain it.	**Yes, the act granted citizens the right to a locally elected legislature, including a Senate and a House of Representatives.**
● **Ask for help** from your group with any writing problems you are having.	**Does the ending clearly explain the importance of the Jones Act?**

The Listener's Role

Listeners should show an interest in the writing and be respectful to the writer.

GUIDELINES	SAMPLE RESPONSES
● **Listen carefully.** Take brief notes so that you can make helpful comments.	**What was life like for Puerto Ricans before the Jones Act?**
● **Look for what is good** about the writing. Give positive comments. Be sincere.	**Your explanation of the limitations of the act is very clear.**
● **Tell what you think could be improved.** Be polite, but don't be afraid to give an honest opinion.	**I think you should say more about the feelings of the Puerto Ricans at the time.**
● **Ask questions** if you are confused about something or want to know more.	**You say that Puerto Rico is a territory. What does that mean?**
● **Make helpful suggestions.** Try to help the writer improve his or her work.	**I think you should include a time line in your report.**

Helpful Comments

Make your comments as specific as possible. This will help the writer concentrate on the parts that need fixing.

Instead of . . .	Try something like . . .
Your writing is boring.	Too many of your sentences begin with "There" or "It."
I don't understand what you're talking about.	The part about due process of the law isn't very clear.
I don't think you've got your facts right.	I think you've got the Spanish-American War and World War I mixed up.

Using a Response Sheet

Use a response sheet, such as the one below, to make comments about another person's writing. (You may not have a comment for every category.)

Response Sheet

Writer's name: _____ Your name: _____

Title: _____

_____

I noticed . . . _____

_____

_____

I liked (enjoyed, appreciated) . . . _____

_____

_____

I would suggest . . . _____

_____

_____

Strong words, phrases, and images in the writing: _____

_____

_____

_____

Editing and Proofreading

What's the difference between an above-average essay and one that really shows you at your best? Sometimes, it's the final changes you make. For example, you might . . .

- combine a series of short sentences;
- replace some general adjectives with more specific ones; and
- correct the spelling and grammar errors that a peer editor found.

Final changes like these are the finishing touches your writing needs before you share it.

You make these types of changes when you edit and proofread your revised writing. When you *edit*, you make sure that all of the words and sentences in your writing are clear and correct. When you *proofread*, you check the final copy of your writing for errors.

What's Ahead

This chapter shows you how to edit for sentence style and word choice. It also contains a helpful checklist that serves as a guide when you edit and proofread your writing for correctness.

- **Checking for Sentence Style**
- **Checking for Word Choice**
- **Editing in Action**
- **Editing & Proofreading Checklist**

Checking for Sentence Style

When you edit for sentence style, check for too many short, choppy sentences and for too many sentences beginning in the same way.

Combine Short, Choppy Sentences

If you use too many short sentences, your writing may not read smoothly. Correct this problem by combining some of your sentences.

> **Four Short Sentences:**
> **Harris works after school. He works at a local grocery store. He started working last month. His family needs financial help.**
>
> **Two Longer, Smoother Sentences:**
> **Harris works after school at a local grocery store. He started working last month because his family needs financial help.**

Vary Sentence Beginnings

Your writing may sound boring if too many sentences start in the same way. To correct this problem, vary your sentence beginnings.

> **Original Passage** (Every sentence begins in the same way.)
> **Harris bagged groceries as soon as he arrived at work. Harris also stocked shelves in the cereal aisle. Harris worked in the storeroom for the final two hours.**
>
> **Edited Passage** (The sentence beginnings are varied.)
> **Harris bagged groceries as soon as he arrived at work. He also stocked shelves in the cereal aisle. For the final two hours, Harris worked in the storeroom.**

Here are two ways used to vary the sentence beginnings above:

1. Replace a noun with a pronoun.
   He also stocked shelves in the cereal aisle.
   (The pronoun *he* is used in place of the noun *Harris*.)

2. Start with a phrase or clause.
   For the final two hours, Harris worked in the storeroom.
   (The phrase *for the final two hours* is moved to the beginning of the sentence.)

Checking for Word Choice

Make sure that the words in your narratives and essays match your purpose and audience. For example, when you are writing a narrative, your voice should be personal, as if you were talking to a group of your classmates. When you are writing an essay, your voice should be more serious and objective. (*Objective* means "not including personal feelings.")

Locating Problems

When you check for word choice, watch for the following problems: (Also see pages 132-133 and 415-432 for help.)

Incorrect Usage

Using the wrong word, like *there* or *they're* instead of *their.*

The firefighters grabbed there (instead of *their*) **axes and charged into the house.**

Using General Adjectives

Using vague modifiers like *nice, big, pretty,* or *neat.*

One firefighter discovered a nice case containing pretty jewelry.

Overusing Adjectives or Adverbs

Using too many modifiers in a sentence.

Our neighbor's brand-new, shiny, chrome-plated motorcycle suddenly and unexpectedly exploded from the intense, powerful heat.

Using General Action Verbs

Using general action verbs instead of more-specific ones.

The fire moved through the old house. *(General verb)*
The fire leaped through the old house. *(Specific verb)*

Evaluating Your Editing for Word Choice

You should be able to make these statements about your writing after editing for word choice:

- I know the meaning of every word in my writing.
- I've double-checked for correct usage.
- The adjectives in my writing are specific.
- I haven't overused adjectives or adverbs.
- My action verbs are specific.

Editing in Action

In the following sample, notice the editing changes made to improve style (*sentences* and *word choice*) and to correct spelling, usage, and punctuation errors. (See the inside back cover of your handbook for an explanation of the editing symbols used in the sample.)

A run-on sentence is corrected.

Suddenly a soft voice comes from overhead, "Good afternoon, ladies and gentlemen. I'd like to welcome you aboard flight 596, nonstop to Chicago. We'll be under way in a few minutes."

A spelling error is corrected.

In the background, behind the voice, I hear many sounds in the cockpit. I smell jet fuel and feel rumbles

An apostrophe is inserted.

under the floor. The whole plane quivers. A woman's voice comes on, "Prepare doors."

A flight attendant up front is fanning herself with one of the safety cards we have in the seat pockets

A usage problem is corrected.

before us. A bell quietly goes "boing." Now there are about six kinds of whines all going at once.

A sentence beginning is varied.

The flight attendant reads us the safety rules over the intercom. Then she tells us to sit back, relax, and enjoy the flight.

Editing & Proofreading Checklist

Use this checklist as a guide when you edit and proofread your writing. **Remember:** Editing becomes important only after you have revised the ideas in your writing.

✳ It's easy to miss errors, so ask a trusted classmate for help.

✔ Sentence Structure

_____ Did I write clear and complete sentences?

_____ Do my sentences flow smoothly?

_____ Did I add style to my sentences?

✔ Word Choice and Usage

_____ Did I use specific nouns and verbs and colorful adjectives? (See pages 132-133.)

_____ Did I use the correct word (*their, there,* or *they're*)? (See pages 415-432.)

✔ Punctuation

_____ Does each sentence have an end punctuation mark?

_____ Did I use apostrophes to show possession (*Cesar's backpack*) or to make contractions (*haven't*)?

_____ Did I punctuate dialogue correctly? (*Christina asked, "Where's my CD player?"*)

✔ Capitalization

_____ Did I start each sentence with a capital letter?

_____ Did I capitalize the names of people, places, and things?

✔ Grammar

_____ Did I use the correct verb forms? (See pages 460-461.)

_____ Do all the subjects and verbs agree in number? Do the singular subjects go with singular verbs and the plural subjects go with plural verbs? (See pages 87-88.)

_____ Did I use pronouns correctly? (See pages 89-90.)

✔ Spelling

_____ Did I check for spelling errors? (See pages 408-414.)

_____ Did I use a spell checker on my computer?

Basic Elements
of Writing

Writing Basic Sentences

Writer Patricia T. O'Connor says that a well-written sentence really is a "triumph of engineering." On its own, an effective sentence states a complete thought using just enough words, and no more. As part of a longer piece of writing, it carries an important idea, and connects readers with the ideas that come before and after it. Since sentences are so basic to writing, you need to learn as much as you can about them.

To become sentence smart, make reading and writing important in your life. Read anything and everything that you can get your hands on, and write regularly on your own. Your personal reading and writing will help you develop an "ear" for good sentences. In addition, follow the guidelines for writing sentences in this chapter and in other parts of the handbook.

What's Ahead

The next seven pages review the basic parts of a sentence, identify sentence errors and problems to avoid, and much more.

- Sentence Review
- Sentence Errors
- Sentence Agreement
- Sentence Problems

> "The sentence's news, what the reader must take away from the sentence, is usually **in the predicate**."
>
> —Scott Rice

Sentence Review

A **sentence** is a group of words that shares a complete thought. It may make a statement, ask a question, or show emotion. A sentence begins with a capital letter and ends with a period, a question mark, or an exclamation point. Here is a guide to understanding sentences.

Basic Parts of a Sentence

All sentences have two basic parts—the subject and the predicate.

Subject. The subject is the part of a sentence that does something or is talked about. In the sample sentence, "our new coach" is the complete subject, and "coach" is the simple subject. (The simple subject consists of the subject without the words that modify it.)

> Our new <u>coach</u> played basketball in college.

Predicate. The predicate is the part of a sentence that says something about the subject. In the sample sentence, "played basketball in college" is the complete predicate, and "played" is the simple predicate or verb. (The simple predicate is the verb without the other words that modify it or complete the thought.)

> Our new coach <u>played</u> basketball in college.

There are two main types of verbs: action verbs (like *played*) and linking verbs (like *is, are, was,* and *were*).

> Our new coach <u>played</u> basketball in college. He <u>was</u> a guard.

Compound Subjects and Predicates. A sentence may have more than one simple subject or predicate (verb).

> <u>Maurice</u> and <u>Gregg</u> play guard, too.

(The sentence contains two simple subjects, *Maurice* and *Gregg*.)

> Theo <u>plays</u> tough defense and <u>rebounds</u> aggressively.

(The sentence contains two simple predicates, *plays* and *rebounds*.)

Basic Sentence Patterns

Sentences in the English language follow these basic patterns.

Subject + Action Verb

S   AV

Mansi dances. (Some action verbs, like *dances*, are intransitive. That means they don't need a direct object to express a complete thought. See page 463.)

Subject + Action Verb + Direct Object

S   AV   DO

Sefton plays the guitar. (Some action verbs, like *plays*, are transitive. That means they need a direct object to express a complete thought. See page 462.)

Subject + Action Verb + Indirect Object + Direct Object

S   AV   IO   DO

Patrice offers elementary students singing lessons. (The direct object *lessons* names who or what receives the action; the indirect object *students* names to whom or for whom the action is done.)

Subject + Action Verb + Direct Object + Object Complement

S   AV   DO   OC

The orchestra director named Marisa assistant conductor. (The object complement *conductor* renames or describes the direct object.)

Subject + Linking Verb + Predicate Noun

S LV   PN

Ravi is a juggler. (The predicate noun *juggler* renames the subject.)

Subject + Linking Verb + Predicate Adjective

S LV   PA

Our jazz band was creative.
(The predicate adjective *creative* describes the subject.)

In all of the sentence patterns above, the subject comes before the verb. However, there are a few types of sentences in which the verb comes before the subject. Here are two examples:

LV S   PN

Is Cesar a drummer? (A question)

LV   S

There were no bass players. (A sentence beginning with *There*)

Sentence Errors

Sentence Fragment A sentence fragment does not express a complete idea. It is missing one or more important parts.

Incorrect: **Writes in a personal journal.** (There is no subject.)

Correct: **Orlinda writes in a personal journal.**
(The subject *Orlinda* has been added.)

Incorrect: **His original songs at the talent show.**
(There is no subject and no verb.)

Correct: **Akira performed his original songs at the talent show.**
(The subject *Akira* and the verb *performed* have been added.)

Run-on Sentence A run-on sentence is two sentences joined without punctuation or without a connecting word (*and, but, or*).

Incorrect: **The art show starts today the sophomore's artwork is on display.** (Punctuation is needed.)

Correct: **The art show starts today. The sophomore's artwork is on display.** (A period has been added after *today*.)

Comma Splice A comma splice is an error made by joining two sentences with a comma instead of a conjunction, a period, or a semicolon.

Incorrect: **Lila loves fashion, she even designs her own clothes.**
(A comma incorrectly connects two sentences.)

Correct: **Lila loves fashion, and she designs her own clothes.**
(The conjunction *and* has been added.)

Rambling Sentence A rambling sentence happens when you put too many little sentences together with the word *and*.

Incorrect: **Our school choir traveled to New York and we sang at a performing-arts center and we toured important attractions like the Statue of Liberty and we saw a musical on Broadway and most importantly, we competed in a musical contest with other high schools.**

Correct: **Our school choir traveled to New York and sang at a performing-arts center. Later, we toured important attractions like the Statue of Liberty and saw a musical on Broadway. Most importantly, we competed in a musical contest with other high schools.**

Sentence Agreement

Make sure that the parts of your sentences "agree" with one another. If you use a singular subject, use a singular verb. If you use a plural subject, use a plural verb. See the samples below and on the next page.

One Subject In most basic sentences, a single subject is followed by the verb.

Incorrect: **Lamarr travel to South Carolina every summer.**

(*Lamarr* is singular; *travel* is plural.)

Correct: **Lamarr travels to South Carolina every summer.**

(Both *Lamarr* and *travels* are singular.)

Incorrect: **His grandparents lives in Charleston.**

(*Grandparents* is plural; *lives* is singular.)

Correct: **His grandparents live in Charleston.**

(Both *grandparents* and *live* are plural.)

The following chart shows additional sentences with one subject. (The verb agrees with the subject in each sentence.)

SINGULAR SUBJECTS	PLURAL SUBJECTS
The man loves the outdoors.	**The men love the outdoors.**
She takes him fishing.	**They take him fishing.**

Compound Subjects Connected by AND If a sentence contains a compound subject connected by *and,* it needs a plural verb.

Cyrus and Theo wait for their friend.

Compound Subjects Connected by OR If a sentence has a compound subject connected by *or,* the verb must agree in number with the subject nearer to it.

The Johnson sisters or Alicia baby-sits for the neighbors.

(The verb *baby-sits* is singular because the subject *Alicia,* which is closer to the verb, is singular.)

Alicia or the Johnson sisters baby-sit for the neighbors.

(The verb *baby-sit* is plural because the subject *sisters,* which is closer to the verb, is plural.)

Unusual Word Order   When the subject is separated from the verb by words or phrases, check carefully to see that the subject agrees with the verb.

Paulo, along with his cousins, works for a messenger service.

(*Paulo*, not *cousins*, is the subject, so the singular verb *works* is used.)

A pack of dogs runs wild in the park.

(*Pack*, not *dogs*, is the subject, so the singular verb *runs* is used.)

The Patels, a new family, are from India.

(*Patels*, not *family*, is the subject, so the plural verb *are* is used.)

When the subject comes after the verb (or part of the verb), you must check carefully to see that the subject agrees with the verb, as in the following examples:

From the back of the bus comes a loud laugh.

From the back of the bus come two loud voices.

Has your friend returned the video?

Have your friends returned the videos?

Indefinite Pronouns   Use a singular verb with these indefinite pronouns: *each, either, neither, one, everyone, everybody, everything, someone, somebody, something, anybody, anything, anyone, nobody, no one, nothing,* and *another.*

Nobody likes the hamburgers in the cafeteria.

(*Nobody* is a singular subject, so the singular verb *likes* is used.)

Everybody chooses the salad bar on Mondays.

(*Everybody* is a singular subject, so the singular verb *chooses* is used.)

Some indefinite pronouns (*all, any, most, none, some*) can be singular or plural. You must study the words that come between the subject and verb to decide.

Most of my friends love the chocolate chip cookies.

(Because the sentence talks about most of the *friends,* a plural noun, the plural verb *love* is used.)

Some of my lunch looks unappetizing.

(Because the sentence talks about some of the *lunch,* a singular noun, the singular verb *looks* is used.)

Sentence Problems

Wordy Sentences Check your sentences for words that repeat what you've said, but in a different way. (See the words in blue below.)

Incorrect: **Zoe will swim laps** in the pool **at 6:00 p.m.** in the evening **to prepare for the conference tournament** featuring all of the teams in the conference.

Correct: **Zoe will swim laps at 6:00 p.m. to prepare for the conference tournament.**

Double Subjects Do not use a pronoun immediately after the subject. (See the pronouns in blue below.) The result is usually a double subject.

Incorrect: **Felix's letter jacket** it **needs to be cleaned. My mother** she **will take care if it.**

Correct: **Felix's letter jacket needs to be cleaned. My mother will take care of it.**

Pronoun-Antecedent Agreement Make sure the pronouns in your sentences agree with their antecedents. (*Antecedents* are the words replaced by the pronouns. See page 451.)

Our principal cleared her throat; then she began her report. (Since the noun *principal* is singular, the singular pronouns *her* and *she* are correct.)

The council members listened to the report, and then they asked a few questions. (Since *members* is plural, the plural pronoun *they* is correct.)

Everyone left the meeting knowing his or her job for the upcoming dance. (Since the indefinite pronoun *everyone* is singular, the singular pronouns *his* or *her* are correct.)

Confusing Pronoun Reference When you use a pronoun, be sure the reader knows who or what the pronoun refers to.

Confusing: **When Ferrin drove his** car **up to the service** window, it **made a strange rattling sound.** (What does the pronoun *it* refer to—the car or the window?)

Clear: **Ferrin's car made a strange rattling sound as he drove it up to the service window.** (The pronoun *it* clearly refers to the car.)

Pronoun Shift Make sure your pronoun agrees in person (*first, second,* or *third*) with the noun it replaces. It is incorrect to shift to another person. (See page 452.)

Incorrect: **If my** classmates **do not understand an assignment, you should ask for help.** (The second-person pronoun *you* does not agree in person with the noun *classmates* that it replaces. Classmates needs a third-person pronoun.)

Correct: **If my classmates do not understand an assignment, they should ask for help.** (The third-person pronoun *they* agrees in person with the noun it replaces, *classmates.*)

Double Negative Do not use two negative words together, like *never* and *no,* or *not* and *no.*

Incorrect: **She** never **saw** no one **run so fast.**

Correct: **She never saw anyone run so fast.**

Do not use *hardly, barely,* or *scarcely* with a negative word.

Incorrect: **I** don't hardly **know what to do.**

Correct: **I don't know what to do.** *or* **I hardly know what to do.**

Confusing OF and HAVE Do not use *of* in a sentence when you really mean *have.* (When *have* is said quickly, it can sound like *of.*)

Incorrect: **He** should of **studied last night.**

Correct: **He should have studied last night.**

Misplaced Modifiers Make sure that your modifiers are close to the words they describe. Otherwise, the sentence may not say what you mean.

Incorrect: After finishing the drill, Coach James **met with the team.** (This sentence says that the coach finished the drill.)

Correct: **After finishing the drill, the team met with Coach James.** (Now the phrase *after finishing the drill* correctly modifies the team.)

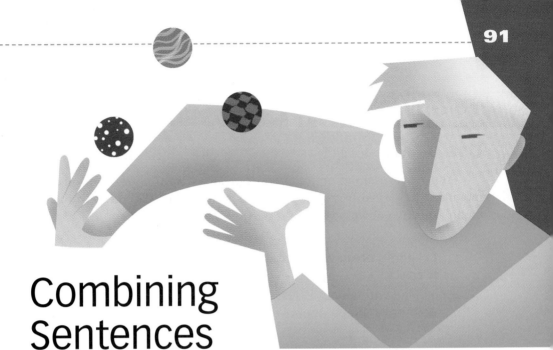

Combining Sentences

Sentence combining is the act of making one smoother, more detailed sentence from two or more short sentences. Read the three short sentences that follow:

Carlos loves to play video games.
He loves to watch movies.
He loves to surf the Net.

These are all acceptable sentences, but see what happens when they are combined. The ideas flow more smoothly.

Carlos loves to play video games, watch movies, and surf the Net.

Sentence combining can help you improve your writing fluency (smoothness) and gain a better understanding of word combinations that you can use. It will also help you write with more style, which will make your papers more enjoyable to read.

What's Ahead

In this chapter, you will learn about different ways to combine sentences to make them read more smoothly. Remember that using effective sentences is one of the traits of good writing. (See page 20.)

- **Combining with Key Words**
- **Combining with Phrases**
- **Combining with Longer Sentences**

Combining with Key Words

Use a Key Word

You can combine, or put together, ideas from short sentences by moving a key word from one sentence to the other. This key word may be an adjective or an adverb.

Two Short Sentences:
> Belindra's poem was printed in the school bulletin.
> It was a shape poem.

Combined with an Adjective:
> Belindra's shape poem was printed in the school bulletin.

Two Short Sentences:
> I'll finish my essay in the computer lab.
> I'll finish it tomorrow.

Combined with an Adverb:
> Tomorrow, I'll finish my essay in the computer lab.

Use a Series of Words

Ideas from short sentences can be combined into one sentence using a series of words or phrases.

Three Short Sentences:
> Study hall is hot. Study hall is stuffy. Study hall is smelly.

Combined with a Series of Words:
> Study hall is hot, stuffy, and smelly.

All of the words or phrases in a series should be **parallel**, or stated in the same way. If you don't do this, your sentence will sound like it is out of balance. Look at the example below.

Incorrect: **Our library contains** study tables, computer stations, **and** it has a reading corner. (The third idea is not parallel to the first two.)

Correct: **Our library contains study tables, computer stations, and a reading corner.** (The series is now parallel, or stated in the same way.)

Combining with Phrases

Use **Phrases**

You can put ideas from short sentences together into one sentence by using prepositional or appositive phrases. (See pages 470 and 386.)

Two Short Sentences:
> **Sergio studied for the math test.** **The test is** on fractions and percentages.

Combined with a Prepositional Phrase:
> **Sergio studied for the math test on fractions and percentages.**

Two Short Sentences:
> **Khadra completed her report.** **It is** about diets for athletes.

Combined with Two Prepositional Phrases:
> **Khadra completed her report about diets for athletes.**

Two Short Sentences:
> *Hoop Dreams* **is** my favorite book of all time.
> *Hoop Dreams* **is also a TV documentary.**

Combined with an Appositive Phrase:
> *Hoop Dreams***, my favorite book of all time, is also a TV documentary.**

Use **Compound Subjects and Verbs**

A compound subject has two or more subjects in one sentence. A compound verb has two or more verbs in one sentence.

Two Short Sentences:
> Carmela **likes romance novels.**
> Elena **likes romance novels, too.**

Combined with a Compound Subject:
> **Carmela and Elena like romance novels.**

Two Short Sentences:
> **Kristos** listened **to the history lecture. He** took **brief notes.**

Combined with a Compound Verb:
> **Kristos listened to the history lecture and took brief notes.**

Combining with Longer Sentences

Use **Compound Sentences**

A compound sentence joins two or more simple sentences. The conjunctions *and, but, or, nor, for, so,* and *yet* are used to connect simple sentences. (Place a comma before the conjunction.)

Two Short Sentences:
> Coach Lloyd supervises the weight room.
> He keeps it open until 5:30 in the evening.

Combined with "and":
> Coach Lloyd supervises the weight room, **and** he keeps it open until 5:30 in the evening.

Two Simple Sentences:
> Mrs. Stephens knows a lot about literature.
> She knows very little about movies.

Combined with "but":
> Mrs. Stephens knows a lot about literature, **but** she knows very little about movies.

Use **Complex Sentences**

A complex sentence joins two or more ideas using subordinating conjunctions—*after, when, since, because*—or relative pronouns—*who, whose, which,* and *that.* (See pages 471 and 454 for a complete list of these words.)

Two Short Sentences:
> My mom is on her feet a lot. She is a nurse.

Combined with the subordinate conjunction "because":
> My mom is on her feet a lot **because** she is a nurse.

Two Short Sentences:
> Life Skills helps us plan for our future.
> Life Skills is a required course.

Combined with the relative pronoun "which":
> Life Skills, **which** is a required course, helps us plan for our future.

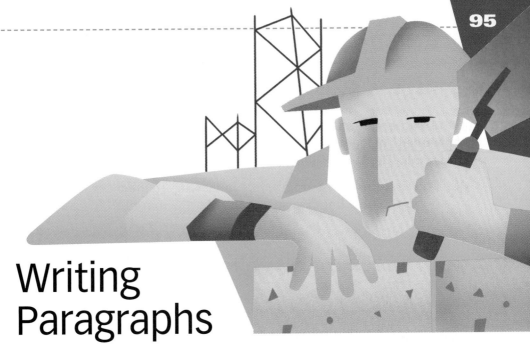

Writing Paragraphs

Writer Donald Hall calls a paragraph a "maxi-sentence" or a "mini-essay." What he means is this: A paragraph is a special unit of writing that does more than the typical sentence and less than the typical essay. Think of the paragraph as an important building block for all of your writing assignments. If you can write strong paragraphs, you can develop effective essays, narratives, and reports.

A **paragraph** is made up of a group of sentences focused on one topic. A paragraph can be an explanation, an opinion, a description, or a narrative. Whatever form a paragraph takes, it must contain enough information to give readers a complete picture of the topic. The first sentence usually identifies the topic; the other sentences support it.

What's Ahead

This chapter will help you write effective paragraphs. It deals with everything from the parts of paragraphs to the linking words or transitions used to connect ideas.

- **The Parts of a Paragraph**
- **Types of Paragraphs**
- **Writing Guidelines**
- **Details in Paragraphs**
- **Organizing Your Ideas**
- **Transition Words and Phrases**

The Parts of a Paragraph

A paragraph has three main parts. It usually begins with a **topic sentence**. The sentences in the middle part make up the **body** of a paragraph. The last sentence is called the **closing sentence**.

✳ The first line in a paragraph is indented. (To *indent* means "to begin the first line five spaces in from the margin.")

Topic Sentence

Body

Closing Sentence

Striking It Rich

Blue jeans are definitely the most recognizable piece of American clothing. They were invented by a man named Levi Strauss. In 1850, during the California gold rush, Strauss took bolts of canvas to San Francisco, in hopes that he could make tents and wagon covers to sell to the miners. When that didn't work out, Strauss decided to use the canvas to make pants that miners could wear for their rough work. Miners bought these pants as fast as Strauss could make them. These pants became the very first Levi jeans, and they changed the world of fashion forever. Later, Strauss made the pants out of blue denim instead of canvas, and in 1870, he added the trademarked copper rivets. Since that time, Levi jeans have become a symbol of the American West and are worn around the world.

A Closer Look at the Parts

Topic Sentence

The topic sentence tells what a paragraph is going to be about. A good topic sentence (1) *names the topic* and (2) *states your feelings about it*. Here is a simple formula for writing good topic sentences:

> **An interesting subject**
> **+   your specific feeling about it**
> ──────────────────────────
> **=   a good topic sentence.**

Topic Sentence   *Blue jeans* (interesting subject) *are definitely the most recognizable piece of American clothing* (specific feeling).

The Body

The sentences in the body give readers the information they need to understand the topic.

- Use specific details to make your paragraph interesting. The details are shown in red in the sentence that follows.

  Later, Strauss made the pants out of blue denim instead of canvas, and in 1870, he added the trademarked copper rivets.

- Organize your sentences in the best possible order. There are three main ways to organize sentences: chronological (*time*) order, order of location, and order of importance.

The Closing Sentence

The closing sentence comes after all of the details have been included in the body. This sentence should remind readers about the paragraph topic. The following example reminds readers about the topic of the sample paragraph.

Closing Sentence   *Since that time, Levi jeans have become a symbol of the American West and are worn around the world.*

Types of Paragraphs

You can write four types of paragraphs: *narrative, descriptive, expository,* and *persuasive.* Each of these requires a different type of thinking and planning.

Narrative Paragraph

In a **narrative paragraph**, you share a memorable event, a short story, or an important experience. The details in a narrative should answer the 5 W's (*who? what? when? where?* and *why?*) about the event.

Topic Sentence

Body

Closing Sentence

Looking Perfect

I was surprised, but happy with the way that I looked on my big day. My mom made my Quinceanera dress, but it wasn't the one that I wanted. I wanted the dress to be a sexy, white strapless gown with lavender flowers. Instead, she made a simple white dress with small pearls. It was attractive, but it wasn't what I wanted to wear on the day that I officially became a lady. Earlier that day, I had my hair, nails, and makeup done. Then I spent a lot of time worrying about the dress. Finally, I couldn't wait any longer, so I had to put it on. Surprisingly, the dress that I didn't want fulfilled all of my dreams. My mom knew how I needed to look on this day, and she had made a dress that made me look perfect. I was beautiful and stylish, a sophisticated young lady ready to enter into adulthood.

Descriptive Paragraph

In a **descriptive paragraph,** you give a clear, detailed picture of one person, place, or object. The following sample describes a popular outfit from an earlier generation. The description is organized by order of location, starting at the top with the hat and ending with the shoes.

Topic Sentence

Body

Closing Sentence

Dressing for Swing

The zoot suit became an important fashion symbol during the big-band swing era of the 1940s. The total ensemble (*complete outfit*) begins with a stylish wide-brimmed, soft-felt hat, usually with the brim turned down. The classic jacket is oversized, double-breasted, and long. It starts with wide-padded shoulders and large pointed lapels, and ends with a tapered fit, beginning at the waist. A formal dress shirt is usually worn under the jacket, accented with a matching silk tie and hanky set. The pleated suit pants start baggy, but taper down from the knee, ending with tight-cuffed bottoms. Two accessories are worn with the pants, a thin leather belt and a long looping chain. The outfit ends with two-toned, thin-soled leather shoes. Because of a renewed interest in swing music, zoot suits have made a comeback and may be rented for special occasions.

Expository Paragraph

In an **expository paragraph,** you share information. You can explain a subject, give directions, or show how to do something. Linking words like *first, second, then,* and *finally* are used to help readers follow the ideas in expository writing. (See page 106 for more linking words.)

Topic Sentence

Body

Closing Sentence

How to Put "Twisties" in Your Hair

The hairstyle called "twisties" is great if you're involved in sports. To style your hair into twisties, first dampen your hair and work a little gel into it to make the style hold. Then use the edge of a comb to part your hair slightly off center. Next, part it again on the other side of the center so you have a section of hair. Starting at your forehead, pick up some of the hair and twist it close to the head. To continue, pick up some hair behind it and twist both together. Then pick up some hair behind that and twist it . . . and keep going as far back on your head as you want. Finally, fasten it at that point with an elastic band or a small butterfly clip. Repeat this process with other sections of your hair. With a little practice, your twisties will look fabulous, and you'll be able to run down the court without your hair flying in your face.

Persuasive Paragraph

In a **persuasive paragraph,** you give your opinion about a topic. To be persuasive, you must include plenty of facts and details to support your opinion.

Topic Sentence

Body

Closing Sentence

No to School Uniforms

Individual choice in clothing, rather than school uniforms, will best serve the students at Starr Tech. First of all, allowing students to wear regular clothes is more economical. If students had to wear uniforms, they would have to buy two sets of clothing, one for school and one for evenings and weekends. Secondly, giving students a choice in their wardrobe sends the proper message. The goal of a school like Starr should be to help students develop their individual talents, not to enforce a strict dress code. Thirdly, and most importantly, having a choice helps students practice being responsible individuals. Instead of requiring uniforms, our school should set some guidelines for what can and cannot be worn. Students who decide to ignore these guidelines must be willing to face the consequences. In other words, students must show that they can make responsible decisions to maintain an important individual right. For these reasons, students at Starr Tech should be allowed to wear regular clothing.

Writing Guidelines

Make sure that you understand the assignment before you plan and write your paragraph. Then follow the steps listed below.

Prewriting Choosing a Topic

- Select a specific topic that meets the requirements of the assignment. (Your teacher may give you a general subject area to choose a topic from.)

Gathering Details

- Collect ideas and details about your topic.
- Write a topic sentence that states what your paragraph is going to be about. (See page 97 for help.)
- List ideas and details that support the topic sentence. Decide on the best way to arrange these details.

Writing Writing the First Draft

- Start your paragraph with the topic sentence. (Indent the first line.)
- Follow with sentences that support your topic. Use your list of details as a guide.
- End with a sentence that reminds readers about your topic.

Revising Improving Your Writing

- Add information if you need to say more about your topic.
- Rewrite any sentences that sound confusing or awkward.

Editing Checking for Style and Correctness

- Check the revised version of your writing for style as well as capitalization, punctuation, and spelling errors. Also have someone else check for errors.
- Then write a neat final copy of your paragraph to share.

Details in Paragraphs

No paragraph is complete without effective facts and details that support your topic sentence. Some of this information may come from personal knowledge and memories. However, you will often refer to books, magazines, Web sites, and experts for the facts you need.

Personal Details

- **Sensory details** are things that you see, hear, smell, taste, and touch. (These details are especially important in descriptive paragraphs.)

    The classic jacket is oversized, double-breasted, and long.

- **Memory details** are things you remember from past experiences. (These details are especially important in narrative paragraphs.)

    My mom made my Quinceanera dress, but it wasn't the one that I wanted.

- **Reflective details** are things you think about or hope for. (These details are often used in narrative and descriptive paragraphs.)

    I wanted the dress to be a white strapless gown with lavender flowers.

Other Sources of Information

To collect facts and details from other sources, keep the following tips in mind. (See pages 254-256 for more information.)

1 Talk with someone you know.
Parents, neighbors, and teachers may know about your topic.

2 Contact an expert.
Meet with an expert to discuss your topic, or contact this person by phone, letter, or e-mail.

3 Write for information. If you think a museum, business, or government office has information you need, send for it. You may also visit these places and gather facts for yourself.

4 Refer to print or on-line resources.
Gather details from books, magazines, newspapers, and the Internet.

Organizing Your Ideas

The sentences in the body of a paragraph must be organized in the best possible way to support the topic. Below are three basic ways to organize your sentences.

Chronological Order   Use chronological order to organize your narrative paragraphs. (Chronological means "according to time.") Words like *first*, *second*, and *next* are used to arrange ideas according to time. (See page 98 for a narrative paragraph.)

> **Early that day, I had my hair, nails, and makeup done. Then I spent a lot of time worrying about the dress. Finally, I couldn't wait any longer, so I had to put it on.**

You should also use chronological order in some expository paragraphs. (See page 100 for an expository paragraph.)

> **To style your hair into twisties, first dampen your hair and work a little gel into it to make the style hold. Then use the edge of a comb to part your hair slightly off center. Next, part it again on the other side of the center so you have a section of hair.**

Order of Location   In most cases, organize descriptive details by order of location to help readers follow the details. For example, a description may move from left to right or from top to bottom. If needed, use words like *above* and *below* to move from one part of the description to the next. (See page 99 for a descriptive paragraph.)

> **The total ensemble (*complete outfit*) begins with a stylish wide-brimmed, soft-felt hat, usually with the brim turned down. The classic jacket is oversized, double-breasted, and long. It starts with wide padded shoulders and large pointed lapels, and ends with a tapered fit, beginning at the waist.**

Order of Importance   Organize persuasive paragraphs by order of importance. You can arrange your argument by starting out with your most important point, or you can lead up to it. (See page 101 for a persuasive paragraph.)

> **Thirdly, and most importantly, having a choice helps students practice being responsible individuals. Instead of requiring uniforms, our school should set some guidelines for what can and cannot be worn. Students who decide to ignore these guidelines must be willing to face the consequences.**

"An **effective** piece of **writing has focus**. There is a controlling vision which orders what is being said."
—Donald Murray

Organizing Paragraphs in Essays

Essays and reports include several paragraphs. This means that you have to organize the ideas within each paragraph, and then organize the paragraphs within the essay. Here are some tips to follow. (See pages 107-125 and 219-235 for more helpful hints.)

1 **Make sure that each paragraph is complete.** Each of your paragraphs should contain an effective topic sentence and supporting details.

2 **Identify the topic and focus of your writing.** In most cases, you should begin with some interesting details to get the reader's attention. Then share the specific topic and focus of your writing.

3 **Develop your writing idea in the middle paragraphs.** Each middle paragraph should include information that explains and supports your focus. Often, the paragraph that contains the most important information comes right before the final paragraph.

4 **End with a concluding paragraph.** This paragraph is usually a review of the main points in the essay. In the last sentence, the importance of the topic is emphasized.

5 **Use transition words or phrases to connect the paragraphs.** (See page 106.) In the sample below, the transitions are shown in red.

> . . . **Since that time, Levi jeans have become a symbol of the American West and are worn around the world.**
>
> **In addition to jeans, other symbols of American culture include athletic shoes and sports jerseys. These two symbols have become especially important with the international popularity of basketball. . . .**
>
> **For many reasons, many fashion trends have begun in the United States. Because of our wealth, free time, and technology, it's easy to understand why . . .**

Transition Words and Phrases

Use the words and phrases in this chart to help you connect your ideas in paragraphs and in longer forms of writing.

Words that can be used to show location:

above	around	between	inside	outside
across	behind	by	into	over
against	below	down	near	throughout
along	beneath	in back of	off	to the right
among	beside	in front of	on top of	under

Words that can be used to show time:

about	during	yesterday	until	finally
after	first	meanwhile	next	then
at	second	today	soon	as soon as
before	third	tomorrow	later	when

Words that can be used to compare things (show similarities):

likewise	as	in the same way
like	also	similarly

Words that can be used to contrast things (show differences):

but	otherwise	on the other hand	although
yet	however	still	even though

Words that can be used to emphasize a point:

again	in fact	for this reason

Words that can be used to add information:

again	and	for instance	as well
also	besides	next	along with
another	for example	finally	in addition

Words that can be used to conclude or summarize:

as a result	finally	in conclusion
therefore	lastly	in summary

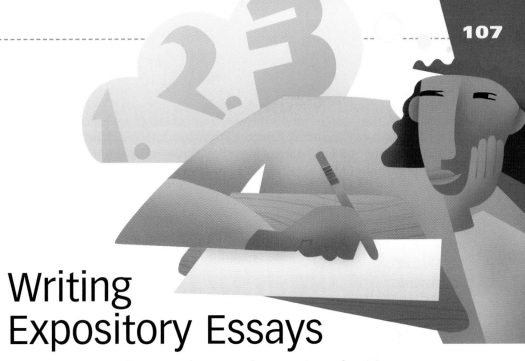

Writing Expository Essays

When you explain or inform in a longer piece of writing, you are writing an expository essay. (Expository writing is sometimes called "informational writing.") It is the most common form of writing assigned in your classes. To write an effective expository essay, you must learn as much as you can about your topic, and then share this knowledge with your readers as clearly and completely as you can.

In most cases, you will write essays about the subjects you are studying in your classes. You will use two main types of thinking to complete expository assignments: *recalling* and *understanding* details.

What's Ahead

This chapter contains everything you need to know to write an expository essay, including a sample essay and step-by-step writing guidelines. A rubric for assessing expository writing is also included.

- Sample Expository Essay
- Writing Guidelines
- Gathering Details for Essays
- Developing Two-Part Essays
- Evaluating Expository Essays

Sample Expository Essay

In this essay, Landon Smith explains what it takes to become a leader. As you read it, notice how the three parts of the essay—the beginning, the middle, and the ending—work together.

Becoming a Leader

BEGINNING

A question and quotation lead up to the thesis (highlighted in yellow).

Who is a leader? The simple answer is "someone who leads." But there isn't anything simple about leadership. As basketball coach Howard Brown states, "Leading a team, and getting the players to work toward a common goal, takes skill and a lot of effort." So how does someone take on this important role? To become a leader, a person must develop three main traits.

MIDDLE

Each middle paragraph discusses a leadership trait.

First of all, leaders must be confident. They must believe in their own abilities and know that these abilities will help the group reach its goals. This confidence comes mainly through training and experience. True leaders are willing to make decisions and stand behind them even when faced with detractors. They know what needs to be done, and they act accordingly. They also make decisions based on good personal judgment, plus the wise input of others.

Secondly, leaders must display good work habits. Effective leaders lead by example, working longer and harder than the rest of the group. In many cases, a group's effort, or lack of it, will be a direct reflection of the leader's example. Leaders also keep up with the latest developments related to the group's work. In other words, true leaders change with the times, and grow as individuals.

Each leadership trait is fully explained.

Thirdly, and most importantly, leaders must earn the respect of the group. This respect is earned in a number of ways. Leaders must be organized, laying out an effective plan or schedule for the group to follow. They help the individuals in the group improve and grow. In addition, effective leaders treat everyone fairly and honestly. They offer praise when earned and criticism when it is necessary.

ENDING

The ending summarizes the main points and shares a proverb.

Becoming a good leader truly does take a lot of effort. A person earns that position by being confident, hardworking, and respected by others. There is an English proverb that says, "A smooth sea never made a skilled mariner." A leader, like a skilled mariner, has sailed and conquered rough seas and, from that experience, has learned how to lead.

Essay Structure

This graphic shows the three main parts of the sample essay.

Becoming a Leader

BEGINNING Who is a leader? The simple answer is "someone . . .

First of all, leaders must be confident. . . .

MIDDLE Secondly, leaders must display good work habits. . . .

Thirdly, and most importantly, leaders must earn the respect of the group. . . .

ENDING Becoming a good leader truly does take a lot of effort.

Writing Guidelines

Prewriting Choosing a Topic

Your teacher will probably identify a general subject area for your essay. Your first job is to select a specific writing topic to explore. Try to select a topic that really interests you.

General Subject Area: *A personal goal*
Specific Writing Topic: *Becoming a leader*

Gathering Details

Follow these steps when you are ready to collect details: (Also see pages 50-51 and 112-113 for collecting strategies.)

1. List all of your ideas about the topic.

2. Review your list to determine how well you know your topic.

3. Collect additional information as needed. When gathering details, look for facts, examples, and quotations that will support or explain your topic.

- Facts are statements and statistics that add support and meaning to your essay. They help you explain your main points.
- Examples are a way of "showing" your readers what you mean. They often follow statements of fact and help to complete an idea.
- Quotations are the exact words of an expert. They add authority to your writing.

Forming a Thesis Statement

Then form a thesis statement. A thesis may be based on your main feelings about a topic, or on a part of the topic that you want to emphasize. Here is a formula for writing a thesis statement.

A specific topic (*To become a leader*)

+ **a main feeling about it, or a part you want to emphasize,** (*a person must develop three main traits.*)

= **an effective thesis statement.** (*To become a leader, a person must develop three main traits.*)

Organizing the Details

Before writing your essay, decide on the best way to organize the details. The **line diagram** below is one type of graphic organizer that will help you arrange your supporting ideas. (See pages 52-53 for other ideas.)

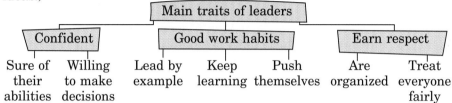

Writing   Writing the First Draft

When you write your essay, pay careful attention to each of the main parts—the beginning, the middle, and the ending.

Beginning ■ Start with general comments about your topic to get your readers interested. Then state your thesis.

Middle ■ In the middle paragraphs (the *body*), share information that supports your thesis. Develop a separate paragraph for each main point.

Ending ■ In the closing paragraph, review the main points covered in the body. Also remind readers why the subject is important.

Revising   Improving Your Writing

Review the first draft of your essay using the checklist below as a guide; also have your teacher or a classmate review your work.

___ Does the opening paragraph introduce the topic in an interesting way and state the thesis of the essay?

___ Does all of the information in the middle paragraphs support the topic?

___ Does the last paragraph signal the end of the essay and remind readers about the importance of the topic?

Editing   Checking for Style and Correctness

Make sure that all of your sentences read smoothly and clearly and that you have used the best words to express your ideas. Then check your revised writing for errors.

Gathering Details for Essays

On the next two pages, you will find tips that will help you collect details when you write about people, places, objects, events, and so on.

Writing About a Person

When writing about or describing a person, make sure you collect plenty of information. The following guidelines will help you collect specific details for your writing.

Observe ■ If possible, carefully watch the person. Maybe the person laughs in a special way or wears a certain type of clothing.

Investigate ■ Talk with your subject. Before the talk, write down a few questions to ask. Then listen closely to the answers.

Remember ■ Recall a story that tells something important about your subject.

Compare ■ Could your subject be compared to some other person?

Writing About a Place

When describing or writing about a place, use details that help readers understand why the place is important to you. The following guidelines will help you collect the best details for your essay.

Observe ■ Study the place you plan to write about. Use photos, postcards, or videos if you can't observe the place in person.

Remember ■ Think of a story about this place.

Analyze ■ What is the most important thing about this place? When is the best time to go there?

Compare ■ Compare your topic to other places.

Writing a Definition

Put the term you are defining (*coyote*) into a class or category of similar objects or ideas (*wild member of the dog family*). Then list special characteristics that make this object different from other objects in that class (*lives in a variety of environments*).

Term—*A coyote*

Class—*is a wild member of the dog family*

Characteristic—*that lives in a variety of environments.*

Writing About an Object

When writing about an object, tell your readers why this object is important or special to you. Use the following guidelines to collect ideas and specific details for your writing.

Observe ■ Think about these questions as you study your object: How is it used? Who uses it? How does it work? What does the object look like?

Research ■ Learn about the object. Try to find out when it was first made and used. Ask other people about it.

Define ■ What class or category does this object fit? (See "Writing a Definition" on page 112.)

Writing About an Event

When writing about or describing an event, include enough details to make the event come to life. Focus on the important actions or on one interesting part. The guidelines below will help you collect details.

Observe ■ Study the event carefully. What sights, sounds, tastes, and smells come to mind when you think of this event? Listen to what people around you are saying.

Remember ■ When writing about something that happened to you, list or cluster as many of the event's details as you can recall. (See page 42 for help with clustering.)

List ■ Answer the *who? what? when? where?* and *why?* questions for the event. (See page 52 for a 5 W's chart.)

Writing an Explanation

When writing an explanation, make your topic easy to understand. You may be asked to explain how to do or make something, how something works, or how to get from one place to another. The following guidelines will help you gather details for your writing.

Observe ■ If possible, either observe or follow the steps you plan to share in your writing. Pay close attention to the details so you can include them in your explanation.

Ask ■ Talk to people who know about your subject. Ask them questions about anything you don't understand.

Research ■ If necessary, learn more about your topic. Find out what makes it different or important.

Developing Two-Part Essays

The most challenging expository essays contain two parts: problem *and* solution, cause *and* effect, comparison *and* contrast. The guidelines that follow will help you develop two-part essays.

- **Collect** your own thoughts and additional information about your topic. Use one of the graphic organizers on the next page to keep track of your collecting.
- **Create** a starter sentence (*thesis statement*) for your essay after you have gathered enough facts and details. Below is a sample thesis statement from a cause-and-effect essay. The first part identifies the cause, and the second part identifies one of the main effects.

  Budget cuts in our school district (part 1: cause)
  have led to fewer extracurricular activities (part 2: effect).

- **List** ideas or write freely about each part of your starter sentence. Keep the ideas flowing for 5 minutes or more.
- **Review** your writing and mark any ideas that you would like to explore further or use in your essay.
- **Write** your essay by connecting the ideas you've marked to include in your writing.
- **Revise** and **edit** your draft after setting it aside for a while.

Starter Sentences

To develop a starter sentence for a two-part essay, complete one of the starter ideas below.

> **For problem and solution essays:**
> . . . could be fixed if . . .
> . . . won't change until . . .
>
> **For cause and effect essays:**
> Because of . . . we now . . .
> When . . . happened, I (*we, they*) . . .
>
> **For comparison and contrast essays:**
> _____ and _____ are both . . . , but they differ in . . .
> While _____ and _____ have . . . in common, they also . . .
>
> **For before and after essays:**
> Once I (*we, they, it*) . . . , but now . . .
> I (*we, they, it*) . . . until . . .

Using Graphic Organizers

Here are four graphic organizers you can use to plan a two-part essay. (See page 52 for other organizers.)

Problem/Solution

Problem:

Causes of the Problem
.
.
.
.
.
.

Possible Solutions
.
.
.
.
.

Cause/Effect

Subject:

Causes	Effects
(Because of...)	(... these conditions resulted)
.	.
.	.
.	.
.	.

Comparison/Contrast

Features of Subject A	Features of Subject B

Circle the similarities and underline the differences.

Before/After

Subject:

Before
After

Evaluating Expository Essays

Use this rubric as a checklist to evaluate the qualities of your expository essays. The rubric follows the traits of effective writing. (See pages 19-24.)

Assessment Rubric

___ **STIMULATING IDEAS**

The essay . . .
- contains an effective thesis statement.
- contains specific facts, examples, or quotations to support the thesis.
- thoroughly informs readers.

___ **LOGICAL ORGANIZATION**
- includes a clear beginning, a strong middle, and an effective ending.
- presents ideas in an organized manner.
- uses transitions to link sentences and paragraphs.

___ **ENGAGING VOICE**
- speaks clearly and knowledgeably.
- shows that the writer is truly interested in the topic.

___ **ORIGINAL WORD CHOICE**
- explains or defines any unfamiliar terms.
- contains specific nouns and active verbs.

___ **EFFECTIVE SENTENCE STYLE**
- flows smoothly from one idea to the next.
- shows a variety of sentence lengths and structures.

___ **CORRECT, ACCURATE COPY**
- observes the basic rules of writing.
- follows the format required by the teacher, or follows some other effective design. (See pages 26-27.)

Writing Persuasive Essays

When you develop an opinion in a longer piece of writing, you are composing a persuasive essay. (*Persuading* means "arguing for or against something.") It is the most challenging form of writing assigned in your classes. Persuasive essays usually follow a pattern: You state your opinion, support it, deal with any opposing viewpoints, and, in closing, restate your opinion.

Persuasive writing requires all of the understanding and clear thinking that you can manage. First, you must learn as much as you can about your topic and, in the process, form an opinion about it. Then, as you develop your essay, you must sound convincing to your readers. Two higher levels of thinking are required for this type of writing: You must *analyze* and *evaluate* the information you collect.

What's Ahead

This chapter will help you write effective persuasive essays. It includes a student sample, writing guidelines, tips for thinking through an argument, and much more.

- Sample Persuasive Essay
- Writing Guidelines
- Using a Graphic Organizer
- Thinking Through an Argument
- Evaluating Persuasive Essays

Sample Persuasive Essay

In this essay, the writer argues that teens need cell phones. He includes three main points to support his opinion. He also includes a concession (opposing viewpoint) in the second to last paragraph.

Teens Dial Up

BEGINNING

Opening statistics lead up to the opinion statement (highlighted).

Cell phone companies predict that by 2005 68 percent of teens in this country will have cell phones (Sewell, 2002). Many schools, politicians, and other officials don't see this as a good thing. However, there are at least three good reasons for teens to have them. Cell phones can make teens safer, healthier, and more responsible.

Parents purchase cell phones for their teens primarily as a safety measure. A recent marketing survey found that 60 percent of parents plan to purchase cell phones for their children for this reason (del Rosario, 2001). Teens can call parents if they need a ride, have car trouble, or experience some other type of emergency. Cell phones can also help to keep teens safe at school. During the Columbine and other high school shootings, students with cell phones called the police.

MIDDLE

Each main point is developed in a separate paragraph.

Not only do cell phones make teens safer, they can, in one important way, also make them healthier. According to a British medical journal study, cell phones may help teens stop smoking. The number of 15-year-old smokers in England dropped as cell-phone use went up ("Cell Phone Chic"). Teens smoke to socialize and act like adults. The study says cell phones are used in the same way. Generally speaking, teens don't have a lot of money. Instead of using their cash to buy cigarettes, they may save it for their cell phones.

Additional studies and statistics are cited.

By using cell phones in the right ways, teens can show adults they are responsible. Approximately 500 teens answered a Website questionnaire about cell phones. The results of the questionnaire showed that 55 percent of teens bought their own cell phones, and more than 35 percent pay their own phone bills. The Web site concluded that, with cell phones, teens feel safer and "more responsible regarding timely payment of bills" ("Teen Cell Survey").

An opposing viewpoint is covered.

It is true that there are times when teens shouldn't use cell phones. Driving is one of these times. Teens certainly don't need the added distraction of using a cell phone while behind the wheel. They also shouldn't use them during class. A cell phone ringing in a classroom is an obvious disruption and shouldn't be tolerated.

ENDING

The writer restates his opinion and main points.

Even with these two problems, the benefits of cell phones for teens are clear. Cell phones in the hands of teens can be very positive for the right reasons and in the right settings. Teens with cell phones will likely be safer, healthier, and more responsible. Officials should do everything they can to promote the meaningful use of these devices.

 For information on giving credit to the sources you use in your writing, turn to pages 232-234 in your handbook.

Writing Guidelines

Prewriting Choosing a Topic

The purpose of a persuasive essay is to convince readers to agree with your opinion about your topic, so it is important to choose a topic that you have strong feelings about. Your teacher may suggest a few writing ideas to get you started. (Also see the topics listed on page 46.)

Make sure that your topic is specific and timely. (*Timely* means "important at the present time.") The brief chart below shows the difference between topics for informational essays and topics for persuasive essays. The persuasive topics are stated as opinions.

Topics for an Informational Essay	Topics for a Persuasive Essay
Cell phone use by teens	Cell phones can make teens safer, healthier, and more responsible.
Four ways to rate movies	Movie ratings improve the viewing habits of young adults.

 See pages 123 and 283-284 for guidelines for writing opinion statements.

Gathering Details

List, cluster, or freewrite to gather support for your opinion. After reviewing your details, collect additional information as needed. Support your opinion with at least two or three main points. There are three main supporting points in the sample essay:

Opinion: **Cell phones can make teens safer, healthier, and more responsible.**

Main Supporting Points:

1. **Promote safety**
2. **Promote better health**
3. **Promote responsibility**

 Organize your information before you write your first draft. (See the graphic organizer on page 122 for help.)

Writing / Writing the First Draft

Beginning ■ In the opening paragraph, get your reader's attention with some interesting comments about your topic; then state your opinion. You may also share the main points you plan to cover in your essay. (See the opening paragraph on page 118.)

Middle ■ Write about the supporting points for your opinion, using one main point per paragraph. Use your outline, list, or other organizer as a guide. **Remember:** In a persuasive essay, the strongest argument is often presented first or last.

(You may need to make a concession in your essay. When you make a concession, you discuss an opposing viewpoint about your topic. Doing so can make your overall argument stronger.)

Ending ■ The last paragraph should restate your opinion, summarize the main points in your argument, and, perhaps, make a call to action. (See the closing paragraph on page 119.)

Revising / Improving Your Writing

Review your first draft using the following checklist as a guide. Also have at least one other person review your work. Then make the necessary changes or improvements in your essay.

___ Does the opening paragraph give background information and state my opinion?

___ Do the main points in the middle paragraphs support my opinion?

___ Are the main points organized so that readers will be able to follow my argument?

___ Did I address any opposing viewpoints?

___ Does the closing paragraph tie everything together and help readers see the value of my opinion?

Editing / Checking for Style and Correctness

Check your revised writing first for sentence style and word choice, and then for errors in spelling, grammar, and punctuation. Also have one other person check your writing for errors. Then complete a neat final copy to share.

Using a Graphic Organizer

Using an outline is a precise, highly organized way to plan your writing. Using a graphic organizer, like the web below, is a much more open way to organize your writing. It's as if you were laying your main ideas and details on a table in order to find the best way to arrange them.

In the planning web below, the opinion appears in the center oval; each main supporting point is linked to this opinion statement. The numbers tell the order in which the main points will appear in the essay. A concession (opposing viewpoint) is indicated by the dotted line around the box.

Planning Web

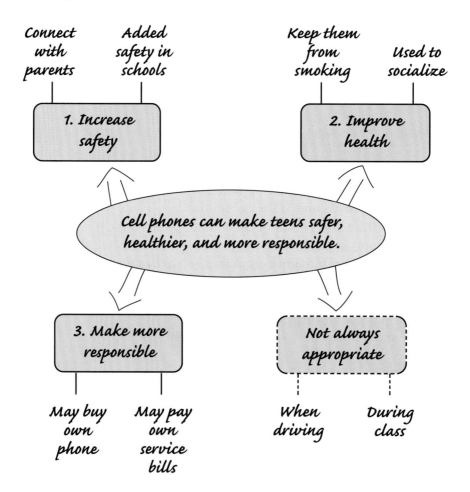

Thinking Through an Argument

The next two pages will help you state and support opinions, as well as make concessions for any opposing arguments.

Stating an Opinion

An effective persuasive essay starts with a reasonable opinion statement. Opinion statements fall into three categories: statements of fact, statements of value, and statements of policy.

Statements of fact claim that something is true or not true.

> **Despite what you might think, most hunters are friends of the environment.**

Statements of value claim that something does or does not have worth.

> **Cell phones can make teens safer, healthier, and more responsible.**

Statements of policy claim that something should or should not be done.

> **The North Section School Board should approve metal detectors for all schools.**

Using Qualifiers

Qualifiers are terms that make an opinion easier to support. See the difference between these two statements:

> **Despite what you might think, hunters are concerned about safety.**

> **Despite what you might think, *most* hunters are concerned about safety.**

"Most" qualifies the opinion stated above so that it is no longer an all-or-nothing idea. Here is a list of useful qualifiers that you can use.

almost	**usually**	**maybe**	**probably**
often	**some**	**most**	**in most cases**

Opinion statements that include words that are strongly positive or negative—such as *all, but, every, always, never,* or *none*—are often difficult to support.

Adding Support

You need convincing facts and details to support your opinion. The more types of support you offer, the stronger your argument will be. Here are some effective types of support.

Predictions: **More and more teens will own cell phones in the future.**

Statistics: **A recent marketing survey found that 60 percent of parents plan to purchase cell phones for their children.**

Comparison: **In the past, teens were usually stuck if they had car trouble or needed some other kind of help. Today, they can quickly and easily use their cell phones to contact help.**

Observation: **The participants in the hunter safety course asked many important questions.**

Expert Testimony: **According to Dr. Gregory Nathan, director of the Department of Parks and Resources, accidental hunting deaths from gunshot wounds have been declining in recent years.**

Making Concessions

When you make a concession, you identify an opposing opinion or viewpoint about your topic. It's important to know that making a concession can actually strengthen your argument. The following concession was made in the sample essay on pages 118-119.

It is true that there are times when teens shouldn't use cell phones.

The phrase *It is true that* introduces this opinion in a way that shows respect for the other side of the argument. Here are some other useful expressions for making concessions:

even though	I agree that	I cannot argue with
I realize that	admittedly	granted
I will admit	you're right	I accept the fact

Evaluating Persuasive Essays

Use this rubric as a checklist to assess your persuasive essays. The rubric is arranged according to the traits of effective writing described in the handbook. (See pages 19-24.)

Assessment Rubric

_____ **STIMULATING IDEAS**

The essay . . .

- states an opinion about an important subject.
- contains convincing reasons to support the opinion.

_____ **LOGICAL ORGANIZATION**

- includes a clear beginning, middle, and ending.
- arranges ideas in an organized manner (perhaps offering the strongest point first or last).
- presents a logical argument.

_____ **ENGAGING VOICE**

- speaks in a convincing, positive way.
- shows that the writer feels strongly about his or her opinion.

_____ **ORIGINAL WORD CHOICE**

- explains important terms.
- uses language that shows an understanding of the subject.

_____ **EFFECTIVE SENTENCE STYLE**

- flows smoothly from sentence to sentence.
- displays varied sentence beginnings and lengths.

_____ **CORRECT, ACCURATE COPY**

- observes the basic rules of writing.
- follows the form suggested by the teacher.

The **Art** of Writing

Writing with Style

Writing Techniques and Terms

Writing with Style

You might think that style is something you add to your writing—a fancy phrase here or a long, complex sentence there. But that is not how style works. In fact, trying to add style usually just clutters things up. It's much more effective to keep things simple and sound like the real you. When it comes to style, the two best words to live by are "be yourself."

Think of writing style as the way you express yourself on paper. It is your words, your sentences, your paragraphs—nobody else's. Your writing style will develop naturally as you continue to write and learn about the language. There are, however, some things that you can do right now to improve it.

What's Ahead

This chapter describes the basic elements of style and explains different ways to develop style. It also covers using colorful words and knowing what to change to make your writing more stylistic.

- Understanding Style
- Developing a Sense of Style
- Modeling the Masters
- Using Strong, Colorful Words
- Knowing What to Change

Understanding Style

Words   The words that you use show your style. In the sample below, Sharee Pearson uses specific words and phrases that reveal the pain of childhood accidents. (Many of these words and phrases are highlighted in red.)

> I had suffered my share of injuries when I was little. Once, when I was playing cars, I toppled over my steering wheel and gashed my chin. My dad rushed me to the doctor to get stitches. Another time, I spied a strange object under the couch. I grabbed the object only to discover too late that it was a large fishing hook, and it was biting fiercely into my thumb. I howled, and my mom came running. She tried to pull it out, but succeeded only in jamming it in further. Once again I was rushed to the doctor, and he had to cut the hook out.

Details   The details and ideas that you share also create your style. In the following sample, writer Gary Sawyer includes many specific details about his topic, a sudden storm on the Kansas prairie. (Many of the details are shown in red.)

> I noticed a menacing black line on the northwest horizon. Soon, a solid purple-black filled the sky. The morning sun to the southeast beamed bright on the squall (storm) line. In the middle of the wall, bearing down toward us, was a giant tower of bright white snow. For miles to either side, there was only the black wall of clouds with a column of snow, lit beautifully by the sun.

Sentences   The way you develop your sentences is also part of your style. In this sample, Scott Mouw expresses his ideas in sentences that read very smoothly. He varies the beginnings and lengths of his sentences. He also uses a variety of sentence types (*simple*, *compound*, and *complex*).

> When I was younger, I would page through the photo albums in our living room. (complex) The red album was by far my favorite. (simple) This album contained black-and-white photos of a time when my grandfather had a flat-top haircut and drove low-rider '57 Chevys. (complex) Most of the photos were taken in the late '50s and early '60s, and they clearly showed the importance of cars in Grandpa's life. (compound) My favorite photos showed the cars my grandfather owned as he got older. (complex) Grandpa did not care for school, but he loved cars and anything else with a motor. (compound) So he always took great care of his wheels. (simple)

Developing a Sense of Style

Here's how you can develop your style—your special way of saying something.

■ **Write with pride.** Good writing begins and ends with your own interest in it. If you care about your writing and put forth your best efforts, your writing will have style.

■ **Write clearly.** Clarity is one of the most important principles of style. It is also one of the hardest to achieve.

■ **Keep things simple.** Writer E. B. White advises writers to approach style with simplicity, plainness, and orderliness. This is good advice from someone known for his pleasing writing style.

■ **Keep things focused.** Writing with style means writing with a clear focus in mind. Writing is "in focus" when it stresses an important part of a topic or a specific feeling you have about it. All of the facts and details in the writing should support the focus. (See page 56.)

■ **Be sincere.** Writing has style when it sounds like one person (*you*) sincerely communicating with another person. It doesn't try to impress readers with a lot of big words. Rather, it is honest and natural.

■ **Know when to cut.** Delete sentences that don't support your main point, and cut any words or phrases that don't strengthen your sentences.

■ **Acquire a writer's sixth sense.** Know when your writing needs work. Watch for groups of sentences that sound too much alike and individual sentences that hang limp like wet rags.

■ **Write active, forward-moving sentences.** Make it clear in your sentences that your subject is actually doing something.

> Out of Style:
> **Plenty of calories are necessary for growth in children.**
> (This thought is wordy and passive.)
> In Style:
> **Children need plenty of calories for growth.**
> (This revised sentence is direct and active.)

"Read! Read! **Read!** And then read some more. When you find something that thrills you, **take it apart paragraph by paragraph**."

—K. P. Kinsella

Modeling the Masters

You can learn a lot about writing by studying the sentences and ideas of some of your favorite authors. When you come across sentences that you really like, practice writing sentences of your own that follow the author's pattern. This process is called modeling. Use the basic guidelines below to practice this helpful technique.

Guidelines for Modeling

- Find a sentence or a short passage that you would like to use as a model.
- Copy it in your writing notebook or on a separate piece of paper.
- Think of a topic for your practice writing.
- Follow the pattern of the sentence or passage as you write about your own subject. (You do not have to follow the model passage exactly.)
- Build each sentence one part at a time. (Don't try to work too quickly.)
- Review your work and change any parts that seem confusing or unclear.
- Save your writing. Share it with a classmate.
- Find other sentences or passages to use as models, and keep practicing.

Morrison

Twain

Modeling Samples

Modeling Sentences. Here is a smooth-reading sentence from "Wings" by Thylias Moss. Notice the modifying phrases beginning with "breaking" and "cutting."

> **"I bought a jug of milk and fell off my bike, breaking the glass jug, cutting my leg."**

■ Here is a student sample following this same pattern:

> **I found an album of family photographs and paged through it, enjoying each photo, losing track of time.**

Modeling Short Passages. Here is a short passage from *Always Running* by Luis J. Rodriguez. The three sentences in this passage vary in terms of length and word order.

> **Although we moved around the Watts area, the house on 105th Street near McKinley Avenue held my earliest memories, my earliest fears and questions. It was a small matchbox of a place. Next to it stood a tiny garage with holes through the walls and an unpainted barnlike quality.**

■ Here is a student sample following this pattern:

> **Although we practiced for the softball tournament, the first game at Island Park on Jefferson Avenue showed our main weaknesses, our poor pitching and fielding. It was a completely one-sided game. Next to our dugout stood our coach with a frown on his face and a disappointed tone in his voice.**

Additional Modeling Ideas

- Search through your own writing for sentences that you really like. Then see how many ways you can rewrite them.
- Keep a file of favorite sentences from your classmates' writing. Or exchange favorite sentences with a classmate and practice modeling these sentences.
- Rewrite a section of one of your old stories to resemble the style of one of your favorite authors.
- Write a story in the style of a favorite author.

Using Strong, Colorful Words

Your writing will have style if you choose the words that best fit your purpose. The best words are ones that add to the overall meaning, feeling, and sound in a piece of writing. Pay special attention to the nouns, verbs, and modifiers (adjectives and adverbs) that you use. The guidelines that follow will help you use strong, colorful words.

> In order to make the best word choices, you need to build your vocabulary. The more words you know, the more words you have to choose from. (See pages 315-330 for help.)

Choosing Specific Nouns

Some nouns are general (*motorcycle, fruit, bird*). Other nouns are specific (*dirt bike, lemon, goldfinch*). Specific nouns give readers clearer, more detailed pictures. As you read down each list in the chart below, the nouns become more specific. The last noun in each list is the type that can make your writing clear and colorful.

person	place	thing	idea
woman	park	drink	feeling
actress	city park	coffee	positive emotion
Halle Berry	Central Park	cappuccino	happiness

Choosing Specific Verbs

Specific action verbs tell readers exactly what is happening. For example, the specific verbs "sprinted" and "jogged" say much more than the general verb "run." The statement "Lawrence jogged around the bases" is clearer than "Lawrence ran around the bases."

✳ Try not to use the "be" verbs (*is, are, was, were*) too often. Many times a stronger action verb can be made from another word in the same sentence.

A "be" verb: **Gabriela Sanchez is the choreographer for the school musicals.**

A stronger verb: **Gabriela Sanchez choreographs the school musicals.**

✳ Use active rather than passive verbs. (See page 459.)

A passive verb: **Another hot dog was eaten by Devon.**

An active verb: **Devon ate another hot dog.**

> "Don't say the old lady screamed—
> bring her on and let her scream."
>
> —Mark Twain

Choosing Effective Modifiers

Adjectives. Use specific adjectives to describe the nouns in your writing. Strong adjectives make the nouns you choose even more interesting and clear. For example, you may tell your readers that Blake's car is a subcompact, but describing it as a *rusty*, *run-down* subcompact says so much more.

✳ Some adjectives are used so often that they carry little meaning: *neat*, *big*, *pretty*, *small*, *cute*, *fun*, *bad*, *nice*, *good*, *dumb*, *great*, and *funny*. Don't overuse these words in your writing. Also be selective with adjectives in your writing. Too many adjectives will make your essays and reports sound unnatural.

Adverbs. Use adverbs when they are needed to describe the action in a sentence. For example, the adverb "barely" clarifies the action in the following sentence: "He barely finished the test before the bell rang."

✳ Don't use two words—a verb and an adverb—when a single vivid verb would be better.

> Verb and adverb: **Mora suddenly yelled when her friend spilled coffee on her.**

> A single vivid verb: **Mora shrieked when her friend spilled coffee on her.**

Choosing Words with Feeling

The words you use in your writing should have the right feeling or connotation. (*Connotation* means "the feeling that a word suggests.") Let's say you are recalling a very close basketball game that your team won in double overtime. It would probably not be enough to say that the game was *exciting* or *action packed*. For this type of game, the word with the right connotation would be *tense* or *gut-wrenching*.

If you need help finding the best words for your writing, use a thesaurus. It will help you pick the word with the right meaning and feeling. (See page 318.)

Knowing What to Change

How can you make a piece of writing more interesting, colorful, and clear? The five points listed below show you how. (See pages 65-72 for more ideas.)

1 **Ideas:** Your topic is too general or uninteresting.
If you're not satisfied writing about the traits of an effective leader, try something a bit more creative. Maybe you could respond to the following quotation: "Leaders are made, not born."

2 **Organization:** Your writing lacks focus (a main point).
If your writing covers too many different ideas, put it into better focus by finding a more specific, interesting way to write about your topic. (See page 56 for more information.)

3 **Voice:** Your writing doesn't sound like you.
If your writing sounds as though it came out of a textbook, try again. This time, be honest and share your real feelings.

4 **Word Choice:** Your writing doesn't say enough.
If your first draft is all skin and bones, flesh it out with details, examples, dialogue, and personal feelings.

5 **Sentence Style:** Your sentences all sound the same.
If your writing seems boring, check your sentences. You may have started too many of them in the same way, used too many "be" verbs (*is, are, was*), or repeated a certain word too many times. You can improve your style by varying your sentence beginnings and changing some of the words you've used.

Special Feature of Style

Writer Donald Murray suggests that you use anecdotes in your writing. (An *anecdote* is a brief story used to make a point.) Anecdotes show readers something in a lively way, rather than telling them.

In the following passage, student writer Amy Douma shares an anecdote about a homeless man.

> **On a cold February afternoon, an old man sits on the sidewalk outside a New York hotel. At the man's feet is a sign that reads: "Won't you help me? I'm cold and homeless and lonely. God bless you." He spends his days alone on the street begging for handouts. He has no job, no friends, and nowhere to turn.**

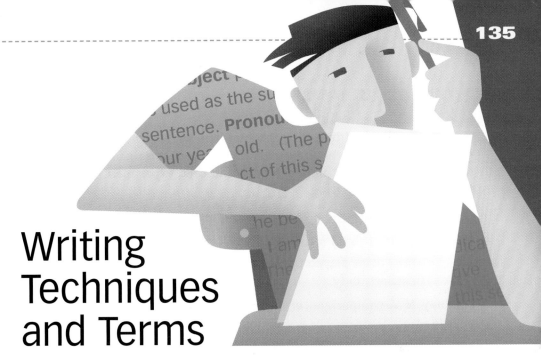

Writing Techniques and Terms

Pay careful attention to the requirements for each of your writing assignments. For one assignment, you may be asked to write an *essay* that includes plenty of *supporting details*. For another one, you may be asked to write a *poem* that includes *figurative language*. To complete these assignments, you would have to know the meaning of each italicized word.

This chapter explains many of the important words associated with writing—including those in the previous paragraph. The first part lists *techniques*, or special devices, that can add style to your writing. The second part lists basic *terms* related to writing. As your knowledge of these techniques and terms grows, so will your ability to express yourself on paper.

What's Ahead

Think of the following pages as your own writing dictionary. Whenever you have a question about a writing-related word, turn here for help.

- **Writing Techniques**
- **Writing Terms**

Writing Techniques

Writers use different techniques to write stories, essays, and reports. (Techniques are methods or ways of doing something.) Look over the following writing techniques and then experiment with some of them in your own writing.

Allusion ■ A reference to a well-known person, place, thing, or event that the reader should recognize.

> **Ms. Foster played Uncle Sam, encouraging us to do our patriotic duty.**

Analogy ■ A comparison of similar objects to help clarify one of the objects.

> **Personal journals are like photograph albums. They both hold pictures of people doing different things.**

Anecdote ■ A little story used to illustrate or make a point.

> **At the height of his baseball career, hall-of-famer Ted Williams flew combat missions in World War II and the Korean War.**
> (This anecdote shows Williams' patriotism and willingness to sacrifice for his country.)

Antithesis ■ Antithesis means "exact opposite." In writing, it usually means using opposite ideas in the same thought or sentence.

> **"Humankind must put an end to war, or war will put an end to humankind."**

Colloquialism ■ A common word or phrase that is used when people talk to one another. Colloquialisms are usually not used in a formal speech or in most assigned writing.

> **"What's up?" and "What's happenin'?" are colloquialisms for "What are you doing?"**

Dramatic monologue ■ A speech in which a character gives a lot of information about himself or herself. The character usually does this by talking alone, but as if someone else were there.

Exaggeration ■ An overstatement or stretching of the truth used to emphasize a point or paint a clearer picture. (See *hyperbole* and *overstatement*.)

> **I slept for a month after getting home from summer camp.**

Flashback ■ A technique in which a writer interrupts a story to go back and explain an earlier event.

Foreshadowing ■ Hints or clues that a writer uses to suggest what will happen next in a story.

Hyperbole ■ An extreme exaggeration or overstatement that a writer uses for emphasis. (See *exaggeration* and *overstatement*.)

> **My heart melted when I saw the Labrador puppy.**

Irony ■ A technique that uses a word or phrase to mean the opposite of its normal meaning.

> **Marshall's favorite activity is cleaning his room.**

Juxtaposition ■ Putting two ideas, words, or pictures together to create a new, often ironic meaning.

> **Oh, the delight of scraping paint!**

Local color ■ The use of details that are common in a certain place (a local area). A story taking place on a seacoast would contain details about the water and the life and people near it.

Metaphor ■ A figure of speech that compares two things without using the word *like* or *as*.

> **In our community, high school football is king.**

Overstatement ■ An exaggeration or stretching of the truth. (See *exaggeration* and *hyperbole*.)

> **When he saw my grades, my dad hit the roof.**

Oxymoron ■ A technique in which two words with opposite meanings are put together for a special effect.

> **small fortune, original copy, tough love, cruel kindness**

Paradox ■ A statement that is contrary to common sense yet may, in fact, be true.

> **Her coach considered this a good loss.**

Parallelism ■ Repeating similar grammatical structures (*words, phrases,* or *sentences*) to give writing rhythm.

> **We will lie on the beach, swim in the ocean, and sleep under the stars.**

Personification ■ A figure of speech in which a nonhuman thing (an *idea, object,* or *animal*) is given human characteristics.

> **Rosie's old car coughs and wheezes on cold days.**

Pun ■ A phrase that uses words in a way that gives them a funny effect.

> **"I have come to believe that opposing gravity is something not to be taken—uh, lightly."** —Daniel Pinkwater

Sarcasm ■ The use of praise to make fun of, or "put down," someone or something. The expression is not sincere and is actually intended to mean the opposite thing.

> **Kobe's a real gourmet; his favorite food is peanut butter and jelly sandwiches.** (A *gourmet* is a "lover of fine foods.")

Satire ■ Using sarcasm, irony, or humor to make fun of people's habits or ideas. Satire is often used to raise questions about a current event or political decision. (See *sarcasm* and *irony*.)

Sensory details ■ Specific details that are usually perceived through the senses. Sensory details help readers see, feel, smell, taste, and/or hear what is being described.

> **As Lamont took his driver's test, his heart thumped, his hands got clammy, and beads of sweat ran down his face.**

Simile ■ A figure of speech that compares two things, using the word *like* or *as*.

> **Faye's little brother darts around like a water bug.**
> **Yesterday, the lake was as smooth as a mirror.**

Slang ■ Informal words or phrases used by particular groups of people when they talk to each other.

> **chill out   hang loose   totally awesome**

Symbol ■ A concrete (or real) object that is used to stand for an idea.

> **The American flag is a symbol of the United States. The stars stand for the 50 states, and the stripes stand for the 13 original U.S. colonies.**

Understatement ■ The opposite of *exaggeration*. By using very calm language, an author can bring special attention to an object or an idea.

> **" . . . except for an interruption caused by my wife falling out of the car, the journey went very well."**
> —E. B. White

Writing Terms

This glossary includes terms that are often used to describe parts of the writing process. It also includes terms that explain special ways of stating an idea.

Argumentation ■ Writing or speaking that uses reason and logic to prove a point or support an opinion.

Arrangement ■ The order in which details are organized in a piece of writing. Arrangement is also known as *organization*.

Audience ■ The people who read or hear what has been written.

Balance ■ Arranging words and phrases in a similar way to give them equal importance. Balance gives writing a pleasing flow or rhythm.

"The thrill of victory, and the agony of defeat . . . "

Beginning ■ The first or opening part in a piece of writing. In a paragraph, the beginning is the topic sentence. In an essay or a report, the beginning is the first paragraph, including the thesis statement.

Body ■ The main or middle part in a piece of writing. The body comes between the *beginning* and the ending (*closing*) and includes the main points that support the writer's thesis.

Brainstorming ■ Collecting ideas by talking freely about all the possibiliti

Central idea ■ The main idea or point in a piece of writing, usually stated in a thesis statement or topic sentence. (See *thesis statement* and *topic sentence.*)

Cliche ■ A phrase or sentence that has been overused. It is usually better to find a new way of saying the same thing. (See *trite.*)

Cliche: **When it comes to numbers, she is** as sharp as a tack.

Better: **When it comes to numbers, her mind works like a calculator.**

Closing ■ The summary or final part in a piece of writing. In a paragraph, the closing is the last sentence. In an essay or a report, the closing is the final paragraph.

Coherence ■ Putting ideas together in such a way that the reader can easily follow them.

Composition ■ Writing in which a series of ideas are combined into one unified piece.

Descriptive writing (description) ■ Writing that uses details to help the readers clearly imagine a certain person, place, thing, or idea.

> **With no one to hold our ankles, sit-ups are nearly impossible to do, especially when Coach Brown barks out the pace we have to follow.**

Dialogue ■ Written conversation between two or more people.

Diction ■ A writer's choice of words. Diction helps create a formal writing style (for reports and business letters), or an informal, everyday writing style (for *personal* and *narrative writing*).

Emphasis ■ Giving great importance to a specific idea in a piece of writing. Emphasis can be achieved by placing the idea in a special position, by repeating a key word or phrase, and so on.

Essay ■ A piece of factual writing in which ideas on a single topic are presented, explained, argued, or described in an interesting way.

Expository writing (exposition) ■ Writing that explains something.

Extended definition ■ A piece of writing that goes beyond the basic definition of a term. An extended definition can include personal definitions, similes, metaphors, quotations, and so on.

Figurative language ■ Special comparisons, often called figures of speech, that make your writing more creative. (See page 207.)

Fluency ■ The ability to express yourself freely and naturally.

Focus ■ The specific part of a topic that is written about in an essay.

Form ■ The way a piece of writing is structured or organized; a type of writing. (See *structure*.)

> **poem   essay   report   news story**

Freewriting ■ Writing whatever comes to mind about any topic.

Generalization ■ A general statement that gives an overall view, rather than focusing on specific details.

Grammar ■ The structure of language. The rules and guidelines that you follow in order to speak and write acceptably.

Idiom ■ Words used in a special way that may be different from their literal meaning. (See pages 433-439.)

> **Mom has *an axe to grind* with the owners of that German shepherd**. (This idiom means "a problem to settle.")
>
> **Carmen always *gives me the cold shoulder***. (This idiom means "ignores me.")

Issue ■ A topic that people have different opinions about.

> **Should our school have a dress code?**

Jargon ■ The technical language of a certain group, occupation, or field.

Computer jargon:	**byte**	**floppy disk**	**mainframe**
	software	**cursor**	**icon**
	modem	**upload**	

Journal ■ A notebook for writing down thoughts, experiences, information, and ideas. (See pages 145-148.)

Limiting the subject ■ Taking a general subject and narrowing it down to a specific topic.

General subject			Specific topic
golf →	**golf skills** →	**driving** →	**correcting a slice**

Literal ■ The actual or dictionary meaning of a word. Language that is literal means exactly what it appears to mean.

Loaded words ■ Words that make people feel for or against something. Loaded words are often used in persuasive writing such as ads.

> **The new tax bill helps the rich and hurts the poor.**
> (The blue words are loaded words.)

Logic ■ The science of reasoning. Logic uses reasons, facts, and examples to prove or support a point. (See page 284.)

Modifiers ■ Words, phrases, or clauses that describe another word.

> **Our black cat slowly stretched in the sunroom and then leaped onto the wicker chair**. (Without the blue modifiers, all we know is that a "cat stretched and leaped.")

Narrative writing (narration) ■ Writing that tells about an event or a story.

Objective ■ Writing that gives factual information without adding feelings or opinions. (See *subjective*.)

Personal narrative ■ Writing that shares an event or experience in the writer's personal life.

Persuasive writing (persuasion) ■ Writing that is meant to get readers to agree with you about someone or something.

Plagiarism ■ Taking someone else's words or ideas and using them as your own.

Poem ■ Writing that uses rhythm, rhyme, and imagery. (See *prose*.)

Point of view ■ The position or angle from which a story is told. (See page 334.)

Process ■ A method of doing something that involves steps or stages.

> **The writing process includes prewriting, writing the first draft, revising, editing and proofreading, and publishing.**

Prose ■ Writing or speaking in the usual sentence form. Prose becomes poetry when it takes on rhyme and rhythm. (See *poem*.)

Purpose ■ The specific reason that a person has for writing.

> **to narrate   to persuade   to explain   to describe**

Revision ■ Making changes in a piece of writing to improve the ideas (content), organization, and *voice*.

Spontaneous ■ Writing or speaking that is not planned or thought out in advance.

Structure ■ The way a piece of writing is organized. (See *form*.)

Style ■ How an author writes (his or her choice of words and sentences).

Subjective ■ Writing that includes personal feelings, attitudes, and opinions. (See *objective*.)

Summary ■ Writing that presents only the most important ideas in something you have read. (See pages 215-218.)

Supporting details ■ The facts or ideas that are used to make or prove a point, or explain or describe a topic.

Syntax ■ The order of words in a sentence. The chapter "Writing Basic Sentences" will help you understand the syntax of sentences in English. (See pages 83-90.)

Theme ■ The central idea or main point in a piece of writing.

teenage dieting	**graduation requirements**
animal rights	**neighborhood watch groups**
driver's safety	**community service**
teen centers	**capital punishment**
peer pressure	**school internships**

Thesis statement ■ A statement that gives the main idea of an essay. (See *central idea*.)

Tone ■ A writer's attitude toward his or her subject.

serious   objective   humorous   subjective

Topic ■ The specific subject of a piece of writing.

Topic sentence ■ The sentence that contains the main idea of a paragraph. (See *central idea*.)

Blue jeans are the most recognizable piece of American clothing.

Transition ■ A word or phrase that connects or ties two ideas together smoothly. (See page 106.)

also   however
lastly   later   next

Trite ■ An expression considered to be an overused and ineffective way of saying something. (See *cliche*.)

honest Abe   red-hot   cute as a button

Unity ■ A sense of oneness in writing in which each sentence helps to develop the main idea.

Universal ■ A topic or idea that appeals to everyone, not just people of a particular age, race, income, or gender group.

Usage ■ The way in which people use language. *Standard language* generally follows the grammar rules; *nonstandard language* does not. Most of the writing you do in school will require standard usage.

Voice ■ A writer's unique, personal tone.

Personal
Writing

Journal Writing

Autobiographical Writing

Journal Writing

More than anything else, journal writing is a way to explore your personal thoughts and feelings . . . and doing so on a regular basis. It is putting pen to paper or fingers to a keyboard day in and day out, writing about your recent experiences and current concerns. If you get into a writing routine and stick to it, you'll gain from the writing in three important ways:

Writing for Meaning Journal writing helps you better understand the daily experiences in your life.

Writing for Practice Writing regularly in a journal develops your writing fluency—the ability to put your thoughts on paper freely and smoothly.

Writing for Learning Writing in a journal about the subjects you are studying helps you become a better learner. (In your writing, you can ask questions and put new ideas into your own words.)

What's Ahead

This chapter will help you learn more about journal writing, including how to get started and how to get the most out of your writing. You'll also learn about different types of journals.

- Getting Started
- Sample Journal Entry
- Types of Journals

Getting Started

Journal writing gives you an opportunity to discover new ideas and new ways of thinking. Follow these steps to get the most out of your journal writing:

1 **Collect the proper tools.** If you're writing by hand, use a spiral notebook and a favorite pen or pencil. Use a computer, but only if you know how to keyboard. Otherwise, you won't be able to explore your thoughts freely enough.

2 **Establish a regular routine.** Write early in the morning, late at night, or sometime in between. It's your choice. Also find a comfortable place to write that is free of distractions.

3 **Keep the ideas flowing.** Try to write for at least 5 to 10 minutes at a time. Write as freely as you can, but make sure that your ideas are written neatly enough to read later.

> If you regularly write for the same amount of time—let's say 10 minutes—count the number of words you produce. That number should increase over time, which means you are gaining fluency as a writer.

4 **Write about things that are important to you.** Here are some general subject areas to get you started:
- interesting things you see or hear
- personal thoughts and feelings
- daily happenings
- important events
- books you've read
- subjects you are studying

> Don't plan your writing or try to figure out what you will say in the beginning, middle, and ending. You don't need to know where your writing is going to take you. Just record your thoughts as they come to mind.

5 **Keep track of your writing.** Date your journal entries, and save them. Read through your journal from time to time. Underline ideas that you would like to write more about in the future. Also make comments in the margins: "What do I really mean by this idea?" or "Why do I feel this way?"

Sample Journal Entry

In this entry, Peter Davis reflects on an important decision that he will soon have to make—what he will do with his life after high school.

October 24

I am trying to decide what I will do when I graduate. I like working on cars, but I also like airplanes. My high school counselor says that there are very good trade schools for mechanics. I could probably work on cars without extra training, but I would get better pay if I were a certified mechanic. Then the big dealerships would be interested in me. Of course, working on airplanes would require special training.

A good friend of mine went to a state college last year and really liked it. So maybe I should at least try college for one year. I'd be the first one in my family to go to college. That would be pretty cool.

Also, I would like to travel, so I could always start school later. The trouble is I don't know if I can afford to hit the road. One of my cousins is enlisting in the Marines when he is done with school. He says he will learn a lot and get to travel. Maybe I should think about enlisting.

I've got two years of high school left, but I want to have things planned long before I graduate. That's my goal, at least for now.

✳ Asking questions and wondering are two ways to reflect in your journal writing. (*Reflect* means "to think very carefully about something.")

Ask questions. As you write, ask yourself questions: *"What was interesting about this experience?" "How do I feel about it now?"*

Wonder. Think about what you have learned from a certain experience. Compare it to other experiences. Predict what it might mean to you in the future.

Types of Journals

If you enjoy keeping a personal journal, you may want to keep other types of journals as well.

Dialogue Journal

In a dialogue journal, two individuals (you and a teacher, family member, or friend) converse in writing. A dialogue journal can help you and your partner learn about each other, work through a problem, or share a common interest.

Learning Log

A learning log (classroom journal) gives you the opportunity to explore concepts, facts, and ideas covered in a specific class. Learning logs are very helpful in your math and science classes, especially when the material is difficult. (See page 348.)

Reader Response Journal

A response journal is a kind of learning log. In this type of journal, you write about your reactions to the books you are reading. Here are some questions that will help you write about literature:

1. What were you feeling after reading the opening chapter(s)? After reading half of the book? After finishing the book?
2. Did the book make you laugh? Cry? Smile? Cheer? Explain.
3. What connections are there between the book and your life? Explain.
4. What is the most important event in the book? The most important passage? The most important word? Explain.
5. Who else should read this book? Why?

Specialized Journal

When you write in a journal about an extended event or experience, you are writing in a specialized journal. You may want to explore your thoughts and feelings while at summer camp, while participating in a team sport, while involved in a school production, or while working on a group project.

Travel Log

In a travel log, you simply explore your thoughts and feelings while vacationing or traveling. It's a way to preserve memories and make use of time while waiting in lines or in transit. (*Transit* means "moving from one location to another.")

Autobiographical Writing

Student writer Jeffrey Carter states, "A story I wrote about my life is my best piece because I was able to control what I wrote." Do you know why Jeffrey felt in control? He was writing about something he truly cares about, one of his own experiences. And he probably put a lot of effort into his work because he was sharing a part of his own life.

When you write about your own experiences, you are involved in autobiographical writing. This can be one of the most satisfying types of writing because it allows you to . . .

- relive important times in your life,
- learn about yourself, and
- establish your special place in the world.

What's Ahead

This chapter contains two types of autobiographical writing, easy-to-follow writing guidelines, and an assessment rubric that you can use to evaluate your writing.

- **Sample Personal Narrative**
- **Writing Guidelines**
- **Sample Phase Autobiography**
- **Evaluating Autobiographical Writing**

Sample Personal Narrative

In this narrative, Justin Hughes recalls a basketball tournament that changed his attitude about life. After you read this narrative, you may think of some life-changing experiences in your own life.

When Basketball Became Less Important

BEGINNING

The opening paragraph sets the scene.

At one time, my whole life revolved around basketball. Then an incident during my eighth-grade basketball season changed all of that. This incident made me realize that I should focus more of my attention around God, family, and friends.

My eighth-grade basketball team was playing in the South Milwaukee Tournament. We had won our first three games in a very impressive way. That put us in a three-game championship series against St. Lucy's Lightnings. We went into the first game of this series very confident. In the first game, my best friend Jermaine scored 25 points, and I scored 27 points. We won that game by a large margin.

MIDDLE

The middle part shares the details of the experience.

Immediately following the game, Jermaine complained about chest pains. He still had the pains the next day at school and was thinking about not playing that night. I told him it was probably nothing but indigestion or heartburn. I finally convinced him to play. I was more worried about the game than I was about Jermaine.

It was a tight game, and Jermaine was playing well. Then, in the third quarter, Jermaine collapsed after setting a pick for our point guard. The team trainers from both sidelines rushed to his aid. They got him off

The writer adds his own feelings.

the court and into an ambulance. For the rest of the game, I couldn't focus, and we lost. The next day, I was hoping to see Jermaine at school, but he didn't show up. I felt really bad because I had persuaded him to play.

Our team went into the last game thinking about Jermaine. The last thing on our minds was winning the championship. At halftime, we were down by 12 points, and my teammates were hanging their heads. When we came out of the locker room, we saw Jermaine sitting on the bench. He said he was suffering from a mild heart murmur. I was ecstatic to see him there. Luckily, I hit a game-winning three pointer with no time left on the clock. I immediately grabbed the game ball and gave it to Jermaine. Then I apologized for making him play the night before.

ENDING

The closing explains the importance of the experience.

My best friend was too ill to play in a game that, in the big picture, meant very little. Ever since this incident, I have changed my priorities. I continue to play basketball, but it no longer runs my life.

Narrative Structure

This graphic shows how the parts of a narrative fit together. Each part—an explanation or action—helps tell the complete story.

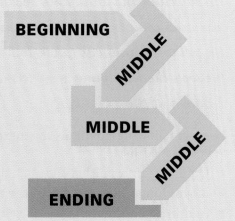

BEGINNING

MIDDLE

MIDDLE

MIDDLE

ENDING

Writing Guidelines

Prewriting Choosing a Topic

Any memorable event that took place over a short period of time is a good topic for a personal narrative. (Just make sure that it meets the requirements of your assignment.) If you have trouble thinking of a topic, use a selecting strategy from your handbook (see pages 41-48).

Gathering Details

If the experience for your narrative is very clear in your mind, you may not need to do much collecting. A simple listing of the basic facts may be enough. Just jot down things as you remember them. See the sample quick list below.

Sample Quick List

Our team was in the South Milwaukee Tournament.

We won the first three games.

~~The games were easy.~~

Then we faced St. Lucy's in a 3-game championship series.

We won the first game; Jermaine and I had good games.

He played in the 2nd game because I asked him to.

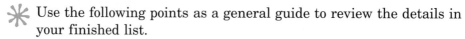

Jermaine complained of chest pains.

He collapsed and was taken to a hospital, and we lost.

We won the last game after Jermaine showed up to watch.

I gave him the game ball.

✳ Use the following points as a general guide to review the details in your finished list.

- Omit any information that is not truly important.
- Move things that are not in the right order.
- Add important details you forgot.
- Use your corrected list as a guide for writing your first draft.

Writing ◢ Writing the First Draft

When writing a first draft, include all of the important details related to the experience. Don't worry if you miss a few things because you can always add them later when you revise your writing. Here are two different ways to write your first draft:

1. **Place yourself right in the middle of the action.**
   "This was it. There was no turning back. As the well-greased wheels on the roller coaster pulled slowly up the track . . . "
   Then share the details of the experience.

2. **Set the scene by beginning with background information.**
   "At one time, my whole life revolved around basketball. . . . "
   Once you complete the beginning part, then continue writing about the experience.

Revising ◢ Improving Your Writing

Review your writing after you finish your first draft. Decide if you have left out any important details or have put things in the wrong order. Also have someone else check your writing to see if any parts are unclear. Then revise your writing as necessary. Here is a sample:

Revising in Action

Immediately following the game,

Jermaine complained about chest pains. He
and was thinking about not playing that night.
still had the pains the next day at school.

An important detail is added.

I told him it was probably nothing but

indigestion or heartburn. I was more

worried about the game than I was about

An idea is reordered.

Jermaine. I finally convinced him to play.

Editing Checking for Style and Correctness

Once you have completed all of your revisions, you are ready to edit your narrative. First make sure that your sentences read smoothly and that you have used the best words. Then check for spelling, grammar, punctuation, and capitalization errors. (Have a trusted classmate check your writing as well.)

After that, write a neat final copy of your narrative. Proofread this copy for errors before you share it. Here are several sample editing changes:

Editing in Action

A comma is added.

A spelling error is corrected.

A verb is made more specific.

> *It was a tight game and Jermaine was*
>
> *playing well. Then, in the third quarter,*
>
> *Jermaine collapsed after setting a pick for*
>
> *our point* ~~gaurd.~~ guard *The team trainers from*
>
> *both sidelines* ~~went~~ rushed *to his aid. They got him*
>
> *off the court and into an ambulance. . . .*

Transition and Linking Words

Narratives are almost always organized *chronologically* (by time). Words and phrases like *first, next,* and *as soon as* are used in narratives to link or connect the related actions. Here is a list of linking words that show time.

about	during	yesterday	until	finally
after	first	meanwhile	next	then
at	second	today	soon	as soon as
before	third	tomorrow	later	when

Sample Phase Autobiography

In this sample phase autobiography, Lisa Servais remembers a time in her life when she enjoyed dressing up. In a phase autobiography, you write about an extended period of time in your life that affected you—made you better or made you different. The key to writing an effective phase autobiography is sharing just the key details. Otherwise, your writing will go on and on, and it won't be very enjoyable to read.

BEGINNING

The writer introduces her phase in the opening line.

MIDDLE

The writer highlights key details.

Fashionation

When I was younger, I was notorious for my strange dress-up games. One of these games was "Keeku." When I played Keeku, I would pin my hair up with plastic barrettes and hold a pair of red sunglass frames that only had one handle. With my costume complete, I would run around the house saying "Keeku! Keeku! Keeku!" It wasn't much of a game, but I guess I enjoyed it because I did it all the time.

I also spent a lot of time playing "Ginger," a character from the old *Gilligan's Island* show, which was one of my favorite reruns when I was little. The main thing I needed to play this was my Ginger dress, or squiggly skirt, as it was sometimes called. It was a multicolored tank top nobody wore anymore, and it was like a dress on me. I would put it on, tie a belt around it, and an amazing change would take place. I was no longer Lisa; instead, I was beautiful, glamorous Ginger from *Gilligan's Island.* I'd walk around the house calling my sisters and brothers Mary Ann, Gilligan, Skipper, or Mr. and Mrs. Howell. The title Professor was reserved for the St. Agnes statue in our living room.

MIDDLE

The writer focuses on important features of the phase.

Once when I was playing Ginger, I added something new to the game; it was my Ginger hairstyle. This delicate design was created by sucking my hair up into the vacuum cleaner hose until it stood on end. I thought I was pretty beautiful until the neighbor boys began teasing me about it. I gave up my Ginger hairdo.

My days of make-believe sometimes included my sister Mary, who was my constant companion. We played long dresses or dressed up in our ballerina dresses. Hers was blue and mine was pink. They itched worse than poison ivy, but we'd wear them for hours. We wore them when we played house and store and restaurant . . . and even when we rode our bikes around the neighborhood.

ENDING

In closing, she reflects on this time in her life.

I guess all kids go through a pretending stage. Why dressing up was so important to me, though, I don't know. Today I wouldn't be caught dead looking like that.

Evaluating Autobiographical Writing

Use this rubric as a checklist to evaluate the quality of your autobiographical writing. The rubric is arranged according to the traits of effective writing described on pages 19-24.

Assessment Rubric

_____ **STIMULATING IDEAS**

The writing . . .

- focuses on a specific experience or extended period of time in your life.
- contains specific details and, if possible, dialogue.
- makes readers want to know what happens next.

_____ **LOGICAL ORGANIZATION**

- includes a clear beginning that pulls readers into the story.
- presents the ideas chronologically (according to time).
- reflects on the importance of the experience or time.

_____ **ENGAGING VOICE**

- shows that the writer is truly interested in the subject.
- speaks with enthusiasm and energy.

_____ **ORIGINAL WORD CHOICE**

- contains specific nouns, verbs, and modifiers.

_____ **EFFECTIVE SENTENCE STYLE**

- flows smoothly from one idea to the next.
- includes sentences that vary in length and in the way they begin.

_____ **CORRECT, ACCURATE COPY**

- follows the basic rules of writing.
- uses the format suggested by the teacher.

Subject
Writing

Biographical Writing

Writing Explanations

Writing News Stories

Writing About Literature

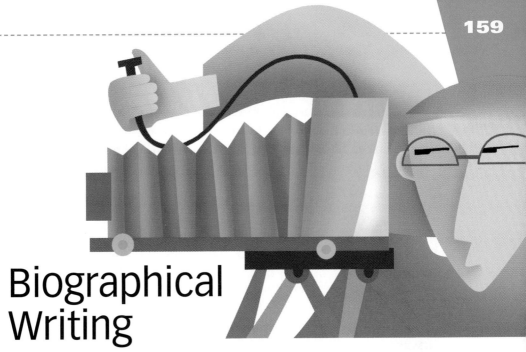

Biographical Writing

Writer William Zinsser says, "Of all the topics available to you as a writer, the one you know best is yourself." Zinsser is absolutely right. You know your own thoughts, feelings, and experiences better than anything else. The topic that you know second best would probably be someone you are close to—a friend, a family member, or a neighbor.

When you write about another person—someone you know or someone who simply interests you—you are involved in biographical writing. Your goal as a biographer is to share a story from that person's life in an appealing way. If the person is new to you, you will have to learn as much as you can about him or her before you start your writing. All types of biographical writing can give you a better understanding of the people and world around you.

What's Ahead

This chapter contains two types of biographical writing along with step-by-step writing guidelines. After reviewing this information, you will be ready to write about another person—someone you know well or someone you would like to learn about.

- Sample Biographical Essay
- Writing Guidelines
- Sample Phase Biography

Sample Biographical Essay

In this biographical essay, Frances Kuhn writes about a person she admires. Frances based her writing on information that she gained by interviewing her subject and by observing him in the classroom.

He D.A.R.E.s to Make a Difference

BEGINNING

The writer uses a story to introduce her subject.

"My mom came into my room and gently woke me up. She was crying and told me to come into the kitchen. I saw my brothers sitting on a bench in the kitchen, crying too, and I knew something was wrong. My mom sat me down and told me that my father was not coming home that night. He was never coming home."

Officer Robert Filley tells this story to his students in the Drug Abuse Resistance Education (D.A.R.E.) classes. This incident was one of the reasons why Robert became a D.A.R.E. officer. Robert's father had been killed in a drunken-driving accident. Alcohol abuse can ruin lives, and Robert knows about this firsthand.

MIDDLE

She shares the exact words of her subject.

Robert has had numerous people to look to for inspiration in his life. His brother has been a police officer for almost 20 years. He was an officer when Robert was growing up in Spring Valley: "My brother was a major role model for me, and he still is." But the biggest inspiration in Robert's life has been his mother. She raised her three boys by herself after his father's death, and she taught them everything she knew about faith, family values, and the meaning of life.

Robert sometimes worries that his children may also have to grow up without a father.

During one experience, he thought his family was going to lose him. "I was working the graveyard shift, and my partner and I got a call saying that there was a motel on fire. When we arrived, there were no fire trucks, just us. Elderly people who couldn't walk were trapped inside, so we kicked down the doors and carried them out over our shoulders. I thought I was going to die during that emergency. But obviously I made it, even though I had to spend two days in the hospital."

She also includes specific details about her subject.

As a D.A.R.E. officer, Robert works four days a week, 10 hours a day, so he has a lot of time to spend with his family on the weekends. He is the choir director at his church and loves to sing and play the guitar. His goal is to move up the ranks within the police force, becoming a detective, then a sergeant, and finally a lieutenant. He would like to retire at the age of 50 and become a teacher.

Robert gets letters all the time from high-school students saying, "Oh, I was at a party last weekend, and someone offered me marijuana. I remembered the things we talked about in D.A.R.E. class. I just wanted to tell you that I said no. You were part of that decision."

ENDING

The writer closes with an important piece of advice.

I asked Robert if he could give advice to young people today, what would it be? He thought about it for a while and replied, "Think about what you are doing before you do it. Then listen to your gut feelings and do what you know is right. If you remember one thing, remember this, 'What is popular is not always right, and what is right is not always popular.' "

Writing Guidelines

Prewriting Choosing a Topic

When you are planning a biography, you have three basic choices for a topic. (Make sure to choose a person that truly interests you—someone you can find plenty of information about.)

1. Think of a person you know very well—a family member or a friend.

2. Think of a person who has had a big influence in your life—perhaps a teacher, a coach, an employer, or a religious leader.

3. Think of an interesting person you have heard about—an explorer, a scientist, an inventor, a leader, an artist, or a musician.

Gathering Details

Your choices for collecting details for a biography are pretty much the same, except if you are writing about an interesting or famous person that you do not personally know. Here are your basic choices:

Type of Subject	Sources of Information
For family members and friends . . .	*search your memory, observe the person, interview him or her, and ask others about the person.*
For teachers, coaches, or employers . . .	*search your memory, observe the person, interview him or her, and ask others about the person.*
For interesting people you have heard about . . .	*interview and observe the person (if possible), read about him or her, and ask others about the person.*

Listing, freewriting, and clustering work well when you collect memory details. A gathering grid (page 53) or a 5 W's chart (page 52) works well for collecting details from reading material. If you plan to conduct an interview, see page 176 for help.

Writing | Writing the First Draft

Follow the guidelines below when you write the first draft of your biographical essay.

- Review the facts, details, and ideas that you have collected, highlighting the ones that interest you the most.

- Make the most interesting details the focus of your writing, and think of the best way to share these details. For example, the writer of the sample essay on pages 160-161 highlights important events in her subject's life and shares some of the person's exact words.

- Here are a few additional ways to develop your writing.

  - Share the details of one important event in the person's life and explain its significance.

  - Focus on the person's outstanding physical characteristics and/or personality traits.

  - Explain how the person fits into a larger group—a family, a team, a business, a school.

  - Analyze the person's importance to the community in which he or she lives, or analyze his or her place in history (if you're writing about a famous person).

- Organize your biographical essay in the following way:

  Beginning In the beginning paragraph, say something interesting about the person to get your reader's attention. Also introduce the focus of your essay.

  Middle In the middle part of your essay, include information that supports or develops your focus. Organize this information either according to time or importance.

  Ending In the last paragraph, come to some conclusion about the importance of the person and his or her story.

Revising Improving Your Writing

Use this checklist as a general guide when you revise your first draft. (Also see page 189.)

___ Does the opening part introduce my focus and capture the reader's interest?

___ Do all of the details in the middle part relate to my focus?

___ Are all of my details specific and clear?

___ Is every detail necessary?

___ Does my ending discuss the person's importance?

Revising in Action

Important details are added.

> Robert's mother raised her three boys by
>
> herself after his father's death, and she
> about faith, family values, and the meaning
> taught them everything she knew∧ of life⊙

Editing Checking for Style and Correctness

Check your revised writing first for style—the smoothness of your sentences and the effectiveness of your word choice. Then check it for correctness—spelling, punctuation, usage, and capitalization errors.

After you complete your editing, write a neat final copy of your essay. Proofread this copy before you share it. (Have somebody else check your writing for errors, too.)

Editing in Action

Two short sentences are combined.

A spelling error is corrected.

> Elderly people who couldn't walk were
>
>   so
> trapped inside,∧ We kicked down the doors
>   shoulders
> and carried them out over our sholders.

A Closer Look at Biographical Writing

The information that follows gives additional planning and writing tips. Refer to these tips if you need extra help with your writing.

Planning Tips

- **Consult several sources of information**. If you find conflicting facts or details about the person, use the source that seems the most reliable.

- **Use a variety of sources**. Use an important print resource, one or two Web sites, an interview, and so on. This will allow you to learn about the person from different perspectives.

- **Double-check facts and details for accuracy**. Even a small factual error can affect the overall quality of your writing.

- **Carefully plan any interviews that you conduct**. If you are well prepared and sound knowledgeable and interested, the person you are interviewing will probably talk more freely with you.

Writing Tips

- **Work in background information**. Give readers the full story.

  Robert has had numerous people to look to for inspiration in his life. . . .

- **Use transitions and introductory words**. Using the right words will make your writing smooth and easy to follow. The introductory words in the passage below are highlighted in red.

  I asked Robert if he could give advice to young people today, what would it be? He thought about it for a while and replied, "Think about what you are doing before you do it. Then listen to your gut feelings and do what you know is right. . . . "

- **Explain or summarize less important information**. If you try to give equal attention to all the details about the person, your essay may lose its focus and appeal. In the sample below, the writer summarizes her subject's interests:

  As a D.A.R.E. officer, Robert works four days a week, 10 hours a day, so he has a lot of time to spend with his family on the weekends. He is the choir director at his church and loves to sing and play the guitar. His goal is to move up the ranks . . .

Sample Phase Biography

A phase biography focuses on a specific time, or phase, in a person's life. In the sample, Jesse Niebor recalls a long-ago winter when his sister "experienced a kindergartner's greatest temptation."

Please Excuse Leah

BEGINNING

The opening paragraph sets the scene.

When my sister Leah was young, winter was a magical time of year for her. She loved the pure, cold air on her face, and the snow that crunched beneath her boots. That is, until Leah experienced a kindergartner's greatest temptation: freezing metal. She had seen playground heroes test fate by licking the flagpole in January and end up sobbing, with a mouthful of tissue. She had heard how Mom, herself, had more than one "sled incident." But in spite of these warnings, Leah was still tempted by metal in winter.

MIDDLE

The middle part focuses on one event.

One frigid morning, when Leah and I were in front of the house waiting for the bus, she noticed our two-year-old brother inside and trotted to the window. There she saw the metal window ledge—Eden's forbidden fruit! Slowly, she stuck out her tongue, ready to pull away. But the window ledge grabbed her tongue and held fast.

As Leah screamed and Mom hurried outside, the bus turned the corner. Mom tried to pull Leah away, but that only caused louder screams. As I hopped on the bus, I joined the rest of the kids watching the spectacle.

ENDING

In closing, the writer adds a touch of humor.

Later that day, my sister made it to school with a swollen tongue, a bruised ego, and a note that said, "Please excuse Leah for being late. She was stuck to the house."

Writing Explanations

Many publications contain explanations—including instructional manuals, cookbooks, and guidebooks. Some explanations tell you how something works or how to make something. Other explanations tell you how to do something or how to get somewhere. Well-written explanations are clear, concise, and easy to follow. (*Concise* means "brief and to the point.")

At first, writing an explanation may seem like an easy process. You simply share a set of facts and details with your readers. But once you get started, you'll find that explanations require a lot of work. The details must be clearly stated and logically arranged. Writing an explanation may, in fact, challenge you more than any of your other writing assignments.

What's Ahead

This chapter provides two sample explanations plus easy-to-follow writing guidelines. Once you review this information, you will be ready to write explanations that truly inform your readers.

- Sample Explanation: How to Make Something
- Writing Guidelines
- Sample Explanation: How Something Works

Sample Explanation

How to Make Something

A recipe is one kind of explanation. In the following sample, Chen Wei Wu explains how to prepare a traditional Chinese food.

BEGINNING

The title and opening part identify the topic.

MIDDLE

The steps are carefully explained.

Making Jiaozi

Chinese dumplings, or jiaozi, is a popular food in China. There is a common saying in China: "There is nothing more delicious than jiaozi." So you can see that Chinese people have great love for this food. To make your own jiaozi with a basic meat filling, follow these directions:

Making the Dumpling Skins

To make the dumpling skins, you will need three basic ingredients: a small package of white flour, very cold water, and salt. Combine the ingredients in this way:

1. Stir a teaspoon of salt into two cups of very cold water.
2. Then add the water to the flour, a little at a time. Use only as much water as necessary to make a workable dough.
3. Knead the dough very well before refrigerating it. (*Kneading* means to work and press the dough with your hands.)

When you are ready to use the dough, break off a piece about the size of a walnut. Form the piece of dough into a ball and with a rolling pin, flatten it into a thin, three-inch circle. Continue this process until you have made enough dumpling skins.

Subheadings and bulleted lists help readers follow the explanation.

Making the Meat Filling

A basic meat filling contains the following ingredients mixed together:

- ground pork (one pound)
- finely chopped cabbage (one cup)
- finely chopped onion (a few tablespoons)
- grated ginger
- soy sauce (two tablespoons)
- minced garlic (one or two cloves)
- salt and pepper (to taste)

Completing the Dumplings

Form the dumplings in this way:

1. Place one tablespoon of filling in the middle of each skin. Then fold the skin over, and seal the dumpling by pressing together both sides. Continue until you have made all of your dumplings.
2. Next, bring a large pot of water to a boil. Add enough dumplings to cover the bottom of the pot. Cover the pot.
3. When it returns to a boil, add a cup of cold water. Cover until the dumplings again come to a boil. Repeat this process one more time, and then the jiaozi are ready. Serve with rice vinegar or soy sauce.

ENDING

The ending adds interest to the writing.

There are more than 3,000 kinds of stuffing that Chinese people put into their dumplings. The ones made in the United States usually are stuffed with a meat filling or with vegetables. By trying this recipe, you will get to enjoy one of the most popular tastes of China.

Writing Guidelines

Prewriting / Choosing a Topic

Pick a topic that interests both you and your readers. Make sure that you know a lot about the topic and that it meets the requirements of your assignment: explaining how to make something, how something works, how something happened, and so on.

Gathering Details

Collect all of the details your readers will need to understand your explanation. (If possible, actually do what you are explaining. Then you will know for sure which steps to include.)

Using a Time Line

If you are explaining how to make something, it may help to use a time line to organize your details. Here's how a time line was used to organize part of the sample essay on pages 168-169.

Making the Dumpling Skins

— *Stir a tsp. of salt into 2 C. of cold water.*
— *Slowly add water to flour to form a dough.*
— *Knead the dough and chill it for . . .*

Writing / Writing the First Draft

Beginning ■ In your beginning paragraph, identify your topic and say something interesting about it to gain your readers' interest.

Middle ■ In the middle paragraphs, explain your topic by using background information, instructions, steps, and so on. Use linking words such as *first, second, next,* and *then.* Use design elements such as subheads and bulleted lists to make your explanation easy to follow. (See the sample on page 27.)

Ending ■ In the closing paragraph, make some final comments about your topic—how you feel about it, why it's important, and so on

Revising / Improving Your Writing

Use the following checklist to review and revise your first draft. (Also see page 189.)

___ In the beginning part, do I clearly identify my topic and say something interesting about it?

___ Do I include a complete explanation or set of instructions in the middle part?

___ Will readers be able to follow every step?

Revising in Action

An important detail is added.

An idea is made clearer.

> *When you are ready to use the dough,*
>
> *break off a piece about the size of a*
> *Form the piece of dough into a ball and,*
> *walnut. With a rolling pin, flatten it into*
>
> *a thin, three-inch circle. Continue this*
> *until you have made enough*
> *process dumpling skins*

Editing / Checking for Style and Correctness

Edit your revised explanation first for sentence smoothness and word choice. Do all of your ideas read smoothly and clearly? Did you use specific nouns and verbs? Then check for punctuation, grammar, and spelling errors.

Editing in Action

A sentence fragment is corrected.

A more specific verb is used.

> *Place one tablespoon of filling. In the*
> *i*
>
> *middle of each skin. Then fold the skin over,*
> *seal*
> *and close the dumpling by pressing together*
>
> *both sides.*

Sample Explanation

How Something Works

In this sample, student Kelli Whitson explains how lightning works.

How Lightning Works

BEGINNING

The topic is
clearly
introduced.

Lightning starts with friction in clouds. The friction comes from updrafts of warm vapor and downdrafts of water and ice. The particles collide, breaking electrons loose. The loose electrons stay at the bottom of the cloud, making a negative charge, and the vapor goes to the top, making a positive charge. In this way, the cloud becomes a huge battery.

The air at the bottom of the cloud conducts electricity as well as metal does. This charged air is called *plasma*, and it dribbles down from the cloud in pathways called *step leaders*. They hang from the cloud like tentacles.

MIDDLE

The steps in
the process
are
explained.

Other tentacles called *positive streamers* reach up from the ground. Once a positive streamer meets a step leader, the path is open for lightning.

As electricity sails through the path, it heats the air hotter than the sun's surface and causes the flash that we call lightning. The air explodes, and the shockwave is called thunder. Up to 40 electrical charges can jump between the cloud and the ground. That's what makes some lightning strikes last a long time.

ENDING

The ending
connects
with the
reader.

Think about this process the next time you shuffle your shoes on the carpet. You're creating friction when you do this, just like a cloud fully charged and ready to create lightning.

Writing News Stories

News is information about recent events and happenings. News appears in print and on-line. It can be seen on television and listened to on the radio. In other words, you can find news just about anywhere at anytime in any form.

Writing effective news stories requires three basic reporting skills. You must . . .

- recognize a newsworthy topic—an event or a happening that readers should know about,
- gather all of the facts about the event by making visits and asking questions, and
- write about the event in a clear and complete story.

When it comes to newswriting, most of your work is done *before* the actual writing. If you gather all of the important facts, you'll have a good chance of developing an effective news story.

What's Ahead

This chapter will help you develop basic news stories and editorials, two common forms of newswriting.

- **Sample News Story**
- **Writing Guidelines**
- **Sample Editorial**
- **Tips for Writing an Editorial**

Sample News Story

In this sample story, Janelle Amos reports on an awards ceremony in her high school. Her story provides all of the basic information related to the event.

Ramos Wins Award

BEGINNING

The reporter opens with the key facts.

Elena Ramos is the 2002-2003 winner of the Delmer High School Senior-of-the-Year Award. She received the award on Tuesday, May 27, at a dinner at Hacket's Supper Club sponsored by the Delmer Parent/Teacher Organization (PTO).

A panel of PTO members, teachers, and students made the selection. Panel members said that choosing the winner was extremely difficult. Finalists for the award included Rob Butler, Michael Gutter, Meagan Pearson, Jessica Johnson, and Ramos.

MIDDLE

Additional information is provided.

Ramos has maintained a 4.0 average throughout her high school career. This past year, she has served as senior editor of the yearbook staff and captain of the girl's basketball team. In addition, she is a volunteer for the "Meals on Wheels" program and a spokesperson for the school's anti-smoking campaign.

PTO Chairperson Ms. Ruth Williams presented Ramos with an engraved plaque and a scholarship worth $1000. In her acceptance speech, Ramos expressed her gratitude for the award and scholarship and thanked everyone who helped her in high school. The award winner will attend New York University, majoring in English.

ENDING

The closing gives the final details.

This annual award was started 20 years ago by the PTO to recognize the achievements of a graduating senior.

Writing Guidelines

The headline should grab the reader's attention, but the beginning or lead paragraph must hold that attention. In most news stories, the lead paragraph gives the key details about the event—*who? what? when? where?* and *why?* The rest of the story is filled with other information organized according to the order of importance (most important to least important). Only when a story is very complex or complicated will details near the end of the piece be truly important to the reader.

Prewriting / Choosing a Topic

If you are a reporter for the school newspaper, you will be assigned stories, so choosing a topic won't be an issue. But when you do have to search for a topic, consider the following points:

- **Importance**. Will this news be of value to your readers? (*Why is the price of lunch tickets increasing so much? Why are teens attracted to the local coffeehouse?*)

- **Timeliness**. Readers want to know what is happening now and what is going to happen. For the most part, old news is no news.

- **Local News**. The best news usually takes place close to home. For students, that means school and community news. However, if you come from another country, you may want to write about news from your homeland. Most readers will find these stories interesting.

- **Human Interest**. Readers enjoy stories about people. Would you rather read a story about a recent rock concert, or a story about the musicians that play in the group?

Finding News Stories . . .

The headlines below show the difference between topics that are newsworthy, and those that are not.

News:	Not News:
Artist Visits Classroom	Students Draw in Class
Girls Win Basketball Title	Girls Practice Free Throws
School Security Increased	Students Use Their Lockers

Gathering Details

Collect details for your story by interviewing people, searching the Internet, making observations, and so on. Take good notes so you have plenty of information to draw from when you are ready to write.

■ To make sure that you have the key facts and details for your lead paragraph, complete a 5 W's chart. The chart below relates to the sample news story on page 174.

5 W's Chart

Who?	What?	When?	Where?	Why?
Elena Ramos	won Senior-of-the-Year Award	Tuesday May 27	Hacket's Supper Club	annual award sponsored by Delmer PTO

Interviewing Tips

Interviewing is one of the best ways to collect information for a news story. Use the following tips as a general guide.

■ **BEFORE . . .**

Be prepared. Set up a time for an in-person or telephone interview. Then write out the questions you want to ask. State your questions so they cannot be answered with a "yes" or "no."

■ **DURING . . .**

Be in control. Politely ask your questions, and listen carefully to the interviewee's answers. If you're doing a phone interview, give feedback, such as "Yes," "Okay," or "I see." Ask ahead of time for permission if you want to tape-record your interview.

Take careful notes. Record key pieces of information, and don't be afraid to ask the person to repeat something or to clarify an important point. Before you finish the interview, ask follow-up questions, check the spellings of names and places, confirm dates, and so on. When you're finished, thank the person.

■ **AFTER . . .**

Review your notes. Go over your notes right after the interview. Then you'll know if you covered all of your questions or if you need to contact the person again.

Writing / Writing the First Draft

- Write the lead paragraph, making sure that it includes the key points you identified in the 5W's chart.

  > The paragraphs in news stories are usually short—often just two or three sentences in length. This makes it easier for readers to follow the main points.

- Then develop the rest of your news story. This part must include all of the important facts and details that you didn't cover in the lead paragraph. The further you get into the story, the less important the information should be.

- Include quotations whenever possible, but always check your notes to make sure that you quote people accurately.

Revising / Improving Your Writing

Use the following checklist as a general guide when you are ready to revise your first draft. (Also see page 189.)

___ Does the lead paragraph cover the key points about the story and gain my readers' interest?

___ In the remaining part, have I included the information that "fills in" the rest of the story?

___ Is the information in the story clearly stated and effectively organized?

___ Is the story written objectively—meaning that I haven't included any of my own thoughts and feelings?

Revising in Action

Key details are added.

2002-2003
Elena Ramos is the winner of the

Delmer High School Senior-of-the-Year

Award. She received the award on Tuesday,

May 27, at a dinner at Hacket's Supper Club sponsored by the Delmer Parent/Teacher Organization (PTO).

Editing ▸ Checking for Style and Correctness

First edit your revised writing for style, making sure that all of your sentences read smoothly and that you have used the best words to express your ideas. Then check for punctuation, spelling, and grammar errors.

> If you are writing for a school newspaper, you will have an editor or an adviser check your story for errors before it is printed. But remember that you are responsible for the accuracy of your story.

Editing in Action

A spelling error is corrected.

A more specific noun is used.

A sentence fragment is corrected.

A capitalization error is corrected.

PTO Chairperson Ms. Ruth Williams

presented Ramos with an engraved (plack) *plaque*

and a scholarship worth $1000. In her

acceptance ~~talk~~ *speech*, Ramos expressed her

gratitude for the award and scholarship, *and*

∧ Thanked everyone who helped her in high

school. The award winner will attend New

York university, majoring in English.

Sample Editorial

The following editorial by student writer Eboni Lewis expresses an opinion about parents of high school athletes. **Remember:** Editorials address current events, situations, and stories.

BEGINNING

The writing opens with an opinion.

MIDDLE

The details in the body support the opinion.

ENDING

The closing reflects on the topic of the editorial.

Parents: Keep Your Distance

Pro athletes have agents because pro sports are often about money. High school sports should be about the game. Parents who act like agents, criticizing coaches and storming into school-board meetings, rob their sons and daughters of the true benefit of sports.

Players who have a problem with playing time should be mature enough to discuss it with the coach. The experience will probably make them better people. Players shouldn't expect their parents to get involved with every problem.

Of course, parents do have an important role. They should support their children in sports and in all of their activities. They should cheer the team during the games, and they should congratulate or console their sons or daughters afterward. Then, when there is a truly serious issue involving their children, parents should step in. But a concern about playing time is not a serious issue.

Athletes must be willing to make sacrifices, work together, and help their teams succeed. Minutes played and points scored should be secondary concerns. Let's leave our sports teams in the hands of our coaches and players. They will do just fine without overbearing parental involvement.

Tips for Writing an Editorial

In an editorial, you express your opinion about a recent event or action. An effective editorial gets readers to accept your point of view. The following tips will help you write editorials.

Choose a current topic.

Make sure that you have strong feelings about the topic and that it will interest your readers.

State your opinion.

Let readers know your position right away. Being direct is the best course of action in all newswriting.

Plan a strong argument.

Plan the main part of your editorial so that your argument is strong from start to finish. Use the questions that follow as a guide:

1. What facts and details support your opinion?
2. Can you get an expert to agree with your opinion?
3. Can you make a comparison to strengthen your argument?
4. Can you effectively counter any key opposing viewpoints? (To *counter* means "to argue against.")
5. Is the action that you suggest reasonable?

Carefully consider your strongest argument.

Place your strongest argument first or last so that it has a lasting impression on your readers.

Speak with confidence.

Speak honestly and show that you really care about the topic. Also make sure that you present a logical, reasonable argument.

Keep things simple.

Don't try to impress readers with your high-powered vocabulary. Instead, use words that everyone can understand.

Act responsibly.

The purpose of an editorial is to express your feelings about an action or event, not to attack a person or a group.

Writing About Literature

It's easy to tell someone that you like or dislike a certain book, but it's not always easy to explain why. That's because forming your thoughts as you speak is difficult to do. You have a much better chance of expressing yourself on paper because the process of writing helps you think more clearly and completely.

Writing a review is one way that you can express your thoughts about a book that you've read. A review states your opinion about a book's value and highlights key parts without giving the whole story away. You can also share your thoughts about a book in a *literary analysis*. An analysis discusses an important feature of a book—the author's main point, the causes of a character's actions, and so on.

What's Ahead

This chapter provides a sample book review and a sample literary analysis. It also includes easy-to-follow writing guidelines and helpful writing ideas.

- Sample Book Review
- Writing Guidelines
- Ideas for a Literary Analysis
- Sample Literary Analysis
- Writing Guidelines
- Evaluating Subject Writing

Sample Book Review

In this sample, Kelly Beaton reviews *The Color Purple* by Alice Walker. Beaton's review reveals just enough about the book to help readers decide if they should read it.

The Color Purple

BEGINNING

The opening introduces the book.

The Color Purple by Alice Walker is an excellent book for anyone interested in a lesson about life. It is a story of hard work and deep feelings. Readers of all ages will find it both heartbreaking and heartwarming.

The novel focuses on the life of Celie and her family in the rural South. They are stuck in a way of life that should have destroyed them, a life involving poor marriages, abuse, racism, and many other seemingly unsolvable problems. Yet, as hardships pile up, the family discovers an inner strength that keeps them going.

MIDDLE

The body highlights the book's story and main character.

Celie, in particular, becomes a stronger person as the story unfolds. Throughout the first part of *The Color Purple,* Celie's life is extremely difficult, almost hopeless, but slowly she discovers her true self and begins to experience periods of happiness and wholeness.

The Color Purple is written as if taken straight from Celie's letters to God. At first, the text may seem difficult to understand, but the story is so appealing that you soon forget that it is written in a rural dialect.

ENDING

The closing reflects on the book's value.

Alice Walker's novel reveals much about the dark side of human nature. Yet it is also a story that celebrates all that is good in life, including family, affection, and individual self-worth. Anyone interested in stories about the full scope of life should read this book.

Writing Guidelines

Prewriting ❯ Choosing a Topic

Review a book or short story that you have recently read, one that you have strong feelings about.

❯ Gathering Details

Collect your thoughts and feelings by freewriting about the book. You may also choose to list the main points about the book's plot, theme, and main characters as they come to mind.

The Color Purple

- *story of hard work and deep feelings*
- *focuses on the life of Celie and her family*
- *life of poor marriages, abuse, racism, etc.*
- *Celie becomes stronger*
- *discovers her true self, experiences happiness*

Read through your ideas and put a check next to the ones that you would like to include in your review. You may have to reread certain parts of the book to make sure that you have all of your facts straight.

Writing ❯ Writing the First Draft

Beginning ■ In the opening paragraph, identify the title and author of the book and make a few general comments about the book. You may want to comment on what the book is about, where it takes place, your main feeling about the book, and so on.

Middle ■ In the middle paragraphs, highlight the book's key features (plot, characters, theme) to give readers a good understanding of the book. But don't give the whole story away!

Ending ■ In the closing paragraph, come to some conclusion about the book's value or importance.

Revising / Improving Your Writing

As you read through your first draft, make sure that you have stated your ideas clearly and completely. Use the following checklist to evaluate the quality of your first draft. (Also see page 189.)

_____ Did I introduce the book and author in the opening paragraph?

_____ Did I highlight the book's key features in the middle paragraphs?

_____ Did I explain the book's value in the closing paragraph?

_____ Does my review help readers decide if they should read the book?

Revising in Action

An idea is made clearer.

An idea is reordered.

> _The Color Purple_ by Alice Walker is an
> ~~for anyone interested in a lesson about life.~~
> excellent book. Readers of all ages will find
>
> it both heartbreaking and heartwarming.
>
> It is a story of hard work and deep feelings.

Editing / Checking for Style and Correctness

First check your revised writing for style. Then edit it for correctness. (Also have a trusted editor check your writing for errors.)

Editing in Action

Spelling and capitalization errors are corrected.

Punctuation is added.

A more specific adjective is used.

> *novel*
> The ~~novul~~ focuses on the life of Celie
>
> and her family in the rural South. They are
>
> stuck in a way of life that should have
>
> destroyed them, a life involving poor
>
> marriages, abuse, racism, and many other
> *unsolvable*
> seemingly ~~hard~~ conflicts.

Ideas for a Literary Analysis

This list of ideas for a literary analysis is arranged according to the four main elements of literature: plot, characterization, setting, and theme. (Also see pages 331-335 for more ideas.) Focus on one or two of these ideas when you write an analysis.

Plot *The action of the story*
- _____ (a main problem or conflict) begins the action.
- The climax (the most important event) happens when . . .
- Suspense or interest is built into the story in these ways:
- _____ is a surprising twist in the plot. (What does it add to the story?)
- The ending is surprising . . . predictable . . . unbelievable.

Characterization *The individuals in the story*
- The main character changes from _____ to _____ by the end of the story.
- A certain person, place, event, or idea influences the main character.
- A certain character acts believably/unbelievably when . . .
- _____ is the most revealing trait of one of the characters.
- The main character relies on _____ for guidance. (How helpful is this person?)

Setting *The time and place of the action*
- The setting affects the main character in the following ways:
- The setting affects the plot in the following ways:
- The setting helped me better understand a specific time and place.

Theme *The message about life*
- Courage . . . peer pressure . . . growing up . . . greed . . . jealousy is a theme in _____.
- _____ shows what it means to experience racism . . . loneliness . . . success . . . .
- The author makes this point about a specific period in history:
- This piece of literature showed me what it is like to be . . .

Sample Literary Analysis

In this analysis of *The Contender*, Lee Benin explores the relationship between the main character and a retired boxer. This relationship helps the main character straighten out his life.

A Positive Influence

BEGINNING

The opening introduces the reading and states the thesis (highlighted).

In *The Contender*, by Robert Lipsyte, a young man battles to succeed against all odds. At the beginning of the novel, Alfred Brooks, a high school dropout, has few prospects. He is terrorized by a local gang and worries about losing his best friend to a world of drugs and crime. Then, surprisingly, Brooks decides to try boxing. While getting started, he meets Vito Donatelli, who becomes the most important influence in his life.

MIDDLE

Details and examples explain the focus.

Donatelli is a retired boxer who owns a gym and works as a trainer of young fighters. Right from the start, Donatelli seems to know Brooks almost better than Brooks knows himself. The main part of the story deals with the relationship between the two men.

The ex-pro leads Brooks in the right direction, helping him discover the best things to do for himself. He tells Brooks that "nothing is ever promised," that he will have to work for everything in life, and even then, there will be no guarantees. He also teaches Brooks that "it's the climbing that makes the man. Getting to the top is an extra reward."

ENDING

The closing reflects on the importance of the relationship.

As their relationship grows, Brooks understands what Donatelli has known all along—that the discipline needed in the ring is also needed in daily life. By the end of the novel, Alfred becomes a contender—ready to deal with any problem life presents.

Writing Guidelines

Prewriting / Choosing a Topic

Select a novel or short story that you have recently read for your analysis. Then review "Ideas for a Literary Analysis" (page 185). Base your analysis on one or two of the ideas listed on that page, or discuss other possible writing ideas with your teacher. Select an idea that you can clearly support with examples from the book or short story.

Stating Your Focus

State the focus of your analysis before you collect any details. Express your focus in a *working thesis statement*. The writer of the sample analysis of *The Contender* (page 186) focuses on the following idea from page 185: *The main character relies on _____ for guidance.* With that idea in mind, he came up with the following thesis statement for his analysis.

Working Thesis Statement

Alfred Brooks meets Vito Donatelli, who becomes the most important influence in his life.

✳ The final version of your thesis statement may not be worded in exactly the same way as your working thesis statement.

Gathering Details

Then list details from the reading that you will use to support or explain your thesis.

Support Details

- *Donatelli works as a trainer and manager of young fighters.*
- *The story deals with the relationship between the trainer and Brooks.*
- *Donatelli leads Brooks in the right direction.*
- *He tells the young fighter to work hard.*
- *Brooks grows as a person with Donatelli's help.*

Writing ⟩ Writing the First Draft

Beginning ■ Your opening paragraph should name the title and author of your reading, identify the theme or thesis of your analysis, and gain your reader's attention. (See the sample analysis on page 186.)

Middle ■ Then develop the main part of your analysis. Make sure to include specific details or direct quotations from the book or short story to support your thesis.

Ending ■ In the closing paragraph, restate your thesis, summarize your main points, and/or briefly discuss the results of your analysis.

Revising ⟩ Improving Your Writing

As you review your first draft, carefully check the three main parts of your analysis. All of the information in your analysis should clearly and completely support your thesis. Revise your writing as needed.

Revising in Action

Information is added.

An idea is made clearer.

> Donatelli is a retired boxer who owns a
> and works as a trainer of young fighters⊙
> gym. Right from the start, Donatelli knows
>   knows himself⊙
> Brooks almost better than Brooks.

Editing ⟩ Checking for Style and Correctness

Check your revised writing for style and for spelling, grammar, punctuation, and capitalization errors.

Editing in Action

A hyphen is added.

Word choice is varied.

> The ex-pro leads Brooks in the right
>   best
> direction, helping him discover the right
>
> things to do for himself.

Evaluating Subject Writing

Use the rubric below as a checklist to evaluate the quality of your writing about literature and other subject writing (biographical essays, explanations, and news stories). The rubric is arranged according to the traits of effective writing described on pages 19-24.

Assessment Rubric

_____ **STIMULATING IDEAS**

The writing . . .

- focuses on an interesting topic (book, person, event, process, etc.).
- contains effective supporting information—details, examples, quotations, and so on.
- informs and entertains the reader.

_____ **LOGICAL ORGANIZATION**

- includes a clear beginning, a strong middle part, and an effective ending.
- uses transitions to link main ideas.

_____ **ENGAGING VOICE**

- displays a clear understanding of the topic.
- speaks with strong feelings and confidence.

_____ **ORIGINAL WORD CHOICE**

- contains specific nouns and vivid verbs.
- defines or explains any unfamiliar terms.

_____ **EFFECTIVE SENTENCE STYLE**

- flows smoothly from one idea to the next.
- shows variation in sentence structure.

_____ **CORRECT, ACCURATE COPY**

- follows the basic rules of grammar, spelling, and punctuation.
- meets the required formatting guidelines.

Creative
Writing

Writing Stories

Writing Poetry

Writing Stories

Writing about your own experiences is fairly easy, and so is writing about people that you know very well. You simply tap into your memory and write. But writing made-up stories is another matter. While the starting point for a story may be a real experience, the end result should be something new and imaginative.

To write effective stories, you must understand how stories develop: In most stories, there is a main character doing some activity, and a problem, or conflict, occurs. The story then unfolds around the main character's attempts to solve the problem. To gain a good understanding of the basic story structure, you should read plenty of short stories and novels.

What's Ahead

This chapter contains all of the information you need to write effective short stories. It includes a sample story, writing guidelines, a list of basic story patterns, and more.

- The Shape of Stories
- Sample Story
- Writing Guidelines
- Story Patterns
- Evaluating Stories

The Shape of Stories

Think of a great experience in your life: a concert, family trip, school play, championship game, or some other special event. The best experiences gradually build in excitement to a high point—a big pay-off—that really makes the event memorable. The best fictional stories do the same thing; they follow a classic plot line that builds to a climax.

Plot

The plot refers to the events or actions that move a story along from start to finish. A plot has five parts: *exposition, rising action, climax, falling action,* and *resolution.* The plot line below shows how these parts work together.

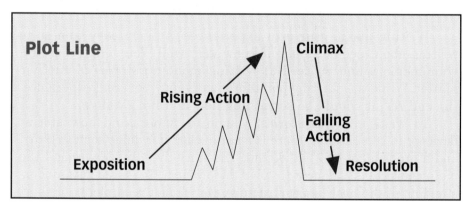

Plot Line

Climax

Rising Action

Falling Action

Exposition

Resolution

A Closer Look at the Parts

Exposition The *exposition* is the beginning part of a story in which the main character, conflict, and setting are introduced. The conflict is the problem that the main character faces. The setting is where and when the action takes place.

> Juan Lopez is about to leave school and head to the park. In one hand, he carries a copy of Conrad Richter's *The Light in the Forest,* and in the other hand, a suspension slip. He's been skipping classes, and now the principal has made his skipping official. "What do you want to do with your life?" the principal yells after him, the same thing Juan's father yelled that morning.

Rising Action   In a short story, the *rising action* usually includes at least two or three important actions involving the main character and his or her problem. This builds suspense into the story.

> **First Action: Juan finishes *The Light in the Forest*, the story of a young man in Colonial America who is torn between two cultures. Juan, who recently moved here from Puerto Rico, understands that feeling.**
>
> **Second Action: Juan remembers hearing about a vision quest, in which a young Native American leaves his family and travels into the wilderness to discover his guardian spirit. (*Guardian* means "one who protects.")**
>
> **Third Action: Juan looks for a guardian spirit. He sees a squirrel looking for food, and wishes he weren't stuck here, cold and hungry, on the park bench. He sees geese flying south and wishes he could fly to Puerto Rico.**

Climax   The *climax* is the moment of truth or the most exciting action, when the character confronts his or her problem head-on. All the action leads up to the climax. In the best stories, the main character is changed by the climax.

> **A crow lands in front of Juan. The big, strong bird stares at him with calm confidence. The crow nods at Juan and then flies off, leaving a black feather. Juan uses the feather to mark his favorite part in the novel. He has just found his guardian.**

Falling Action   The *falling action* involves the main character as he or she learns how to deal with life after the moment of truth.

> **Juan walks home through the cold dark streets and knows that he, like the crow, will overcome this harsh northern place. He'll show his principal, his father, and himself that he can succeed.**

Resolution   The *resolution* brings the story to a natural, thought-provoking, or surprising conclusion. (In some stories, it's hard to tell the difference between the falling action and resolution because they are so closely related.)

> **Juan arrives home, and his father meets him at the door. "Where've you been?" Juan holds up the suspension slip and says, "I've been in a bad place, but I'm not there anymore. And it's more important where I'm going."**

Sample Story

Read and enjoy the sample story by Gabe Roberts. The side notes indicate how the story develops from the exposition to the resolution.

Ghosts in the House

EXPOSITION

The writer identifies the main character, setting, and conflict.

More than anything, I'll miss this.
Terrell sat on an old crate by the attic window and watched the sun set. It turned his neighborhood gold. From this window, even the worn-out rooftops shone like the streets of heaven.

"This is my house." The words sounded hollow. Somebody had bought the place to make it a parking lot. "This is *my* house."

Actually, it wasn't. The house had been abandoned for 10 years, and most of the neighborhood kids called it the "haunted house." Four years ago, Terrell explored it and liked it so well, he made it his own. He and his friends called themselves "the Ghosts," and they fixed up their Haunt and hung there every afternoon.

RISING ACTION

Dialogue moves the story along.

" 'Sup?" said Junior, coming up the stairs.

Terrell knocked knuckles with him. "Last day for the Ghosts."

Junior flopped down on the old beanbag. "Nah, we'll always be the Ghosts."

"What're Ghosts without a Haunt?"

Bill climbed in through the fire escape. " 'Sup?"

"I'm surprised you came," Terrell said.

Bill slouched against the wall. "It couldn't last forever, T. Two more years, and we'll graduate anyway."

Terrell said, "This is *our* house. We grew up here. Who can grow up in a parking lot?"

There was nothing more to say. Outside, the rooftops gave up their gold and became cracked black asphalt. Bill left, and then Junior. That left

RISING ACTION

Additional actions add suspense.

only Terrell and his window and the house that wasn't his.

On the next day, the house was padlocked, and a sign was taped on the door: "PRIVATE PROPERTY. KEEP OUT. VIOLATORS WILL BE PROSECUTED."

The Ghosts weren't violators. They took care of this place, and it took care of them.

On Saturday, a truck pulled up, and strangers went in with tools to rip out everything valuable before they tore the house down.

Terrell gathered the Ghosts. They'd always been a group of friends, never a gang, but they felt like a gang walking over there. Terrell led the Ghosts into the house and went to the man who drove the truck— a guy with sandy hair and a nervous smile.

CLIMAX

Terrell and his friends confront their problem.

"This is our house," Terrell blurted. "We belong here. This is a good house, and it should be for people, not cars."

The guy nodded slowly, pressing his lips together. "All right. Why don't you guys start by tearing off the old siding?"

"We don't want this place torn down."

"Neither do I," said the man. "Aren't you guys here to help?"

"Help what?"

"This is a Habitat for Humanity project. We're fixing this place up so a family can live here. I thought you guys were volunteers."

FALLING ACTION AND RESOLUTION

The story comes to a satisfying end.

Terrell glanced at Junior and Bill. They were smiling, looking at the house the way they'd looked at it four years ago.

"Yeah," Terrell said. "We're volunteers."

"Great," said the guy. "I'm Gunthar. Sign in on that sheet, grab a donut, and then pick up a crowbar and get to work on that old siding."

Half an hour later, Terrell was on a ladder by the old attic window, and even in the middle of the morning, his neighborhood looked like gold.

Writing Guidelines

Prewriting / Planning Your Writing

Professor John Tolkien was grading exams when he scribbled a now-famous line: "In a hole in the ground there lived a Hobbit." Tolkien didn't know what a Hobbit was or why it lived in the ground. Even so, a single character in a setting inspired him to write *The Hobbit* and *The Lord of the Rings*.

As stated in the introduction on page 191, most short stories start with a main character doing some activity, and a conflict occurs. Before you start your writing, identify at least the main character and a problem for this person to deal with.

- **Create a main character.** Base your main character on people you know or on people that you create in your imagination. Remember, though, not to embarrass anyone by making a character too much like that person.

  > Think of other characters to include. The best stories have characters that you enjoy reading about and sometimes caring about. Don't, however, include so many characters that the reader becomes confused.

- **Develop a conflict.** Your main character can be in conflict with another person, with him- or herself, with nature, with society, or with fate. (See page 333 for more information.) The main character in the sample story on pages 194-95 is primarily in conflict with himself: He is having a hard time giving up the Haunt.

Other Elements to Consider . . .

- **Establish a setting.** *The Hobbit* was set in "a hole in the ground" long ago. Your setting can be anyplace that allows your main character to deal with the conflict, but limit yourself to one main location and a brief span of time.

- **Consider the action.** The conflict requires the main character to act, so list two or three actions that could move your story along. Also consider the climax, or moment of truth.

  > Use a story map to plan your story. (See page 54.) But remember that you don't have to fill in the complete map before you start your first draft.

Writing   Creating the First Draft

Use your story map as a general guide when you write your first draft. (Also review pages 192-193 for help.)

Exposition

To get the reader's attention, start your story in one of these ways:

■ **Start with an exciting action.**

> The dog lunged at Ming, and she climbed higher in the tree.

■ **Begin with dialogue.**

> "I need to see some I.D.," said the security guard.

■ **Make a surprising statement.**

> David wasn't worried about the trees along the ski trail;
> it was the bear that concerned him.

As you develop this part of your story, you should name the setting, introduce the main character, and identify the conflict. Once this is done, you're ready to move on to the middle part of your story.

Rising Action and Climax

Place your characters in the first challenging action. Then build suspense with each new action or struggle, leading up to the climax. Follow these writing tips:

■ Pay special attention to your verbs, making them strong (*vaulted* instead of *jumped*) and active (*collided* instead of *was hit*).

■ Create dialogue that sounds real and natural. Let the words reflect what the characters think and feel.

■ Include sensory details. What do the characters see, hear, smell, taste, or feel?

■ *Show* instead of *tell* what is happening. For example, instead of writing "Joe was happy," write "Joe's face split into a grin." Instead of writing "The boat was in trouble," write "A wave crashed over the side and swamped the boat."

Falling Action and Resolution

After the climax, work quickly through the rest of the story. Show how the climax has changed your main character, and tell how he or she will act or live from now on. The ending of your story will fall into place if the other parts of your story work well together.

Revising / Improving Your Writing

Ask yourself the following questions when you review and revise your first draft. (Also see page 200.)

___ Do my characters talk and act like real people?

___ Does the conflict really test my main character?

___ Do all the actions build toward the climax?

___ Did I show rather than tell most of the time?

___ Does my story contain any holes or confusing parts?

Revising in Action

An unneeded idea is deleted.

An idea is added.

> "This is our house," Terrell blurted.
> ~~He meant it.~~ "We belong here. It should be
> *This is a good house, and*
> for people, not cars."

Editing / Checking for Style and Accuracy

When you edit your revised story, first pay attention to sentence style and word choice. Then check for capitalization, punctuation, usage, and spelling errors. Also have a trusted classmate check your story for errors.

Editing in Action

Word choice is improved.

A usage error is fixed.

Punctuation is added.

> *pressing*
> The guy nodded slowly, ~~putting~~ his lips
> *All right*
> together. "~~Alright.~~ Why don't you guys start
> by tearing off the old siding?"
> "We don't want this place torn down."

Story Patterns

Here are brief descriptions of popular short-story patterns. These patterns may give you ideas for your own stories.

The Quest

The main character goes on a journey into the unknown, overcomes a number of obstacles, and returns either victorious or wiser. Heroic myths follow this pattern, but so do many modern stories.

A young woman fights for the right to join an all-male sports team.

The Discovery

The main character follows a trail of clues to discover an amazing secret. Mystery and suspense novels use this pattern.

A curious young man discovers that the bully at school is . . .

The Rite of Passage

A difficult experience changes the main character in a significant and lasting way. These stories are also called "Coming of Age" stories.

A young soldier learns about responsibility while on the battlefield.

The Choice

The focus in this type of story is a decision the main character must make. Tension builds as the decision approaches.

A teenage mother must decide whether to keep her child or give him up for adoption.

The Union

Two people fall in love, but they are held apart by a number of obstacles. Their struggle to come together only causes their love to grow stronger. Sometimes they succeed, and sometimes they fail.

A young deaf man falls in love with a gifted violinist and then struggles to understand the music he can't hear.

The Reversal

In this pattern, the main character follows one course of action until something causes him or her to think or act in a different way.

A young woman quits school, but then discovers her true love is painting and enrolls in an art school.

Evaluating Stories

Use the rubric below as a checklist to evaluate the quality of your story writing. The rubric is arranged according to the traits of effective writing described on pages 19-24.

Assessment Rubric

____ **STIMULATING IDEAS**

The story . . .
- contains an entertaining or engaging plot.
- brings the action alive with dialogue and details.
- develops interesting characters.

____ **LOGICAL ORGANIZATION**
- builds to a climax that changes the main character.
- develops with the characters' words and actions moving things along.
- comes to a natural, satisfying, or surprising close.

____ **ENGAGING VOICE**
- uses language that holds the reader's interest.
- sounds realistic in terms of the characters' dialogue.

____ **ORIGINAL WORD CHOICE**
- contains specific verbs and nouns.
- uses sensory details.

____ **EFFECTIVE SENTENCE STYLE**
- flows smoothly from one idea to the next.
- includes sentences of varied lengths and beginnings.

____ **CORRECT, ACCURATE COPY**
- follows the basic rules of grammar, spelling, and punctuation.
- meets the required formatting guidelines.

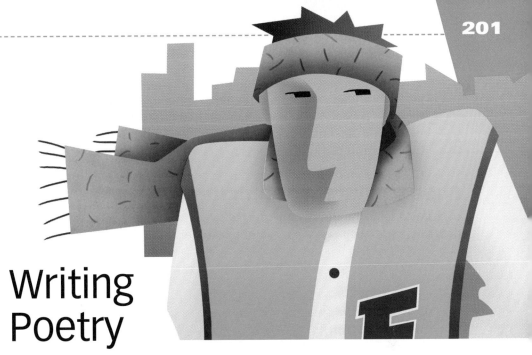

Writing Poetry

Moviemakers capture images on film, and poets capture images in words. (*Images* are mental pictures.) If you enjoy movies and video games, you have visual skills that will help you write poetry. In the following free-verse poem, student writer Devon Jackson captures the image of waiting at a station for the elevated train.

PASSAGE HOME
Gray walls of glass ram at the charcoal sky.
My fists jam in jacket pockets.
My teeth hiss steam.
Beneath my feet, the platform rumbles.
I wait behind the yellow line for my passage home.

What's Ahead

This chapter gives all the information you need to write a free-verse poem, plus much more.

- **What Is Poetry?**
- **Writing Guidelines**
- **Special Poetry Techniques**
- **Evaluating Poetry**

What Is Poetry?

Poetry is different from prose—the regular writing in which you use sentences and paragraphs. Here are some of the differences.

Poetry paints word pictures.

Poets focus on creating word pictures, or images, using details that describe what they see, hear, smell, taste, and touch.

> The sun sits,
> orange and pulpy,
>   on the horizon.
>   —Hector Hernandez

> Locusts breathe
> the rice-rich air.
>   —Reiko Kurisawa

> Cool.
> Moist.
> Heavy with life.
> Earth.
>   —Dixon Smith

> I shriek
>   and the tires shriek
>   and the bumper argues
>   with the old oak tree.
>   —Shauntay Roberts

Poetry speaks to the heart.

Poems speak to the mind and to the heart. It's the heart part that separates poetry from prose. You can feel the poet's hurt in this poem.

> You smile at the edge of sight, and I turn to see you.
>   No more.
> You whisper between words, and I hush to hear you.
>   No more.
> Without you, I am in darkness,
>   and the sun hides beneath the world.
>   —Declan Kelly

Writing / Creating the First Draft

Study the details you gathered. Which details provide the strongest image? Make that image the focus of your poem.

Alana decided to focus on the fiery colors of autumn leaves. She wrote her first draft freely from the point of view of the leaves themselves. It only took Alana a few lines to create an effective image.

> *WE WERE GREEN*
>
> *On the tree, we were green,*
> *but now we fall*
> *in fiery colors.*
> *We shine with flame in the world.*

Revising / Improving Your Writing

Review your first draft and ask a friend or classmate to read and react to it. Use the following checklist to help you make improvements.

___ Did I create a clear image, or word picture?

___ Did I use the best words to describe my subject?

___ Does my poem express my real feelings?

___ Do my words and phrases have pleasing sounds?

___ Does my poem have a pleasing form?

___ Does my ending deepen the meaning?

Revising in Action

The order of ideas is changed.

New imagery is added.

> *On the tree, we were green,*
> *one shade, one shape, one size,*
> *but now we fall*

Editing / Checking for Style and Correctness

Check your revised poem for style and errors. In a free-verse poem, you do not have to capitalize the first word in each line. The choice is yours. Use end punctuation at the end of complete thoughts. Use other punctuation only as needed.

Editing in Action

Line breaks are added for effect.

Word choice is improved.

in fiery colors.

    glow
We shine with flame before the world

turns white.

Sample Free-Verse Poem

The final version of Alana's poem captures an image of autumn leaves.

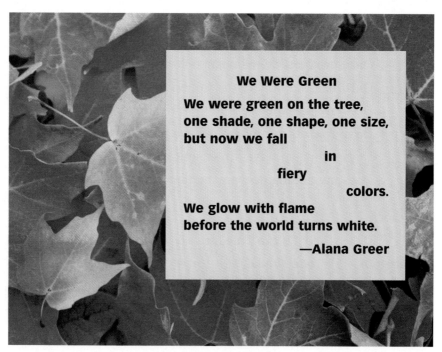

We Were Green

We were green on the tree,
one shade, one shape, one size,
but now we fall
                            in
                    fiery
                            colors.
We glow with flame
before the world turns white.

—Alana Greer

Special Poetry Techniques

Listed below are common techniques or devices that poets use to develop effective poems.

Figures of Speech

Poets use the following techniques to create strong images in their poems. These techniques are called *figures of speech*.

A **simile** *('si-mə-lē)* makes a comparison using *like* or *as*.

> **The scrap of paper fought like a fish on a hook.**

A **metaphor** *(me-tə-fŏr)* compares two different things without using a word of comparison, such as *like* or *as*.

> **Her eyes were searchlights.**

Personification *(pər-sä-nə-fə-'kā-shən)* is a technique that gives human traits to something that is nonhuman.

> **The leaves gossiped among themselves.**

Hyperbole *(hī-pər-bə-lē)* is an exaggerated statement.

> **When Guadalupe showers, the Pacific goes dry.**

The Sound of Poetry

Poets use the following techniques to include pleasing sounds in their poems.

Alliteration *(ə-li-tə-'rā-shən)* is the repetition of consonant sounds at the beginning of words.

> **The kids rode a cute little carousel.**

Assonance *('a-sə-nən(t)s)* is the repetition of vowel sounds in words.

> **A green apple gleams at me.**

Consonance *('kän(t)-sə-nən(t)s)* is the repetition of consonant sounds anywhere in words.

> **They plucked the anchor from the aching deep.**

End Rhyme *(end\rīm)* is the use of rhyming words at the ends of two or more lines.

> **Flowers grow in sidewalk <u>cracks</u>,**
> **and children grow near railroad <u>tracks</u>.**

Internal Rhyme *(in-'tər-nəl\rīm)* is the use of rhyming words within a line of poetry.

> **The <u>smoke</u> could <u>choke</u> a chimney.**

Onomatopoeia *(ä-nə-mä-tə-'pē-ə)* is the use of words that sound very much like the noise they name.

> **The <u>crackling</u> bag <u>crumpled</u> in his fist.**

Repetition *(re-pə-'ti-shən)* is the technique of repeating a word or phrase for rhythm or emphasis.

> **She forced <u>her tired</u> feet, <u>her tired</u> soul, to slog along.**

Rhythm *('ri-thəm)* is the way a poem flows from one idea to the next. In free-verse poetry, the rhythm follows the poet's natural voice. In traditional poetry, a regular rhythm is created. Notice how the accented syllables in the following lines create the poem's regular rhythm.

> **Ĭn Lóndŏntoẃn, whĕre úrchĭns híde,**
> **Thĕre líves ă mán ŏf wóefŭl mínd.** (a regular rhythm)

Reading Poetry . . .

Now that you understand the techniques of poetry, you'll get more enjoyment out of reading poems. Here are a few additional points to keep in mind. (Also see page 297.)

- A poem usually focuses on some part of life. It could focus on an ordinary event (waiting for a bus), a difficult situation (the passing of a loved one), or something in between.
- Since poems are usually brief, every word and phrase is important. Regular writers think in terms of words and sentences; poets think in terms of word pictures.
- How the poem is arranged on the page depends on the type of poem and the message the poet wants to communicate.
- To get the most out of a poem, read it several times—a few times to yourself and a few times out loud.

Evaluating Poetry

Use this rubric as a checklist to evaluate the quality of your poetry. The rubric is arranged according to the traits of good writing described on pages 19-24.

Assessment Rubric

____ **STIMULATING IDEAS**

The poem . . .

- focuses on a specific memory, feeling, image, or person.
- brings the subject to life.
- contains strong images (word pictures).

____ **LOGICAL ORGANIZATION**

- forms a meaningful whole—an idea creatively presented and developed.
- deepens its meaning in the final lines.

____ **ENGAGING VOICE**

- uses words and phrases to effectively create images.
- maintains a consistent voice throughout.

____ **ORIGINAL WORD CHOICE**

- contains specific sensory details.
- employs poetic techniques (See pages 207-208).

____ **EFFECTIVE SENTENCE STYLE**

- moves smoothly from one line or idea to the next.
- sounds pleasing when read out loud.

____ **CORRECT, ACCURATE COPY**

- is free of careless errors.
- follows the required formatting guidelines (if it is a traditional poem).
- looks interesting on the page (if it is a free-verse poem).

Report
Writing

Writing Observation Reports

We experience the world in five basic ways: We see, hear, touch, taste, and smell things around us. A person with a "sharp eye" sees details others miss. A person with "an ear for music" hears the notes more clearly. But being a skilled observer requires much more than sensory awareness. Skilled observers like scientists, artists, and musicians have fine-tuned the most powerful organ of observation, the brain.

Experienced writers are also effective observers. They notice details that other people often miss, and these details give them many ideas for their writing. Writing an observation report requires you to view the world in the same way that the pros view it. You must carefully gather and share information about a place, an event, an action, or an experiment.

What's Ahead

This chapter contains a sample observation report that shares the results of a science experiment, plus easy-to-follow writing guidelines.

- **Sample Science Observation Report**
- **Writing Guidelines**

Sample Science Observation Report

In this sample, Manny Barker reports on the connection between getting a car washed and the probability of rain. Notice that his report contains five parts.

BEGINNING

The first two parts identify the focus of the experiment.

SCIENTIFIC QUESTION: Is there a connection between getting a car washed and the probability of rain?

HYPOTHESIS: There is no connection between getting a car washed and the probability of rain.

MIDDLE

In the next two parts, the writer identifies his process.

PROCEDURE: For three weeks (April 5-April 26), I contacted the Neptune Car Wash to find out how many cars were washed each day. I also charted the weather (temperature, precipitation, air pressure) for each day during that time. (*Precipitation* means "the amount of rain.")

OBSERVATIONS: The three days that had the highest number of cars washed were April 6 (31), April 18 (38), and April 21 (28). These three days were also among the warmest days with the lowest pressure during this time. The three days that had the most rain were April 7 (.27 inches), April 20 (.6 inches), and April 22 (.18 inches).

ENDING

In the closing, the writer explains what he learned.

CONCLUSION: People do tend to wash their cars a day or two before it rains, but washing a car doesn't cause the rain. People wash their cars when the weather is warmest (high temperatures and low pressure), and unusually warm weather is often followed by rain.

Writing Guidelines

Prewriting ▸ Choosing a Topic

In most cases, you will write a science observation report based on an in-class lab experiment. If you are asked to create your own experiment, think about the subjects that you have studied in class. Then select a specific idea for an experiment based on one of those subjects.

The sample report on page 212 is based on weather, a common subject in high school science classes. The writer of the sample report decided to focus on the following idea, which he restated in the form of a question:

Idea: *It always seems to rain shortly after people wash their cars.*

Question: *Is there a connection between getting a car washed and the probability of rain?*

Gathering Details

Before you begin your gathering and observing, state what you think your experiment will prove. This statement is called a *hypothesis* (hī-pö-thə-səs). Here is the hypothesis for the sample report:

Hypothesis: *There is no connection between getting a car washed and the probability of rain.*

> Conduct your experiment by making your observations and taking notes. Upon completion, decide if your observations prove or disprove your hypothesis. Make sure that you have information that clearly supports your conclusions or findings.

Writing ▸ Writing the First Draft

As you write your first draft, include all of the important facts and observations you've collected. Follow your teacher's instructions for the form of your report, or follow the format of the sample report. This report includes five parts: *scientific question, hypothesis, procedure, observations,* and *conclusion*.

Revising / Improving Your Writing

Use the following checklist as a guide when you review and revise your first draft.

___ Did I cover all of the key parts in my report?

___ Do my observations clearly support my conclusion?

___ Are my ideas easy to follow and arranged in the best order?

___ Did I use a serious tone of voice?

Revising in Action

A more serious tone is used.

Important details are added.

For three weeks (April 5-April 26), I
contacted
~~hooked up with~~ the Neptune Car Wash to find
cars
out how many ~~sets of wheels~~ were washed
(temperature, precipitation, air pressure)
each day.   I also charted the weather for

each day during that time.

Editing / Checking for Style and Correctness

Edit your revised report for style by making sure that every sentence reads smoothly and that you have used the best words to express your ideas. Then check your writing for errors.

Editing in Action

Words replace numerals.

A plural verb is used.

A spelling error is corrected.

three
The ~~3~~ days that had the highest
were
number of cars washed ~~was~~ April 6 (31),
three
April 18 (38), and April 21 (28).   These ~~3~~
warmest
days were also among the (wormest) days

with the lowest pressure during this time.

Writing Summaries

A summary is a short piece of writing that captures the main point of a reading selection. You should paraphrase the main ideas, which means you put them in your own words. A summary should be no more than one-third as long as the original text. Writing a summary is an effective writing-to-learn or study technique because it tests how well you understand what you have read.

A good summary includes only the necessary facts. Names, dates, times, places, and similar information are usually necessary, but examples and descriptive details are not. To identify the important ideas, pay attention to the title and to the *italics* and **boldfaced** words in the reading. Also ask yourself these questions as you read: *What is the biggest or most important idea in the reading? What information supports this idea?*

What's Ahead

This chapter will help you write summaries of reading material. It includes a summary of a brief magazine article and easy-to-follow writing guidelines.

- ● **Sample Summary**
- ● **Writing Guidelines**

Sample Summary

MAIN IDEA

IMPORTANT DETAILS

Information uncovered 56 years after World War II has led the Navy to reclassify the cause for the sinking of the U.S. patrol boat PE-56 from accidental to caused by "enemy action." Originally, a boiler-room explosion was blamed for the sinking despite reports of a U-boat sighting. New evidence presented by naval historian Paul Lawton reveals that PE-56 was sunk by the German submarine U-853, killing 49 of its 62 sailors. Ironically, less than two weeks later, that submarine was the last to be destroyed during the war, and lies only seven miles off the shore of Rhode Island.

Original Reading Selection

Truth Surfaces About a Nazi Submarine

Anxiety about homeland security is nothing new: In World War II, German submarines haunted America's East Coast. *U-853*, the last U-boat sunk in the war, was among them—it lies only seven miles off Rhode Island, one of two dozen known German U-boat wrecks in U.S. waters. Now the ghost of *U-853* is back. After 56 years the U.S. Navy has acknowledged one of the U-boat's last kills, a Navy ship that sunk late in the war.

On April 23, 1945—two weeks before Germany surrendered—an explosion ripped the U.S. patrol boat *PE-56* as it sat off the coast of Maine, sending a geyser of water 300 feet in the air and killing 49 of its 62 crewmen. A 200-foot-long World War I era "sub chaser," the craft was being used that day to haul targets for bombing practice by Navy pilots.

A Navy Court of Inquiry ruled that *PE-56's* boiler had exploded and that the cause was "not enemy action," despite the accounts of crewmen who saw a sub surface soon after the explosion. Some described a conning tower carrying red and yellow markings like the insignia of *U-853* (the image of a red horse on a yellow shield). Twelve days—and one additional kill—later the sub was destroyed by a massive barrage of depth charges near Block Island.

Paul Lawton, a Brockton, Massachusetts, naval historian, began investigating the case in 1998 and gave his findings to the Navy, which has finally reclassified *PE-56's* sinking as an enemy sub attack.

—Cliff Tarpy

Writing Guidelines

Prewriting Choosing a Topic

You may decide to summarize a challenging reading selection on your own, or your teacher may ask you to summarize a specific reading assignment.

Gathering Details

Learn as much as you can about the reading selection by reading it at least twice.

- Skim the selection once to get the general, overall meaning. (*Skim* means "to read quickly.") Remember to pay special attention to the titles, headings, and *italics* or **boldfaced** words.
- Look up any key words that are new to you.
- Then read the selection again; list the main idea and important supporting points as you identify them.

> *Main Idea:* **The Navy has reclassified the cause of the sinking of a World War II ship**
>
> *Supporting Points:* – *the patrol boat PE-56*
> – *sinking changed from accidental to caused by "enemy action"*
> – *discovery made 56 years later*

Writing Writing the First Draft

Write your summary, using your own words as much as possible.

- The first sentence should be the topic sentence of your summary, stating the main point of the reading.
- In the remaining sentences, include the important details that support or explain the main point.
- Arrange your sentences in the most logical order.
- Add a closing sentence if one seems to be needed.

Revising / Improving Your Writing

Carefully review your first draft, using this checklist as a guide. Then make the necessary changes.

___ Have I clearly stated the main idea in the first sentence?

___ Have I included the important details needed to understand the main idea?

___ Are my ideas in the best order?

Revising in Action

An important detail is added.

A detail is reordered.

> uncovered 56 years after World War II
> Information has led the Navy to
>
> reclassify the cause from accidental to
>
> caused by "enemy action" for the sinking of
>
> the PE-56.

Editing / Checking for Style and Correctness

Use the following checklist as a basic editing guide.

___ Do my sentences read smoothly and clearly?

___ Do I use my own words as much as possible?

___ Is my summary free of careless errors?

Editing in Action

A spelling error is corrected.

A specific verb is added.

> explosion
> Originally, a boiler-room exploshun was
>
> blamed for the sinking despite reports of a
>
> U-boat sighting. New evidence presented by
> reveals
> naval historian Paul Lawton says that . . .

Writing Research Reports

Teachers assign reports because they want you to experience the complete researching process—investigating a worthwhile topic, organizing the information you have collected, and compiling the results in a paper. Most reports are at least three to five pages long and may require a title page, an outline, and graphics or charts.

Three things separate research reports from most types of school-related writing. In a research report, you must . . .

- refer to a variety of sources (books, magazines, Web sites, experts, and so on),
- identify the sources that you use in your paper, and
- follow special formatting guidelines.

What's Ahead

This chapter will help you develop an effective research report. It covers everything from selecting a topic to preparing a works-cited page.

- Sample Research Report
- Writing Guidelines
- Giving Credit for Information
- Adding a Works-Cited Page
- Evaluating Research Reports

Sample Research Report

Student writer Dean Karas wrote this research report about one of his favorite musicians, Bruce Springsteen. Karas's report focuses on the business side of Springsteen's career.

Karas 1

The writer provides a complete heading.

Dean Karas

Ms. Smith

World Issues

March 12, 2004

Bruce Springsteen

BEGINNING

The writer introduces his topic and states his thesis (highlighted).

In The Rolling Stone Encyclopedia of Rock & Roll, Bruce Springsteen is described as a "rock and roll working-class hero" (Holly and Romanowski 930). His memorable career has earned him a place among rock's elite performers such as Carlos Santana, Jimi Hendrix, and Mick Jagger. To his credit, Springsteen has remained a great rock performer despite poorly timed publicity, bad management, and corporate interference.

MIDDLE

He uses headings to help readers follow the report.

Poorly Timed Publicity

When a rock singer begins his career, he needs publicity, but too much of it too early can have a negative effect. When Columbia Records signed Springsteen, they promoted him as the new Bob Dylan on his first album. As Orth, Huck, and Greenberg explained in Newsweek, "The promotional overkill had a negative effect. Disc

Karas 2

jockeys resented the overinflated hype and ignored the record, refusing to give it air time." The album sold only around 25,000 copies. Springsteen's second album received good critical reviews, but sold even fewer copies and got less radio play, probably because Springsteen's manager sent a nasty letter to disc jockeys.

Then The Rolling Stone critic Jon Landau, in his now famous review of Springsteen, wrote, "I have seen the future of rock and roll, and it is Bruce Springsteen" (qtd. in Orth, Huck, and Greenberg). Columbia used Landau's positive review to promote the first two albums and build interest in the next album, Born to Run. This review, plus Springsteen's memorable live performances, helped to sell a million copies of the album. The success of Born to Run also spiked sales of the previous two albums. In other words, when the timing was right, the publicity helped make Springsteen a star.

The writer cites someone's remarks published in another text. (See page 232.)

He also adds his own summary thoughts.

Bad Management

The music industry abounds with stories about problems between musicians and their managers. Two of those stories deal with Springsteen's relationship with his managers. His first one, Mike Appel, was devoted to Springsteen and managed to sign him with Columbia Records. However, Appel did not effectively manage his client's money. In fact, Appel spent most of Springsteen's

Karas 3

first advance from Columbia on a new office for himself. According to Goodman's analysis, Appel was a poor choice as a manager because he was too limited in his experiences to handle Springsteen's success (273-274).

After a series of legal disputes involving Springsteen and Appel, critic Jon Landau eventually coproduced an album with Springsteen and became his manager. Goodman suggests that there was a constant conflict between the performer and his new manager (305). Landau was very concerned about his client's commercial success, while Springsteen himself was much more concerned about his music and maintaining fan loyalty. Springsteen may have had problems with his two managers, but the problems have never stopped the musician from focusing all his efforts on his music.

Corporate Interference

From the start of his career, Springsteen had doubts about the commercial side of rock and roll. Referring to the publicity surrounding the release of his third album, Springsteen said, "The hype just gets in the way. . . . It's weird. All the stuff you dream about is there, but it gets diluted by all the other stuff that jumped on you by surprise" (qtd. in Orth, Huck, and Greenberg). But he always believed in his abilities as a musician and the value of his music. Springsteen made this clear when he

Karas 4

said, "The pressures of business are powerless in the face of what is real" (qtd. in Goodman 353).

In discussing his relationship with his record company, Springsteen stated, "It's okay as long as it stays out of the way and helps" (qtd. in Goodman 302). Springsteen refuses to perform in large arenas to make more money at the expense of his music. The same distaste for commercialism has led Springsteen to refuse to sell T-shirts and other concert souvenirs (Goodman 304). His fans see him as a throwback to the early days of rock. Springsteen explains his relationship with his fans in this way: "I was always concerned with writing to my age at a particular moment. That way I would keep faith with the audience that supported me" (qtd. in Morse).

More than almost any other performer, Bruce Springsteen has managed to hold on to his music despite the distractions that come with being a rock star. Most importantly, he has never been frozen into a single marketing package that is simply recycled again and again. He continues to produce music that appeals to his huge following of fans.

Specific details add interest to the report.

ENDING

In closing, the writer restates his thesis and adds a final idea.

Works Cited

Goodman, Fred. The Mansion on the Hill. New York:
    Vintage Books, 1998.

Holly, George-Warren, and Patricia Romanowski, eds.
        The Rolling Stone Encyclopedia of Rock & Roll. 3rd
        ed. New York: Rolling Stone Press, 2001.

Morse, Steve. "Bruce Looks Back." Boston Globe. 20 Nov.
        1998. 10 Apr. 2004 <http://home.theboots.net/
        theboots/articles/bostonglobe98.html>.

Orth, Maureen, Janet Huck, and Peter S. Greenberg.
        "Making of a Rock Star." Newsweek. 27 Oct. 1975.
        12 Apr. 2004 <http://home.theboots.net/theboots/
        articles/newsweek75.html>.

"Works Cited" is centered one inch from the top.

The sources cited in the report are listed alphabetically.

Double-space throughout.

Indent the second and third lines five spaces.

Writing Guidelines

Prewriting / Selecting a Topic

Your teacher may offer one or more *general* subjects for you to consider for your report. It will be up to you to choose a *specific* topic to explore, a topic that truly interests you and meets the requirements of the assignment.

The writer of the sample report on pages 220-224 was interested in music. His teacher suggested that he consider a musician who has made an important contribution during his or her career. To search for a topic, he simply listed some of his favorite classic rock stars, and then selected the one that interested him the most, Bruce Springsteen.

Favorite classic rock stars

Carlos Santana

Bruce Springsteen

Jimi Hendrix

Eric Clapton

Organizing Your Research

Once you select a specific writing idea, it's important to learn as much as you can about it. Start by freely recording your thoughts and feelings about the topic. Then, to help you organize your reading and note taking, list questions that you would like to answer during your research. Think of questions that cannot be answered with a simple "yes" or "no."

Dean Karas, the writer of the sample report, listed these questions about his topic. (For a sample gathering grid, see page 53.)

Sample Questions

— *How did Bruce Springsteen get started?*

— *How did he become a star?*

— *What makes him different?*

— *What are his strengths as a musician?*

— *How has he maintained his popularity?*

— *How will he be remembered?*

Prewriting Gathering Details

Identifying Sources

Your teacher will provide you with guidelines, listing the number and types of resources you should use. For example, you may be asked to use at least four sources, two of which must be books or magazines. List your sources on note cards or on your computer. Include all the important publishing information for each one. Arrange and number the sources alphabetically by the author's last name. (See the example below.)

Taking Notes

As you conduct your research, take notes and write out quotations related to your topic. (*Quotations* are someone's exact words.) Follow these guidelines for your note taking. (Also see pages 344 and 346.)

- Take notes on 4- by 6-inch cards or on half sheets of paper.
- Write each research question at the top of a separate note card.
- When you find answers to a question, record that information on the right card.
- Record the page number where each piece of information was found. Also place the number of the resource (from the resource note cards) on the note card.
- If you run out of room on one note card, start another note card related to that question.

Sample Resource Card

> Goodman, Fred. *The Mansion on the Hill.* New York: Vintage Books, ②

Sample Note Card

> What makes him different? ②
> - doesn't get caught up in business of music
> - refuses to perform in large arenas and refuses to sell T-shirts and other souvenirs at concerts (page 304)

Prewriting / Planning Your Writing

Focusing Your Thinking

Review your research to determine what you have learned about your topic. Then decide on a focus for your writing. (A *focus* is a special feeling you have about the topic, or a specific part of it that you would like to write about.) Express your focus in a *working thesis statement*. The writer of the sample report decided to focus on the difficulties Bruce Springsteen has had with the business side of his career.

Working Thesis Statement

Bruce Springsteen has remained a great rock performer despite poor publicity, bad managers, and corporate interference.

Arranging Your Notes

Then arrange your note cards in the best possible order to support your focus. Set aside any note cards that don't relate to your writing idea.

Organizing the Supporting Information

The next step is to develop a writing plan, listing the main points and important supporting details that you will use in your report. (Don't include specific examples and quotations.) Here is the start of a plan for the sample research report.

Sample Writing Plan

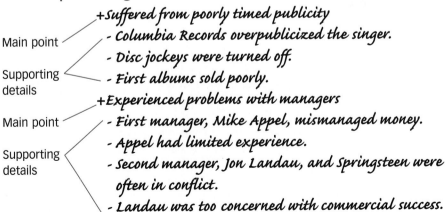

Main point
+ Suffered from poorly timed publicity
- Columbia Records overpublicized the singer.
- Disc jockeys were turned off.
Supporting details
- First albums sold poorly.
Main point
+ Experienced problems with managers
- First manager, Mike Appel, mismanaged money.
- Appel had limited experience.
Supporting details
- Second manager, Jon Landau, and Springsteen were often in conflict.
- Landau was too concerned with commercial success.

Creating an Outline

If you are required to write an outline for your research report, use your writing plan as a starting point. (See page 58 for samples.)

Writing ⟩ Writing the First Draft

If you have carefully planned your report, the actual writing should go smoothly. Keep these two points in mind as you write:

- Use your own words as much as possible. Include the ideas of others or direct quotations only when they add important support to your thesis.
- Keep your audience in mind at all times: What do they already know about your subject, and what do they need to know?

Writing the Opening Paragraph

The first part of the opening paragraph should say something interesting, surprising, or important about the topic to gain the reader's interest. The second part should identify the thesis of your research. Here are four ways to gain a reader's attention:

1 Begin with a revealing quotation.

2 Start with a surprising fact.

3 Give an interesting description.

4 Ask a question.

In the first line of the sample report on page 220, the writer uses a brief quotation to gain the reader's attention. He then adds an interesting detail about his topic before stating his thesis.

Opening quotation —
Interesting detail —
Thesis statement —

> In <u>The Rolling Stone Encyclopedia of Rock & Roll</u>, Bruce Springsteen is described as a "rock and roll working-class hero" (Holly and Romanowski 930). His memorable career has earned him a place among rock's elite performers such as Carlos Santana, Jimi Hendrix, and Mick Jagger. To his credit, Springsteen has remained a great rock performer despite poorly timed publicity, bad management, and corporate interference.

(There is a good chance that the final version of your thesis statement will not be worded in exactly the same way as your working thesis statement.)

Writing the Middle Paragraphs

Write the body of your research report using your writing plan and note cards as a guide. Each main idea in your plan will serve as the topic sentence of a paragraph in your report. The details listed under each main idea become the sentences that help develop the paragraph. Include additional details, examples, or quotations as needed.

Notice how the writer of the sample report developed the following middle paragraph:

> Topic sentence — When a rock singer begins his career, he needs publicity, but too much of it too early can have a negative effect. When Columbia Records signed Springsteen, they promoted him as the new Bob Dylan on his first album. Supporting detail — As Orth, Huck, and Greenberg explained in Newsweek, "The promotional overkill had a negative effect. Disc jockeys resented the overinflated hype and ignored the Quotation — record, refusing to give it air time." The album sold only around 25,000 copies. Springsteen's second album Supporting detail — received good critical reviews, but sold even fewer copies and got less radio play, probably because Springsteen's manager sent a nasty letter to disc jockeys.

You can also try writing your report without following your plan. To do this, turn over your plan and note cards, and write as much as you can on your own. Refer to your notes only when you need a quotation or a specific fact. After completing your writing, review your plan and notes to see if you have missed anything.

Writing the Closing Paragraph

The final paragraph in your report should do one or more of the following things: (1) Restate the thesis of your report. (2) Summarize the main points covered in the middle paragraphs. (3) End with one or more important thoughts about the topic. Here is the closing paragraph in the sample report:

> Restatement of thesis — More than almost any other performer, Bruce Springsteen has managed to hold on to his music despite the distractions that come with being a rock star. Most importantly, he has never been frozen into a single marketing package that is simply recycled again and Important final thought — again. He continues to produce music that appeals to his huge following of fans.

Revising / Improving Your Writing

A research report takes time to revise because it is a complex piece of writing. During this step in the process, remember to focus on the ideas, organization, and voice in your writing. Use the information that follows as your guide to revising:

Beginning ■ Does your opening paragraph introduce the topic in an interesting way and state the thesis, or focus, of your report?

Middle ■ Does the information in each middle paragraph support your thesis? Are these paragraphs organized in the best order? Does any information need to be added, cut, or made clearer?

Ending ■ Does the final paragraph do one or more of the following things: Restate the focus, summarize the supporting points, and/or make important final points about the topic?

Other Revising Concerns: For the most part, did you use your own words? Did you include any quotations or examples? Are any charts or drawings you may have included clear?

Revising in Action

A specific detail is added.

An idea is reordered.

An awkward sentence is rewritten.

Then The Rolling Stone critic Jon Landau , *in his now famous review of Springsteen,* wrote, "I have seen the future of rock and roll, and it is Bruce Springsteen." This review, plus Springsteen's memorable live performances, helped to sell a million copies of Born to Run. Columbia used Landau's positive review to promote the first two albums and build interest in the next album, Born to Run. The success of Born to Run also spiked sales of the previous two albums. ~~So the timing came right and publicity started a star.~~ *In other words, when the timing was right, the publicity helped make springsteen a star.*

Editing ⟩ Checking for Style and Correctness

Edit your revised report for style by making sure that all of your sentences read smoothly and clearly and that you have used the best words to express your ideas.

Then edit your writing for correctness by checking for spelling, grammar, punctuation, and capitalization errors. Also make sure that you have accurately given credit for information taken from the sources that you used in your report. (See pages 232-234 for help with giving credit for information.)

Editing in Action

A more vivid verb is used.

A spelling error is corrected.

A lowercse letter is capitalized.

An apostrophe is added to show possession.

A verb tense error is corrected.

abounds
The music industry ~~is filled~~ with stories about

problems between musicians and their managers.

Two of these stories deal with Springsteen's
relationship
(relasionship) with his managers. His first manager,

Mike Appel, was devoted to Springsteen and

managed to sign him with Columbia records.

However, Appel did not effectively manage his

clients money. In fact, Appel spent most of

Springsteen's first advance from Columbia on a

new office for himself. According to Goodman's

analysis, Appel was a poor choice as a manager
was
because he ~~is~~ too limited in his experiences to

handle Springsteen's success (273-274).

Completing the Final Copy

Once you have completed your editing, write a neat final copy of your report using the sample report on pages 220-224 as a formatting guide. Proofread this copy before you share it.

Giving Credit for Information

Follow your teacher's guidelines, and the information below and on the next two pages, for giving credit to the authors whose ideas or exact words you have used in your writing. If you don't give the proper credit, you may be guilty of **plagiarism** ('plā-jə-'ri-zəm)—the act of presenting someone else's ideas as your own.

Citing Sources in the Writing

To give credit in the body of your report, place (in parentheses) the author's last name and the page number(s) on which you found the information. Place this information at the end of the last sentence or idea taken from that author. (See the examples below.)

> The same distaste for commercialism has led Springsteen to refuse to sell T-shirts and other concert souvenirs **(Goodman 304)**.

If you already name the author in your paper, simply indicate the page number on which the information was found.

> According to **Goodman's** analysis, Appel was a poor choice as a manager because he was too limited in his experiences to handle Springsteen's success **(273-274)**.

If you use someone's exact words as they are published in another text, give the abbreviation *qtd. in* (quoted in) before the source in your reference.

> Springsteen made this clear when he said, "The pressures of business are powerless in the face of what is real" **(qtd. in Goodman 353)**.

If you refer to an Internet source, cite the author's name if it is given. If no author is given, then cite the title of the source. You will not have a page number to cite.

> "I was always concerned with writing to my age at a particular moment. That way I would keep faith with the audience that supported me." **(qtd. in Morse)**.

✳ For the author's full name and the title of the material, the reader can check the works-cited page at the end of the research report.

Adding a Works-Cited Page

A works-cited page lists, in alphabetical order, the materials you actually used in your research report. Double-space this information and indent the second and third lines of each entry five spaces. Use the sample entries that follow as a guide. Also see page 224 for a sample works-cited page.

> **BOOKS** Author or editor (last name first). Title (underlined). City where the book was published: Publisher, copyright date.

One Author

Zubrin, Robert J. Entering Space: Creating a Spacefaring
   Civilization. New York: Tarcher/Putnam, 1999.

Two or Three Authors

Diehl, Daniel, and Mark Donnelly. Medieval Furniture: Plans
   and Instructions for Historical Reproductions.
   Mechanicsburg: Stackpole, 1999.

> **ENCYCLOPEDIAS** Author (if available). "Article title" (in quotation marks). Title of the encyclopedia (underlined). Edition or version (if available). Date published.

One Author

Pettigrew, Thomas F. "Racism." The World Book Encyclopedia.
   1998 ed.

> **MAGAZINES** Author (if available). "Article title" (in quotation marks). Title of the magazine (underlined) Date (day, month, year): Page numbers of the article.

Signed Article in a Magazine

Anderson, Kelli. "Going to the Dawgs." Sports Illustrated 15 Nov.
   1999: 116-19.

Unsigned Article in a Magazine

"Seven Tips About Portable Generators." Consumer Reports
   Nov. 1999: 10.

ELECTRONIC SOURCES Author (if available). "Article title" (if available, in quotation marks). Source title (underlined). Date published. Name of sponsor (if available). Date found <URL> (address).

Web Site (Professional)

ESPN.com. 12 Nov. 1999. ESPN Internet Ventures. 24 Nov. 1999
<http://espn.go.com>.

Article Within a Web Site

Devitt, Terry. "Flying High." The Why Files. 9 Dec. 1999. U of
Wisconsin, Board of Regents. 4 Jan. 2000
<http://whyfiles.news.wisc.edu/shorties/kite.html>.

Article Within a Web Site (No author)

"Becoming a Meteorologist." Weather.com. 12 Nov. 1999. The
Weather Channel. 24 Nov. 1999 <http://weather.com/
learn_more/resources/metro.html>.

✳ Because the availability of information on computer networks can change from day to day, print out a copy of the material you are citing. Then you and your teacher can check the accuracy of quotations and facts cited in your paper.

OTHER SOURCES Author (if available). "Article title" (if available, in quotation marks). Source title (underlined). Medium (CD-ROM, DVD, Diskette). Edition (if available): Manufacturer or publisher's name, year of development.

Publication on CD-ROM, Diskette, or Magnetic Tape

"Sepoy Rebellion." Microsoft Encarta 98 Encyclopedia. CD-ROM.
1998 ed. Microsoft, 1998.

Filmstrip, Slide Program, Videocassette, DVD

Going Back: A Return to Vietnam. Videocassete. Virginia
Productions, 1982.

✳ Visit our Web site for updates and additional information about citing sources. Our address is <thewritesource.com>. The formats for all works-cited samples in this section are based on the latest edition of the MLA handbook.

Evaluating Research Reports

Use this rubric to evaluate the quality of your research writing. The rubric is arranged according to the traits of good writing on pages 19-24.

Assessment Rubric

____ **STIMULATING IDEAS**

The research report . . .

- shares information about an interesting topic.
- effectively supports your thesis or focus.
- keeps the reader's interest.
- gives credit, when necessary, for ideas from other sources.

____ **LOGICAL ORGANIZATION**

- includes a clearly developed beginning, middle, and ending.
- presents supporting information in an organized manner (one main point per paragraph).

____ **ENGAGING VOICE**

- speaks in a knowledgeable voice.
- shows that the writer is truly interested in the topic.

____ **ORIGINAL WORD CHOICE**

- explains or defines any unfamiliar terms.
- uses a serious or formal level of language.

____ **EFFECTIVE SENTENCE STYLE**

- flows smoothly from one idea to the next.

____ **CORRECT, ACCURATE COPY**

- follows the basic rules of writing.
- meets the required guidelines for formatting and documentation (giving credit).

Workplace
Writing

Writing Business Letters

Writing E-Mail, Memos, and Proposals

Writing Business Letters

Memos, e-mail messages, and business letters are common forms of workplace writing. People in the workplace usually send memos and messages to people they know. They are brief and quickly composed forms of business writing. On the other hand, people send business letters to individuals they may not know very well. Business letters are formal in tone and carefully worded.

Effective business letters get the reader's attention and prompt some action—a meeting, an agreement, a contract, or a solution to a problem. Business letters can also help students get things done—both in and out of school. For example, in school you can write a letter requesting information for a project; at home you can write a letter of application for a job.

What's Ahead

This chapter includes everything that you need to know about writing business letters, from understanding the basic parts to sending the final copy.

- Parts of a Business Letter
- Sample Business Letter
- Writing Guidelines
- Types of Business Letters
- Sample Letter of Complaint
- Sending Your Letter

Parts of a Business Letter

A business letter is made up of six basic parts: the **heading, inside address, salutation, body, closing,** and **signature.**

1 The **heading** gives the writer's complete address, plus the date.

2 The **inside address** gives the name, title, and address of the person or organization you are writing to.

- If the person has a title, make sure to include it. (If the title is short, write it on the same line as the name, separated by a comma. If the title is long, write it on the next line.)

- If you are writing to an organization or a business, rather than to a specific person, begin the inside address with the name of the organization or business.

3 The **salutation** is the greeting. Place a colon after the salutation.

- If you know the person's name, use it in your greeting. Use Mr. or Ms. plus the person's last name. (Do not guess at Miss or Mrs.)

- If you don't know the name of the person, use a salutation like one of these:

  Dear Museum Director: (the person's title)

  Dear Waterford Chamber of Commerce: (the organization)

  Dear Customer Service: (the department)

4 The **body** is the main part of the letter. Single-space each of the paragraphs, and double-space between each one. Do not indent the paragraphs.

- If the letter is two pages long, make a heading on the second page. List Page 2, the reader's name, and the date at the top left-hand margin.

5 The **closing** comes after the body. Use **Yours truly** or **Sincerely** as the closing for a business letter. Capitalize the first word of the closing, and put a comma after it.

6 The **signature** completes the letter. If you are using a computer, leave four spaces after the closing; then type your name. Write your signature between the closing and the typed name.

Sample Business Letter

1 2025 Rupert Avenue
Denver, CO 80222
March 12, 2004

———— Four to Seven Spaces

2 Ms. Maria Alvarez-Gonzales
College-Bound Director
Hispanic Chamber of Commerce
23 Merten Street
Denver, CO 80222

———— Double Space

3 Dear Ms. Alvarez-Gonzales:

———— Double Space

I am a sophomore at Bradford High School in Denver. My guidance counselor, Mr. T. J. Belliard, suggested that I contact you about your college-bound program.

Mr. Belliard told me that the program helps Hispanic students prepare for college, and that is just the kind of help I need. I will be the first member of my family to attend college, so we are not sure of everything I should be doing. Could you please send me information about the program? I'd be especially interested to know if you help students prepare for entrance exams and apply for

4 scholarships.

Please contact Mr. Belliard at 200-2442, extension 16, if you need to know about my high school record. He will answer any questions you may have.

Thank you for considering my request.

———— Double Space

5 Sincerely,

———— Four Spaces

Rosa Hernandez

6 Rosa Hernandez

Writing Guidelines

Prewriting / Choosing a Topic

Think about the goal or purpose for your letter. Are you requesting information, making a complaint, or expressing an opinion? You might find it helpful to state the purpose for your letter—what you want the reader to know or to do. Then state who the reader is.

Gathering Details

Gather all of the facts and details that you will need to write an effective letter. Keep your purpose and reader in mind as you collect information.

Purpose: *I am requesting information about a college-bound program.*

Reader: *Ms. Maria Alvarez-Gonzales*

Details: – *suggested by Mr. Belliard*
– *need guidance for college*
– *need to know more about the program*
– *help with entrance exams and scholarships*

Writing / Writing the First Draft

Always think in terms of the beginning, middle, and ending when you write a letter.

Beginning ■ In the opening paragraph, state the reason for your letter.

Middle ■ Present the important facts and details in short, clearly stated paragraphs.

Ending ■ Explain what action you would like the reader to take.

> You will have a better chance of getting action if you speak politely and positively in your letter.
>
> *Impolite:* Give me information about the program.
> *Polite:* **Could you please send me information about the program?**

Revising / Improving Your Writing

As you review your first draft, make sure that you have made all of the key points and that the information is clear and in the best order. Your letter should leave your reader with no unanswered questions.

Revising in Action

A detail is added.

An idea is made clearer.

> Mr. Belliard told me that the program
> helps Hispanic students prepare for college.
> ∧ and that is just the kind of help I need.
>
> I will be the first member of my family to
> attend college, so we ∧ ~~need help with things.~~
> are not sure of everything I should be doing.

Editing / Checking for Style and Correctness

Make sure that all of the sentences in your revised letter read smoothly. Then edit your writing for errors. Double-check the spelling and accuracy of names and addresses.

Use the sample letter on page 239 as a guide when you write the final, edited copy of your letter. Send your letter as soon as possible after completing it. (See page 244 for help.)

Editing in Action

A spelling error is corrected.

A misused word is replaced.

A run-on sentence is corrected.

> Please contact Mr. Belliard at 200-2442,
>   extension   know
> ~~extention~~ 16 if you need to ~~no~~ about my high
>
> school record ∧ he will answer any questions
>   ○≡
> you may have.

Types of Business Letters

Three common types of business letters include *letters of request, letters of complaint,* and *letters of opinion.*

Letter of Request

In a letter of request, you ask for information or answers to your questions. (See page 239 for an example.)

- Explain why you are writing.
- Ask questions if necessary.
- State what you would like to receive.
- Thank the person for helping you.

Letter of Complaint

In a complaint letter, you discuss a problem that you need help solving. (See page 243 for an example.)

- Identify the problem and possible causes. (You may have bought something that is damaged.)
- Discuss the problem. (Explain any action you have already taken.)
- Explain what you would like the reader to do about the problem.
- Be honest and polite. Express your concern, but do so in a mature and fair way.

Letter of Opinion

In an opinion letter, you share your feelings about something with a school official, a public official, the local newspaper, and so on.

- Explain the situation that concerns you.
- Express your opinion about this situation.
- Support your opinion with facts and examples.
- Suggest a change, reinforce your opinion, or make a call for action.

Sample Letter of Complaint

Starr High School
625 Island Avenue
Fort Worth, TX 76102
October 12, 2004

All parts of
the letter
are properly
presented.

Customer Service Manager
Rightway Fund-Raisers
2525 Capital Drive
Springfield, IL 62701

Dear Customer Service Manager:

BEGINNING

The problem
is explained.

At the beginning of the semester, we ordered T-shirts
from your company for a fund-raiser sponsored by our
school's marching band. We experienced quite a shock
when we unpacked the T-shirts. The lettering is
blurry on all of the extra-large shirts.

MIDDLE

The problem
is discussed.

We showed the T-shirts to our band director. He
suggested that we return the defective shirts along
with a letter explaining the problem and a copy of
our purchase order.

ENDING

A solution
is offered.

I'm sure that once you read this letter and inspect the
T-shirts, you will replace them with new shirts that
are printed correctly. We would appreciate receiving
the replacements as soon as possible to fulfill our
student orders.

Sincerely,

Scott Thompson

Scott Thompson
Band Club President

Sending Your Letter

Addressing the Envelope

Follow these guidelines when addressing an envelope:

- Begin the name and address of the person you are writing to slightly to the left of the middle of the envelope.
- Write your name and address in the upper left-hand corner.
- Place a stamp in the upper right-hand corner.

MS ROSA HERNADEZ
2025 RUPERT AVE
DENVER CO 80222

MS MARIA ALVAREZ-GONZALES
COLLEGE-BOUND DIRECTOR
HISPANIC CHAMBER OF COMMERCE
23 MERTEN ST
DENVER CO 80222

Using the U.S. Postal Service Guidelines

The postal service prefers that you address envelopes in this way:

- Capitalize everything and leave out all punctuation.
- Use the list of common abbreviations found in the National ZIP Code Directory. (See page 405.)
- Use numerals rather than words for numbered streets and avenues (7TH AVE, 2ND ST NE).

Folding the Letter

Fold the letter so that it fits neatly in the envelope.

1. Fold the bottom third of the letter up and crease it.
2. Fold the top third of the letter down and crease it.
3. Insert the letter—with the open end at the top—into the envelope.

Writing E-Mail, Memos, and Proposals

People in the workplace spend a lot of time communicating with one another. They meet in person, talk on the phone, exchange memos and e-mail messages, and so on. Communicating makes it possible for people to complete their work.

Written communication plays a special role in the workplace. With writing, individuals have time to think—to be sure the message is clear. Then once the message is sent, both the sender and the receiver have a hard copy for handy reference. And because a written message is a "permanent" form of communication, people are likely to consider it carefully and to take action.

What's Ahead

This chapter contains samples and writing guidelines for three forms of workplace writing: e-mail messages, memos, and proposals. The samples show how you can use these special forms of writing right now in school.

- Sample E-Mail Message and Writing Guidelines
- Sample Memo and Writing Guidelines
- Sample Proposal and Writing Guidelines

Sample E-Mail Message

In this e-mail message, the writer asks his teacher to consider his writing idea—explaining how to make jiaozi (Chinese dumplings).

The subject line identifies the topic.

The main part of the message discusses the topic.

In closing, the writer asks for approval of his idea.

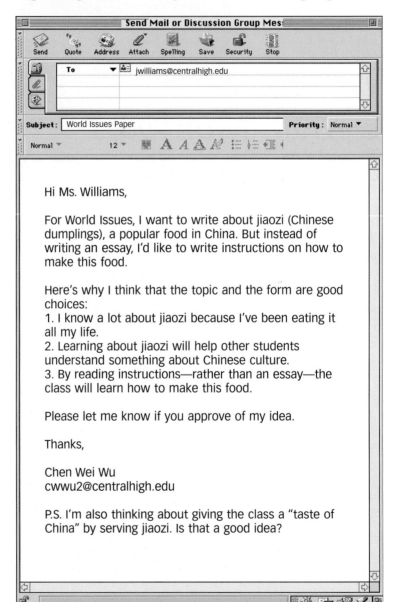

Send Mail or Discussion Group Mes

Send Quote Address Attach Spelling Save Security Stop

To ▼ jwilliams@centralhigh.edu

Subject: World Issues Paper   Priority: Normal ▼

Normal ▼   12 ▼

Hi Ms. Williams,

For World Issues, I want to write about jiaozi (Chinese dumplings), a popular food in China. But instead of writing an essay, I'd like to write instructions on how to make this food.

Here's why I think that the topic and the form are good choices:
1. I know a lot about jiaozi because I've been eating it all my life.
2. Learning about jiaozi will help other students understand something about Chinese culture.
3. By reading instructions—rather than an essay—the class will learn how to make this food.

Please let me know if you approve of my idea.

Thanks,

Chen Wei Wu
cwwu2@centralhigh.edu

P.S. I'm also thinking about giving the class a "taste of China" by serving jiaozi. Is that a good idea?

Writing Guidelines: E-Mail Messages

An e-mail message is a note sent through a computer network to a reader (or many readers). It is a fast way to write, send, reply to, and store messages. However, it's still important to write a good message in the first place.

Prewriting / Planning Your Message

Consider both the reader and the purpose for your message. Then gather all the details you will need.

Writing / Writing the First Draft

Organize your e-mail message in three parts.

Beginning ■ Enter an address on your e-mail form, and type a subject line that tells your reader the topic of the message.

Middle ■ Briefly greet your readers and then discuss the topic. Provide the necessary, basic details in a logical order, and keep all paragraphs short.

Ending ■ If you need the reader to do something, state so clearly. Then end politely.

Revising / Improving Your Writing

Ask yourself these questions as you review your first draft:

___ Is my message clear?

___ Did I use short, well-organized paragraphs?

___ Is my message accurate? Are all addresses, dates, actions, and details correct?

___ Is my message complete?

___ Does the message fit on one or two screens?

Editing / Checking for Style and Correctness

Before clicking the "send" command, carefully check for spelling, punctuation, and usage errors.

Sample Memo

In this sample memo, the writer updates his math teacher about his work on an extended project.

Memo

Date: April 19, 2003

To: Ms. Lavinski

From: Roberto Trevino   *RT*

Subject: Mid-Project Report

The goal for my math project is to figure out if the new locker rooms will have enough locker space for the swim team's big meets. So far I've done three things:

1. I interviewed Coach Delgazo about the swim team's needs.

2. I met with Dr. Matthews to explain my project.

3. I studied the blueprints for new locker rooms.

This week I plan to write a letter to Dr. Matthews and Coach Delgazo explaining my findings.

Please let me know if you have any questions.

Writing Guidelines: Memos

A memo is a short message in which you ask or answer questions, give a short report, send a reminder, or describe a procedure.

Prewriting / Planning Your Message

Consider who your reader will be and your reason for writing. Then gather the necessary details to write your memo.

Writing / Writing the First Draft

Organize your memo in three parts.

Beginning ■ Form a heading that contains the following information:

Date: Month, day, and year
To: Reader's name
From: Your full name
(You may initial this part before you send it.)
Subject: Memo's topic

Middle ■ Explain the reason for the memo, and provide the necessary details. Use short paragraphs, or list the most important points.

Ending ■ If any follow-up action is needed, state it clearly and politely.

Revising / Improving Your Writing

Ask yourself these questions as you review your first draft:

___ Is my memo clear and complete?
___ Did I use short paragraphs and/or well-organized lists?
___ Are all the details accurate?

Editing / Checking for Style and Correctness

Check your memo for the proper format, accurate spelling, and correct punctuation and usage. Prepare your final copy and proofread it. Get someone else to double-check your final proofreading.

Sample Proposal

In this sample, the writer provides his teacher with a detailed plan for a math project.

The heading clearly sets up the proposal.

Date: March 21, 2003
To: Ms. Lavinski
From: Roberto Trevino
Subject: Proposal for Math Project

The opening briefly describes the project.

Project Description
I want to see if the new locker rooms will include enough locker space for big swim meets.

Materials Needed
1. Blueprints for the locker rooms
2. Calculator
3. Computer and printer

The middle part gives details about the project.

Deadlines
April 11   Interview Coach Delgazo about the swim team's needs.
April 14   Meet with Dr. Matthews to get his permission to review the blueprints and to discuss the size of the lockers.
April 18   Study the blueprints to determine if there will be enough locker space.
April 25   Send letters to Dr. Matthews and Coach Delgazo explaining my findings.
May 2   Share my findings with the class.

Outcome
I will learn if the new locker rooms provide enough locker space for big swim meets.

The closing asks for approval of the project.

Please approve my proposal, or suggest needed changes.

Writing Guidelines: Proposals

A proposal is a detailed plan for completing a long-term project. Writing a proposal will help you think about and organize your efforts so that you complete a project on time.

Prewriting / Planning Your Proposal

To get started, carefully think about the project: Consider what you need to do, divide the project into doable parts, and describe what you hope to accomplish. Then carry out as much research as needed.

Writing / Writing the First Draft

Organize your proposal in three parts.

Beginning ■ Form a heading that contains the following information:

> **Date:** Month, day, and year
> **To:** Reader's name
> **From:** Your full name
> **Subject:** Proposal's topic

Middle ■ State your main point—what you are trying to do. Then explain your plan. Include details about the equipment, materials, and other resources needed. Outline the steps to be taken and, finally, describe the expected results.

Ending ■ Ask for approval of the proposal.

Revising / Improving Your Writing

Ask yourself these questions as you review your first draft:

___ Does my proposal include enough details?
___ Did I state and organize my points effectively?

Editing / Checking for Style and Correctness

As you review your revised proposal, make sure that you have used effective words and sentences to express your ideas. Then check for spelling, grammar, and punctuation errors. Write a neat copy of your proposal, and carefully proofread this copy before sharing it.

Searching
to Learn

Types of Information

You've been assigned to write a research paper about a specific food of the United States. Since you like hot food, you decide to write about Southwestern food, but how do you find information? You could look in the library for a book about Southwestern cooking or search the Internet for background information. You could also refer to your family's favorite recipes and cookbooks or talk to the cooks at local restaurants that serve Southwestern dishes.

As you search for information, one source often points you to other sources. You may even end up with more information than you need. Then you will have to sort through the materials and decide which are best for your paper.

What's Ahead

There are two general sources of information—primary sources and secondary sources. This chapter describes the differences between the two. It also explains how to use primary sources and how to judge the usefulness of all your sources.

- Primary vs. Secondary Sources
- Types of Primary Sources
- Evaluating Sources of Information

Primary vs. Secondary Sources

Primary sources are direct sources of information. You obtain the information firsthand, or directly from the source. You are using a primary source when you . . .

- visit a place or attend an event related to your topic,
- talk to knowledgeable people about your subject,
- conduct a survey, or
- carry out an experiment.

Secondary sources are indirect sources of information. You obtain the information secondhand, from a text that gathered it from various primary sources. Examples are encyclopedias, newspapers, nonfiction books, and CD-ROM's. You are using a secondary source when you . . .

- read an article about your subject,
- look up your subject in a reference book,
- visit a Web site, or
- search a CD-ROM for information.

Primary Sources

1
Talk to your mom about recipes.

2
Take part in a chili cook-off.

3
Interview a local chef.

4
Conduct a survey about favorite Southwestern foods.

Secondary Sources

1
Read a review of a local restaurant.

2
Look through a Southwestern cookbook.

3
Scan an article about cowboy cooking.

4
Watch a TV cooking show.

Types of Primary Sources

Primary sources give you firsthand details and information. First-hand research can be fun, and the information itself can make your paper far more direct and interesting for your readers. Here are five types of primary resources.

Observation and Participation

You can gather information by just watching people or places: If you see that a restaurant is always crowded, you can assume that people like to eat there. You could also take part in an event: You could go to the restaurant and order one of its Southwestern dishes, or you could cook one of your favorite recipes for yourself.

Surveys and Forms

An easy way to collect firsthand information from many people is to conduct a survey. Create a questionnaire or an easy-to-fill-in form that asks for the information you need. Deliver it to the "right" people to fill out, and then collect the completed surveys. For example, you could survey people about their favorite Southwestern foods.

Interviews

In an interview, you talk to someone who knows about your subject. Talking in person works best, but you can also interview someone through the mail, over the phone, or by e-mail. An interview with a local chef could give you valuable information for your paper on Southwestern food. (For tips on interviewing, see page 176.)

Presentations

Special classes, museum exhibits, or displays can provide you with valuable information. A class on Southwestern cooking, for example, could give you some interesting facts for your paper. Remember to take good notes during presentations.

Diaries, Journals, and Letters

Diaries, journals, and letters are interesting to read. They are also excellent sources of information. A cowboy's diary or a farmwife's letter could help explain the history of Southwestern cooking. Look for these sources in libraries, bookstores, and museums, or on the Internet.

Evaluating Sources of Information

You will probably find a lot of information about your topic. But before you use any of it, you must decide whether or not the information is dependable. Use the following questions to help you decide about the reliability of your sources.

1. Is the source a primary source or a secondary source ?

You can usually trust the information you've collected yourself, but be careful with secondary sources. Although many of them are reliable, they can contain outdated or incorrect information.

2. Is the source an expert ?

An expert knows more about a subject than other people. Using an expert's thoughts and opinions can make your paper more believable. If you aren't sure about a source's authority, ask a teacher, parent, or librarian what he or she thinks.

3. Is the information accurate ?

Sources that people respect are usually very accurate. Big-city newspapers (*New York Times* or *Chicago Tribune*) and well-known Web sites (CNN or ESPN) are reliable sources of information. Little-known sources that do not support their facts or that contain errors may not be reliable.

4. Is the information fair and complete ?

A reliable source should provide information fairly, covering all sides of a subject. If a source presents only one side of a subject, its information may not be accurate. To make themselves sound better, politicians and advertisers often present just their side of a subject. Avoid sources that are one-sided, and look for those that are more balanced.

5. Is the information current ?

Usually, you want to have the most up-to-date information about a subject. Sometimes information changes, and sources become outdated quickly. Check the copyright page in books, the issue date of magazines, and the posting date of on-line information.

Using Electronic Sources

The Internet and other electronic sources hold an amazing amount of information. On the Internet, you can search the entire world for the facts and details you may need. Searching the world for information may sound like an overwhelming task; but once you're familiar with using the Internet, your search can be simple and exciting.

Many people, in fact, just hop on the Internet when they need to know something. They overlook other electronic sources like CD-ROM's, which are also packed with information and may be easier to use than the Internet. This chapter will help you use both the Internet and CD-ROM's efficiently.

What's Ahead

First you will learn some basic facts about the Internet, including tips for searching the Web and using message boards and e-mail. Then you'll find an explanation of CD-ROM's—what they are, how to use them, and how to find the right ones for your research needs.

- **Understanding the Internet**
- **Using the Internet**
- **Using CD-ROM's**

Understanding the Internet

The Internet is made up of many interconnected computers. It lets you look for information anywhere in the world without leaving your desk. Two important parts of the Internet are the World Wide Web and e-mail. The Web can provide you with many different informational sites, including message boards. Message boards offer comments and facts from people who are especially interested in a certain subject. (See page 259.) E-mail allows you to send messages, greetings, or questions to other people.

The World Wide Web

The World Wide Web is like a huge library, and its "books" are Web sites. Each site contains a number of Web pages, like the pages of a book. Web pages are ordinary computer files, but besides words and pictures, they can also hold sound and video footage.

Because a Web page is a regular computer file, almost anyone can create one. Many businesses, schools, and individuals have their own Web sites filled with information. The hardest part is finding the site you need, but learning how to use your computer's Web browser will help you make a successful search of the Web.

Points to Remember . . .

- **Each Web site has its own address.** If you know it, key it into your browser's address bar. For example, **http://www.newmexico. org/culture/food.html** is the address of a site about Southwestern food found in New Mexico.

- **Web pages and sites are linked together.** This makes it easy to find the information you want. For example, while visiting a site about Southwestern food, you could click on a link that would take you to a page of recipes. Some Web sites also provide links to other sites about the same subject.

- **Special search tools help you find information.** Key your subject into your Internet browser's search tool. For example, if you would key in *Southwestern food,* your browser would provide you with a list of related Web sites. If you want an even more detailed search, you can use a search engine.

Message Boards

Many Web sites maintain message boards where visitors can post questions about a topic. Other visitors can read and react to the questions. A message board usually includes a search function so that later visitors with similar questions can quickly find the answers they need.

Finding a message board about your topic is easy. When you type a search term into a major search portal, the results include postings from message boards. It is worth visiting a message board even if the postings don't directly help you. You can do another search from there; the results (links) may be more up-to-date than the original postings.

Points to Remember . . .

- **Read the FAQ's.** FAQ's means "frequently asked questions." Many message boards have a section of FAQ's and answers that can give you a good idea of a board's purpose.
- **Get to know the board.** Read a portion of some current discussion within a board. This will help you decide if the board can provide useful information about your topic.
- **Don't believe everything you read.** Remember that anybody can take part in a message board. Although these people may be interested in the board's topic, they are not necessarily experts. They can get their facts wrong.

Netiquette

Netiquette is a word that was created by Internet users who combined "Net" and "etiquette." (*Netiquette* means "using good manners on the Net.") Here are a few basic rules of netiquette:

1. **Don't use the Internet to waste people's time.** Don't send or forward e-mail that is inappropriate or of no interest to others.

2. **Use your time on the Internet wisely.** There may be other students waiting to use the computer. The Internet is a highway. Don't hold up traffic!

3. **Respect the law.** Some material on the Internet is covered by laws that limit how you may use the information. Make sure you know what the rules are, and then follow them.

E-Mail

E-mail is perhaps the most familiar part of the Internet. It is an easy and quick way to talk to people around the world. Besides sending messages, you can attach a document to your e-mail. A survey sent by e-mail is a good way to acquire information from many people.

Points to Remember . . .

- **Use e-mail wisely.** Don't send unimportant e-mail that clutters up people's mailboxes or wastes their time.
- **Make your message clear.** Take your time when composing a message. Be sure to include all necessary information, and ask the questions you need answered. If you are sending a survey or questionnaire, make sure it is attached properly.
- **Be accurate.** Although writing and sending e-mail is fast and easy, take time to proofread your message. Treat your e-mail message as you would an important letter. Use capital letters, punctuation, and paragraphs. If your e-mail program has a spelling and grammar check, use it.

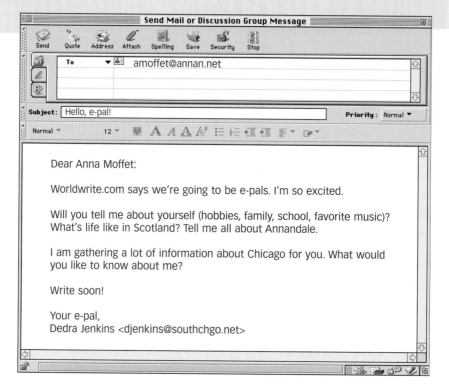

Using the Internet

Using the Internet can be both fun and frustrating. Here are some tips for making your time on-line more rewarding.

Work carefully. Always check your typing. If you mistype a Web address, your browser won't take you there. Even one wrong, forgotten, or extra character can make a difference.

Be patient. The Internet is vast, and searches can get complicated or frustrating. You may type in the address of a promising Web site only to find it's gone. This happens because Web sites are like businesses. Old ones disappear, and new ones take their place. You just have to keep searching.

Keep learning. Internet browsers have tutorials that help you use your browser and surf the Web. You may also get help from people who are more experienced in using the Internet.

Store important information. Use your e-mail program's address book to store the e-mail addresses that you use often. With your browser, bookmark frequently visited Web sites. Finally, write down important e-mail and Web-site addresses in case they are accidentally deleted.

Where to Learn More

These Web sites will help you learn about electronic sources. (Internet sites change from time to time. Whenever a Web site changes, there will be a link from the old address to the new one.)

- **http://www.pbs.org/uti/begin.html**
  Beginner's Guide: Understanding and Using the Internet. This site provides an effective starting point for learning about and using the Internet.
- **http://www.wiredguide.com/**
  Wiredguide: A Beginner's Guide to Computing and the Internet. Wiredguide provides you with links to Web sites designed to guide your computer and Internet use.
- **http://www.livinginternet.com/**
  The Living Internet. This site provides in-depth information about the Internet.

Using CD-ROM's

The CD-ROM is another valuable electronic source of information. A CD-ROM is a compact disc packed with data—an entire encyclopedia set, for example. Many reference books come in CD-ROM versions that include sounds, videos, and music in addition to the usual photos and text. They even include links to Web sites for additional information. The following print sources have been put on CD:

- encyclopedias
- dictionaries
- atlases
- study guides
- directories
- guides to magazine and newspaper articles

CD-ROM's are very simple to use. Just slide one into your computer's CD player. Type in or click on the subject you are looking for, and the information appears on your computer screen.

Points to Remember . . .

- **Each CD-ROM has its own rules for finding information.** Make sure you know how to search the CD-ROM you are using. Ask for help if you need it. Many CD-ROM's ask you to use keywords to search for information. Think of the best keywords for your topic. Use *and, or,* and *not* to narrow your search.

Topic:	Keywords:
African elephants	Elephants *and* African
	Elephants *not* Asian

- **Know the time covered on the CD-ROM.** Find out how far back the information goes. If a CD-ROM lists magazine articles for the past year, you won't find an article that was published two years ago. Also find out how up-to-date the CD-ROM is.
- **For the latest information, use the Internet.** Just like a book, a CD-ROM can become outdated. If you need the most up-to-date information, the Internet may be a better source.

Using the Library

Although the Internet is a wonderful resource, so is a good library. A school or public library contains books, the latest (and older) issues of magazines and newspapers, and helpful reference texts. It also has CD-ROM's, videos, and, in many cases, access to a computer for Internet searches and e-mailing. It's all there for you to use.

The Internet may be a good starting point for research, giving a lot of up-to-date information about almost any topic. The problem is finding this information and checking its reliability. On the other hand, library material contains in-depth and reliable materials on almost any topic. The library also has trained professionals to help you find what you need.

What's Ahead

This chapter provides basic guidelines for conducting library research, including using the computer catalog, locating books on the shelves, and much more.

- Searching for Information
- Using a Library Catalog
- Finding Books
- Using Reference Books
- Using the *Readers' Guide*

Searching for Information

Every library has a catalog that lists its collection of books, videos, DVD's, and CD's. While most libraries use computer catalogs, some may still have card catalogs as well. Using one of the catalogs is the best way to start your search for information.

Catalog Entries

A library catalog contains three types of entries for a book: title, author, and subject.

1 **Title entries** start with the book's title. If the title begins with *A*, *An*, or *The*, skip that word and look for the book under the next word of the title. Titles beginning with an abbreviation are filed as though the abbreviation were spelled out.

> ### *The Feast of Santa Fe:*
> ### *Cooking of the American Southwest*
> (This title would be filed under *Feast* in the card catalog.)

2 **Author entries** feature the name of the book's author. The author's last name is listed first.

> ### Dent, Huntley

3 **Subject entries** begin with the subject of the book.

> ### Southwestern cooking

Using a Library Catalog

A computer catalog and a card catalog contain the same type of information. Using each involves a slightly different process.

The Computer Catalog

With a computer catalog, you can find information on the same book in three ways. (Also check the library's instructions for using the computer catalog.)

1 If you know the book's **title**, enter it in the title search bar. You may enter just the first few words of a very long title. Also, if you remember only a few words of a title (*Santa Fe Feast*), enter them in a "keyword title search." The computer will give you a list of titles containing those words.

2 If you know the book's **author**, enter the name in the author search bar according to the catalog's instructions (*Dent, Huntley* or *Huntley Dent*). The computer will return a list of all the books by that author in the library's collection.

3 If you know neither the title nor the author, search for the book by **subject**. Enter the subject or a word related to it (keyword). Try to use very specific words (*Southwestern cooking*, not just *cooking*).

Sample Computer Catalog Entry

Author:	Dent, Huntley
Title:	The Feast of Santa Fe: Cooking of the American Southwest
Published:	New York, Simon and Schuster, 1985.
Subjects:	Cookery—New Mexico—Santa Fe. Santa Fe (N.M.)—Social life and customs.
Notes:	Illustrations by Susan Gaber.
Format:	397 pages.

STATUS:	CALL NUMBER:
Available	641.5979D

LOCATION:
General stacks

The Card Catalog

A library's card catalog is usually found in a cabinet of drawers. The drawers contain **title**, **author**, and **subject cards**, which are arranged in alphabetical order.

1 To find a book's title card, ignore a beginning *A*, *An*, or *The* and look under the next word of the title.

2 To find a book's author card, look under the author's last name. Then find the author card with the title of the book in question.

3 To find a book's subject card, look up an appropriate subject.

All three cards will contain important information about your book—most importantly, its call number. This number will help you find the book on the library's shelves.

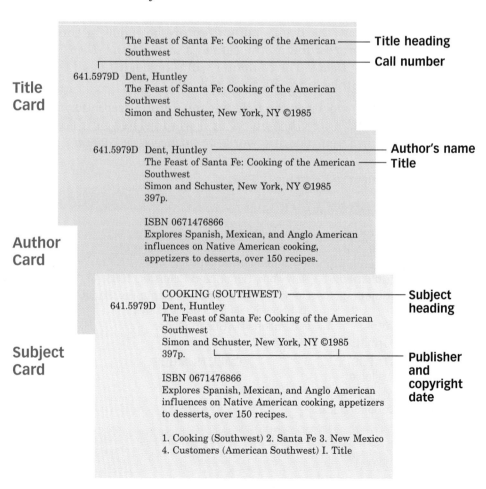

Finding Books

All nonfiction books in the library have **call numbers**. The books are arranged on the shelves according to these numbers. Call numbers are usually based on the **Dewey decimal classification** system, which divides nonfiction books into 10 subject categories.

000-099 **General Works** (includes encyclopedias)

100-199 **Philosophy** (includes psychology)

200-299 **Religion** (includes mythology)

300-399 **Social Sciences** (includes education and government)

400-499 **Languages** (includes dictionaries)

500-599 **Sciences** (includes math, biology, chemistry)

600-699 **Technology** (includes inventions, medicine, and cookbooks)

700-799 **Arts and Recreation** (includes music and sports)

800-899 **Literature** (includes essays and famous speeches)

900-999 **History and Geography** (includes travel)

- **Call numbers often contain decimals.**
  The number 641.5979 is smaller than the number 641.6. That's because 641.6 is actually 641.6000, but the zeros aren't written. This means that a book numbered 641.5979 would be shelved before a book numbered 641.6.

- **Call numbers can contain letters.**
  The D in 641.5979D is the first letter of the author's last name (Dent). This book would be shelved before a book with the call number 641.5979E, whose author's name begins with E.

- **More about using call numbers.**
  You would find the book with the call number 641.5979D (*The Feast of Santa Fe*) in the "Technology" section.

Biographies Books about people's lives are shelved under the call number 921. They are arranged in alphabetical order according to the name of the person the book is about.

Fiction Books These books are located in a separate section from the nonfiction books. They are arranged in alphabetical order according to the first three letters of the author's last name. (Some classic fiction books may be shelved in the "Literature" section—800-899.)

Using Reference Books

A reference book is a special kind of nonfiction book that contains specific facts or background information. The reference section includes encyclopedias, dictionaries, almanacs, and so on. Usually, reference books cannot be checked out, so you must use them in the library.

Using Encyclopedias

An encyclopedia is a set of books (or a CD-ROM) that contains basic information on almost every topic from *A* to *Z*. Topics are arranged alphabetically.

Tips for Using Encyclopedias

- **At the end of an article, there is often a list of related articles.**
  You can read these other articles to learn more about your topic.
- **The index can help you find out more about your topic.**
  The index is usually in a separate volume or at the end of the last volume. It lists every article that contains information about a topic. For example, if you look up "chili pepper," you would find a list of articles—*New Mexico, Pepper, Spices, United States Culture,* and so on—that include information about that subject. (Besides giving you a similar list, a CD encyclopedia may link you to Web sites for more information.)
- **Libraries usually have several sets of encyclopedias.**
  Different encyclopedias may contain different information. Review each set and decide which one best serves your needs. (In most cases, your teachers will not want you to use more than one encyclopedia for an essay or a report.)

Sample Encyclopedia Index

Encyclopedia volume

New Mexico N: 256 *with pictures and maps*
  Hispanic Americans (In the Southwest) H:**252-253**
  Mission Life in America (Western Missions) M:**618-619**
  Peonage P:**276**

Page numbers

  United States. History of the *picture on* U:**141**
  See also the list of Related Articles in the New Mexico
    article
New Mexico, University of N:**277**; U:**214**

Related topics

    New Mexico *picture on* N:**260**
New Mexico Highlands University U:**212**

Other Reference Books

Most libraries contain several types of reference books besides encyclopedias.

Almanacs are books filled with facts and statistics about many different subjects. *The World Almanac and Book of Facts* contains celebrity profiles; statistics about politics, business, and sports; plus consumer information. There is also a special edition for kids.

Atlases contain detailed maps of the world, continents, countries, and so on. They also contain photographs and related information. Specialized atlases cover topics like outer space and the oceans.

Dictionaries contain definitions of words and more. Biographical dictionaries focus on famous people. Specialized dictionaries deal with science, history, medicine, and other subjects.

Directories list information about groups of people, businesses, and organizations. The most widely used directories are telephone books.

Periodical Indexes list articles in magazines and newspapers. These indexes are arranged alphabetically by subject. Look for one of these indexes:

- *Readers' Guide to Periodical Literature*
  Lists articles from many publications. (See page 271).
- *New York Times Index*
  Lists articles from the *New York Times* newspaper.

Other Familiar Reference Books do not fit into any one category but are recognized by their names:

- *Famous First Facts* includes almost 10,000 facts about events, discoveries, and other "firsts" in the United States.
- *Facts About the Presidents* presents information about all the American presidents.
- *Bartlett's Familiar Quotations* lists thousands of quotations from famous people.
- *Guinness Book of World Records*, published annually, contains facts about nature, sports, and the strange things people do to gain attention.

Understanding the Parts of Nonfiction Books

Nonfiction books have many parts. Knowing the contents of each part can help you find the information you need. Provided below is a short description of each part, starting at the front of the book.

- The **title page** is usually the first page with printing on it. It gives the title of the book, author's name, publisher's name, and the city where the book was published.

- The **copyright page** follows the title page. It tells the year that the book was published. This date helps you decide if the book's information is current enough for your purpose.

- A **preface, foreword, introduction,** or **acknowledgement** sometimes follows the copyright page. These parts often give a short history about how the book came to be published—including what the book is about, why it was written, and who or what circumstances may have helped the process along.

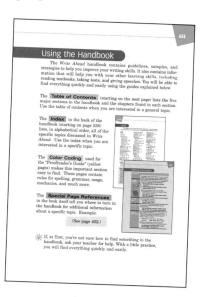

- The **table of contents** shows how a book is organized. It lists the chapter or section titles and their page numbers. This list serves as an outline, giving you an idea of what the book is about.

- The **body,** also called the text, is the main part of the book.

- An **appendix** may follow the body. It contains extra information such as maps, tables, and lists.

- A **glossary** lists and explains any special words that are used in the book.

- The **bibliography** may contain sources that the author used when putting the book together. It may also give suggestions for other books and articles to read about the subject.

- The **index** is an alphabetical list of all the important topics presented in the book. It gives the page numbers where each topic is found. By looking through a book's index, you can easily decide if the book has the information you need.

Using the *Readers' Guide*

Since magazines are published more often than books, they can be good sources of up-to-date information. Libraries carry periodical indexes that list articles from more than 200 popular magazines. Instead of searching every magazine for information on a subject, you can use a periodical index to find articles in several magazines. Periodical indexes can be found on CD-ROM or in book format. The *Readers' Guide to Periodical Literature* or a similar index is found in every library. Here are some tips on using the *Readers' Guide:*

1   **Check your library's collection of magazines.** Find out which ones your library subscribes to. You will save time by searching only for magazines that are in the library.

2   **Use the correct edition of the *Readers' Guide*.** To find information in the very latest magazines, use the most recent issue of the *Readers' Guide*. Different issues cover different time periods; so if you need information about a certain event, look in the issues that correspond to that event's date.

(At the end of the year, all the monthly issues of *Reader's Guide* are published together in one book.)

3   **Look up your subject.** Subjects are listed alphabetically. If you can't find enough articles about your subject, try looking under another word. One subject listing may also be cross-referenced, sending you to another subject. For example, if you look up *hot peppers,* the *Readers' Guide* may send you to *chili peppers.*

4   **Look up an author.** If you know the name of an author who writes about your topic, look up the name. Articles are listed under authors' names, too.

5   **Write down information.** Once you've found an article that sounds interesting, write down the information you need to find it—the name of the magazine, the issue date, the name of the article, and its page numbers.

6   **Find the magazine.** Finding the magazine may take some work. If it is a recent issue, it will be easy to find. If it is an older issue, it may be harder to find. Some libraries put a year's worth of magazines in a big binder. Other libraries store older magazines on CD's or on microfilm. If you're not sure where to look, ask a librarian for help.

Thinking
to Learn

Thinking and Writing

Becoming a good thinker is one of the most important things you can do for yourself. Good thinking can improve your writing—after all, writing is, basically, putting your thoughts on paper. In addition, effective thinking can improve your reading skills as well as your speaking and problem-solving skills.

Part of becoming a good thinker is learning about the different kinds of thinking, also known as thinking strategies. Understanding each strategy and how to apply it will prepare you to take on most writing and learning tasks.

What's Ahead

This chapter explains six kinds of thinking and gives you a sample assignment for each. A helpful chart on page 280 reviews basic guidelines for thinking and writing.

- **Recalling Information**
- **Understanding Information**
- **Applying Information**
- **Analyzing Information**
- **Synthesizing Information**
- **Evaluating Information**
- **Guidelines for Thinking and Writing**

Recalling Information

When you **recall**, you remember and repeat information. You recall when you . . .

- remember specific facts and details, and
- share the information, either by speaking or by writing.

Tips for Recalling

■ Listen carefully in class and take notes, writing down facts, terms, and definitions.

■ Read your texts carefully, taking notes on important pieces of information.

■ Review and study the information until you know it well.

Most writing assignments combine a higher level of thinking with recalling. However, on a test, you may be asked simply to recall information for a multiple-choice, matching, or fill-in-the-blank question. Imagine you've just learned about Cesar Chavez and the United Farm Workers movement in history class. The test questions below would require you to recall what you learned.

Assignment: Fill in the blanks below with the correct answers.

1. What year did Cesar Chavez establish the National Farm Workers Association? __1962__

2. The organization later came to be called _____
   __United Farm Workers__.

3. List three nonviolent protest tactics that Chavez employed in the struggle to gain justice for farm workers.
   __strikes, fasts, marches__

Understanding Information

When you **understand** information, you know what it means. You can put the ideas into your own words. You understand when you . . .

- explain something,
- tell how something works,
- tell what something means, or
- summarize information by restating the main details.

Tips for Understanding

▪ Use study-reading and note-taking strategies (see pages 344-346).

▪ Rewrite the information in your own words.

▪ Explain the information to someone else.

▪ Display the information using a drawing, graphic organizer, chart, or map.

Often, you will be asked to show understanding by writing a paragraph or an essay. To develop the paragraph below, the student had to recall important facts and details and use this information to show understanding.

Assignment: Explain how his religious upbringing had an impact on Cesar Chavez's life.

Early in his life, Cesar Chavez's father lost his land, and his family went to live with his abuelita, or grandmother. She taught the young Cesar to appreciate the ceremonies and teachings of the Catholic Church. Every day she would tell him stories and proverbs with morals to teach him how to live well. From her, he learned how important it was to persist in the quest for justice. Later in life, his love for the poor, like that of Jesus in the Bible, inspired him to act as an advocate for the mostly Mexican American migrant laborers in California. He organized the workers to seek fair wages and better treatment. One time before a strike he said, "We're going to pray a lot and picket a lot." His faith strengthened him for the many struggles he had as a labor leader.

Applying Information

When you **apply** information, you use it. You apply when you . . .

● explain a process or show how something works.
● use information to solve problems in school and in daily life, such as
   – following a sheet of directions to complete a class project or
   – using a subway map to get someplace new.

Tips for Applying

■ Select the most important facts and details.
■ Write about new information in a journal to discover its usefulness.
■ Answer any questions that you have about the information.
■ Organize the information in a clear way.

Some assignments ask you to apply information to your own life. To do this, you need to know the main facts and understand the overall theme. The assignment below asks students to apply what they have learned about Cesar Chavez's life to their own struggles.

Assignment: What do you find most inspirational about Cesar Chavez's many achievements? Apply this to your own life.

I am most inspired by the obstacles Cesar Chavez overcame during his childhood. At the age of 12, living in a poor barrio in California, Cesar decided that somehow he would work his way out of poverty. When he went to Anglo school, he was made fun of for speaking Spanish; and during his youth, he moved so much that he attended 37 schools. After 8th grade, he had to work in the fields because his father had been hurt in an accident.

My family moved a lot while I was growing up, and I didn't always like the schools I went to. But Cesar Chavez's life shows me that education is very important—whether it happens in or out of school. Although I don't have to deal with discrimination, I also believe, as Chavez did, that serving others is important.

Analyzing Information

When you **analyze** information, you break it down into parts. There are many ways to do this. You analyze when you . . .

- tell how things are alike and different,
- tell which parts are most important,
- divide information into different groups, or
- give reasons for something.

Tips for Analyzing

■ Identify the different parts that make up the whole.
■ Consider how the parts are related to one another.

When you analyze material, figure out what kind of analysis is needed (comparing, ranking, giving reasons, and so forth). Then decide which facts and details to use and how to organize them.

✳ A Venn diagram can help you organize your thoughts when you are asked to compare and contrast, as in the paragraph below. (Also see page 296.)

Assignment: Compare Cesar Chavez and Martin Luther King, Jr.

Cesar Chavez and Martin Luther King, Jr., fought similar fights. Both men were part of a nationwide struggle for civil rights in the 1960s. They both drew heavily from the teachings of Ghandi, who promoted nonviolence as a way to protest injustice. Using their strong religious upbringings as a basis for their work, both Chavez and King used Biblical language and religiously motivated speeches to bring people together for the cause of justice. Chavez worked to promote justice for exploited migrant workers, mostly Mexican Americans, while King worked for justice and equality for African Americans, who had been discriminated against for so long. Because of their skin color and their ethnicity, both men had to face the ugly realities of racism as they were growing up.

Synthesizing Information

When you **synthesize**, you create something new using ideas and information you have already learned. You synthesize when you . . .

- add new ideas to what you already know,
- use the information in a new way, or
- predict what may happen in the future because of this information.

Tips for Synthesizing

- Combine one body of information with another in order to make a prediction. (For example, when you understand a situation like Chavez's organization of migrant workers, you can make predictions about what might happen in similar situations today.)
- Ask "what if" questions about the information.
- Put information into a new form.

Synthesizing is both challenging and fun. Basically, you get to use your imagination to reshape information. The free-verse poem below is the result of an assignment in which students were asked to think in a new way about what they had learned.

Assignment: Turn what you know about Cesar Chavez's mission into a play, poem, or children's story.

SOUR GRAPES

Some people eat grapes without thinking twice
Others don't even want to see them after working
Up in the fields all day, every day,
Receiving minimum wages for their labors
Getting out of bed before the crack of dawn
Racing out to the fields
And facing a full day of backbreaking labor,
Pushed on by supervisors and managers
Ever demanding they harvest more and more
Shiny red grapes

Evaluating Information

When you **evaluate** information, you decide on its worth. You tell how effective or ineffective something is. You evaluate when you . . .

● give your opinion about something, or
● discuss the good points and the bad points about something.

Tips for Evaluating

■ Learn as much as you can about the topic.
■ Know and understand the main points about it.
■ Think about the value of the topic.

A good evaluation is based on good information. Start with a sentence that identifies your overall opinion, or evaluation; then add facts and details that prove your evaluation is a good one. Note how the sample paragraph contains a great deal of supporting ideas.

Assignment: In a paragraph, evaluate the overall effects of unionizing on the lives of California migrant workers.

The impact of unionizing on the lives of California migrant farm workers was overwhelmingly positive. Under the leadership of Cesar Chavez, the United Farm Workers (UFW) made many historic achievements for farm workers. Among them were the first genuine collective bargaining agreement between farm workers and growers in the history of the United States, the first and only pension plan for retired farm workers, the first credit union for farm workers, and the first health plan for farm workers. Before these agreements, farm workers had no health plans, pension provisions, or banking capabilities. The UFW also helped establish the first union contracts requiring rest periods, clean drinking water, hand-washing facilities, and protective clothing against pesticide exposure. Thanks to much hard work, the UFW contracts helped improve workers' health and earnings and helped decrease their long hours and dangerous work conditions.

Guidelines for Thinking and Writing

Whenever you are asked to . . .

Be ready to . . .

RECALL	
underline	circle
list	match
name	label
cluster	define

Remember what you have learned.
- collect information
- list details
- identify or define key terms
- remember main points

UNDERSTAND	
explain	review
summarize	restate
describe	cite

Explain what you have learned.
- give examples
- restate important details
- share the main ideas

APPLY	
change	illustrate
do	model
demonstrate	show
locate	organize

Use what you have learned.
- select the most important details
- organize information
- explain a process
- show how something works

ANALYZE	
break down	rank
examine	compare
contrast	classify
tell why	

Break down information.
- carefully examine a subject
- divide it into groups
- make connections and comparisons

SYNTHESIZE	
combine	connect
speculate	design
compose	create
predict	develop
invent	imagine

Reshape information.
- invent a better way of doing something
- blend the old with the new
- predict or hypothesize (make an educated guess)

EVALUATE	
recommend	judge
criticize	argue
persuade	rate
convince	assess

Judge the worth of information.
- point out a subject's strengths and weaknesses
- evaluate its clearness, accuracy, and value
- convince others of its value or worth

Thinking Clearly

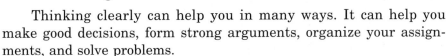

Thinking clearly can help you in many ways. It can help you make good decisions, form strong arguments, organize your assignments, and solve problems.

Clear thinking is especially important when you must plan a major assignment like a speech, persuasive essay, or research paper. For these kinds of assignments, your ideas must be logical *(supported with good reasons)* and reliable *(supported with solid evidence)*. So how do you think more clearly and logically? Generally speaking, you must organize, support, and present your points so well that your audience cannot question what you have said or written.

What's Ahead

This chapter will guide you through the decision-making process and explain how to use facts and opinions to persuade. It will also show you how to avoid unclear thinking, give you a step-by-step process for solving everyday problems, and more.

- Making Good Decisions
- Using Facts and Opinions
- Using Logic to Persuade
- Avoiding Unclear Thinking
- Solving Problems
- Asking Questions

Making Good Decisions

Deciding what flavor of ice cream to buy is usually easy. For one thing, you know what you like. For another, if you try a new flavor and don't like it, you may be disappointed, but you really haven't lost much of anything. Certainly, some other decisions are more important . . . and harder to make.

Here's how to think clearly when you have a hard decision to make:

1 **Write down what it is you must decide.**

2 **Write down your choices.** Under each choice, write down the facts about it, your feelings, and any questions you may have.

3 **Find the answers to your questions,** asking others for help if necessary.

4 **Add up the "pros" (positives) and "cons" (negatives).** Sometimes it helps to put a ✔ next to each good thing and an ✗ next to each bad thing.

5 **Make a decision.** You could decide to make the choice with the most checks, but you could also find that one point, good or bad, is more important to you than anything else.

Sample Decision

Should I go to the basketball game or finish my math homework?

BASKETBALL GAME	MATH HOMEWORK
All my friends will be there, so it will be fun.	I have to get a passing grade, or I won't be able to play football.
It's the last home game of the season.	The assignment will take at least an hour.
I'll get home at 10:30 p.m., and I'll be tired.	Can I get an extension and turn it in later? [NO]

Decision: *Because I can't turn my homework in later, I need to stay home and finish it so I can pass the course. Being able to play football next season is more important to me than one night of fun at the basketball game.*

Using Facts and Opinions

A **fact** is a detail about something that exists or something that really happened. An **opinion** is a feeling or belief about something. Facts can be checked or proven to be true; opinions are neither true nor false and cannot be checked.

When you have a persuasive speaking or writing assignment, you are trying to persuade someone that your opinion makes sense. To do this, you must rely heavily on facts. A persuasive assignment asks you to do two things: (1) Research a topic so that you can come up with an intelligent opinion about it; and (2) Support or prove your opinion using facts.

Facts

"It is 20 degrees Fahrenheit outside today."
"I am wearing a bright yellow coat."

Opinions

"It is too cold to run for track practice today."
"This coat is the coolest one in school."

Facts Support Opinions

It is often necessary to share your opinions when you speak and write. But listeners and readers expect you to back up your opinions with facts. Here are two examples:

Opinion: The expensive new developments will hurt our neighborhood.

Facts that support the opinion:

As wealthier people move into the area, working-class residents will find their property taxes and rents rising very quickly.

Opinion: This skirt is way too tight!

Facts that support the opinion:

The waistband is digging into my skin and leaving big red marks.

Using Logic to Persuade

Use the following tips for writing a successful persuasive essay or speech:

1 **Thoroughly research your subject.** Use books, magazines, the Internet, and interviews to find out as much as you can about your topic.

2 **Form an opinion.** Make sure you understand and believe the opinion so you can write or speak in a sincere, honest style.

3 **Write an opinion statement,** following this simple formula.

> **Formula:** **A specific subject**
> *(Low-income residents)*
> **+ a specific opinion**
> *(need stable, affordable housing.)*
> _____
> **= a good opinion statement**
> *(Low-income residents need stable, affordable housing.)*

> Avoid opinions that include strongly positive or negative words such as *all, best, every, never, none,* or *worst.* Exaggerated statements like "All the new homes built in this area should be affordable for poverty-level families" are impossible to support.

4 **Support your opinion with clear, provable facts.**

Opinion: "Wild animals in Yellowstone, even dangerous species, should be protected from hunters."

Provable fact: "Some of the dangerous species, such as grizzly bears, are endangered." (You can prove this with an official list).

Unprovable fact: "Grizzly bears attack humans only when they are afraid." (This statement is difficult to prove.)

5 **Organize your facts in one of two basic ways:** (1) State your opinion or belief in the topic sentence or thesis statement, and then support it with specific facts; or (2) Begin by presenting specific facts, and then lead up to a concluding or ending statement that contains your opinion.

Avoiding Unclear Thinking

Certain thinking "shortcuts" lead to misleading ideas, which can confuse readers. The examples that follow will show you types of unclear thinking, also called "logical fallacies," that you should avoid in your own writing.

Avoid statements that jump to a conclusion.

Because crime has increased in recent years, we need to start imposing strict curfews to limit teenagers' activities at night.

This statement assumes that teen curfews will solve crime problems, when, in fact, the majority of crimes are not committed by teens.

Avoid statements that are supported with nothing more than the simple fact that most people agree with them.

Teen curfews are good because most people agree that young people out after 10:00 p.m. are up to no good anyway.

Most people may think this, but, in reality, there are good reasons for young people to be out after 10:00 p.m.—jobs, study groups, athletic events, plays, concerts, and so on.

Avoid statements that exaggerate the facts or mislead the reader.

Curfews give teens the idea that no one trusts them, isolating them and making them angry, thereby turning them into criminals.

This statement is an exaggeration. While curfews may make some teens angry, it does not follow that these same teens will go out and commit crimes.

Avoid statements that contain a weak or misleading comparison.

Trying to enforce teen curfew laws is like trying to herd stray cats. It won't work.

This is a weak, unfair comparison; human beings should not be compared to stray cats.

Avoid statements that appeal only to the reader's feelings.

Teen curfews take advantage of our youth by severely violating their legal rights and viciously discriminating against minorities and the poor.

This statement uses words appealing to the emotions rather than to the reasoning powers of the reader. If the writer had facts to back up this statement, he or she would probably not use such emotional language.

Avoid statements, called half-truths, that contain only part of the truth.

Teen curfews use up valuable police time to remove the law-abiding youth from the public streets, leaving the streets open to crime.

It is a half truth to say that only "the law-abiding youth" would be removed from the streets. While studies of cities in the United States vary, some places that have imposed curfews have experienced a reduction in crime.

Avoid statements that reduce a solution to two possible extremes: "America, love it or leave it." "Put up or shut up."

Either we establish a curfew in our city, or teen crime will skyrocket.

This statement doesn't allow for a logical discussion of the issue. Obviously, there are other crime-reduction or prevention plans that could be considered.

Solving Problems

Does your life sometimes seem like it's made up of one problem after another? Guess what? That's true for most of us. Here's how you can use your thinking skills to solve some of the problems you face.

1 **Name the problem.** Figure out what it is. Also remember that although the problem may make you feel angry, your feelings aren't the problem. Rather, the problem is the situation that is causing your feelings.

2 **Think about and write down everything you know about the problem.** What caused it? Has it happened before? When? Has it happened to anyone you know? What did he or she do about it?

3 **Consider ways to solve the problem.** Think of as many solutions as you can. Write these down so you can compare them. Also, don't expect quick, easy solutions to every problem.

4 **Predict what may happen if you try each solution.** If the solution will cause more trouble than the problem itself, forget about it! Consider whether you can use two solutions together. Also think about what will happen if you do nothing.

5 **Choose the best solution and try it.** If you've thought of more than one good solution, try the easiest one first.

6 **Evaluate the solution.** How did things work out? If this problem happens again, what will you do?

The Scientific Method

The scientific method is a special process that will help you come to a conclusion about, or solve, a specific problem. Here are the steps in this process:

Identify the problem.

Make observations about it.

Advance a hypothesis (educated guess) or solution.

Gather data and test it against your hypothesis.

Investigate further, observing and collecting more data.

Note the data and draw possible conclusions.

Establish a single conclusion.

Asking Questions

Be curious! Find an interesting subject and let your curiosity take over. Write down as many questions as you can think of, and then try to answer them by gathering information about your subject. The chart below offers questions you can use as models for your own questions about different subjects, including **problems** (*like teenage smoking*), **policies** (*like a new dress code*), or **concepts** (*like community service*).

Problems

Description: What is the problem? What are the signs of the problem?

Function: Who or what is affected by it? What new problems may it cause in the future?

History: What is the current status of the problem? What or who caused it?

Value: What is its significance? Why is it more (or less) important than other problems?

Policies

Description: What type of policy is it? What are its most important features?

Function: What is the policy designed to do? What is needed to make it work?

History: What brought this policy about? What are the alternatives to this policy?

Value: Is the policy workable? What are its advantages and disadvantages?

Concepts

Description: What type of concept is it? Who or what is related to it?

Function: Who has been influenced by the concept? Why is it important?

History: When did it originate? How has it changed over the years?

Value: What practical value does it hold? What is its social worth?

Thinking Better

Thinking begins with careful observation—noticing the details of a situation and storing them for later use. The more information you have available to you, the better you will be able to plan, work, and solve problems—from figuring out how much time you'll need to complete a research report to putting up a new basketball hoop on your garage.

Becoming a better thinker also requires that you get involved in the world around you. As you experience more and more new things, old ideas will give way to new, original ideas; and you'll improve your ability to be creative, logical, and thoughtful.

What's Ahead

In this chapter, you'll find tips for becoming a better thinker. Learning and practicing these suggestions will strengthen your thinking skills and help you tackle difficult problems. The chart on page 291 efficiently links thinking strategies with writing in general.

- Becoming a Better Thinker
- Basic Writing and Thinking Moves

Becoming a Better Thinker

There is no magic formula for becoming a better thinker. Like everything worthwhile, it takes practice. However, the suggestions that follow should start you off on the right track.

1 **Be patient.** Don't expect quick solutions to every problem or challenge you face. Good thinking often takes time and requires you to plan, listen, and discuss.

2 **Set goals.** Separate the tasks you can do now (short-term goals) from those you must work on step-by-step to accomplish (long-term goals).

3 **Get involved.** Read books, magazines, and newspapers; watch documentaries; participate in sports, join a club; look at art, create your own art.

4 **Think logically.** Think beyond your "knee-jerk" emotions or the first answer that pops into your head. Look at all sides of a problem and consider all the possible solutions.

5 **Ask questions.** Be curious about what you read, what you hear, even what you see. If you think you know "what" it is, then ask "why, who, when, where, how, how much, why not, what if?"

6 **Be creative.** Do not settle for the obvious answer or the usual way of doing things. Look at things in a new way—redesign, reinvent, reenact, rewrite. (See "Answering Offbeat Questions," page 50).

7 **Make connections.** Pay attention to the details and how they are tied together. Use what you have learned to help you solve new problems. Use comparisons, analogies, metaphors.

8 **Write things down.** Writing can help you clarify ideas and remember them longer. It can help you discover things you didn't know you knew. It can help you sort through your thoughts and "see" them in a new light.

Your basic writing and thinking moves. On the next page is a "process chart" showing the kinds of thinking (from simple to complex) that go on when you write. However, you shouldn't expect to think in a straight line. Thinking goes up and down, backward and forward.

Basic Writing and Thinking Moves

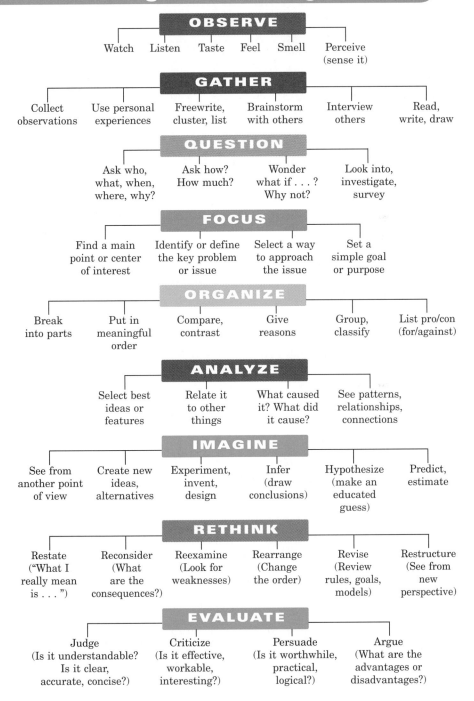

OBSERVE

Watch   Listen   Taste   Feel   Smell   Perceive
(sense it)

GATHER

Collect | Use personal | Freewrite, | Brainstorm | Interview | Read,
observations | experiences | cluster, list | with others | others | write, draw

QUESTION

Ask who, | Ask how? | Wonder | Look into,
what, when, | How much? | what if . . . ? | investigate,
where, why? | | Why not? | survey

FOCUS

Find a main | Identify or define | Select a way | Set a
point or center | the key problem | to approach | simple goal
of interest | or issue | the issue | or purpose

ORGANIZE

Break | Put in | Compare, | Give | Group, | List pro/con
into parts | meaningful | contrast | reasons | classify | (for/against)
| order

ANALYZE

Select best | Relate it | What caused | See patterns,
ideas or | to other | it? What did | relationships,
features | things | it cause? | connections

IMAGINE

See from | Create new | Experiment, | Infer | Hypothesize | Predict,
another point | ideas, | invent, | (draw | (make an | estimate
of view | alternatives | design | conclusions) | educated
| | | | guess)

RETHINK

Restate | Reconsider | Reexamine | Rearrange | Revise | Restructure
("What I | (What | (Look for | (Change | (Review | (See from
really mean | are the | weaknesses) | the order) | rules, goals, | new
is . . . ") | consequences?) | | | models) | perspective)

EVALUATE

Judge | Criticize | Persuade | Argue
(Is it understandable? | (Is it effective, | (Is it worthwhile, | (What are the
Is it clear, | workable, | practical, | advantages or
accurate, concise?) | interesting?) | logical?) | disadvantages?)

Reading
to Learn

Reading with Purpose

Good readers usually read for specific purposes. For example, they may read to . . .

- enjoy an exciting story,
- learn about a specific topic,
- study for a test, or
- catch up on the news.

It's also true that good writers usually write for specific purposes. Recognizing those purposes as well as the patterns that writers commonly use can empower your reading. When you understand how a piece of writing is put together, you are much more likely to grasp its meaning.

What's Ahead

In the following pages, you will learn how to spot patterns in writing, enabling you to read everything from paragraphs to poetry with greater purpose. You will also consider some of the special challenges Web pages can present for the reader.

- **Reading Signal Words**
- **Reading Paragraphs**
- **Reading Nonfiction**
- **Reading Fiction and Poetry**
- **Reading Web Pages**

Reading Signal Words

Good writers include transition or linking words to clarify details (see page 106), and good readers pay attention to those transition words. Like traffic signals, transitions offer direction: *keep going, turn around, stop and take note,* and so on.

Signal-word category	Examples	The reader should . . .
Emphasis	most important, the chief reason, especially noteworthy, a key element, the primary concern	pay special attention (the writer wants you to remember this)
Addition	first, second, third, next, one more, another, in addition, also, finally, last	look for a list of items (two or more)
Comparison	similarly, just as, like	see how items match
Contrast	different, yet, but, however, in contrast, on the other hand, even though	see how items differ, or expect a change of direction
Cause/ Effect	because, since, as a result, consequently, therefore, thus	look for a cause and the results that follow (sometimes the results come first and the cause follows)
Example	for example, such as, to illustrate, for instance	look for a specific example following a general statement or concept (to clarify)

Reading Paragraphs

All of your writing assignments consist of a series of paragraphs. Most paragraphs address one main idea. Often, that main idea is stated in one sentence, called the **topic sentence**:

> **A dog can be a wonderful companion.**

The sentences in the **body**, or middle part, of a paragraph provide details supporting the main idea:

- **My dog always has time for me.**
- **He is sad when I leave and happy when I return.**
- **He loves me no matter what I do, what grades I get, how I look, or whether I make the team.**

In most paragraphs, there is also a **closing sentence** that brings a paragraph to a logical stopping point.

> **My dog is truly my best friend.**

Location of the Topic Sentence

Identifying a topic sentence will help you determine the purpose behind each paragraph. Usually the topic sentence comes first in a paragraph (before the details).

> **January in northern Wisconsin can be bitterly cold.** . . .

Sometimes the topic sentence comes last (after the details).

> . . . **Clearly, January in northern Wisconsin can be bitterly cold.**

Occasionally the topic sentence falls in the middle of the paragraph. It can also be *implied:* The writer provides all the details, and the reader comes to understand the main idea even without a topic sentence.

FYI

Just as a topic sentence states the main idea of a paragraph, a thesis statement states the main idea of an essay, an article, or a report.

Reading Nonfiction

Paragraphs, sections, and even whole chapters of nonfiction are often organized according to predictable patterns. Recognizing these patterns will help you (1) understand what you read, and (2) organize any notes you may take. (See page 52 for more on graphic organizers.)

Pattern Type and How to Use It	What to Look For	Suggested Graphic Organizer (for notes)

Description

Focus on the senses
- The general topic
- References to sight, sound, smell, taste, and/or touch

SENSORY CHART

Sights	Sounds	Smells	Tastes	Textures

Chronological Order

List events according to time
- First event
- Second event
- Third, and so on

TIME LINE

Spatial Order

Describe object or place according to location of parts
- First part
- Second part
- Third, and so on

DESCRIBING WEB

Comparison/Contrast

Tell how two or more topics are the same and/or different

1. Characteristics of only topic 1
2. Characteristics of only topic 2
3. Characteristics both (or all) topics share

VENN DIAGRAM

Cause/Effect

Explain what caused something or explain the effects of one or more causes
- Cause (or causes)
- Effect (or effects)

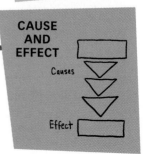

CAUSE AND EFFECT

Causes

Effect

Reading Fiction

Fiction uses made-up characters and events to explain some truth or theme about life. Here are some tips to help you understand fiction in all of its different forms.

Before you read . . .

- Try to find out something about the author.
- Think about the title.

As you read . . .

- Try to predict the plot. (*What is going to happen next?*)
- Try to analyze the characters. (*Why is he/she acting like that?*)
- Connect the characters and events to your own life where possible.
- Notice the author's choice of words and sentence style. (*Take note of passages that interest or puzzle you.*)

After you read . . .

- Talk to others who have read the story; compare reactions.
- Focus on the main character. (*Did he/she change? Why?*) Often, this is the key to understanding a piece of fiction.
- Try to state the story's thesis (main idea) in one sentence.
- Evaluate: Did the author get this main idea across?

Reading Poetry

Poetry tends to be densely packed, like a stick of dynamite ready to explode with meaning. That meaning is carried in the words, but also in the rhythm, rhyme, line length, sounds, and punctuation in the poem. Many poems also use metaphors or similes (page 207) to connect images to ideas. Here are two tips for understanding a poem.

- Read the poem several times, out loud if possible. The more often you read it, the more meaning you will gain.
- Relax and react to the poem on your own terms. Instead of always asking, "What does the poet mean?" ask "What does this poem mean to me?" Most poems have more than one "correct" interpretation.

The words (lyrics) of songs often read like poems. Try using the tips above the next time you want to figure out the meaning of a particular song.

Reading Web Pages

Ask yourself the following two questions in order to identify the most important information in a Web site.

1. Why am I reading this Web page ❓

Knowing why you are reading a Web page is important when you are looking for specific information. (It's less important when you're just surfing for fun.) Web sites are different from textbooks:

A textbook is usually clearly organized.

- Headings tell you what information is most important and what information is less important.
- You start at the beginning and work through the pages in order.

A Web site is usually loosely organized.

- A list of choices to click on may not give you a clear sense of what is most important.
- You often work your way around the site in any order you choose.
- You may even surf over to other related (or unrelated) Web sites.

✳ Keep your purpose clearly in mind when reading Web pages. Take notes or print out your most significant findings.

2. Who wrote this Web page ❓

Knowing who is behind a Web site is also very important. Anyone who understands the technology can create a Web site—the question is whether you should accept that "anyone" as an authority. Before accepting a Web site as truth, ask yourself the following questions. (Also see page 256.)

- Whose Web site is this?
  (It may take detective work to find the answer.)
- Why did this person or group create this site?
  (Do they have a specific purpose in mind?)
- When was this site last updated?
  (The date is usually listed at the bottom of the home page.)
- Do you notice any mistakes or misinformation on this site?
  (A Web site with too many errors is a poor source of information.)

Reading Graphics

When *USA Today* first came out in 1982, people were surprised to see so many colorful graphics. Critics wondered if a newspaper so easy to read could make it. The answer is yes. *USA Today* is now the largest-selling newspaper in the United States; over two million copies are sold each day. *USA Today* is designed to share information so that it is easy to follow. That's why the paper uses so many graphics.

A good graphic can make complex data easy to understand. It can show in a single picture or chart what it might take many paragraphs to tell. That's why an effective graphic works so well. It immediately makes sense to readers, and the information it presents sticks with them.

What's Ahead

All graphics show how facts relate to one another. Different graphics show different kinds of relationships. This chapter will help you read and understand the most common kinds of graphics, including graphs, tables, diagrams, and maps.

- **Understanding Graphs**
- **Understanding Tables**
- **Understanding Diagrams**
- **Understanding Maps**
- **Checklist for Reading a Graphic**

Understanding Graphs

Graphs are pictures of information, not pictures of things. The information in graphs is often called *data*. The most common kinds of graphs are *line graphs, pie graphs,* and *bar graphs.*

Line Graph A line graph shows how things change over time. The horizontal line (across the bottom) of the graph stands for *passing time* (seconds, minutes, years, etc.). The vertical line (up the left side) shows the subject. Check out the line graph below.

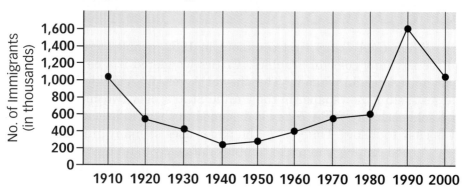

Legal Immigration to the United States

Pie Graph A pie graph shows how all the parts of something add up to make the whole. A pie graph often shows percentages. (A percentage is the part of a whole stated in hundredths: 10% = $\frac{10}{100}$.) It's called a pie graph because it is usually a circle.

If percentages are used, they should add up to 100 percent; if numbers are used, they may add up to some other total.

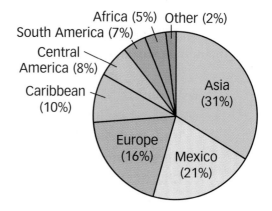

U.S. Legal Immigrants: Region of Origin
(1980-2000)

Bar Graph   A bar graph uses bars to show how different things compare to one another. When bar graphs examine how something changes over time, the horizontal line (across the bottom) usually marks *time periods,* and the vertical line (up the left side) marks *amounts.*

Growth of Internet Users
Estimated number of Americans age 3 and older
with access to the Internet, 1997-2001

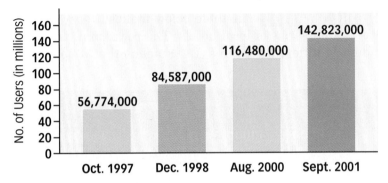

Horizontal Bar Graph   In a bar graph, the bars or columns may run horizontally (across) rather than vertically (up and down).

2000 Population in the United States

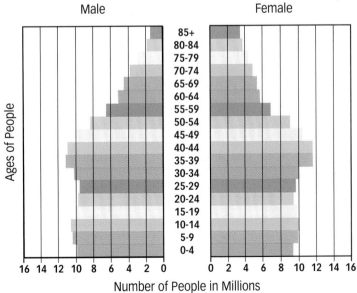

Understanding Tables

Tables organize words and numbers so that it's easy to see how they relate to one another. Each table has *rows* (going across) and *columns* (going down). Rows contain one kind of information, while columns contain another type of information. Some common kinds of tables include comparison tables, distance tables, and conversion tables.

Comparison Table The table below makes it easy to review the main features in a series of local hotels. The rows name the hotels; the columns identify different features. (A ● means that a hotel offers this feature.)

Hotel	Features				
	In-Room Cable	Indoor Pool	Restaurants	Nearby Shopping	Internet Service
Four Kings	●		●		●
Rainbow	●	●		●	
Golden Palm	●	●	●		●
Badger	●		●	●	●

Distance Table Another common kind of table is a distance, or mileage, table. To read a distance table, find your starting point in one row or column. Then find your destination in the other direction. Where the row and column meet, you find the distance between locations.

Mileage Table			
	Los Angeles	Seattle	Boston
Los Angeles	0	1,141	3,026
New York	2,787	2,912	211
Miami	2,752	3,334	1,486
Chicago	1,989	2,043	1,015
Houston	1,581	2,498	1,858

Conversion Table   Another very useful table is a conversion table. This is a table that converts (changes) information from one form to another. The table below converts degrees Fahrenheit to the nearest degree Celsius (Centigrade).

Degrees Fahrenheit*	to	Degrees Centigrade
0		-18
32		0
40		4
50		10
60		16
70		21
80		27
90		32
100		38

*To convert, subtract 32, then multiply by .56.

Custom-Made Tables   Tables are used to show all kinds of information. They are often a good way to record information you gather. Imagine that you need to gather facts about several different countries and compare some of the information you have gathered. You could make a custom-made table like the one below.

Comparing Countries			
	Canada	**Mexico**	**U.S.**
Size (Sq. Miles)	3.85 million	759,000	3.8 million
Type of Government	Parliamentary	Republic	Republic
Voting Age	18	18	18
Literacy	99%	87%	98%

Understanding Diagrams

A diagram is a drawing showing how something is constructed, how its parts relate to one another, or how it works.

Picture Diagram A picture diagram is just that—a picture or drawing of the subject. Often, some parts of the subject are left out in order to emphasize others.

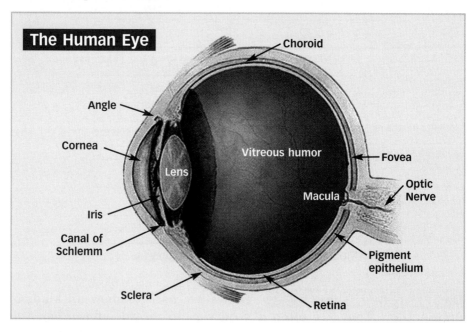

The Human Eye

Choroid

Angle

Cornea

Lens

Iris

Canal of Schlemm

Sclera

Vitreous humor

Macula

Retina

Fovea

Optic Nerve

Pigment epithelium

Line Diagram A line diagram uses lines, symbols, and words to show the relationship among ideas. The diagram below shows how the Germanic languages relate to one another.

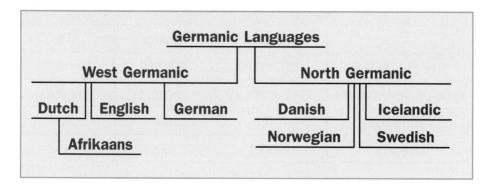

Germanic Languages

West Germanic

North Germanic

Dutch   English   German

Afrikaans

Danish

Norwegian

Icelandic

Swedish

Understanding Maps

There are many kinds of maps, each serving a different purpose.

Weather Map   A weather map has a language all its own, made up of words, symbols, and colors.

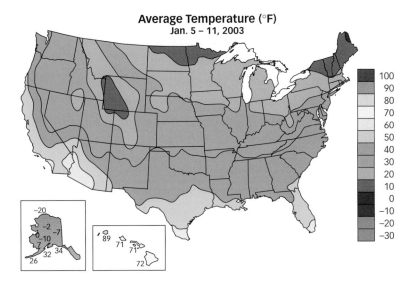

Average Temperature (°F)
Jan. 5 – 11, 2003

Population Map   This type of map shows the population density in the United States.

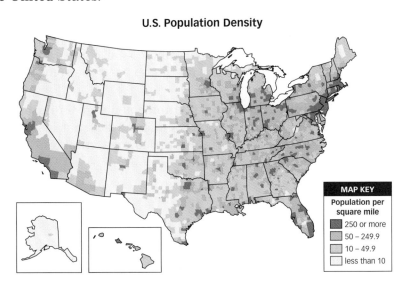

U.S. Population Density

Checklist for Reading a Graphic

Whether you are reading a textbook or a magazine, graphics can help you understand the information. Here's how to use a graphic and words together to understand what you are reading.

✔ First, scan the words and the graphic.

_____ Read the titles, the subtitles, the first sentence of each paragraph, and the summary, if there is one.

_____ Determine what the text is about.

_____ Look at the titles of the graphic.

_____ Be sure about the subject of the graphic.

_____ Notice the type of graphic (bar graph, diagram, pie graph, comparison table, and so forth).

✔ Next, read the text and the graphic.

_____ Read the paragraph above or below the graphic to get background information.

_____ Read every word, including the captions and labels.

_____ Read the key or legend which give details about how the graph works.

✔ Finally, ask yourself these questions.

_____ What does the graphic tell me?

_____ What part of the text does the graphic relate to? (Each graphic probably gives more information about one part of the text.)

_____ What information in the graphic is also given in the text? (Sometimes a graphic and the text tell the same thing, but in different ways.)

_____ What information in the graphic is not given in the text? (Sometimes a graphic gives information that is not in the text. That's why it's important to read graphics.)

Reading
Textbooks

Does this ever happen to you? You read a paragraph, page, or chapter in a textbook—put the book down—and say, "I can't remember a thing!" Many students have that experience. The good news is, you *can* remember important information that you read. The way to do that is by taking control of your reading assignments. You control the type of music you listen to, so do the same with your reading.

The secret to reading textbooks is to be an active reader. Have a plan in mind, and make sure you carry it out—before, during, and after the reading. The plan may begin with thinking about the reading and end with writing in your own words about the material.

What's Ahead

This chapter will help you improve your textbook reading. You will learn about helpful strategies that you can use throughout the reading process to become a more effective and efficient reader. Although this chapter is about reading textbooks, many of the suggestions apply to reading all nonfiction selections.

- **Taking Control of Your Reading**
- **Before You Read**
- **As You Read**
- **After You Read**
- **Taking-Control Summary**

Taking Control of Your Reading

How do you react when your teacher assigns a textbook chapter for you to read? What do you say to yourself?

- *Why bother? I won't understand it anyway.*
- *I could read the whole chapter and not remember one thing!*
- *I hate reading this textbook!*

Or . . .

I'm going to conquer this material!

Maybe the last reaction is hard to believe—but it's the attitude that a successful reader takes. Rather than being controlled by the chapter, this reader is in control. How can you tell who or what is in control?

The book is in control if you do the following:

- Read just because you have an assignment.
- Open the book and simply start on the first sentence.
- Skip over the titles and subheads.
- Accept the words automatically.
- Always read at one speed.
- Just read (don't write anything down).
- Close the book after reading and forget all about it.

You are in control if you do the following:

1 Consider why the material was assigned.

2 Preview the material.

3 Break up your reading into sections.

4 Slow down if the material is challenging; speed up if the material is easy.

5 Take notes as you read.

6 Think about the material and review your notes.

Follow the steps above to be a take-control reader. Your reading skills will begin to improve even if you apply just a few of these suggestions. Imagine how well you will read if you apply them all!

Before You Read

1 Consider why the materials was assigned.

When you are asked to read a textbook chapter, ask yourself these questions:

- What does the reading have to do with everything else we're doing in this class?
- What am I supposed to get out of the reading—background information, general knowledge, or specific facts?
- What do I need to do with the material when I finish—write a paper, participate in a discussion, or take a test?

✳ This step won't take long, but even a few minutes of thought will effectively prepare you to read.

2 Preview the material.

Previewing the material means looking it over before you begin to read. Look carefully at . . .

- titles, headings, and subheadings,
- pictures and their captions,
- graphs and tables, and
- vocabulary words if they are highlighted.

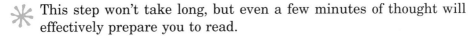

Also skim through the introduction and conclusion if those are provided. "Wow," you're thinking, "that could take up to 15-20 minutes!" You're right. Previewing, done well, can takesome time.

The truth is, until people try it, they often think previewing is a waste of time. In fact, the time you spend previewing a chapter actually saves time in two ways: (1) The chapter will be easier to read, and (2) You will better remember what you've read when you finish.

As You Read

The three steps discussed on the next three pages will help you carry out the actual reading.

3   Break up your reading into sections.

Instead of reading through the whole chapter, break your reading into sections. Identify the major headings, and use them to divide your reading. Each heading begins a new section, a new purpose for reading. It is often best to read only a few of these sections at a time.

If you see the chapter as one long reading, you might feel overwhelmed and not finish. If, on the other hand, you see the chapter as a series of short readings (divided by headings), you will probably feel more in control. What's more, you can use the headings to guide your reading.

If a heading says . . .	Read to find out . . .
• The First Americans	• who these individuals are.
• The Greatest Invention Since the Wheel	• what the invention is and the story behind it.
• What Is Electricity?	• what the key features of electricity are.
• Geographical Features of Hawaii	• what the geographical features are.
• Becoming a Better Reader	• how to read better.
• Immigration Laws	• what these laws are and how they work.

Hint: Many readers like to turn headings into formal questions:
- Who were the first Americans?
- What is the greatest invention since the wheel?
- How can I become a better reader?

Hint: If a heading is plural ("Geographical Features of Hawaii"), you should read to find a list of information:
- Feature one
- Feature two
- Feature three

4 Slow down if the material is challenging; speed up if the material is easy.

Some people read everything at the same rate of speed. But if you take control, you will vary your speed to match what you are reading.

Challenging material: If the section is difficult for you because it contains new vocabulary and complicated sentences, then slow down. This kind of reading is a challenge, so take your time. Concentrate on difficult ideas to see if you can understand them. Write down questions to ask in class. Take notes; consider how new information and ideas fit with what you already know about the topic.

Easy material: If the section is easy for you—familiar words and recognizable material, then you can read faster. You may even be able to skip some of the short words (*a, an, the, of, with, and*, for example) and still understand the section. Be careful, though, not to be overly confident.

FYI

Do you "say" every word in your head as you read? That is called "subvocalizing." It slows you down. Consider these points:

- You can probably *say* about 150 to 200 words per minute. If you subvocalize, that's about how fast you can read.

- You can probably *think* about 1,000 words per minute— or more! If you avoid subvocalizing, you greatly increase your reading speed.

Unless what you're reading is especially difficult, subvocalizing isn't necessary. But changing that habit will take practice. Start with very easy reading material.

What does all this mean? It means that reading speed is like driving speed. You slow down for dangerous roads and crowded areas; you speed up on straightaways and highways. Good readers, like skilled drivers, know the difference and control their speed accordingly. Good readers are in control.

5   Take notes as you read.

If you are serious about studying the chapter, taking notes is not an option; it is a necessity. Why? Taking notes will . . .

- keep you alert.
- help you remember what you read.
- help you see relationships within the chapter.
- help you relate the chapter to your classwork—and to your life.
- give you a handy study guide for tests.

The chart below lists common note-taking methods. Experiment to see what works best for you.

Method	Description	Advantages	Disadvantages
Highlighting	• Use a colored highlighter to mark words in the text.	• Easy	• Allows your brain to relax ("I'll come back and study this later!"). • Is not allowed in most school-owned textbooks.
Writing main points in a notebook	• Write major ideas in your own words. • Copy terms and their definitions.	• Requires you to concentrate. • Provides review sheets for tests.	• Relationships between ideas may not be clear.
Using graphic organizers (See page 52.)	• Make picture diagrams of sections of the chapter.	• Requires you to concentrate. • Shows relationships between ideas. • Provides review sheets for tests.	• Works best for parts of chapters, but often is difficult to use for the chapter as a whole.
Preparing double or triple columns	• Divide note pages in half or thirds. • Take notes on (1) the reading, (2) your response to it, and/or (3) the class lecture.	• Requires you to concentrate. • Helps you relate the reading to lecture materials. • Gives you space to react to the text. • Provides review sheets for tests.	• The lecture column can be difficult to coordinate with the reading notes.

After You Read

Use this information as a guide when you finish your reading.

> **6** **Think about the materials and review your notes.**

Thinking about and reviewing what you have read will help you understand and remember the material. Putting it out of your mind will lead to forgetting.

When to review.

- **Read over your notes immediately after the reading.** Without doing this, you'll forget more than 50 percent of what you've learned within the first hour of reading it.
- **After the initial review, look at your notes and/or the chapter every few days** (until you've learned the information). With each review, you will recall more and understand more.

How to review.

When it comes time to review what you've read, choose one (or several) of the methods described below.

- **Read the material out loud.** When you use more senses, you are employing more of your brain to remember and understand.
- **Test yourself using your notes.** This works especially well if you've taken double-column notes or prepared certain graphic organizers.
- **Teach the material to someone else.** Studies show that when you teach—especially when you use your own words—you retain or remember more information. If you can explain the material, you understand it. If you can't find someone who's willing to be your pupil, explain the material out loud anyway.
- **Read important points into a tape recorder.** Listen to the recording when you're doing something mindless.
- **Write about the material in your own words.** Don't worry too much about grammar or spelling; just get your thoughts on paper.
- **Study with a partner or a group.** It can be fun and helpful to learn in a group. (Just don't let the "fun" overtake the review!) Hearing what someone else learned from the reading can improve your understanding of the material.

Taking-Control Summary

Before You Read

- Consider why the material was assigned.
  - How does it relate to school? To the rest of my life?
  - What do I need to learn? For what purpose?
- Preview (look over) the material.
  - Titles, headings, subheadings
  - Pictures, captions
  - Graphs, tables
  - Vocabulary
  - Introduction and conclusion

As You Read

- Break up the chapter—reading one or two main points at a time.
- Adjust your reading speed to the difficulty of the material.
  - Hard? Slow down.
  - Easy? Speed up.
- Take notes.

After You Read

- Review the material.
  - Review right away; then every few days.
  - Talk, test, teach, tape-record, and/or write about the material; consider studying with a group.

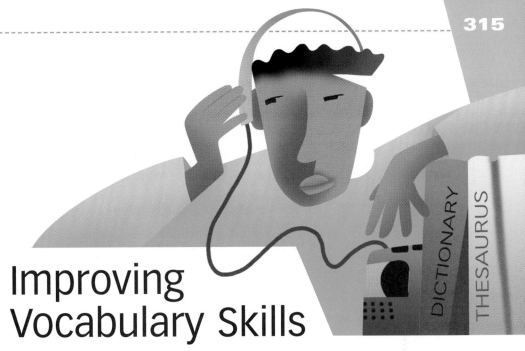

Improving Vocabulary Skills

How important is vocabulary? Very! The ability to use many words helps you read, write, listen, speak—even think. In fact, many experts believe that the fastest way to estimate someone's IQ is to check his or her vocabulary.

You can improve your vocabulary by reading books, listening to speakers, having new experiences, or watching educational programs. (Learning about any new subject requires learning the vocabulary that goes with it.)

What's Ahead

In this chapter you will learn about many strategies to improve your vocabulary. Try a number of these strategies as you work on future reading assignments.

- **Building Your Vocabulary**
- **Using Context**
- **Referring to a Thesaurus**
- **Checking a Dictionary**
- **Keeping a Personal Dictionary**
- **Prefixes, Suffixes, and Roots**
- **Understanding the Levels of Diction**

Building Your Vocabulary

The following chart lists six methods that you can use to improve your vocabulary.

Method	Description	Why It Works
Use context.	Look at the passage surrounding the words you don't know. (See page 317.)	Words and ideas around a word often give hints as to what the word means.
Learn common roots, prefixes, and suffixes.	If you're familiar with common word parts, you will be able to figure out many new words.	Tens of thousands of English words come from common Greek and Latin word parts. (See pages 322-329.)
Look up words in the dictionary.	Read the dictionary meaning. Also read the word history, which appears in square brackets. (See page 320.)	Sometimes the word history helps you connect the new word with one you already know.
Keep a vocabulary notebook.	Write down words you don't know. Include the pronunciation and meaning, and use each word in a sentence.	Writing reinforces your learning. The notebook is also a handy study guide.
Say your new words out loud.	Read your vocabulary notebook out loud, or look for places in conversation where you can use your new words.	Saying new words out loud means you hear them. Using that extra sense helps you remember.
Use your new words often.	Concentrate on using new words when possible in your writing.	Research shows that you need to use a new word to make it your own.

Using Context

When you come across a word you don't know, you can often figure out its meaning from the other words in the sentence. The other words form a familiar context, or setting, for the unfamiliar word. Looking closely at these surrounding words will give you clues to the meaning of the new word.

When you come to a word you don't know . . .

■ **Look for a synonym**—a word that has the same meaning as the unknown word.

> **Sara had an ominous feeling when she woke up, but the feeling was less threatening when she saw she was in her own room.** (An *ominous* feeling is a threatening one.)

■ **Look for an antonym**—a word that has the opposite meaning as the unknown word.

> **Boniface had always been quite heavy, but he looked gaunt when he returned from the hospital.** (*Gaunt* is the opposite of *heavy*.)

■ **Look for a comparison or contrast.**

> **Riding a mountain bike in a remote area is my idea of a great day. I wonder why some people like to ride motorcycles on busy six-lane highways.** (A *remote* area is out of the way, in contrast to a *busy* area.)

■ **Look for a definition or description.**

> **Manatees, large aquatic mammals (sometimes called sea cows), can be found in the warm coastal waters of Florida.** (An *aquatic* mammal is one that lives in the water.)

■ **Look for words that appear in a series.**

> **The campers spotted sparrows, chickadees, and indigo buntings on Saturday morning.** (An *indigo bunting*, like a *sparrow* or *chickadee*, is a bird.)

■ **Look for a cause and effect relationship.**

> **The amount of traffic at 6th and Main doubled last year, so crossing lights were placed at that corner to avert an accident.** (*Avert* means "to prevent.")

Referring to a Thesaurus

A thesaurus is a reference book (or on-line resource) that gives many synonyms and antonyms for words. A thesaurus helps you in two ways:

1. It helps you find just the right word for a specific sentence.

2. It keeps you from using the same words again and again.

If a thesaurus is organized alphabetically, look up the word as you would in a regular dictionary. If you have a traditional thesaurus, look for your word in the book's index.

Finding the Best Word

A thesaurus would be helpful if you needed one effective word to mean *overly proud* in the following sentence:

In many fables and tales, the kings and queens were

_____ , which made the common men and women

feel a mixture of emotions, including anger and hopelessness.

Sample Thesaurus Entry

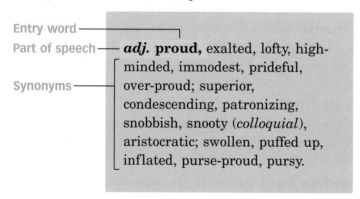

Entry word
Part of speech —— **adj. proud,** exalted, lofty, high-
minded, immodest, prideful,
Synonyms —— over-proud; superior,
condescending, patronizing,
snobbish, snooty (*colloquial*),
aristocratic; swollen, puffed up,
inflated, purse-proud, pursy.

(*Colloquial* means "informal or conversational.")

After reading the list of synonyms and studying the definitions of the unfamiliar ones in a dictionary, you might decide on *condescending* because it best describes the type of pride in this sentence. (*Condescend* means "to act like you are superior.")

In many fables and tales, the kings and queens were
condescending **, which made the common men and women**
feel a mixture of emotions, including anger and hopelessness.

Checking a Dictionary

The dictionary is, of course, your most reliable source for learning the meanings of new words. Remember, too, that a word often has more than one meaning, so read them all. In addition to the meanings of words, the dictionary offers the following aids and information:

Guide words are words located at the top of every page. They show the first and last entry words on a page, and they help you check whether the word you're looking up is listed on that page.

Entry words are the bold words that are defined on the dictionary page. Entry words are listed in alphabetical order.

Syllable divisions show where you can divide a word into syllables. Some dictionaries use heavy black dots to divide the syllables. Other dictionaries put extra space between syllables.

Parts of speech labels tell you the different ways a word can be used. For example, the word *grief* is used only as a noun. On the other hand, the word *griddle* can be used as a noun (*The griddle was ready for the pancakes*) or as a verb (*I'll griddle the pancakes*).

Pronunciations are phonetic respellings of a word. (*Phonetic* means "relating to speech sounds.")

Spelling and **capital letters** (if appropriate) are given for every entry word. If an entry is capitalized, capitalize it in your writing, too.

Illustrations are often provided to make the definition clearer.

Accent marks show which syllable or syllables should be stressed when you say a word.

Synonyms are words with similar meanings. **Antonyms** are words with opposite meanings and may be listed last.

Etymology gives the history of a word [in brackets]. Knowing a little about a word's history can make it easier to remember.

Pronunciation keys give symbols to help you pronounce the entry words.

> *Remember:* Each word may have several definitions. That's why it's important to read all of the meanings and then select the one that is best for you.

Model Dictionary Page

Entry word —————————— **lan·ta·na** (lăn-tă′nə, -tăn′ə) n. Any of various aromatic chiefly tropical shrubs of the genus *Lantana*, having dense spikes or heads and small colorful flowers. [NLat. *Lantana*, genus name < Ital. dial. *lantana*, wayfaring tree, viburnum.]

Syllable divisions — **lan·tern** (lăn′tərn) n. **1.a.** An often portable case with transparent or translucent sides for holding and protecting a light. **b.** a decorative casing for a light, often of paper. **c.** A light and its protective or decorative case. **2.a.** The room at the top of a lighthouse where the light is located. **b.** *Obsolete.* A lighthouse. **3.** A structure built on top of a roof with open or windowed walls to admit light and air. [ME < OFr. *lanterne* < Lat. *lanterna* < Gk. *lampter* < *lampein*, to shine.]

Definition with
two closely
related meanings

lantern fish n. Any of numerous small deep-sea fishes of the family Myctophidae, having phosphorescent light organs along each body wall.

lantern fly n. Any of various chiefly tropical insects of the family Fulgoridae, having an enlarged elongated head, once thought to be luminescent.

lantern jaw n. **1.** A lower jaw that protrudes beyond the upper jaw. **2.** A long think jaw that gives the face a gaunt appearance. — **lan′tern-jawed′** (lăn′tərn-jôd′) adj.

lantern wheel n. A small pinion consisting of circular disks connected by cylindrical bars that serve as teeth.

Pronunciation —————— **lan·tha·nide** (lăn′thə-nīd′) n. See **rare-earth element**. [LAN-THAN(UM) + -IDE.]

lanthanide series n. The set of chemically related elements with properties similar to those of lanthanum, with atomic numbers from 57 to 71; the rare-earth elements.

lan·tha·num (lăn′thə-nəm) n. symbol **La** A soft malleable metallic rare-earth element, obtained chiefly from monazite and bastnaesite and used in glass manufacture. Atomic number 57; atomic weight 138.91; melting point 920°C; boiling point 3,469°C; specific gravity 5.98 to 6.186; valence 3. See table at **element**. [NLat. < Gk. *lanthanen*, to escape notice (< the finding of the element hidden in oxide of cerium).]

lant·horn (lănt′horn′, lăn′tərn) n. *Chiefly British.* A lantern. [Alteration of LANTERN.]

Etymology ——————— **la·nu·gi·nous** (lə-noo′jə-nəs, -nyoo′-) also **la·nu·gi·nose** (-nōs′) adj. Covered with soft short hair; downy. [< Lat. *lanuginosus* < *lanugo, laniugin-*, lanugo. See LANUGO.] — **la·nu′gi·nous·ness** n.

la·nu·go (lə-noo′go, -nyoo′-) n., pl. **-gos**. A covering of fine soft hair, as on a leaf of a newborn child. [ME, pith < Lat. *lanugo*, down < *lana*, wool.]

Accent mark ————— **lan·yard** also **lan·iard** (lăn′yərd) n. **1.** *Naut.* A short rope or gasket used for fastening something or securing rigging. **2.** A cord worn around the neck for carrying something, such as a knife. **3.** A cord with a hook at one end used to fire a cannon. [Perh. alteration of ME *lainere*, strap < OFr. *laniere* < *lasne*, perh. alteration of *nasle*, lace, of Gmc. orig.]

Spelling and ——————— **Lan·zhou** also **Lan·chow** (lăn′jō′). A city of central China on capital letters
the Huang He (Yellow River) N of Chengdu; cap. of Gansu province. Pop. 1,060,000.

Lao (lou) n., pl. **Lao** or **Laos** (louz). **1.** A member of a Buddhist people inhabiting the area bording the Mekong River in Laos and Thailand. **2.** The Tai language of the lao. — adj. Of or relating to the Lao or their language or culture.

La·oc·o·ön (lā-ŏk′ō-ŏn′) n. *Gk. Myth.* A Trojan priest of Apollo who was killed along with his two sons by two sea serpents for having warned his people of the Trojan horse.

La·od·i·ce·a (lā-ŏd′ĭ-se′ə, lā′ə-dī). An ancient city of W Asia Minor in present-day W Turkey; built by the Seleucids in the 3rd cent. B.C.

la·od·i·ce·an (lā-ŏd′ĭ-se′ən) adj. 1. Of or relating to Laodicea. 2. Indifferent or lukewarm esp. in matters of religion. — n. A native or inhabitant of Laodicea. [Adj., sense 2, in reference to Revelation 3:14–16.]

La·om·e·don (lā-ŏm′ĭ-dŏn′) n. *Gk. Myth.* The founder and first king of Troy and father of Priam.

La·os (lous, lä′ōs′). A country of SE Asia; became part of French Indochina in 1893 and gained its independence in 1953. Cap. Vietiane. Pop. 3,811,000.

La·o·tian (lā-o′shan, lou′shan) adj. **1.** Of or relating to Laos or its people, language, or culture. **2.** Of or relating to the Lao people. — n. **1.** A native or inhabitant of Laos. **2.** A Lao.

Lao·tzu (lou′dzŭ′) also **Lao-tse** or **Lao·zi** (-dze′). fl. 6th cent. B.C. Chinese philosopher regarded as the founder of Taoism.

Parts of speech ———— **lap**[1] (lăp) n. **1.a.** The front from the waist to the knees of a seated person. **b.** The portion of a garment that covers the lap. **2.** A hanging or flaplike part. **3.** An area of responsibility, interest, or control. —*idiom.* **the lap of luxury.** Conditions of great affluence or material comfort. [ME *lappe*, lappet, lap < OE *læppa*, lappet.] — **lap′ful′** n.

Parts of speech
(principal parts of
the verb)

lap[2] (lăp) v. **lapped, lap·ping, laps.** — tr. **1.a.** To place or lay (something) so as to overlap another. **b.** To lie partly over or on: *each shingle lapping the next.* **2.** To fold (something) over onto itself. **3.** To wrap or wind around (something); encircle.

Guide words ————— **lantana**
lap

lantern wheel

Laos

Pronunciation key

ă	pat	oi	boy
ā	pay	ou	out
âr	care	ŏŏ	took
ä	father	ōō	boot
ĕ	pet	u	cut
ē	be	ûr	urge
ĭ	pit	th	thin
ī	pie	th	this
îr	pier	hw	which
ŏ	pot	zh	vision
ō	toe	ə	about,
ô	paw		item

Stress marks:
′ (primary);
′ (secondary); as in
dictionary (dĭk′shə-nĕr′ē)

Keeping a Personal Dictionary

You can improve your vocabulary by keeping a personal dictionary. Put each new word in a notebook, in a section of your journal, or on a note card. Include the following items for each entry:

- pronunciation key
- a definition
- a sentence using the word
- synonyms for the word

Social Studies

amend (ə'mend)
    to put right, to change

Will the committee amend the proposal?

Synonyms: correct, revise, adjust

Literature

commotion (ke 'mō shen)
    a condition of unrest, confusion, or disturbance

After the officer barked out a series of orders, there was a general commotion among the prisoners.

Synonyms: excitement, flurry, stir

Music

libretto (lĭ–brĕt´–o)
    the text of an opera or a musical

We found the libretto for Joseph's Amazing Technicolor Dreamcoat on the Internet.

Prefixes, Suffixes, and Roots

On the next several pages, you will find many common prefixes, suffixes, and roots in the English language.

Prefixes

A **prefix** is a word part that is added before a word. (*Pre-* means "before.") A prefix changes the meaning of the word it is added to. For example, the prefix *un-* added to the word *fair (unfair)* changes the word's meaning to "not fair."

ambi- *[both]*
  ambidextrous (skilled with both hands)

anti- *[against]*
  antifreeze (a liquid that works against freezing)
  antiwar (against wars and fighting)

astro- *[star]*
  astronaut (person who travels among the stars)
  astronomy (study of the stars)

auto- *[self]*
  autobiography (writing that is about yourself)

bi- *[two]*
  bilingual (using or speaking two languages)
  biped (having two feet)

circum- *[in a circle, around]*
  circumference (the line or distance around a circle)
  circumnavigate (to sail around)

co- *[together, with]*
  cooperate (to work together)
  coordinate (to put things together)

ex- *[out]*
  exhale (to breathe out)
  exit (the act of going out)

fore- *[before, in front of]*
  foremost (in the first place, before everyone or everything else)
  foretell (to tell or show beforehand)

hemi- *[half]*
  hemisphere (half of a sphere or globe)

hyper- *[over]*
  hyperactive (overactive)

im- *[not, opposite of]*
  impatient (not patient)
  impossible (not possible)

in- *[not, opposite of]*
  inactive (not active)
  incomplete (not complete)

inter- *[between, among]*
  international (between or among nations)
  interplanetary (between the planets)

macro- *[large]*
  macrocosm (the entire universe)

mal- *[bad, poor]*
  malnutrition (poor nutrition)

micro- *[small]*
  microscope (an instrument used to see very small things)

mono- [one]
monolingual (using or speaking only one language)

non- [not, opposite of]
nonfat (without the normal fat content)
nonfiction (based on facts; not made-up)

over- [too much, extra]
overeat (to eat too much)
overtime (extra time; time beyond regular hours)

poly- [many]
polygon (a figure or shape with three or more sides)
polysyllable (a word with more than three syllables)

post- [after]
postscript (a note added at the end of a letter, after the signature)
postwar (after a war)

pre- [before]
pregame (activities that occur before a game)
preheat (to heat before using)

re- [again, back]
repay (to pay back)
rewrite (to write again or revise)

semi- [half, partly]
semicircle (half a circle)
semiconscious (half conscious; not fully conscious)

sub- [under, below]
submarine (a boat that can operate underwater)
submerge (to put underwater)

trans- [across, over; change]
transcontinental (across a continent)
transform (to change from one form to another)

tri- [three]
triangle (a figure that has three sides and three angles)
tricycle (a three-wheeled vehicle)

un- [not]
uncomfortable (not comfortable)
unhappy (not happy; sad)

under- [below, beneath]
underage (below or less than the usual or required age)
undersea (beneath the surface of the sea)

uni- [one]
unicycle (a one-wheeled vehicle)
unisex (a single style that is worn by both males and females)

Numerical Prefixes

deci- [tenth part]
decimal system (a number system based on units of 10)

centi- [hundredth part]
centimeter (a unit of length equal to 1/100 meter)

milli- [thousandth part]
millimeter (a unit of length equal to 1/1000 meter)

micro- [millionth part]
micrometer (one-millionth of a meter)

deca- or dec- [ten]
decade (a period of 10 years)
decathlon (a contest with 10 events)

hecto- or hect- [one hundred]
hectare (a metric unit of land equal to 100 ares)

kilo- [one thousand]
kilogram (a unit of mass equal to 1,000 grams)

mega- [one million]
megabit (one million bits)

Suffixes

A **suffix** is a word part that is added after a word. Sometimes a suffix will tell you what part of speech a word is. For example, many adverbs end in the suffix *-ly*.

-able *[able, can do]*
  agreeable (able or willing to agree)
  doable (can be done)

-al *[of, like]*
  magical (like magic)
  optical (of the eye)

-ed *[past tense]*
  called (past tense of *call*)
  learned (past tense of *learn*)

-ess *[female]*
  lioness (a female lion)

-ful *[full of]*
  helpful (giving help; full of help)

-ic *[like, having to do with]*
  symbolic (having to do with symbols)

-ily *[in some manner]*
  happily (in a happy manner)

-ish *[somewhat like or near]*
  childish (somewhat like a child)

-ism *[characteristic of]*
  heroism (characteristic of a hero)

-less *[without]*
  careless (without care)

-ly *[in some manner]*
  calmly (in a calm manner)

-ology *[study, science]*
  biology (the study of living things)

-s *[more than one; plural noun]*
  books (more than one book)

-ward *[in the direction of]*
  westward (in the direction of west)

-y *[containing, full of]*
  salty (containing salt)

Comparative Suffixes

-er *[comparing two things]*
  faster, later, neater, stronger

-est *[comparing more than two]*
  fastest, latest, neatest, strongest

Noun-Forming Suffixes

-er *[one who]*
  painter (one who paints)

-ing *[the result of]*
  painting (the result of a painter's work)

-ion *[act of, state of]*
  perfection (the state of being perfect)

-ist *[one who]*
  violinist (one who plays the violin)

-ment *[act of, result of]*
  amendment (the result of amending, or changing)
  improvement (the result of improving)

-ness *[state of]*
  goodness (the state of being good)

-or *[one who]*
  actor (one who acts)

Roots

A **root** is a word or word base from which other words are made by adding a prefix or a suffix. Knowing the important roots can help you figure out the meaning of difficult words.

ali, alter *[other]*
  alias (a person's other name)
  alternative (another choice)

am, amor *[love, like]*
  amiable (friendly)
  amorous (loving)

anni, annu, enni *[year]*
  anniversary (happening at the same time every year)
  annually (happening once a year)
  centennial (happening once every 100 years)

anthrop *[human being]*
  anthropoid (like or of a human being)
  anthropology (the study of human-kind)

aster *[star]*
  aster (star flower)
  asterisk (starlike symbol [*])

aud *[hear, listen]*
  audible (can be heard)
  auditorium (a place to listen to speeches and performances)

bibl *[book]*
  Bible (sacred book of Christianity)
  bibliography (list of books)

bio *[life]*
  biography (book about a person's life)
  biology (the study of life)

chrome *[color]*
  monochrome (having one color)
  polychrome (having many colors)

chron *[time]*
  chronological (in time order)
  synchronize (to make happen at the same time)

cide *[the killing of; killer]*
  homicide (the killing of one person by another person)
  pesticide (pest [bug] killer)

cise *[cut]*
  incision (a thin, clean cut)
  incisors (the teeth that cut or tear food)
  precise (cut exactly right)

cord, cor *[heart]*
  cordial (heartfelt)
  coronary (relating to the heart)

corp *[body]*
  corporation (a legal body; business)
  corpse (a dead human body)

cosm *[universe, world]*
  cosmos (the universe or world)
  microcosm (a small world)

cred *[believe]*
  credible (capable of being believed)
  incredible (unbelievable)

cycl, cyclo *[wheel, circular]*
  bicycle (a vehicle with two wheels)
  cyclone (a very strong circular wind)

dem *[people]*
  democracy (ruled by the people)
  epidemic (affecting many people at the same time)

dent, dont *[tooth]*
  dentures (false teeth)
  orthodontist (dentist who straightens teeth)

derm *[skin]*
  dermatology (the study of skin)
  epidermis (outer layer of skin)

Roots (continued)

dic, dict [say, speak]
  dictionary (a book of words that people use or say)
  predict (to tell about something in advance)

dynam [power]
  dynamite (powerful explosive)
  dynamo (power producer)

equi [equal]
  equinox (day and night of equal length)
  equivalent (the same or equal to)

fac, fact [do, make]
  factory (a place where people make things)
  manufacture (to make by hand or machine)

fide [faith, trust]
  confident (having faith or trust in oneself)
  fidelity (faithfulness to a person or cause)

fin [end]
  final (the last of something)
  infinite (having no end)

flex [bend]
  flexible (able to bend)
  reflex (bending or springing back)

flu [flowing]
  fluent (flowing smoothly or easily)
  fluid (waterlike, flowing substance)

forc, fort [strong]
  force (strength or power)
  fortify (to make strong)

fract, frag [break]
  fracture (to break)
  fragment (a piece broken from the whole)

gen [birth, produce]
  congenital (existing at birth)
  genetics (the study of inborn traits)

geo [of the earth]
  geography (the study of places on the earth)
  geology (the study of the earth's physical features)

grad [step, go]
  gradual (step-by-step)
  graduation (taking the next step)

graph [write]
  autograph (writing one's name)
  graphology (the study of hand-writing)

greg [herd, group]
  congregation (a group that functions together)
  segregate (to group apart)

hab, habit [live]
  habitat (the place in which one lives)
  inhabit (to live in)

hetero [different]
  heterogeneous (different in birth or kind)
  heterosexual (having interest in the opposite sex)

homo [same]
  homogeneous (of the same birth or kind)
  homogenize (to blend into a uniform mixture)

hum [earth]
  exhume (to take out of the earth)
  humus (earth; dirt)

hydr [water]
  dehydrate (to take the water out of)
  hydrophobia (the fear of water)

ject [throw]
  eject (to throw out)
  project (to throw forward)

leg *[law]*
   legal (related to the law)
   legislators (people who make laws)

log, logo *[word, thought, speech]*
   dialog (speech between two people)
   logic (thinking or reasoning)

luc, lum *[light]*
   illuminate (to light up)
   translucent (letting light come
      through)

magn *[great]*
   magnificent (great)
   magnify (to make bigger or greater)

man *[hand]*
   manicure (to fix the hands)
   manual (done by hand)

mania *[insanity]*
   kleptomania (abnormal desire to
      steal)
   maniac (an insane person)

mar *[sea, pool]*
   marine (of or found in the sea)
   mariner (sailor)

medi *[middle, between]*
   mediocre (between good and bad;
      average)
   medium (in the middle)

mega *[large]*
   megalith (large stone)
   megaphone (large horn used to
      make voices louder)

mem *[remember]*
   memo (a note or reminder)
   memorial (a reminder of a person or
      an event)

meter *[measure]*
   meter (unit of measure)
   voltmeter (device to measure volts)

migra *[wander]*
   immigrant (person who moves to
      another country)
   migrant (person who moves from
      place to place)

mit, miss *[send]*
   emit (to send out; give off)
   transmission (sending over)

mob, mot *[move]*
   mobile (movable)
   promotion (being moved ahead in
      rank or performance)

mon *[warn, remind]*
   admonish (to warn or remind)
   monument (a structure used as a
      reminder of a person or an event)

mort *[death]*
   immortal (something that never dies)
   mortal (subject to death; causing
      death)

multi *[many, much]*
   multicultural (of or including many
      cultures)
   multiped (an animal with many feet)

nat *[to be born]*
   innate (present from birth)
   nativity (birth)

neur *[nerve, nervous system]*
   neurologist (a doctor who treats the
      nervous system)
   neurosurgery (surgery on part of the
      nervous system)

nov *[new]*
   innovation (a new idea)
   renovate (to make like new again)

numer *[number]*
   innumerable (too many to count)
   numerous (large in number)

Roots (continued)

omni [all, completely]
omnipresent (present everywhere at the same time)
omnivorous (eating all kinds of food)

onym [name]
anonymous (without a name)
pseudonym (false name)

pac [peace]
pacific (peaceful)
pacifist (person who is against war)

path, pathy [feeling, suffering]
empathy (feeling for another)
telepathy (feeling from a distance)

patr [father]
patriarch (the father of the family)
patron (father figure)

ped [foot]
pedal (lever worked by the foot)
pedestrian (one who travels by foot)

pend [hang, weigh]
pendant (a hanging object)
pendulum (a hanging weight that swings back and forth)

phil [love]
Philadelphia (city of brotherly love)
philosophy (the love of wisdom)

phobia [fear]
acrophobia (a fear of high places)
agoraphobia (a fear of public, open places)

phon [sound]
phonics (related to sounds)
symphony (sounds made together)

photo [light]
photo-essay (a story told mainly with photographs)
photograph (picture made using light rays)

pop [people]
population (the number of people in an area)
populous (full of people)

port [carry]
export (to carry out)
portable (able to be carried)

proto [first]
protagonist (the main character in a story)
prototype (the first model made)

psych [mind, soul]
psychiatry (the study of the mind)
psychology (the science of mind and behavior)

rupt [break]
interrupt (to break into)
rupture (to break)

sci [know]
conscious (being aware)
omniscient (knowing everything)

scope [instrument for viewing]
kaleidoscope (instrument for viewing patterns and shapes)
periscope (instrument used to see above the water)

scrib, script [write]
manuscript (something written by hand)
scribble (to write quickly)

sen [old]
senile (showing old age)
senior (an older person)

sequ, secu [follow]
sequence (one thing following another)

spec [look]
inspect (to look at carefully)
specimen (an example to look at)

sphere [ball]
hemisphere (half of a sphere; one of the halves of the earth)

spir [breath]
   expire (to breathe out; die)
   inspire (to breathe into; give life to)

---

strict [tighten]
   boa constrictor (a large snake that coils around its prey and squeezes it to death)
   constrict (to draw tightly together)

---

tact, tag [touch]
   contact (touch)
   contagious (spreading disease by touching)

tele [over a long distance; far]
   telephone (machine used to speak to people over a distance)
   telescope (machine used to see things that are very far away)

---

tempo [time]
   contemporary (from the current time period)
   temporary (lasting for a short time)

---

tend, tens [stretch, strain]
   extend (to stretch and make longer)
   tension (the act of stretching something tight)

---

terra [earth]
   terrain (the earth or ground)
   terrestrial (relating to the earth)

---

therm [heat]
   thermal (related to heat)
   thermostat (a device for controlling heat)

---

tom [cut]
   anatomy (the science of cutting apart plants and animals for study)
   atom (a particle that cannot be cut or divided)

---

tox [poison]
   intoxicated (poisoned inside; drunk)
   toxic (poisonous)

---

tract [draw, pull]
   traction (the act of pulling)
   tractor (a machine for pulling)

---

typ [print]
   prototype (the first printing or model)
   typo (a printing error)

---

vac [empty]
   vacant (empty)
   vacuum (an empty space)

---

val [strength, worth]
   equivalent (of equal worth)
   evaluate (to find out the worth of)

---

ver, vers [turn]
   divert (to turn aside)
   reverse (to turn back)

---

vid, vis [see]
   supervise (to oversee or watch over)
   videotape (record on tape for viewing)

---

viv [alive, life]
   revive (to bring back to life)
   vivacious (full of life)

---

voc [call]
   vocalize (to speak, sing, or call)
   vocation (the way a person earns a living; a person's calling)

---

vor [eat]
   carnivorous (flesh-eating)
   herbivorous (plant-eating)

---

zoo [animal or animals]
   zoo (a place where animals are kept)
   zoology (the study of animal life)

Understanding the Levels of Diction

Knowing about the different levels of diction helps you use the most appropriate language in your writing. (*Diction* is a writer's choice of words.)

Formal English

Your research papers, reports, and academic essays should meet the standards of **formal English**. This formal level of language pays careful attention to word choice and sentence structure. It carefully follows all of the basic rules of grammar and usage, and maintains a serious, objective (factual) tone throughout. The following sample meets the standards of formal English.

> **The Milwaukee Public Museum features an interesting butterfly exhibit. It looks and feels very much like a tropical rain forest. Hundreds of butterflies, from the common Monarch to the electric-blue Morpho, fly freely through the exhibit. Visitors stand quietly, hoping one of the butterflies will land on them. The exhibit also features a learning gallery and garden for young children.**

Informal English

You may write many other forms, such as personal narratives and friendly letters, using a more informal level of language. **Informal English** usually includes some personal references *(I, you, he, she)*, a few popular expressions, and shorter sentences. In addition, informal English sounds friendly in tone and follows all of the basic conventions of grammar and usage. It makes readers feel comfortable and at ease with the writing. The sample below is written using informal English.

> **Last January, I visited the butterfly exhibit with my science class. I couldn't believe it! I felt like I was in a rain forest with lush trees and flowers and a gurgling waterfall. Best of all, the air was full of butterflies—gold, yellow, blue, green, and white. We all stood there like a people-garden, hoping to attract some of the fluttering creatures. I slowly held up my hand, and wouldn't you know it, a yellow butterfly landed on my nose.**

✳ When appropriate, you may also use slang in your creative writing and jargon, or technical language, in your reports and essays.

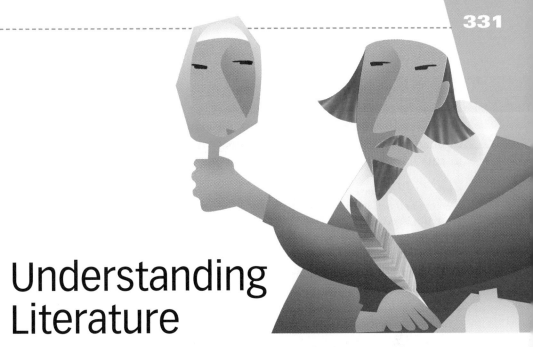

Understanding Literature

Since literature has been written for you, the reader, you won't want to miss what it has to offer. Each of the novels, short stories, poems, and plays that you read has a message to share; but in order to understand this message, you must take your time. You must read the piece carefully, then think about it, and, if possible, discuss it with someone else. Doing these things will give you the best chance of getting meaning and enjoyment from the books that you read.

It is also important to become familiar with the various types of literature and with the vocabulary that has been established to talk about it—terms like *narrator, point of view, conflict, plot,* and so on. Knowing the "language of literature" will help you confidently write and talk about your favorite books.

What's Ahead

This chapter will give you two lists of terms with definitions. One identifies the various types of literature, and the other one explains the elements, or parts, of literature. You'll also find suggestions for discussing the literature you read.

- **Types of Literature**
- **Elements of Fiction**
- **Discussing Literature**

Types of Literature

This list will give you brief descriptions of some of the most common types of literature. If you need more information, see the index in this handbook.

Allegory: A story in which the characters and action represent an idea or a truth about life.

Autobiography: A writer's story of his or her own life.

Biography: A writer's account of some other person's life.

Comedy: Writing that deals with life in a humorous way, often poking fun at people's mistakes.

Drama: A form that uses dialogue to share its message and is meant to be performed in front of an audience.

Essay: A short piece of nonfiction that expresses the writer's opinion or shares information about a subject.

Fable: A short story that often uses talking animals as the main characters and teaches an obvious lesson or moral.

Fantasy: A story set in an imaginary world in which the characters usually have supernatural powers or abilities.

Folktale: A story originally passed from one generation to another by word of mouth only. The characters are usually all good or all bad and in the end are rewarded or punished as they deserve.

Historical Fiction: A made-up story based on something real in history, so fact is mixed with fiction.

Myth: A traditional story intended to explain a mystery of nature, religion, or culture. The goddesses and gods of mythology have supernatural powers, but the humans do not.

Novel: A book-length, fictional prose story. Because of its length, a novel's characters and plot are usually more developed than those of a short story.

Parable: A short story that explains a belief or moral principle.

Play: (See *Drama.*)

Poetry: A literary work that uses concise, often rhythmic language to express ideas or emotions. Examples: ballad, blank verse, free verse, elegy, limerick, sonnet.

Prose: A literary work that uses the familiar spoken form of language, sentence after sentence.

Realism: Writing that attempts to show life as it really is.

Science Fiction: Writing based on real or imaginary science, and often set in the future.

Short Story: A piece of literature that can usually be read in one sitting. Because of its length, a short story has only a few characters and focuses on one problem or conflict.

Tall Tale: A humorous, exaggerated story often based on the life of a real person. The exaggerations build until the character does impossible things.

Tragedy: Literature in which the hero is destroyed because of some tragic flaw (defect) in his or her character.

Elements of Fiction

This list includes many terms used to describe the elements or parts of literature. The information will enable you to discuss and write about the novels, poetry, essays, and other literary works you read.

Action: Everything that happens in a story.

Antagonist: The person or force that works against the hero of the story. (See *protagonist*.)

Character: One of the people (or an animal) in a story.

Characterization: The ways in which a writer develops a character, making him or her seem believable. Here are three methods:

- Sharing the character's thoughts, actions, and dialogue.
- Describing his or her appearance.
- Revealing what others in the story think of this character.

Conflict: A problem or confrontation between two forces in a story. Here are the five basic conflicts:

- **Person Against Person** A problem between characters.
- **Person Against Him- or Herself** A problem within a character's own mind.
- **Person Against Society** A problem between a character and society, school, the law, or some tradition.
- **Person Against Nature** A problem between a character and some element of nature, such as a blizzard, a hurricane, or a mountain climb.
- **Person Against Fate (God)** A problem or struggle that appears to be beyond a character's control.

Dialogue: The conversation between two or more characters.

Foil: The character who serves as a challenge to the main character.

Mood: The feeling a piece of literature creates in a reader.

Moral: The lesson a story teaches.

Narrator: The person or character who actually tells the story, giving background information and filling in details between portions of dialogue.

Plot: The action that makes up the story, following a plan called the plot line.

Plot Line: The planned action or series of events in a story. There are five basic parts: exposition, rising action, climax, falling action, and resolution.

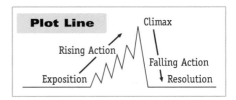

- **Exposition** The part of the story near the beginning where the characters are introduced, the background is explained, and the setting is described.
- **Rising Action** The central part of the story during which various problems arise.
- **Climax** The high point or climax in the action of a story.
- **Falling Action** The action and the dialogue following the climax that lead the reader to the end of the story.
- **Resolution** The part of the story in which the problems are solved and the action comes to a satisfying end.

Point of View: The angle from which a story is told. The angle depends upon the narrator, or person telling the story.

- **First-Person Point of View**
  This means that one of the characters is telling the story: "We're just friends—that's all—but that means everything to us."

- **Third-Person Point of View**
  In third person, someone from outside the story is telling it: "They're just friends—that's all—but that means everything to them." There are three third-person points of view: *omniscient, limited omniscient,* and *camera view.* (See illustration.)

Protagonist: The main character in a story, often a good or heroic type.

Setting: The place and the time frame in which a story takes place.

Theme: The message about life or human nature that is "hidden" in the story that the writer tells.

Tone: The attitude or feeling that comes across in a piece of literature, revealed by the characters, the word choice, and the general writing style. Tone can be serious, funny, satiric, and so forth.

Total Effect: The total impact or influence that a story has on a reader.

Third-Person Points of View

Omniscient point of view allows the narrator to share the thoughts and feelings of all the characters.

Limited omniscient point of view allows the narrator to share the thoughts and feelings of only one character.

Camera view (objective view) allows the storyteller to record the action from his or her own point of view, being unaware of any of the characters' thoughts or feelings.

Discussing Literature

If, after reading and thinking about a book, poem, or story, you feel as though you just don't get it, try talking about it with someone. Choose someone who has read the same piece of literature, and start asking questions. You will find that talking about the literature will give you insights and understanding that you did not have before.

Discussing books in a small group can also be an interesting way to enjoy literature. Start with a few people, decide on a book to read, and afterward, get together to talk about it. The following questions will give you several ways to begin your discussion.

Ideas for Discussion

THE PLOT

What events from the story (book) stand out in your mind? Why?
What is the basic conflict in the story?
What parts of the story remind you of your own life? In what way?
What other books with similar plots have you read?

THE CHARACTERS

Who are your favorite characters?
Do any of the characters remind you of people you know?

OVERALL EFFECT

How does the title fit the book?
What is the tone of the book?
What is the theme of the book?
What is your opinion of the book?
Who else do you think would like to read this book?

Guidelines for Sharing in a Group

- Listen respectfully to one another. Ask questions and give reactions after a group member has finished talking.

- Add to what the others say about the book.

* After you have discussed a book, consider reading favorite parts to each other.

Learning
to Learn

Viewing Skills

Classroom Skills

Group Skills

Speaking and Listening Skills

Test-Taking Skills

Planning Skills

Viewing Skills

Television is the main source of entertainment in today's world, but it is also an important source of news for many people. When the World Trade Center was destroyed, TV brought the event into our homes. It also brings special programming about history, science, nature, and current events. In addition, television commercials try to turn us into "informed" consumers of food, clothes, video games, and on and on.

Research shows that most teens watch more than 10 hours of television every week. As a result, television affects what you know, what you think, and even what you buy. That means you need to be a smart viewer.

What's Ahead

This chapter introduces skills that will help you become a better television viewer. More specifically, it explains how to watch news shows, special programs, and commercials.

- Watching the News
- Watching TV Specials
- Watching Commercials

Watching the News

TV news can inform you about events close to home as well as events around the world. The one disadvantage of TV newscasts is that they are usually short. They cannot cover the story in as much detail as a newspaper or magazine can. The big advantage, however, is that they can sometimes cover events as they happen. Always watch the news for completeness, correctness, and point of view.

Watch for Completeness

A news story should answer the questions *who? what? when? where? why?* and *how?* Listen to be certain that all the answers are given. Notice how the following introduction to a story answers the 5W and H questions.

On early Sunday morning, nine coal miners escaped a
when *who* *what*

flooded mine. For three days, the trapped miners had
what

waited 240 feet beneath the surface of the earth at the
where

Quecreek Mine in Somerset, Pennsylvania. During this
where

time, rescue workers determinedly dug a narrow shaft
how

until they reached them. Eventually, each man was lifted
how

through the shaft to safety.
how

The near tragedy began with an inaccurate map.
why

Miners using this map accidentally ruptured the wall
why

between their shaft and an abandoned mine. The resulting
why

flood trapped the men in a chamber with no escape and

limited air.

Watch for Correctness

Reporters try to get the latest news out quickly so that viewers can know what is happening at the moment. In the rush, misinformation may be shared. When a reporter is unsure about the facts, he or she uses phrases like "according to sources," "we are getting reports," and "it is estimated." If you hear these phrases, keep watching or check back later to be certain you know the complete, accurate story.

Watch for Point of View

In a straight news story, reporters must try to tell the news fairly, with no indication of how they personally feel about it. As a viewer, you must be on the lookout for one-sided stories in which a single viewpoint stands out. Never make a judgment about an event until you've heard "the other side of the story." Here are two ways that point of view can influence what you see on the news.

 The reporter chooses the facts and video footage for the story.

People are debating whether to widen a road in your city. One news story shows bulldozers knocking over beautiful trees and describes how the road will destroy valuable farmland and animal habitat. A story on another station describes how widening the road will make travel along it much safer. Both stories tell about the same event, but from different points of view.

 The reporter chooses whom to interview.

The people a reporter talks to can affect how you think about an event. Say that the reporter interviews both a commuter and a local farmer about widening a busy road. The commuter complains about not being able to get to work fast enough in the morning. The farmer holds a clump of rich soil as he talks about the proposed road putting an end to his sweet-corn crop. This story shares two completely different points of view because it includes interviews from two people with different interests and concerns.

An **editorial** is a special story that shares the reporter's thoughts about a news event. News shows will always identify an editorial so that viewers know they are listening to someone's opinion and not to straight news.

Watching TV Specials

Television specials cover particular topics in history, science, nature, or current events. Longer than news stories, specials may include film clips, interviews with experts, music, animation, and other information. Some TV specials are available on DVD or videotape, and you can also choose to record a special yourself. This allows you to watch it several times to make learning easier. Here are some tips for getting the most out of TV specials.

Before you watch . . .

- **Find out what the special is about.** Make sure the program is about the subject you are interested in. Titles can be misleading, so check TV listings to read a basic summary of the show.

- **Make a list of questions.** Think about what you already know about the subject. Then, in a notebook, list questions that you want answered. Leave enough space between the questions for your answers.

- **Know what to look for.** Your teacher may give you a list of questions to answer or study guides to help you work your way through the show. Make sure you understand what your teacher wants you to look for as you watch.

While you watch . . .

- **Check that the information is complete, correct, and fair.** Make sure that the TV special answers the questions *who? what? when? where? why?* and *how?* in detail. The producers of a special should present information fairly and accurately.

- **Look for the answers to your questions.** As the information is presented, write down a short answer to each question in your list. Afterward, write more complete answers.

- **Write down new questions and other notes.** While watching, you may discover interesting facts or questions that you were not looking for. Write these down so you can find out more after the show.

After you watch . . .

- **Write complete answers to your questions.** Use your notes to write more complete answers to your questions while the information is fresh in your mind.

- **Talk with someone else who watched the program.** A family member or friend may have noticed something that you didn't see or remember. Expand your notes by talking about the special.

- **Write more about the program.** To understand the information well, write a summary, an outline, or a journal entry. Writing about the program will help you remember the special's main ideas and details. (See below.)

- **Find out more about the subject.** For more information, look at the Web sites and books recommended at the end of the special.

Sample Journal Entry

The Fillmore, a TV special on PBS

San Francisco became overcrowded during the California gold rush. The city expanded westward, and the new neighborhood was called "The Fillmore" after its main street. Fillmore Street survived the 1906 earthquake, so people from other parts of the city moved there—especially Japanese Americans.

Between 1907 and 1945 The Fillmore's population grew to include Mexican, African American, and Jewish people. It was one of the most diverse places in the country. When the Japanese Americans were put into camps during WWII, African American shipbuilders from the South moved into their empty houses.

The thriving neighborhood was called "the Harlem of the West." Famous jazz musicians like Count Basie, Louis Armstrong, and Duke Ellington played there. After WWII, the white people left The Fillmore to live in the suburbs.

During the "urban renewal" of the 1950s and 1960s, parts

Watching Commercials

TV commercials have a much different purpose than news shows and specials. While the ads may be fun to watch, their goal is almost always to get you to buy something. The following selling methods explain how commercials accomplish their purpose. Watch for these methods so that you can be a wiser, more informed consumer.

Selling Methods

Slice of Life

Some commercials look like everyday life—a group of kids, for example, playing basketball after school. In the ad, none of the players miss a shot . . . and why? They are all wearing Brand X shoes.
Remember: These are actors, and most of them may never wear those shoes, or play basketball for that matter.

Famous Faces

Advertisers know that average people look up to famous people. You may not be able to hit home runs like Alex Rodriguez or act like Halle Berry, but at least you could wear the same clothes or drink the same soft drink.
Remember: The celebrities are being paid to promote these products.

Just the Facts

Often, commercials use facts and figures to convince you to buy a product. For example, an ad may claim that, according to tests, Brand Y car is safer than Brand Z car. But were these tests fair? Who conducted them—an unbiased consumer group or the automobile manufacturer? Get more information before you decide whether the "facts" presented are true.
Remember: Figures can be misleading if they are not used correctly.

Problem-Solution

Commercials promote some products by showing how easily they can solve big problems for you. For example, no one comes near a boy because his deodorant just doesn't work. He tries Brand K, and he's got friends hanging all over him!
Remember: Real solutions are almost never that easy. Having friends requires being trustworthy, helpful, and kind.

Classroom Skills

In school, your main job is to learn, and good classroom skills can make this job easier. Taking notes and using a learning log are two important skills. They will help you learn as you read your textbooks, think about ideas, listen to your teachers, and do your homework.

Taking notes is especially important when you are listening to a lecture or reading an assignment. This skill keeps you focused on the subject and helps you organize information. Taking notes also helps you understand complicated ideas and remember information.

Keeping a learning log can strengthen your understanding of any subject—even the most difficult ones. It gives you a place to explore your own thoughts, feelings, and questions about your class work.

What's Ahead

In this chapter, you will learn how to take good notes and write in a learning log. These useful skills will help you learn in school as well as in the workplace.

- Setting Up Your Notes
- Taking Lecture Notes
- Taking Reading Notes
- Reviewing Your Notes
- Keeping a Learning Log

Setting Up Your Notes

Keep your notes in a notebook, preferably one for each subject. You can also take notes on loose-leaf paper kept in a three-ring binder, which lets you add or remove pages as needed. Wherever you keep your notes, write only on one side of the paper. This makes your notes easier to read and easier to find.

Leave wide margins.

Skip a line for each new idea.

Make sketches.

How Hot-Air Balloons Fly   Oct. 17

Theory
* Warm air rises in cooler air.
* Wind blows in different directions at different altitudes.

Three parts of a balloon (3 B's)
1. Burner—heats the air
2. Balloon envelope—holds the air
3. Basket—carries pilot and passengers

Steps in launching a balloon
1. Attach propane burner to basket, then basket to envelope.
2. Unroll envelope.
3. Inflate envelope with huge fan.
4. Ignite burner flame to heat air in envelope.
5. Climb into basket.
6. Ground crew lets go.

Flying the balloon
1. Blast large flame to heat air faster and ascend.
2. Open parachute valve at top of envelope to let hot air out and descend.

Taking Lecture Notes

Your teacher may give a lecture to explain an important subject, introduce a new topic, or help the class review for a test. The following tips will help you take clear, organized lecture notes.

1 **Write the topic and date at the top of each page.** You may also number each page of notes to keep them in order.

2 **Listen carefully. This is the key to taking good notes.** Don't get so busy writing that you forget to listen for important clues. For example, if a teacher says, "There are six steps in flying a hot air balloon," you can listen for the six steps. Also listen for key words such as *first, second, next,* or *most importantly.*

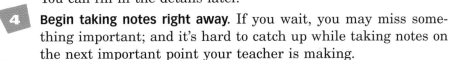

3 **Use your own words.** You can't write down everything your teacher says. Instead, try to put the main points into your own words. You can fill in the details later.

4 **Begin taking notes right away.** If you wait, you may miss something important; and it's hard to catch up while taking notes on the next important point your teacher is making.

5 **Write quickly, but be neat.** Write as fast as you can while still being neat. Your notes won't be much good if you can't read them.

6 **Condense information.** Use lists, abbreviations, and phrases to keep information organized and easy to understand. Skip the small, unnecessary words such as articles and some adverbs and adjectives. Shorten some words—*intro* for introduction, *chap* for chapter, and so on. Combine letters, numbers, and symbols to form words as people do when personalizing license plates. L8R could stand for *later.*

7 **Draw sketches and diagrams.** It may be quicker to draw a sketch or graphic than to explain something in words.

8 **Copy anything your teacher writes on the board.** It is usually important.

Ask questions. If you don't understand something, ask your teacher to clarify it. You can also ask your teacher to repeat something or to please slow down.

Taking Reading Notes

Taking notes while you read an assignment is easier than taking notes during a lecture. You can stop to write at any time, which means you can write more neatly and carefully. Here are some tips for taking reading notes.

1 **Preview the assignment.** Look through your assignment to see what your reading is about. Look at the title, introduction, headings, and chapter summary. Also look at any pictures, maps, or charts. (See page 309.)

2 **Quickly read the entire assignment once before taking notes.** A quick reading gives you an overview of the material and allows you to pick out the main ideas. This will make your note taking easier.

3 **Take notes while reading a second time.** Start taking notes as you read your assignment again. Read the material slowly and stop at new ideas or words.

- **Write down the important information.**

- **Put notes in your own words.** Don't just copy passages from the book. You learn more when you rewrite ideas in your words. (See pages 215-218 for more information on summaries and paraphrases.)

- **Use headings or subtitles.** Headings and subtitles help organize your notes. Write down the important information under each heading or subtitle.

- **Include notes about pictures, charts, and illustrations.** You can also make quick sketches of any photos or illustrations in your notes.

- **Use graphic organizers.** (See pages 296.)

- **List and define any new words.** Look up each word in the glossary or in a dictionary. Write down the appropriate meaning in your notes. Also write down the number of the page where the word is located. This way you can easily find it again.

(**Learn more.** Check "Reading Textbooks" on pages 307-314 for more information on taking reading notes.)

Reviewing Your Notes

As you read over your notes, circle any words that may not be spelled correctly. Also circle any words or phrases that you don't understand. Look up these words in a dictionary or textbook glossary. Then write each word and its meaning in the margin of your notes.

1 **Write any questions you have in the margin.** Then try to find the answers on your own. If you can't find an answer, then ask a teacher or classmate. Write the answer near the question.

2 **Use a highlighter to mark the most important notes.** If you prefer, you can use a different colored pen to circle or underline key ideas.

3 **Rewrite your notes.** Rewriting notes gives you another chance to learn the material. Also copy your notes if they are sloppy or unorganized.

4 **Review your notes again.** Look over your notes before the next class—especially if you are having a test or class discussion.

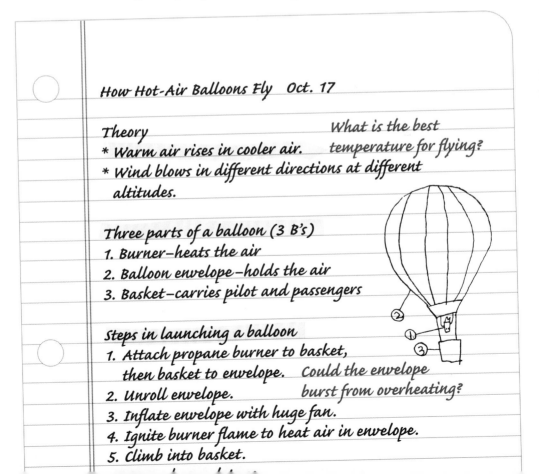

How Hot-Air Balloons Fly   Oct. 17

Theory   What is the best
* Warm air rises in cooler air.   temperature for flying?
* Wind blows in different directions at different
   altitudes.

Three parts of a balloon (3 B's)
1. Burner–heats the air
2. Balloon envelope–holds the air
3. Basket–carries pilot and passengers

Steps in launching a balloon
1. Attach propane burner to basket,
   then basket to envelope.   Could the envelope
2. Unroll envelope.   burst from overheating?
3. Inflate envelope with huge fan.
4. Ignite burner flame to heat air in envelope.
5. Climb into basket.

Keeping a Learning Log

A learning log is a place for you to explore any thoughts, feelings, or questions you may have about what you are studying. It gives you the opportunity to become actively involved in your learning. Here are some suggestions.

1 **Keep a learning log for any subject.** Learning logs are especially good for subjects that are really hard for you.

2 **Keep your learning log in a handy place.** Either use a part of the subject notebook for your learning log, or write in a separate notebook that you always have with you.

3 **Write freely.** Record ideas as they come to mind.

4 **Use graphic organizers and drawings.** Graphics and illustrations can help you remember complex or key points.

5 **Write about any of these ideas:**

● what you learned from an experiment,

● the most interesting ideas from a lecture or reading,

● questions about what you are learning, or

● thoughts about what you still want to learn about a topic.

Oct. 19

Purpose of experiment: See if our homemade hot-air balloon will take off
Results: It did!

Note: Propane is the same gas people use in grills. Can be explosive. Same problem for balloonists?
Questions: What if we had to depend on hot-air balloons to travel around the world? My brother had the experience of not being able to "catch a wind" in a balloon outside of Denver. He could only go up and down. Why? (Talk to Mr. Gatz.)

Group Skills

Teamwork is a big part of playing sports. Players who work well with others contribute to their team's success. This is true for any group. Members who work well together add to the group's success—at home, at school, and at work.

More than anything else, good communication skills will enable you to work well with others. As each group member shares his or her ideas, the group can function smoothly. Effective communication involves listening, observing, cooperating, clarifying, and responding. And learning these skills will put you on the "winning team" wherever you go.

What's Ahead

In this chapter, you will learn the communication skills needed to work in a group. These skills will help you succeed both in and out of school.

- Skills for Listening
- Skills for Observing, Cooperating, Clarifying
- Skills for Responding

Skills for Listening

Being a good listener is the key to communicating within a group. Listening is more involved than you might think. Simply hearing someone talk does not mean you are listening to him or her. Listening means paying attention, staying focused, and thinking about the person's ideas. Listening can be a difficult communication skill to master. Here are some tips for becoming a good listener.

Show that you are listening.

Let the speaker know that you are listening. Your body language reveals whether or not you are listening with interest. Putting your head down on your desk or looking around the room sends the message that you don't care what's being said, even if you are listening. Look at the speaker, make eye contact, nod your head if you agree, and stay attentive. Don't look around or suddenly ask, "What?" When the speaker is finished, ask questions, make a comment, or compliment an idea.

Think while you listen.

While a person is speaking, think about what he or she is saying, not about what you're doing after school or what you're having for lunch. Consider how an idea relates to your group's goals. Is it a good idea? Can you improve on the idea? Take notes to help you remember information. Don't think about what you are going to say next. Keep your mind focused on the person who is speaking.

Interrupt only when necessary.

A good listener lets someone finish speaking. It is the polite thing to do and helps the speaker stay on track. If you think of a question or comment while a person is speaking, write it down for later discussion. If you think an idea needs more explanation, or if a speaker gets off the subject, you may need to interrupt. But be polite. Say, "Excuse me." Then ask the speaker to clear up an idea or return to the subject.

> Remember to listen to others with an open mind, and wait until they are done speaking before offering suggestions or asking questions.

Skills for Observing

Being a careful observer is an important group skill. You can learn what speakers are feeling by their movements and tone of voice.

Watch body language.

People communicate their feelings through body positions, facial expressions, and hand gestures. Leaning forward shows interest, while slouching may indicate boredom. Look for frowns, scowls, or smiles, too.

Listen to the tone of voice.

A person's tone of voice can say as much as a person's words. Tone can tell you if he or she is nervous, angry, happy, sad, or bored.

Skills for Cooperating

In order for a group to complete its task, group members must work together, or cooperate.

Use words of encouragement.

Groups work best when members trust and encourage one another. Never make fun of others' ideas, but be encouraging instead. Say, "I like your suggestion." Or say, "Great idea!" If you want to change an idea, start with a compliment: "That could definitely work, but what if we do this . . . ?"

Avoid put-downs.

Always remain courteous when working in a group. If you don't like someone's idea, don't say, "That's a stupid idea." Instead say, "I don't know if that idea will work."

Skills for Clarifying

Summarizing is an effective way to make ideas clear.

Summarize ideas when necessary.

Repeat what you said in another way to ensure that people will follow your ideas. And if you don't understand a speaker's ideas, politely summarize what you heard, and then ask the speaker if you are correct.

Skills for Responding

To accomplish a task, group members must interact. Someone begins by sharing an idea, others respond with suggestions or questions, and the process continues until the group's task is completed. Certain skills are needed to respond appropriately.

Think before you respond.

There are many ways to respond to a person's idea, and it is always best to think through your choices before responding. When people talk first and think later, arguments are bound to disrupt the group's work. Comments like "That's a dumb idea" or "You don't know what you're talking about" can only lead to hurt feelings and anger.

> To respond tactfully, do one of the following: ask for clarification, make a suggestion to improve an idea, or request that the group move on. Always remember that each group member is entitled to his or her opinion or idea.

Learn how to disagree.

If you disagree with what a person says, just say, "I disagree" or "I disagree with that." Don't say, "I disagree with you." This makes it too personal. Focus on the idea, not the person, and give your reasons for disagreeing. You can also ask questions. These responses will usually lead to discussion, during which the group can decide if an idea is worth considering.

Communicate with respect.

Always treat yourself and other group members with respect and common courtesy.

Respect yourself by . . .
- believing that your own ideas are important,
- sharing your ideas clearly and politely, and
- taking responsibility for what you say.

Respect others by . . .
- encouraging everyone to participate,
- listening openly to what others have to say, and
- complimenting others when you can.

Speaking and Listening Skills

Giving a speech can be exciting, but it can also be scary. If you are afraid to stand up and speak to a group, you are not alone. It is a common fear, but one that you can overcome.

Speaking in public is a type of performing. You may already be familiar with "performing" on the basketball court, in a band, in a play, at a dance, and so on. With planning and practice, you will also be able to give an effective speech.

The purpose of a speech is to share information or feelings about a topic. Being able to share your ideas clearly with others is a skill you will use now in school and at home, and later, when you enter the world of work.

What's Ahead

This chapter will help you plan, write, and present a speech of your own. You will also learn how to listen to other speakers.

- Planning Your Speech
- Creating Note Cards
- Writing Your Speech
- Practicing and Giving Your Speech
- Becoming a Good Listener

Planning Your Speech

There are three basic types of speeches, each one with a different purpose. In an *informational* speech, you inform people about a topic. In a *persuasive* speech, you try to convince listeners to agree with you or do something. In a *demonstration* speech, you show people how to do something.

Your teacher may assign a certain type of speech or allow you to choose for yourself. Follow this step-by-step plan to complete each of your speech assignments:

1 Pick a topic.

- Choose a topic that interests you and will interest your listeners.
- Choose a topic that you know well or would like to learn about.
- Choose a topic specific enough to cover in a short speech.

Possible information topics . . .
an unusual hobby, a famous person, an interesting experience you've had, an important historical event, a type of music

Possible persuasive topics . . .
a new school rule or policy, a community action, an exercise program, teenage reading habits, a new television show

Possible demonstration topics . . . cooking a favorite food, creating a Web page, drawing or sculpting, showing how to grow vegetables in pots, playing an instrument

> Dan Cortez decided to give an informational speech about a situation he thought would interest his classmates: his cousin's struggle to attend high school in the United States.

2 Find information.

Finding information for a speech is the same as doing research for a writing assignment. Here are some suggestions:

- Use your own experiences.
- Read books, diaries, magazines, and newspapers.
- Use the Internet.
- Watch TV specials and videos, and listen to radio talk shows.
- Talk to people who know about your topic—friends, family, teachers, and coaches.
- Look at photographs, museum exhibits, and maps.

Take notes and collect more information than you need. This way you can choose the best facts and details for your speech. Find photos, charts, and other graphics to show during your speech. (Demonstration speeches should include hands-on materials.)

> **Dan got information for his speech by talking to his family. He also added facts from Internet sites and magazines.**

3 Write your beginning.

After thinking about the information, you should have a good idea of what you want to say. First, write an interesting beginning, which is the best way to get the attention of your audience. Here are six ideas for starting your speech:

- Ask a question.
- Tell a joke or funny story (if appropriate).
- Use a surprising fact or statistic.
- Make a strong or surprising statement.
- Share an interesting story or personal experience.
- Start with a meaningful quotation.

> **To begin his speech, Dan shared a personal experience and used a surprising fact: "When the traffic or the weather is bad, it takes me 20 minutes to get to school. . . . [but] Maria has to drive from another country."**

4 Organize your ideas.

Having decided what you want to say, write your main points and supporting facts onto note cards. Follow the tips below and refer to the sample cards on the next pages.

- Write out your beginning word for word on the first card (or cards).
- Use one card for each main idea and its supporting details. You needn't write these points word for word, but use enough words to help you remember what you want to say.
- Use words that sound natural to you. Your speech will be easier to give . . . and easier to understand.
- Review the ideas for your speech by laying out all the cards you've prepared. Decide which points you want to use, and which you want to discard (unnecessary or off-the-subject information).
- Do more research and prepare more note cards if necessary.
- Depending on the purpose of your speech, arrange your ideas in the best order. For example, save your strongest point for the end of a persuasive speech, present a demonstration speech step-by-step, and so on.
- Write out your conclusion word for word on the last card or cards. (See below.)
- Number the cards to keep them in order during your speech.

5 Think of an effective ending.

Never end a speech by saying, "That's it" or "I'm done." Remind the audience of your most important point, tell why your topic is worth considering, or share a personal insight.

> Dan concluded his speech by sharing what his cousin's experience has taught him: "I feel grateful just to be able to go to this high school."

Creating Note Cards

Here are some of the note cards Dan used to plan his speech. The beginning and ending are entirely written out. The other cards contain main ideas.

1

BEGINNING:
When the traffic or the weather is bad, it takes
me 20 minutes to get to school. That's only about
8 minutes more than usual, but I still complain.
Then I think about my cousin Maria, and I stop
grumbling. Sometimes it takes her three hours to
get to school. That's because Maria has to drive

2

Maria drives from Mexico → El Paso, Texas.
— gets up 5:00 a.m.
— waits an hour at border

3

Maria lives during week with father in El Paso.
— both American citizens

4

Other students cross the border illegally.
— some caught by Border Patrol
— guards more worried about drug smugglers

5

ENDING:
Imagine risking your life to go to school! When I
think of Maria and those other kids, I feel
grateful just to be able to go to this high school.

Writing Your Speech

You can give your speech using only your note cards, but you can also write out the entire speech.

The Long Drive

When the traffic or the weather is bad, it takes me 20 minutes to get to school. That's only 8 minutes more than usual, but I still complain. Then I think about my cousin Maria, and I stop grumbling. Sometimes it takes her three hours to get to school. That's because Maria has to drive from another country.

Every Monday morning, Maria drives from a small town in Mexico to El Paso, Texas, to go to high school. She gets up at 5:00 a.m. to get on the road. Then she often waits over an hour to cross the border. Maria says a good education is worth the hassle.

In El Paso, she lives with her father, and they are both American citizens. On the weekends, she goes back to her mom, brothers, and sisters in Mexico. Her father stays and works hard to support his family. It is a big sacrifice to see them only once in a while. Although Maria travels hours to school, she never complains. Like her dad, she wants to get ahead. She knows she is lucky to go to high school as a United States citizen.

Many other students cross the border illegally to go to school. They have more to worry about than a 3-hour drive. Some are caught by the Border Patrol. Luckily, the guards are more worried about drug smugglers, so the students get off easy. Still, crossing the border illegally is risky. Each year about 400 people die trying to cross the border between Mexico and the United States.

Imagine risking your life to go to school! When I think of Maria and those other kids, I feel grateful just to be able to go to this high school.

Practicing Your Speech

Begin practicing a few days before you give your speech. At first, practice alone. Emphasize the important words as if your listeners were present. Practice hand gestures and eye contact. If possible, record or videotape yourself. Then listen or watch for places where you can improve your speech.

After you've practiced several times and feel comfortable, give your speech to a friend or family member. Ask for suggestions to make the speech clearer and more understandable. Then try to memorize as much of your speech as you can, using your note cards only as a guide.

Giving Your Speech

If you've planned your speech carefully and practiced it enough, giving the speech should be a positive experience. Here are some tips:

Before . . .

- Before you start, make sure your note cards are in order.
- Stand up straight, take a deep breath, and relax.

During . . .

- Speak loudly, clearly, and slowly.
- Look up from your note cards and make eye contact with your audience. Look at a friend or at someone who is paying close attention to you. This will help you relax.
- Vary the tone and emotion of your voice. This shows your interest and keeps the audience interested.
- Gesture with your hands to help make a point.
- Stand still. Don't fidget, tap your note cards, or rock back and forth. These nervous movements will make it hard for the audience to pay attention.
- If you lose your place, forget to say something, or drop your note cards, don't panic. Just keep going. **Remember:** The audience doesn't know what's in your speech.

After . . .

- At the end of your speech, wait to see if anyone has questions.
- Calmly gather up your note cards and any other materials and return to your seat.

Becoming a Good Listener

Listening is an important communication skill. If you are a good listener, you help the speaker relax and you also learn more. Listed below are some tips for becoming a good listener. (Also see page 350.)

Be attentive.

Sit up straight, keep your hands still except when taking notes, and pay attention to the speaker. Nod your head occasionally to show the speaker that you are listening.

Watch the speaker.

A person uses more than his or her voice to communicate. A speaker will talk through facial expressions, hand gestures, and body language.

Take notes.

Take brief notes during a speech, especially if you have questions about what the speaker is saying. Write down new words and ideas so you can find out what they mean later. Your notes can help you summarize what you've learned during the speech.

Listen for key words.

Key words such as *first, next,* and *important* help you follow the main ideas in a speech.

Listen to the speaker's tone of voice.

Tone of voice can tell you how the speaker feels about different ideas, especially in terms of their importance or value.

Ask questions.

When the speaker finishes, ask questions about things you don't understand or want to know more about.

Test-Taking Skills

Teachers give tests to check how well you are learning. You may feel nervous while taking tests and have trouble remembering the important information, but this shouldn't happen if you are prepared. This is true of any test—objective, essay, or standardized. Plan properly, and you will perform at your best.

The preparation should start with your class work. Make sure that you understand the subjects you are studying. This means you must pay attention in every class, take good notes, and complete each assignment. (See pages 343-348 for more information about classroom skills.) You must also understand the test-taking process. This means you should know how to study for and take different types of tests.

What's Ahead

This chapter will help you plan your test-taking strategies and make test taking less stressful for you. It includes tips for studying and for taking four types of tests.

- **Preparing for a Test**
- **Test-Taking Tips**
- **Taking Objective Tests**
- **Taking Essay Tests**
- **Taking Standardized Tests**
- **Taking District or State Writing Tests**

Preparing for a Test

1 Ask questions.

Teachers often provide study-guide sheets to help you prepare for tests. If one isn't provided, ask your teacher about the test.

- Find out if the test will cover information from textbook readings, lecture notes, experiments, videos shown in class, or other material.
- Ask what type of questions will be on the test: multiple-choice, true/false, fill-in-the-blanks, matching, or essay questions.
- Find out if you can use your textbook or notes for the test. (Sometimes, essay tests are "open book" and "open note.")

2 Review the material.

To get the best results, set up a study schedule. The more time you spend studying, the better prepared you will be.

- Begin your review at least a few days before the test. Don't wait until the last minute.
- Look over all the test material once. Then make a list of the information that is especially challenging or information you need to memorize. Focus a lot of your study time on this material.
- Continue reviewing your notes until you feel that you really understand everything.

3 Study carefully.

Consider these study strategies when you prepare for a test:

- Use lists, note cards, or graphic organizers to help you study.
- Say the material out loud. First read from your notes or text. Then put the information in your own words.
- Write out the key information from memory. Afterward, check your notes to see how well you remembered it.
- Picture the information in your mind. Then review your notes to see if your "picture" was accurate.
- Study with someone else, or simply explain the material to a friend.

Test-Taking Tips

- **Listen carefully** as your teacher gives any directions, makes any corrections, or provides other information. And don't try to get a head start while your teacher is talking. You may miss important comments such as these:

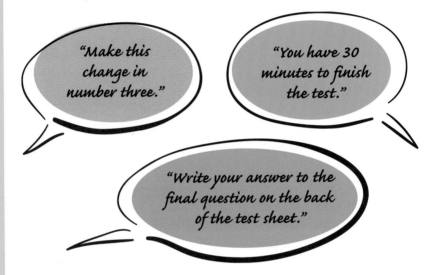

"Make this change in number three."

"You have 30 minutes to finish the test."

"Write your answer to the final question on the back of the test sheet."

- **Put your name on the test right away.** (Then you won't forget!)

- **Take a quick look at the entire test.** This will help you decide how much time to spend on each section or question.

- **Begin the test.** Read the instructions before answering each set of questions. Do exactly what they tell you to do.

- **Read each question carefully.** Be sure you understand the question completely before answering it.

- **Answer all of the questions you are sure of first.** Then go back to the other questions, and do your best to answer each one. Keep track of the time as you work on the more difficult questions.

- **Check over your answers when you finish the test.** If you skipped any really hard questions, try to answer them now.

Taking Objective Tests

There are four basic types of questions on objective tests: true/false, matching, multiple-choice, and fill-in-the-blanks. (*Objective* means "based on facts.") The tips that follow will help you complete each type of objective test.

True/False

To answer a true/false question, you decide if a statement is true or false.

- Read the statement carefully. If any part of the statement is false, the answer is false.

  False **Propane is a gas, but it can also be a solid.** (Propane is a gas, but it can't be a solid.)

- Watch for words such as *always, all, every, never, none,* or *no.* Very few things are *always* true or *never* true.

  False **A pilot can always land a hot-air balloon where he or she wants.** (The word "always" makes this statement false.)

- Pay special attention to words meaning "not": *nothing, not, doesn't, don't, isn't, wasn't,* and so on. Make sure that you understand what the statement means.

  True **Propane is not dangerous when stored properly.**

Matching

Matching consists of two lists. You match an item in one list to an item in the other list.

- Read both lists before beginning. Watch for items that are close in meaning or very similar, since they may be the most difficult to match correctly. Cross out each answer as you find it.

  <u>C</u> 1. **Second president of the United States**
  <u>A</u> 2. **President during World War II**
  <u>B</u> 3. **Sixth president of the United States**

  A. **Franklin Roosevelt**
  B. **John Quincy Adams**
  C. **John Adams**

- If you change an answer after crossing it out, make sure you remember which answers you have left.

- Match the items you are sure of first. Then match the more difficult items using the process of elimination.

Multiple-Choice

A multiple-choice question gives you several possible answers to choose from. You decide which answer (or answers) is correct. For very difficult questions, rule out any obviously wrong answers; then use logic to choose from the remaining answers.

- Read the directions carefully. There is usually one correct answer for each question. Sometimes, however, you may have to mark more than one correct answer.

  Which of the following places are continents?
  A. Australia   **C.** Greenland
  B. Russia   **D.** Europe

- Look for words like *except, never,* and *unless* that may change the meaning of the question.

  None of these countries are in Europe except
  A. France   **C.** China
  B. Mexico   **D.** Australia

- Questions that include possible answers like "Both A and B" or "None of the above" can be hard to answer.

  Which cities are located in California?
  A. San Jose   **D.** San Juan
  B. San Diego   **E.** Both A and B
  C. San Antonio **F.** None of the above

Fill-in-the-Blanks

A fill-in-the-blanks test is made up of sentences or paragraphs with some words left out. You fill in the missing items.

- Each blank usually stands for one missing word. If there are three blanks, you will have to write in three words.

  The branches of government are the legislative, judicial, **and** executive.

- Look for clues in the sentence. For example, if the word before a blank is *an*, the word you have to fill in will begin with a vowel. If the verb after a blank is singular (or plural), you need to write in a singular (or plural) noun.

  Air Force One is an airplane **that the president uses for travel.**

- Try not to leave any blanks empty. If you don't know an answer, make a logical guess.

Taking Essay Tests

Answering essay test questions can be difficult, especially when you have to answer the questions within a limited amount of time. If different questions are worth different points, you may want to start with the questions that are worth more.

Answering an essay test question is really like writing an essay. You must select a writing idea, organize your thoughts, write the essay, and so on. You just have less time to complete your writing.

1 Understand the question.

- Read the question several times.
- Identify the key words that explain what you have to do. Here are some key words and an explanation of what they ask you to do.

Compare	means "tell how things are alike."
Contrast	means "tell how things are different." In some answers, you may have to both compare and contrast items.
Define	means "give a clear, specific meaning of a term or object."
Describe	means "tell how something looks, sounds, and feels."
Diagram	means "explain with lines or pictures—a map, a web, or another graphic organizer."
Evaluate	means "give your opinion about a topic." It is very important to tell why you have this opinion, and to give details that support it.
Explain	means "tell what something means or tell how something works." You should give reasons, causes, or step-by-step details.
Identify	means "answer who? what? when? where? and why? about a topic."
Illustrate	means "show how a law, rule, or principle works through a specific example or examples."
Prove	means "present facts and details that show something is true."
Review	means "give an overall picture about a topic."
Summarize	means "tell the important information about a topic."

2 Plan your answer.

- Make sure that you understand the question, including the meaning of the key word.
- Write a thesis statement or topic sentence for your essay.
- Collect or recall important details that support your thesis. (You may be allowed to use your book or class notes.)
- Consider using an outline, a list, or a graphic organizer to arrange these ideas. (See below.)
- Before writing your essay, make sure that your ideas answer the question.

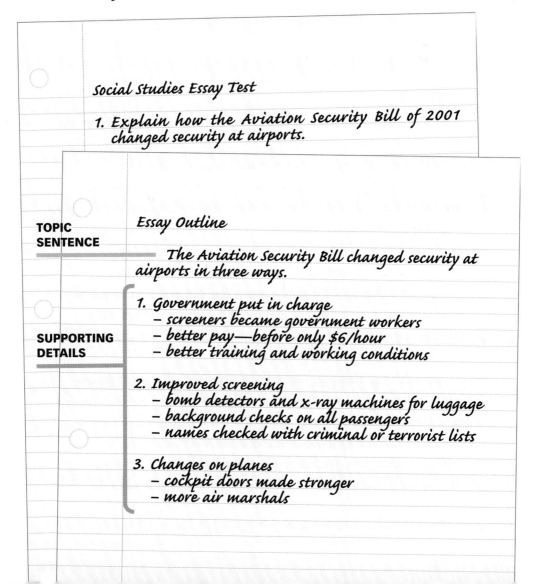

Social Studies Essay Test

1. Explain how the Aviation Security Bill of 2001 changed security at airports.

TOPIC SENTENCE

Essay Outline

The Aviation Security Bill changed security at airports in three ways.

SUPPORTING DETAILS

1. Government put in charge
   – screeners became government workers
   – better pay—before only $6/hour
   – better training and working conditions

2. Improved screening
   – bomb detectors and x-ray machines for luggage
   – background checks on all passengers
   – names checked with criminal or terrorist lists

3. Changes on planes
   – cockpit doors made stronger
   – more air marshals

3 Write your answer.

Be as neat as possible so that your essay is easy to read, but remember that your teacher is most interested in the effectiveness of your response—that your answer is clear and complete.

- Use your planning as a guide as you write.
- Start your answer with the thesis statement or topic sentence.
- Support your thesis with facts and details from your planning.
- After including all of your supporting information, write a closing sentence or conclusion.
- When you have finished, review your essay. Make sure your essay answers the question clearly and correctly.

Explain how the Aviation Security Bill of 2001 changed security at airports.

The Aviation Security Bill changed security at airports in three ways. First of all, a new government agency was put in charge of airport security. As a result, people who checked passengers and bags became government workers receiving better training and better pay. Before, many screeners only made about $6 an hour. The improved training and pay made these workers do their jobs better.

Improved screening procedures also made the security system more effective. Luggage was checked for bombs with special detectors or x-ray machines. Thorough background checks were made on all passengers. Screeners were looking for criminals or suspected terrorists.

In addition, changes were made on the airplanes themselves. For example, doors were made stronger so no one could enter an airplane's cockpit. Also, more air marshals flew on board airplanes to keep passengers as safe as possible. All of this improved security clearly increased the check-in time for passengers, but, more importantly, it greatly improved their safety.

Taking Standardized Tests

Standardized tests measure your skills and progress in English, science, social studies, math, and reading. The questions for these types of tests follow a certain format. Knowing about this format can prepare you for your next standardized-test experience. The guidelines below and the examples on the next page should help.

Guidelines for Standardized Tests

■ **Listen carefully to the instructions.**

Most standardized tests follow very strict guidelines.

■ **Quickly review the test.**

Make sure you have all the pages—and that you understand what you need to do for each section.

■ **Read the directions carefully.**

Most standardized tests have specific directions for each section, and no two sections are exactly alike.

■ **Plan your time.**

Most tests allow you a certain amount of time for each section. If not, plan your time based on the difficulty of each section.

■ **Answer the easy questions first.**

Then address the hard questions.

■ **Read all the choices.**

Don't answer a question until you've read all the choices.

■ **Make educated guesses.**

Unless you're told not to, select an answer for every question. First cross out choices that are clearly incorrect; then use logic to choose from the remaining answers.

■ **Double-check your answers.**

As time permits, check each of your answers to make sure you haven't missed anything or made any careless errors.

> Mark your answer sheet correctly and clearly. If you need to change an answer, erase it completely. Also make sure that your answers line up to the correct numbers on the answer sheet.

Tips for Taking Standardized Tests

Vocabulary ■ The vocabulary part of standardized tests often contains *synonym* and *antonym* questions. Synonym questions ask you to find a word that has the same meaning; antonym questions ask for the opposite meaning of a word.

Synonym TRANSPARENT (A) beautiful (B) helpful (C) rigid
(D) original (E) clear

Antonym RESTRAIN (A) control (B) assist (C) release
(D) confuse (E) rinse

Analogies ■ Analogies ask you to figure out relationships. First look at the pair of words you are given (WARM: HOT::) and decide how they are related. Then read the choices and decide which pair has the same relationship as the first two words. (The colon between the word pair means *is to*; the double colon means *as*.)

Analogy HILL: MOUNTAIN:: (A) lake: ocean (B) cow: goat
(C) career: job (D) hope: despair

Multiple-Choice ■ The key to multiple-choice questions is to read the directions carefully. (The example below requires finding the sentence error.) Always read all the choices before selecting your answer.

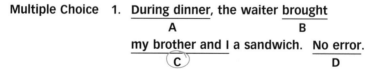

Multiple Choice 1. During dinner, the waiter brought
                        A   B
                    my brother and I a sandwich. No error.
                        C   D

Reading Comprehension ■ Often, you will be asked to read a passage and answer questions about it. The guidelines below can help you answer reading questions.

1. Read the questions before you read the passage.

2. Then read the passage carefully, but as quickly as possible.

3. Review all the choices before choosing the best answer.

Taking District or State Writing Tests

When you are taking a district or state writing test, your goal is to complete a clear piece of writing within a limited amount of time. These tests can vary greatly from one situation to the next.

Keep Up with Your Class Work

Here are some tips to help you prepare for timed writings:

- Keep up with your in-class reading and note taking.
- Work hard on all of your writing assignments. That will increase your writing confidence.
- Understand the writing process, especially writing thesis statements and organizing supporting details.
- Complete timed writings on your own for practice. (See below.)

Practice Timed Writings

The following strategy will prepare you for timed writing tests.

1. Underline the important points in your class notes.

2. Write a question (or two) about one of the main points.

3. Turn the question into a thesis statement (or topic sentence).

> Question: **Did the invention of the atomic bomb shorten World War II?**

> Statement: **The invention of the atomic bomb shortened World War II.**

4. List a few main points in support of the thesis.

5. Develop your essay, always keeping track of the time.

6. Reserve a few minutes for basic revising and editing.

Learn About Writing Prompts

- Some prompts are open-ended: **Share an experience that taught you something about your personality.**
- Some prompts give clearly defined instructions: **Write a letter to a school administrator expressing your opinion about a certain rule or policy.**
- Some prompts require a response to a piece of literature: **Buck in *The Call of the Wild* has a strong will to live. In a brief essay, cite two or three of his actions that reveal this will.**

Completing the Actual Writing

When you must write in a timed situation, follow these steps.

1 **Read the prompt carefully**, looking for key words or the central idea. (See page 366.)

2 **Restate the prompt** in a thesis statement (or topic sentence).

3 **Collect details** that support the thesis.

4 **Organize your details** by numbering them or by using a basic graphic organizer.

5 **Write your essay**, always keeping your thesis clearly in mind.

6 **Add a conclusion** that summarizes your main points and keeps the reader thinking about your topic.

7 **Leave enough time to review the entire essay** and make any necessary changes.

Sample Writing Prompts

Listed below are writing prompts similar to the types used in a state writing test. These samples will give you an idea of what to expect on your own writing tests.

> **Suppose that your school district has decided to cut all art classes because of budget constraints. In a persuasive essay, defend or oppose this idea. The superintendent is your audience.**

> **Write an expository essay in which you explain the value of friendship. Base your thoughts on what you have experienced, observed, or read about.**

> **"He who seeks trouble always finds it." Discuss the truth of these words, presenting examples from some or all of the following: literature, history, current events, or personal experience. Be specific.**

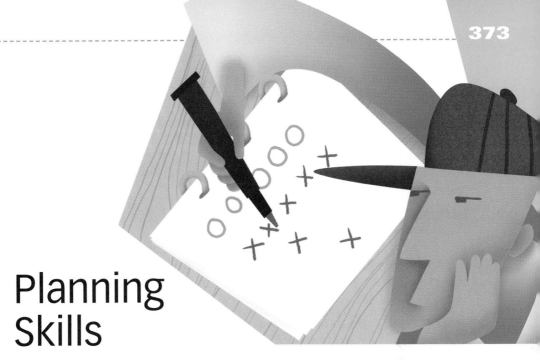

Planning Skills

In the movie *Raiders of the Lost Ark,* Indiana Jones is determined to hijack the truck that holds the Ark. His friend asks him how, and Indy says, "I don't know. I'm making this up as I go." Of course, he succeeds, but in real life very few people succeed without planning.

Everyone knows that Michael Jordon is a world-class basketball player, yet he was passed over for the varsity team as a high-school sophomore. After that, he set his goal: to make varsity as a junior. His plan? Practice every day. Michael recalls, "Whenever I was working out and got tired and figured I ought to stop, I'd close my eyes and see that list in the locker room without my name on it, and that usually got me going again." He made the varsity team as a junior, and the rest is history.

What's Ahead

This chapter shows you how to set goals and provides tips on how to reach them. You will also learn how to manage your time more effectively and how to complete your assignments.

- Setting Goals
- Managing Your Time
- Planning Sheets
- Completing Assignments

Setting Goals

A goal is something that you want to do. You may want to pass your next history test. This is a short-term goal, something you can do soon. Long-term goals, like learning to play an instrument or going to college, are things you can do in the future.

Set your goals.

Setting goals is like making a list. Try making a list of things you want to accomplish tomorrow (*short-term goals*). Next, make a list of 10 things you want to do during your lifetime—fly a helicopter, play the tuba, go to college, whatever (*long-term goals*).

Learn how to reach your goals.

Michael Jordan learned that he had to practice every day in order to become a better basketball player. To reach any goal, you must first find out what is needed to attain it. Passing your next history test, for example, may require several steps: (1) read your notes every day until the test, (2) discuss any questions with your teacher, (3) review the study guide several times, and (4) get plenty of sleep the night before.

Use small goals to reach your big goals.

Michael Jordan attained his goal of being a world-class basketball player by first reaching a number of smaller goals: Jordan (1) made the varsity high school team, (2) won the state championship, (3) received a scholarship to the University of North Carolina, (4) helped UNC win the national championship, and (5) earned a spot in the NBA. You, too, can use smaller goals as stepping stones to meet your big goals.

Keep trying.

If Michael Jordan had decided to quit playing basketball when he didn't make the varsity team as a sophomore, he would not have become a star. Everybody fails sometimes; but as long as you keep trying, your goals are still attainable.

If you skipped reading your notes last night, or didn't practice the tuba, start again today. Don't be afraid, either, to change your goals along the way. Just keep dreaming . . . and planning.

Managing Your Time

Sometimes it seems like you've got so much to do, you'll never get it all done. Managing your time can help. First, learn to break big tasks into smaller ones. Then make a schedule to help you stay on track. Sticking to your schedule will enable you to accomplish everything you must do. You may even end up with free time on your hands.

Goal: *Do well on Friday's history test on chapters 10-12.*

Plan: *Make a study schedule for the week.*

Day	Time	Activity
Monday	*Study hall*	*Reread chapter 10; write any questions in log.*
	After supper	*Read over class notes and do part 1 of review sheet.*
Tuesday	*Before class*	*Talk with Mrs. P. about questions.*
	After supper	*Reread chapter 11; log any questions.*
		Read over class notes and do part 2 of review sheet.
Wednesday	*Before class*	*Talk with Mrs. P. if necessary.*
	Study hall	*Reread chapter 12; log any questions.*
	Before bed	*Read over class notes and finish review sheet.*
Thursday	*Before class*	*Talk with Mrs. P. if necessary.*
	After supper	*Read over class notes and finished review sheet. Get to bed earlier.*
Friday	*Before class*	*Look over any notes that are hard to remember.*
	Class	*Take test.*

Planning Sheets

Planning sheets can help you manage your time during the school year. Daily planners help you organize homework; weekly planners help you keep track of your work for a week.

Daily Planner Each day, list your assignments and due dates.

■ MONDAY, _____

English

Read essay on pages 95-96. Answer questions. Due Wednesday.

Math

Fraction exercise page 58. Due tomorrow.

Social Studies

Read chapter 4. Due tomorrow.

Science

Summarize experiment results. Due Wednesday.

■ TUESDAY, _____

English

Write first draft of narrative essay. Due Friday.

Math

Study fractions for test on Friday (pages 51-58).

Social Studies

Answer questions at end of chapter 4. Due tomorrow.

Science

Watch special about volcanoes tonight on TV.

Weekly Planner On a weekly planner, you usually write down your most important activities and tasks for the week.

Day	Before School	At School	After School	After Dinner
Monday	Pack Grand Canyon photos		B-ball practice homework	Watch Monday night football
Tuesday		Ask Mr. Williams about extra credit	Work until 9	
Wednesday	Bring guitar		B-ball practice	Homework
Thursday		dance committee meeting	Work until 8	Band practice, homework
Friday				Movie

Completing Assignments

At school and at work, everyone has assignments. However, people sometimes put off doing these tasks, which makes completing them more difficult than it has to be. If you do some planning, finishing jobs will be much easier. See the tips below.

Getting It Done

Plan ahead. Look over your daily planner to see what assignments you have and when they're due. Then schedule time for each assignment, and stick to your schedule.

Set small goals. Break big projects into several small steps. Complete one or two of these steps each day.

Read the instructions. Before beginning your work, read over the instructions to make sure that you understand the assignment.

Get help. If you're not sure about an assignment, or if you get stuck, call a friend or ask a family member for help. Talk to your teacher the next day if possible.

Make a special study area. If you are doing your homework at home, create a comfortable work area for yourself. Keep all your study supplies in this special space.

Take breaks. Schedule some short breaks during your study time. Keep your breaks between 5 and 10 minutes in length. Grab a snack, play with a pet, go outside; but don't turn on the TV.

Stay focused. Avoid distractions so that you stay focused and stay on schedule. Turn off the TV and cell phone. The sooner you get your assignments done, the more time you will have for other activities.

> **Stay busy.** Work steadily on your assignments. If you don't have very much homework due for tomorrow, get started on a long-range assignment or begin reviewing for an upcoming test. Spend at least some time every day on schoolwork.

Proofreader's
Guide

Marking Punctuation

Period

A **period** is used to end a sentence. It is also used after initials, after abbreviations, and as a decimal point.

To End a Sentence

Use a period to end a sentence that is a statement, a request, or a command (not an exclamation).

We are going to listen to music tomorrow. (statement)

Please bring your favorite CD to class. (request)

Choose wisely. (command)

✻ It is not necessary to place a period after a statement that has parentheses around it and is part of another sentence.

Pigpen (his real name is Arthur) couldn't wait to play in the fresh mud.

After an Initial

Use a period after an initial.

B. B. King (blues musician)

Octavia E. Butler (writer)

As a Decimal

Use a period as a decimal point and to separate dollars and cents.

New York City has more than 7.5 million people.

I paid $2.25 for a hot dog from a street vendor.

After an Abbreviation

Place a period after each part of an abbreviation—unless the abbreviation is an acronym. An *acronym* is a word that is formed from the first (or first few) letters of words in a phrase.

Abbreviations **a.m. Mr. Jr. Dr. U.S.A.**

Acronyms **NATO NASA laser modem**

✻ When an abbreviation is the last word in a sentence, use one period at the end of the sentence.

I am interested in renewable energy sources, such as sunlight, wind, water, etc.

380

Question Mark

A **question mark** signals the end of an interrogative sentence. (An *interrogative sentence* asks a question.) A question mark can also be used to show doubt about the correctness of a fact or figure.

Direct Question

Use a question mark at the end of a direct question (an interrogative sentence).

Why can't we all just get along?

Indirect Question

Do not use a question mark after an indirect question. (In an *indirect question,* you tell about a question you or someone else asked.)

People often ask me if I'm related to Will Smith.

Tag Question

Use a question mark when you add a short question (a tag question) to the end of a statement.

You would tell me if my hair was messed up, wouldn't you?

Your hair is your own responsibility, don't you think?

Exclamation Point

An **exclamation point** is used after a word, a phrase, or an exclamatory sentence to express strong feeling. (It should not be overused.)

Great!

That is so cool!

What a tough job!

Never write more than one exclamation point in school writing assignments or in business letters.

The bull elephant weighed 12,000 pounds!!!!
(too many exclamation points)

The bull elephant weighed 12,000 pounds!
(correct punctuation)

Comma

Commas are used to indicate a pause or change in thought. They keep words and ideas from running together and make writing easier to read.

Items in a Series

Use commas between words or phrases in a series. (A *series* contains at least three words or phrases in a row.)

A good baseball player must be able to hit, run, and field. (words in a series)

Knowing the pitcher's moves, taking a long lead, and getting a good jump on the catcher are essentials for a good base runner.
(phrases in a series)

> **Important:** A *phrase* is a group of related words, like "knowing the pitcher's moves." A phrase does not express a complete thought.

To Keep Numbers Clear

Use commas to separate numerals in large numbers in order to distinguish hundreds, thousands, millions, and so on. Do note leave a space after commas in numerals.

If I've told you once, I've told you 658,000 times.

Do not use a comma when a number refers to a year, street address, or ZIP code. Also, it is easier to write some numbers in the millions and billions this way: 7.5 million, 16 billion.

Could you write me a check for $10.5 million?

In Dates and Addresses

Use commas to set off the different parts in addresses and dates. But do not use a comma to separate the state from the ZIP code.

Send your check or money order to Smith for Mayor, 1401 Belt Drive, Columbus, OH 43208.

Julio got his license on June 12, 2003.

Do not use a comma if only the month and year are written (July 1776).

Comma

To Set Off Dialogue

Use a comma to set off the exact words of the speaker from the rest of the sentence.

Ms. Arbogast asked, "Do you know how proud you made me?"

✳ If you are telling what someone has said but are not using the person's exact words, do not use commas or quotation marks.

Ms. Arbogast asked if I knew how proud I had made her.

To Set Off Interruptions

Use commas to set off a word or phrase that interrupts or emphasizes the main thought of a sentence.

You may someday, as a matter of fact, own a wristwatch computer.

WORDS Here is a list of words and phrases you can use to interrupt or emphasize main thoughts.

INTERRUPTING WORDS

for example
however
in fact
moreover
as we all know
as a matter of fact

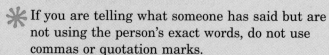

TESTS Try one of these tests to see if a word or phrase needs to be set off with commas:

1. Take the word or phrase out. If the meaning of the sentence does not change, use commas.

2. Move the word or phrase to another place in the sentence. If the meaning does not change, use commas.

To Set Off Interjections	Use a comma to separate an interjection or a weak exclamation from the rest of the sentence. (An *interjection* is a word or phrase showing surprise or strong emotion.)

No kidding, are you saying we've practically won?

Okay, now what do I do?

 If an interjection shows very strong feeling, you may use an exclamation point (!) to separate it from the rest of a sentence.

Wow! The fireworks were incredible!

WORDS Here are some of the words that may be used as interjections.

INTERJECTIONS

Hey	**Wow**
Oh my	**No kidding**
Okay	**Hello**

In Direct Address	Use commas to separate a noun of direct address from the rest of the sentence. A noun of direct address names the person(s) being spoken to.

I'd really like to try out for the track team, Mr. McKeral.

The truth is, Maria, I simply cannot dance.

To Set Off Titles or Initials	Use commas to set off titles or initials (and first names) that follow a person's last name.

Marcus Welby, M.D., was no Dr. Quinn.
(titles following names)

Hickok, J. B., and Cody, William F., are also known as "Wild Bill" and "Buffalo Bill."
(initials following last names)

 If an initial comes at the end of a statement, use only one period.

Her initials are C. J.

Comma

In Compound Sentences

Use a comma between two independent clauses that are joined by coordinating conjunctions such as *and, but, so, nor,* and *yet.* (An *independent clause* expresses a complete thought and can stand alone as a simple sentence.)

> **His skin looked as if it had sparks of fire in it, and the sun played against the red highlights in his body.**
>
> —Gloria Naylor, *The Women of Brewster Place*

Avoid Comma Splices! When two independent clauses are joined with only a comma and no connecting word, it is called a **comma splice**. A comma splice is a sentence error. (See page 86.)

To Separate Introductory Phrases and Clauses

Use a comma to separate a clause or a longer phrase that comes *before* the main part of the sentence.

> **After the practice was over, Kenton walked home.** (clause)
>
> **Throughout the entire meal, Kimya did not say a word.** (long phrase)

✳ You usually do not need a comma when the phrase or the clause comes *after* the main part of the sentence.

> **I'm going to the park because I need a place where I can think.** (No comma is needed after the word *park*.)

✳ Also, you usually do not need a comma after a brief opening phrase.

> **For months I have waited for this moment.** (No comma is needed after the phrase *for months*.)

To Separate Adjectives

Use commas to separate two or more adjectives that modify a noun in an equal way.

Many well-educated, well-respected scientists believe that one of Jupiter's 58 moons shows signs of life.

(*Well-educated* and *well-respected* are separated by a comma because they equally modify *scientists*.)

Angela took her usual morning walk.

(*Usual* and *morning* do not modify *walk* equally. No comma is needed between these two modifiers.)

TESTS Use one or both of these tests to help you decide if adjectives modify equally and need commas:

1. Switch the order of the adjectives. If the sentence is still clear, the adjectives modify equally. Use commas.

2. Put the word *and* between the adjectives. If the sentence sounds clear, the adjectives modify equally. Use commas.

* **Remember:** Do not use a comma to set off the last adjective from the noun.

Healthy-looking, well-dressed people often look away from the homeless.

(There should be no comma between *well-dressed* and *people*.)

To Set Off Explanatory Phrases

Use commas to set off an explanatory word or phrase from the rest of the sentence.

Mr. Gibson, wanting to be fair, gave everyone a chance to view Jupiter through the telescope.

Comma

To Set Off Appositive Phrases

Use commas to set off an appositive from the rest of the sentence. (An *appositive* is a word or a phrase that identifies or renames the noun or pronoun before it.)

My two least favorite subjects, history and math, are the first two classes of the day.
(*History and math* is an appositive phrase.)

> **APPOSITIVE PHRASES**
>
> Sammy Sosa, *the amazing home-run hitter,* . . .
>
> Honda, *one of the most popular cars on the road,* . . .
>
> Television, *a big time waster,* . . .
>
> Fried chicken, *my favorite fast food,* . . .

To Separate Nonrestrictive Phrases and Clauses

Use commas to set off nonrestrictive phrases and clauses (those that are *not* necessary to the basic meaning of the sentence).

Soccer, which has been a favorite sport in Europe and South America, is becoming popular in the United States.
(The clause "which has been a favorite sport in Europe and South America" is nonrestrictive— not necessary to understand the basic sentence— so it is set off by commas.)

＊No commas are needed around a restrictive phrase or clause. (*Restrictive* phrases and clauses are necessary to understand the sentence.)

The soccer that is played indoors is fast paced and high scoring.
(The clause "that is played indoors" is restrictive, or needed to complete the meaning of the sentence.)

Semicolon

A **semicolon** is sometimes used in the same way that a comma is used. However, a semicolon usually means a stronger pause, closer to a full stop.

To Join Two Independent Clauses

Use a semicolon to join two independent clauses when there is no connecting word like *and* or *but*. (*Independent clauses* are simple sentences that can stand alone.)

I did not call myself a poet; I told people I wrote poems.

                                    –Terry McMillan, *Breaking Ice*

With Conjunctive Adverbs

Use a semicolon when two independent clauses are joined by a conjunctive adverb. The semicolon comes before the adverb, and a comma comes after it.

Jorge finished his assignment; meanwhile, the eggs burned.

CONJUNCTIVE ADVERBS	
also	meanwhile
as a result	moreover
besides	nevertheless
for example	similarly
however	then
in addition	therefore
instead	thus

To Separate Groups of Words That Contain Commas

Use semicolons between groups of words in a series when one or more of the groups already contains commas.

Here's a list of things we should be recycling: aluminum, tin, and other metals; cardboard, newspapers, and other paper products; glass bottles, jars, and other glass items.

Colon

A **colon** may be used to introduce a quotation or a list. Colons are also used in business letters and between the numbers expressing time.

To Introduce a Quotation

Use a colon to introduce any quotation that follows a complete sentence. (A *quotation* is someone else's exact words.)

> **Baseball catcher Yogi Berra was famous for his wise sayings, including this one: "It ain't over until it's over."**

> **Movie producer Woody Allen made the following statement: "It's not that I'm afraid to die. I just don't want to be there when it happens."**

To Introduce a List

Use a colon to introduce a list.

> **Lucien has three major dislikes: whiners, bullies, and braggarts.**

When introducing a list, the colon often comes after summary words like *the following* or *these things*.

> **A good student does the following: reads, writes, and remembers.**

✳ Do not use a colon after a verb or preposition.

> **Most shoes are made of: leather, rubber, plastic, or canvas.** (The colon is incorrectly used after the preposition *of*.)

In a Business Letter

Use a colon after the salutation or greeting in a business letter.

> **Dear Dr. Demento: Dear Madam:**

Between Numbers in Time

Use a colon between the parts of a number that show time.

> **4:30 p.m.   11:00 a.m.   12:00 noon**

Hyphen

A **hyphen** is used to divide a word at the end of a line. It is also used to form compound words and to write fractions. In addition, a hyphen is used to join the words in compound numbers from twenty-one to ninety-nine, to join letters and words, and so on.

To Divide a Word

Use a hyphen to divide a word when you run out of room at the end of a line. A word may be divided only between syllables (*el-e-va-tor*). Refer to a dictionary if you're not sure how to divide a word. Here are some additional guidelines.

- Never divide a one-syllable word: *gross, lead, jump, thought.*
- Try not to divide a word of five or fewer letters: *July, study, paper.*
- Never divide a one-letter syllable from the rest of the word: *omit-ted* not *o-mitted.*
- Never divide abbreviations or contractions: *Mrs., Dr., NAACP, don't, haven't.*
- Never divide the last word in a paragraph.
- When a vowel is a syllable by itself, divide the word after the vowel: *ele-vator,* not *el-evator.*

In a Compound Word

Use a hyphen to make some compound words.

all-star
toll-free number
three-year-old sweater
on-line search
baby-sitter

Between Numbers in a Fraction

Use a hyphen between the numbers in a fraction that is written as a word.

one-fourth (1/4)
five-sixteenths (5/16)
seven thirty-seconds (7/32)

Hyphen

To Join Letters and Words	Use a hyphen to join a letter to a word. **PG-rated movie** **T-shirt** **e-mail** **U-turn**
With *self, ex, all, great*	Use a hyphen to form new words beginning with the prefixes *all, self, ex,* and so on; and to join the prefix *great* to names of relatives. Also use a hyphen with suffixes such as *elect* and *free*. **all-conference athlete** **self-learner** **ex-friend** **great-uncle** **mayor-elect** **trouble-free** **half-painted garage**
To Form an Adjective	Use a hyphen to join two or more words that work together to form a single (one-thought) adjective. **sun-dried fruit** **rain-soaked tent** **big-boned man** ✳ When words forming the adjective come after the noun, they are often not hyphenated. **man who was big boned** *Caution:* When the first of the words ends in *ly,* do not use a hyphen. Also, do not use a hyphen when a number or letter is the final part of a one-thought adjective. **newly recorded CD** **number one song on the charts**

Dash

A **dash** is used to show a break in a sentence, to emphasize a word or a group of words, or to show that someone's speech is being interrupted.

To Show a Sudden Break in a Sentence	A dash can show a sudden break in a sentence. **My point is—and I do have a point—that I forgot what I started to say.** **There is one thing—actually several things—that bother me about hot weather.**
For Emphasis	Use a dash to emphasize a word, a series of words, a phrase, or a clause. **After years of trial and error, Belther made history with his invention—the unicycle.** **You can learn about many subjects—customs, careers, sports, and weather—on the Internet.**
To Set Off Parenthetical Material	You can use dashes to set off parenthetical material—material that explains or clarifies a word or phrase. **High-tech jobs—ones that require a lot of training—are popular.**
To Indicate Interrupted Speech	Use a dash to show that someone's speech is being interrupted by another person. **Why, hello—yes, I understand—no, I remember—of course—I'll do that.**
To Set Off an Introductory Series	Use a dash to set off an introductory series from the sentence that explains the series. (A series contains at least three words or phrases in a row.) **Movies, music, and fashion—these are three key parts of American pop culture.**

Quotation Marks

Quotation marks are used for each of the following reasons:

- To set off the exact words of a speaker from the rest of the sentence
- To show the exact words a writer has quoted from a book or magazine
- To set off certain titles
- To note words used in a special way

To Set Off the Exact Words of a Speaker	Place quotation marks before and after a speaker's words in dialogue. **"Why am I so hungry?" asked Lucas. "I just ate two double cheeseburgers."**
To Set Off Quoted Material	Place quotation marks before and after the exact words you quote from magazines, books, and other sources. **Futurist Don Reynolds says, "Today's students will go through an average of four careers."** (A *futurist* predicts what will happen in the future.)
To Punctuate Titles	Use quotation marks to punctuate titles of songs, poems, short stories, lectures, episodes of radio and television programs, book chapters, electronic files, and articles in encyclopedias, newspapers, or magazines. **"Wild Thing"** (song) **"We Real Cool"** (poem) **"Eleven"** (short story) **"How Not to Be Seen"** (television episode) **"Elvis Seen Alive in Antarctica"** (newspaper article) ✳ When you write a title, capitalize the first word, the last word, and every word in between except for articles (*a, an, the*), short prepositions (*of, for, in, on, to, with*), and coordinating conjunctions (*and, or, but*).

For Long Quotations	If a quotation in a report is two or more paragraphs long, place quotation marks before each paragraph and at the end of the last paragraph.

    "_____

_____ .

    "_____

_____ ."

Quotations that are more than four lines in length are usually set off from the rest of the paper by indenting 10 spaces from the left.

    _____

       _____

       _____

       _____

       _____ .

    _____

(**Important:** Quotations that are set off in this way do not require quotation marks unless quotation marks appear in the original copy.)

Placement of Punctuation	When a period or comma ends quoted material, place it inside the quotation marks.

    "Good try," remarked Louis.
    Louis remarked, "Good try."

Place an exclamation point or a question mark *inside* the quotation marks when it punctuates the quotation.

    Bill Cosby used to wonder, "Why is there air?"

Place an exclamation point or a question mark *outside* the quotation marks when it punctuates the main sentence.

    Did Juanita tell Julio, "I'll be there at eight"?

Special Words	Quotation marks may also be used (1) to set apart a word that is being discussed, (2) to indicate that a word is slang, or (3) to point out that a word is being used in a special way.

    1. Little Manda could not pronounce "aluminum."
    2. Shemekia says she is "phat," not overweight.
    3. Fireworks will really "light up" the holiday.

Apostrophe

An **apostrophe** is used to form contractions, to form plurals, or to show possession. (*Possession* means "owning something.")

To Form Contractions

Use an apostrophe to show that one or more letters have been left out of a word to form a contraction.

I'm (I am)   they'd (they would)

COMMON CONTRACTIONS

couldn't (could not)	haven't (have not)	I've (I have)
didn't (did not)	he's (he is, he has)	they're (they are)
doesn't (does not)	I'll (I will)	won't (will not)
don't (do not)	isn't (is not)	wouldn't (would not)
hasn't (has not)	it's (it is, it has)	you'd (you would)

To Form Plurals

Use an apostrophe and *s* to form the plural of a letter or a numeral.

A's   B's   4's   12's

To Form Singular Possessives

To form the possessive of most singular nouns, add an apostrophe and *s*.

Denzel's new movie

the building's roof

✳ When a singular noun with two or more syllables ends with an *s* or a *z* sound, the possessive may be formed by adding just an apostrophe.

Luis' honesty or **Luis's honesty**

But when the singular noun is a one-syllable word, form the possessive by adding both an apostrophe and *s*.

Roz's roses

To Form Plural Possessives	To form the possessive of most plural nouns ending in *s*, add just an apostrophe.
	bosses' orders **the students' exams**
	For plural nouns not ending in *s*, add an apostrophe and an *s*.
	children's sizes **men's room**
	✳ **Remember:** The word that comes before the apostrophe is the owner.
	his sister's room (The room belongs to his sister.)
	his sisters' room (The room belongs to his sisters.)

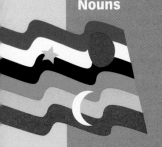

In Compound Nouns	Form the possessive of a compound noun by placing the possessive ending after the last word.
	the secretary of state's speech
	her brother-in-law's second cousin
	✳ If the possessive form of a plural compound noun sounds awkward, you may replace the possessive with an *of* phrase.
	their fathers-in-law's (plural) **nationalities** or
	the nationalities of their *fathers-in-law* (plural)

With Indefinite Pronouns	Form the possessive of an indefinite pronoun (*each, everyone, no one, anyone,* and so on) by adding an apostrophe and *s*. (See page 454.)
	somebody's smelly sneakers **anyone's guess**
	✳ For two-word pronouns, add an apostrophe and *s* to the second word.
	somebody else's smelly sneakers

To Show Shared Possession	Add an apostrophe and *s* to the last noun when the possession is shared.
	Huey, Dewey, and Louie's house
	✳ If possession is not shared, add an apostrophe and *s* to each noun.
	Huey's, Dewey's, and Louie's houses (they live in different houses.)

Italics and Underlining

Italics is a style of type that is slightly slanted. In this sentence the word *sunshine* is printed in italics. In handwritten or typed material, each word or letter that should be in italics is underlined.

Mr. Morton assigned us an article in *Newsweek*. (printed)

Mr. Morton assigned us an article in Newsweek. (handwritten or typed)

In Titles

Underline (or use italics for) the titles of books, plays, long poems, magazines, movies, television programs, record albums, cassettes, CD's, the names of ships and aircraft, and newspapers.

To Kill a Mockingbird (book) Ebony (magazine)
Save the World (album) Men in Black (movie)
Bernie Mac (television show) Titanic (ship)
Chicago Sun Times (newspaper)

Foreign Words

Underline (or use italics for) non-English words and scientific names not used in everyday English.

Semper fidelis means "always faithful." It is the motto of the U.S. Marine Corps.

Nicole approaches life sans souci, that is, "without worry."

For Special Uses

Underline any number, letter, or word that is being discussed or used in a special way. (Sometimes quotation marks are used for this reason. See page 393.)

I hope this letter I stands for incredible instead of incomplete.

Parentheses

Use **parentheses** around words that add or clarify information.

Some of the most popular kinds of music in the world (such as jazz and blues) were born in the United States.

Editing for Mechanics

Capitalization

Capitalize all proper nouns and all proper adjectives. A proper noun names a specific person, place, thing, or idea. A proper adjective is formed from a proper noun.

Common Nouns	president	country	continent
Proper Nouns	Thomas Jefferson	Brazil	Africa
Proper Adjectives	Jeffersonian politics	Brazilian food	African history

A Quick Guide

Days of the week . . . . Friday, Saturday, Sunday
Months . . . . September, October, November
Holidays, holy days . . . . Memorial Day, Kwanza, Easter
Periods, events in history . . . . the Renaissance, the Vietnam War
Political parties . . . . the Democratic Party
Official documents . . . . Emancipation Proclamation
Trade names. . . . . Buick, Nike, Maxwell House
Official titles . . . . Mayor Richard M. Daley
Official state nicknames. . . . . Peach State, Great Lake State
Geographic names
  Planets, heavenly bodies . . . . Earth, Saturn, the Milky Way
  Continents. . . . . Africa, Antarctica, Asia, South America
  Countries . . . . Switzerland, Ethiopia, Argentina, Japan
  States. . . . . New Jersey, Kansas, Nevada, Alabama
  Provinces . . . . Manitoba, Ontario, Newfoundland
  Counties, cities, towns, villages . . . . . . Dade County, Durango, Beaver Dam
  Streets, roads, highways . . . . Sunset Boulevard, Route 31
  Sections of a country or continent. . . . . the South, the Middle East
  Landforms. . . . . the Appalachians, the Sahara Desert
  Bodies of water. . . . . Lake Erie, Tinker Creek, the Persian Gulf
  Buildings. . . . . the Museum of Science and Industry, the Taj Mahal
  Public areas. . . . . Yellowstone Park, the Vietnam Memorial

Capitalization

Titles Used with Names	Capitalize titles used with names of persons and the abbreviations standing for those titles.

Senator Kennedy   **Mayor Martin J. Chavez**
Dr. Amy Lin   **Rev. Martin Luther King, Jr.**

Abbreviations	Capitalize abbreviations of titles and organizations.

M.D.	(Doctor of Medicine)
Dr.	(Doctor)
M.A.	(Master of Arts)
Ph.D.	(Doctor of Philosophy)
Mr.	(Courtesy title before the last name or full name of a man)
Mrs.	(Courtesy title before the last name or full name of a married woman)
Ms.	(Courtesy title before the last name or full name of a woman or a girl)
UN	(United Nations)

Historical Names	Capitalize the names of historical documents, events, and periods of time.

Civil War   **Harlem Renaissance**
Magna Carta   **Bronze Age**
Mayflower Compact

Organizations	Capitalize the name of a team, an organization, or an association.

Sacramento Kings   **Red Cross**
United Nations

Days of the Week	Capitalize the names of days of the week, months of the year, and special holidays.

Friday   **Martin Luther King Day**
Thanksgiving   **August**

Do not capitalize the names of seasons.
winter   **spring**   **summer**   **fall** (or autumn)

First Words	Capitalize the first word of every sentence and the first word in a direct quotation. Do not capitalize the first word in an indirect quotation.

When will this heat wave end? (sentence)

The guest speaker said, "That is a very interesting question." (direct quotation)

Ms. Spivey said that she would not tolerate cruel words. (indirect quotation)

"Why on earth," he asked, "do you insist on cracking your knuckles?" (Notice that *do* is not capitalized because it does not begin a new sentence.)

Names of People	Capitalize the names of people and also the initials or abbreviations that stand for those names.

Tiger Woods	**Sally Ride**
Yo-Yo Ma	**Condoleezza Rice**
Mary J. Blige	**Benito Juárez**

✳ If a woman uses both her maiden name and married name, the maiden name is listed first, and both are capitalized.

Coretta Scott King	**Sandra Day O'Connor**
Martha Ulforts Meyer	**Kimberly Yashiki Smith**

✳ Women or men who use two last names often hyphenate them.

Kathleen Aguilera-Pérez

Devon Grant-Smith

Words Used as Names	Capitalize words such as *mother, father, aunt,* and *uncle* when these words are used as names.

When Uncle Eddie visits, we always have a good time. ("Uncle Eddie" is the name of a person.)

If Grandma comes with him, we have even more fun. ("Grandma" is used as a name.)

✳ Words such as *dad, uncle, mother,* and *grandma* are not usually capitalized if they come after a possessive pronoun such as *my, his, our.*

My mother has decided to go back to school. (Here "mother" is not used as a name.)

400

Capitalization

Letters	Capitalize the letters used to indicate form or shape. **T-shirt U-turn S-curve V-shaped**
Names of Languages, Religions, Nationalities, Races	Capitalize the names of languages, religions, nationalities, and races, as well as the proper adjectives formed from them. **Spanish, Urdu, Serbian** (languages) **Islam, Christianity, Buddhism** (religions) **Chinese, Italian, Polish** (nationalities) **Asian, African, European** (races) **English tea** **Colombian coffee**

✳ Also capitalize nouns that refer to the Supreme Being, the word *Bible*, the books of the Bible, and the names for other holy books.
God, Jehovah, the Lord, Jesus Christ, the Psalms, Allah, Koran

Capitalize	Do Not Capitalize
American	anti-American
July, November	summer, fall
Aviation High School	a New York high school
Governor Janet Napolitano	Janet Napolitano, our governor
President George W. Bush	George Bush, our president
Honda Civic LS	a Honda car
We live on planet **Earth**.	The earth we live on is good.
I'm taking **Introduction to Government**.	It is a civics class.

Titles	Capitalize the first word of a title, the last word, and every word in between except articles (*a, an, the*), short prepositions (*of, at, to*), and coordinating conjunctions (*and, but, or*). Follow this rule for titles of books, newspapers, magazines, poems, plays, songs, articles, movies, works of art, stories, and essays.

> ***Native Son*** (book)
> ***The Miami Herald*** (newspaper)
> ***Ebony*** (magazine)
> **"Billie Jean"** (song)
> **"Kid in the Park"** (poem)
> ***A Raisin in the Sun*** (play)
> ***The Kings of Comedy*** (movie)

Particular Sections of the Country	Capitalize words that indicate particular sections of the country.

> **Many people live on the West Coast.**
> ("West Coast" is a section of the country.)

Do not capitalize words that simply indicate direction.

> **If you keep driving west, you will end up in the Pacific Ocean.** (direction)

✳ Capitalize proper adjectives formed from the names of specific sections of a country.

> **Midwestern work ethic**
> **Southern charm**

✳ Do not capitalize adjectives formed from words that simply indicate direction.

> **the southern part of Florida**
> **flying into western Canada**

Official Names	Capitalize the names of businesses and the official names of their products. (These are called trade names.) Do not, however, capitalize a general, descriptive word like *tissues* when it follows the product name.

> **Energizer** batteries   **Timex** watches
> **McDonald's** cookies   **KFC** restaurants
> **Best Buy** stores   **Kleenex** tissues

Plurals

The **plurals** of most nouns are formed by adding *s* to the singular.

football — **footballs**   bicycle — **bicycles**

The plural form of nouns ending in *sh, ch, x, s,* and *z* is made by adding *es* to the singular.

crash	— **crashes**	ditch	— **ditches**
mess	— **messes**	buzz	— **buzzes**
box	— **boxes**	ax	— **axes**

Plurals That Do Not Change

A few words in English are the same in the singular and in the plural.

Singular: I saw a **deer** disappear into the woods.
Plural: Five **deer** remained in the cornfield.

Singular: That **sheep** always wanders away.
Plural: The other six **sheep** follow it.

Singular: Did you see that **trout**?
Plural: Dad caught three **trout**.

Words Ending in *o*

The plurals of words ending in *o* with a vowel letter just before the *o* are formed by adding *s.*

video — **videos**   studio — **studios**

The plurals of words ending in *o* with a consonant letter before the *o* are mostly formed by adding *es.*

hero — **heroes**   potato — **potatoes**

✳ *Exception:* Musical terms and words borrowed from Spanish form plurals by adding *s.* Use a dictionary for other words of this type.

piano	— **pianos**	taco	— **tacos**
solo	— **solos**	burro	— **burros**
banjo	— **banjos**	burrito	— **burritos**

✳ Other exceptions include the following:

photo — **photos**   yo-yo — **yo-yos**

Nouns Ending in *ful*

The plurals of nouns that end with *ful* are formed by adding an *s* at the end of the word.

two **handfuls**   three **tankfuls**
four **mouthfuls**   five **cupfuls**

Nouns Ending in *f* or *fe*	The plurals of nouns that end in *f* or *fe* are formed in one of two ways: If the final *f* sound is still heard in the plural form of the word, simply add *s*; if the final sound is a *v* sound, change the *f* to *v* and add *es*.

belief — **beliefs**   roof — **roofs**
cuff — **cuffs**   chief — **chiefs**
(plural ends with *f* sound)

life — **lives**   knife — **knives**
calf — **calves**   leaf — **leaves**
(plural ends with *v* sound)

Nouns Ending in *y*	The plurals of common nouns that end in *y* (with a consonant letter just before the *y*) are formed by changing the *y* to *i* and adding *es*.

diary — **diaries**   hobby — **hobbies**
fairy — **fairies**   fly — **flies**

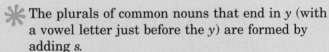 The plurals of proper nouns ending in *y* are formed by adding *s*.

There are two Rudys in our class.

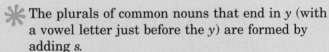 The plurals of common nouns that end in *y* (with a vowel letter just before the *y*) are formed by adding *s*.

boy — **boys**   holiday — **holidays**
stay — **stays**   monkey — **monkeys**

Adding an '*s*	The plurals of symbols, letters, numerals, and words discussed as words are formed by adding an apostrophe and an *s*.

three ?'s and six !'s   three 9's

A's **and** B's   if's, and's, **or** but's

Irregular Spelling	A number of words take on an irregular or new spelling to form a plural. Some words are now acceptable with the commonly used *s* or *es* ending.

child — **children**   tooth — **teeth**
man — **men**   goose — **geese**
foot — **feet**   woman — **women**
ox — **oxen**   crisis — **crises**
index — **indices** (or) **indexes**
cactus — **cacti** (or) **cactuses**

Plurals

Compound Nouns

The plurals of compound nouns are usually formed by adding *s* or *es* to the important word in the compound.

life jackets secretaries **of state**
mothers-**in-law** maids **of honor**

Collective Nouns

A collective noun may be singular or plural depending on how it's used. A collective noun is singular when it refers to a group as one unit; it is plural when it refers to the individuals in the group.

Use a singular pronoun (*its*) to indicate that the collective noun is singular. Use a plural pronoun (*their*) to show that the collective noun is plural.

The team won its first state championship this year. (group as a unit)

The team and their families are invited to an awards dinner. (group as individuals)

Abbreviations

Abbreviations are shortened forms of words. You can use the following abbreviations in all your writing:

Mr. Mrs. Ms. Dr. M.D.
B.C.E. (before the Common Era)
C.E. (Common Era)
a.m. (ante meridiem)
p.m. (post meridiem)

In formal writing assignments, **do not abbreviate** the names of states, countries, months, days, units of measure, or courses of study.

Acronyms

An acronym is a word formed from the first (or first few) letters of words in a phrase.

HUD (Housing and Urban Development)
radar (radio detecting and ranging)
WHO (World Health Organization)
MADD (Mothers Against Drunk Driving)
VISTA (Volunteers in Service to America)

Initialisms	An initialism is like an acronym. However, the initials used to form this type of abbreviation cannot be pronounced as a word. Initialisms are not usually followed by periods.

TV	— Television
CIA	— Central Intelligence Agency
PTA	— Parent-Teacher Association
HMO	— Health Maintenance Organization
IRS	— Internal Revenue Service

State Abbreviations

	Standard	Postal		Standard	Postal		Standard	Postal
Alabama	Ala.	AL	Kentucky	Ky.	KY	North Dakota	N.D.	ND
Alaska	Alas.	AK	Louisiana	La.	LA	Ohio	Ohio	OH
Arizona	Ariz.	AZ	Maine	Maine	ME	Oklahoma	Okla.	OK
Arkansas	Ark.	AR	Maryland	Md.	MD	Oregon	Ore.	OR
California	Calif.	CA	Massachusetts	Mass.	MA	Pennsylvania	Pa.	PA
Colorado	Colo.	CO	Michigan	Mich.	MI	Rhode Island	R.I.	RI
Connecticut	Conn.	CT	Minnesota	Minn.	MN	South Carolina	S.C.	SC
Delaware	Del.	DE	Mississippi	Miss.	MS	South Dakota	S.D.	SD
District			Missouri	Mo.	MO	Tennessee	Tenn.	TN
of Columbia	D.C.	DC	Montana	Mont.	MT	Texas	Tex.	TX
Florida	Fla.	FL	Nebraska	Neb.	NE	Utah	Utah	UT
Georgia	Ga.	GA	Nevada	Nev.	NV	Vermont	Vt.	VT
Hawaii	Hawaii	HI	New			Virginia	Va.	VA
Idaho	Idaho	ID	Hampshire	N.H.	NH	Washington	Wash.	WA
Illinois	Ill.	IL	New Jersey	N.J.	NJ	West Virginia	W. Va.	WV
Indiana	Ind.	IN	New Mexico	N.M.	NM	Wisconsin	Wis.	WI
Iowa	Iowa	IA	New York	N.Y.	NY	Wyoming	Wyo.	WY
Kansas	Kan.	KS	North Carolina	N.C.	NC			

Address Abbreviations

	Standard	Postal		Standard	Postal		Standard	Postal
Avenue	Ave.	AVE	Lake	L.	LK	Rural	R.	R
Boulevard	Blvd.	BLVD	Lane	Ln.	LN	South	S.	S
Court	Ct.	CT	North	N.	N	Square	Sq.	SQ
Drive	Dr.	DR	Park	Pk.	PK	Station	Sta.	STA
East	E.	E	Parkway	Pky.	PKY	Street	St.	ST
Expressway	Expy.	EXPY	Place	Pl.	PL	Terrace	Ter.	TER
Heights	Hts.	HTS	Plaza	Plaza	PLZ	Turnpike	Tpke.	TPKE
Highway	Hwy.	HWY	Road	Rd.	RD	West	W.	W

Common Abbreviations

AC alternating current
a.m. ante meridiem
ASAP as soon as possible
C.O.D. cash on delivery
D.A. district attorney
DC direct current
etc. and so forth
F Fahrenheit
FM frequency modulation

GNP gross national product
i.e. that is (Latin *id est*)
kg kilogram
km kilometer
kw kilowatt
l liter
lb. pound
m meter
M.D. Doctor of Medicine
mfg manufacturing
mpg miles per gallon

mph miles per hour
oz. ounce
pd. paid
pg. page (or p.)
p.m. post meridiem
ppd. postpaid, prepaid
qt. quart
R.S.V.P. please reply
tbs, tbsp, T tablespoon
tsp teaspoon
vol. volume
vs. versus
yd. yard

Numbers

Numbers from one to nine are usually written as words. All numbers 10 and over are usually written as numerals.

> **two   six   nine   11   25   341**

If you're comparing the numbers in a sentence, write them both as numerals or as words.

> **The team members range in age from 9 to 13 years old.**

> **The team members range in age from nine to thirteen years old.**

Very Large Numbers

When writing sentences, you may use a combination of numerals and words for very large numbers.

> **The world's population is expected to be about 7.9 billion by 2020.**

You may spell out large numbers that can be written as two words.

> **two million   nine thousand**

If you need more than two words to spell out a number, write it as a numeral.

> **5,340   9,641**

Sentence Beginnings	Use words, not numerals, to begin a sentence.
	Forty-two states have laws restricting smoking.
	Change the sentence structure if this rule creates a clumsy construction.
	Clumsy: **Two hundred ninety-three students had part-time jobs last year.**
	Better: **Last year, 293 students had part-time jobs.**

Compound Modifier	Use words for numbers that come before a compound modifier if that modifier includes another number.
	The cook made eleven 16-inch pizzas for the party.
	During the summer, Diego worked twelve 10-hour days.

Time and Money	If time or money is expressed with an abbreviation, use numerals; if either is expressed in words, spell out the number.
	3:00 a.m. (or) **three o'clock**
	$20 (or) **twenty dollars**

45

Numerals Only

Use numerals for any numbers in the following forms:

money **$5.10**
decimals **99.5**
dates . . . . **May 10, 2004**
statistics . . . . **65 mph**
addresses . . . . **904 Hosenpud Ave.**
ZIP codes **60202**
identification numbers . . . . **Highway 45**
percentages . . . . **50 percent**
phone numbers **555-8646**
pages . . . . **pages 15-17**

 Always use numerals with abbreviations and symbols.

6'3" 2 in. 84° F 2 tsp 6% 30 mph 7 lbs. 3 oz.

Improving Your Spelling

1. **Be patient.** Becoming a good speller takes time.

2. **Learn the basic spelling rules.** (See page 414.)

3. **Check your spelling** by using a dictionary or list of commonly misspelled words.

4. **Check a dictionary** for the correct pronunciation of each word you are trying to spell. Knowing how to pronounce a word will help you remember how to spell it.

5. **Look up the meaning of each word.** Knowing how to spell a word is of little use if you don't know what it means.

6. **Practice seeing the word in your mind's eye.** Look away from the dictionary page and write the word on a piece of paper. Check the spelling in the dictionary. Repeat this process until you can spell the word correctly.

7. **Make a spelling dictionary.** Include any words you frequently misspell in a special notebook.

A			
	across	aisle	angel
	actual	alarm	anger
abbreviate	adapt	alcohol	angle
aboard	addition	alike	angry
about	address	alive	animal
above	adequate	alley	anniversary
absence	adjust	allowance	announce
absent	admire	all right	annoyance
absolute	adventure	almost	annual
accident	advertise	already	anonymous
accidental	advertising	although	another
accompany	afraid	altogether	answer
accomplish	after	aluminum	antarctic
according	afternoon	always	anticipate
account	afterward	ambulance	anxiety
accurate	again	amendment	anxious
accustom	against	among	anybody
ache	agreeable	amount	anyhow
achieve	agreement	analyze	anyone
acre	aid	ancient	anything

anyway
anywhere
apartment
apiece
apologize
apparent
appeal
appearance
appetite
appliance
application
appointment
appreciate
approach
appropriate
approval
approximate
architect
arctic
aren't
argument
arithmetic
around
arouse
arrange
arrival
article
artificial
asleep
assign
assistance
associate
association
assume
athlete
athletic
attach
attack
attempt
attendance
attention
attitude
attorney

attractive
audience
August
author
authority
automobile
autumn
available
avenue
average
awful
awkward

B

baggage
baking
balance
balloon
ballot
banana
bandage
barber
bargain
barrel
basement
basis
basket
battery
beautiful
beauty
because
become
becoming
before
began
beginning
behave
behavior
being
belief
believe
belong

beneath
benefit
between
bicycle
biscuit
blackboard
blanket
blizzard
bother
bottle
bottom
bough
bought
bounce
boundary
breakfast
breast
breath
breathe
breeze
bridge
brief
bright
brilliant
brother
brought
bruise
bubble
bucket
buckle
budget
building
burglar
bury
business
busy
button

C

cabbage
cafeteria
calendar

campaign
canal
cancel
candidate
candle
cannon
cannot
canoe
can't
canyon
capacity
captain
cardboard
career
careful
careless
carpenter
carriage
carrot
casualty
catalog
catastrophe
catcher
caterpillar
catsup
ceiling
celebration
cemetery
census
century
certain
certificate
challenge
champion
change
character
chief
children
chimney
chocolate
choice
chorus
circumstance

citizen
civilization
classmates
classroom
climate
climb
closet
clothing
coach
cocoa
cocoon
coffee
collar
college
color
column
comedy
coming
commercial
commission
commit
commitment
committed
committee
communicate
community
company
comparison
competition
competitive
complain
complete
complexion
compromise
conceive
concerning
concert
concrete
condemn
condition
conductor
conference
confidence

congratulate
connect
conscience
conscious
conservative
constitution
continue
continuous
control
convenience
convince
coolly
cooperate
corporation
correspond
cough
couldn't
counter
country
county
courage
courageous
court
courteous
courtesy
cousin
coverage
cozy
cracker
cranky
crawl
creditor
cried
criticize
cruel
crumb
crumble
cupboard
curiosity
curious
current
custom
customer

D

daily
dairy
damage
danger
daughter
dealt
decided
decision
decorate
defense
definite
definition
delicious
dependent
describe
description
desert
deserve
design
desirable
despair
dessert
determine
develop
device
devise
diamond
diary
dictionary
difference
different
difficulty
dining
diploma
director
disagreeable
disappear
disappoint
disapprove
discipline
discover

discuss
discussion
disease
dissatisfied
distinguish
distribute
divide
divine
division
doctor
doesn't
dollar
doubt
dough
dual
duplicate

E

eager
economy
edge
edition
eight
eighth
either
electricity
elephant
embarrass
emergency
emphasize
employee
employment
enclose
encourage
engineer
enormous
enough
entertain
enthusiastic
entirely
entrance
envelope

environment
equipment
equipped
escape
especially
establish
every
evidence
exaggerate
exceed
excellent
except
exceptional
excite
exercise
exhaust
exhibition
existence
expect
expensive
experience
explain
explanation
expression
extinct
extraordinary
extreme

facilities
familiar
family
famous
fascinate
fashion
faucet
favorite
feature
February
federal
fertile
field

fierce
fifty
finally
financial
foreign
formal
former
forth
fortunate
forty
forward
fountain
fourth
freight
friend
frighten
fulfill
further
furthermore

gadget
gauge
generally
generous
genius
gentle
genuine
geography
ghetto
ghost
gnaw
government
governor
graduation
grammar
grateful
grease
grief
grocery
grudge
guarantee

guard
guardian
guess
guidance
guide
guilty
gymnasium

hammer
handkerchief
handle
handsome
happen
happiness
hastily
having
hazardous
headache
height
hesitate
history
hoarse
holiday
honor
hoping
hopping
horrible
hospital
humorous
hurriedly
hygiene
hymn

icicle
identical
illiterate
illustrate
imaginary
imagine

imitation
immediate
immense
immigrant
impatient
importance
impossible
improvement
incredible
indefinitely
independent
individual
industrial
inferior
infinite
initial
innocent
instance
instead
insurance
intelligence
intention
interested
interesting
interfere
interpret
interrupt
interview
investigate
invitation
irrigate
island
issue

jealous
jewelry
journal
journey
judgment
juicy

K

kitchen
knew
knife
knives
knock
knowledge

L

label
laboratory
ladies
language
laugh
laundry
lawyer
league
lecture
legal
legible
legislature
leisure
length
liable
library
license
lightning
likely
liquid
literature
living
loneliness
losing
lovable
lovely

M

machinery
magazine
magnificent

maintain
majority
making
manual
manufacture
marriage
material
mathematics
maximum
mayor
meant
measure
medicine
medium
message
mileage
miniature
minimum
minute
mirror
miserable
missile
misspell
moisture
molecule
monument
mortgage
mountain
muscle
musician
mysterious

N

naive
natural
necessary
negotiate
neighbor
neither
nickel
niece
nineteen

nineteenth
ninety
noisy
noticeable
nuclear
nuisance

O

obedience
obey
occasion
occasional
occur
occurred
offense
official
often
omitted
operate
opinion
opponent
opportunity
opposite
ordinarily
original

P

package
paid
pamphlet
paradise
paragraph
parallel
paralyze
parentheses
participant
participate
particular
pasture
patience
peculiar

people
perhaps
permanent
perpendicular
persistent
personal
perspiration
persuade
phase
physician
piece
pitcher
planned
plateau
pleasant
pleasure
pneumonia
politician
possess
possible
practical
prairie
precede
precious
precise
precision
prejudice
preparation
previous
primitive
principal
principle
prisoner
privilege
probably
procedure
proceed
professor
pronounce
pronunciation
protein
psychology
pumpkin

Q

quarter
questionnaire
quiet
quite

R

raise
realize
really
receipt
receive
received
recipe
recognize
recommend
reign
relieve
remember
repetition
representative
resistance
respectfully
responsibility
restaurant
review
rhyme
rhythm
ridiculous
route

S

safety
salad
salary
sandwich
satisfactory
Saturday
scene
scenery

schedule
science
scissors
scream
screen
season
secretary
seize
sensible
sentence
separate
several
shining
similar
since
sincere
skiing
sleigh
soldier
spaghetti
specific
sphere
sprinkle
squeeze
statue
statute
stomach
stopped
straight
strength
stretched
studying
subtle
succeed
success
sufficient
summarize
suppose
surely
surprise
syllable
sympathy
symptom

T

table
teacher
technique
temperature
temporary
terrible
territory
thankful
theater
their
there
therefore
thief
thorough
though
throughout
tired
together
tomorrow
tongue
touch
tournament
toward
tragedy
treasurer
tried
tries
truly
Tuesday
typical

U

unfortunate
unique
unnecessary
until
usable
useful
using
usual

V

vacation
vacuum
valuable
variety
various
vegetable
very
view
violence
visible
visitor
voice
volume
voluntary
volunteer

W

wander
weather
Wednesday
weigh
weird
welcome
welfare
whale
where
whether
which
whole
whose
width
women
worthwhile
writing
written

Y

yellow
yesterday

Spelling Rules

i* before *e	Write *i* before *e* except after *c*, or when sounded like *a* as in *neighbor* and *weigh*. **Exceptions** to the "*i* before *e*" rule include the following: either heir height financier leisure species foreign neither their ✳ Eight of the exceptions are in this sentence: **Neither sheik dared leisurely seize either weird species of financier.**
Silent *e*	If a word ends with a silent *e*, drop the *e* before adding a suffix that begins with a vowel. state — **stating** — **statement** use — **using** — **useful** ✳ Do not drop the *e* when the suffix begins with a consonant. Exceptions include *truly, argument,* and *ninth*. nine — **ninety** — **nineteen**
Words Ending in *y*	When *y* is the last letter in a word, and a consonant is just before the *y*, change the *y* to *i* before adding any suffix, except those that begin with *i*. lazy — **laziness** fly — **flies** — **flying** When forming the plural of a word that ends in *y* and has a vowel just before the *y*, add *s*. toy — **toys** monkey — **monkeys**
Words Ending in a Consonant	When a one-syllable word (*beg*) ends in a consonant (be**g**) preceded by one vowel (b**e**g), double the final consonant before adding a suffix that begins with a vowel (beg**g**ing). beg — **begging** When a multisyllable word (*admit*) ends in a consonant (admi**t**) preceded by one vowel (adm**i**t), the accent is on the last syllable (admít), and the suffix begins with a vowel (ing)—the same rule holds true: double the final consonant (admi**tt**ing). admit — **admitting**

Commonly Misused Words

This chapter lists words that are commonly confused and used incorrectly. First, look over all of the words listed on the next 18 pages. Then, whenever you have a question about which word is the right one to use, turn here for help. (If this chapter doesn't answer your question, refer to a dictionary.)

a, an	**Fifth Avenue is a famous street in New York.** (**A** is used before words that begin with a consonant sound.) **I asked an understanding policeman for directions.** (**An** is used before words that begin with a vowel sound.)
accept, except	**Myron accepted the award.** (**Accept** means "to receive.") **Everyone except Felix attended the banquet.** (**Except** means "other than.")
adapt, adopt	**Malcolm X adapted to a Muslim lifestyle.** (**Adapt** means "to adjust or change to fit.") **He had adopted the Islamic faith.** (**Adopt** means "to choose and treat as your own.")
affect, effect	**The new guidelines will affect the students' work.** (**Affect** is a verb meaning "to influence.") **One effect of the guidelines is longer class periods.** (**Effect** is a noun meaning "the result.")
allowed, aloud	**The teacher allowed the students to read in class.** (**Allowed** means "permitted.") **Each student will read aloud at the end of the period.** (**Aloud** means "in a speaking voice.")
allusion, illusion	**My sister makes allusion to her future fans.** (**Allusion** is an indirect reference to someone or something.) **She is under the illusion that she's going to be a star.** (**Illusion** is a false idea.)
a lot	**There are a lot of reasons for that.** (**A lot** is always two words.)

already, all ready	I **already** finished cleaning the bathroom. (*Already* is an adverb telling when.) So, I'm **all ready** to go skateboarding. (*All ready* is a phrase meaning "completely ready.")
alright, all right	**Alright** is the incorrect spelling of *all right*. Are you **all right**? (*All right* is a phrase meaning "satisfactory or okay.")
altogether, all together	Crenshaw is **altogether** crazy. (*Altogether* is an adverb meaning "completely.") The family was **all together** in the warm apartment. (*All together* describes people or things gathered in one place at one time.)
among, between	The point guard and forwards talked **among** themselves. (*Among* is used when speaking of more than two persons or things.) They debated **between** zone or man-to-man defense. (*Between* is used when speaking of only two.)
amount, number	Bernie ate a huge **amount** of food at the game. (*Amount* refers to things you can measure, but not count.) A small **number** of fans cheered. (*Number* is used when you can count things.)
annual, biannual, semiannual, biennial, perennial	The **annual** blues festival was held in June this year. (*Annual* means "once a year.") Our city has a **biannual** budget meeting. (*Biannual* and *semiannual* both mean "twice a year.") The flower sale is a **biennial** event. (A *biennial* event happens every two years.) My brother has a **perennial** enthusiasm for baseball. (*Perennial* means "continuing without interruption.")
ant, aunt	The **ant** is an industrious insect. My **aunt** is usually very funny.
anyone, any one	**Anyone** could have seen that coming. (*Anyone* is a pronoun meaning "any person at all.") **Any one** of us may be next. (*Any one* refers to a choice of one.)

anyway, anyways	**Anyways** is an incorrect form of **anyway**.
ascared, scared	**Ascared** is not standard English. Use **scared** or **afraid**.
assent, ascent	My mom finally gave her **assent** to the balloon ride. (***Assent*** means "agreement.") The hot-air balloon began its **ascent** at 10 a.m. (***Ascent*** is the act of rising.)
ate, eight	Gregg **ate** a peach. (***Ate*** means "to have eaten.") **Eight** peaches cost only a dollar in 1960. (***Eight*** is a number.)
bare, bear	Her **bare** feet looked cold. (***Bare*** means "without covering.") The **bear** gulîped the trout in midair. (A ***bear*** is a large, furry animal.) Miguel couldn't **bear** listening to his baby sister cry. (The verb ***bear*** means "to tolerate" or "to carry.")
base, bass	The **base** of the building was beginning to crumble. (***Base*** [rhymes with *vase*] is the foundation or lower part of something.) The singer's **bass** voice rumbled like thunder. (A ***bass*** [rhymes with *vase*] voice has a deep, low sound.) Carmen had never seen a **bass** outside of an aquarium. (A ***bass*** [rhymes with *mass*] is a type of fish.)
be, bee	Nikia wants to **be** an artist. (***Be*** is a verb.) A **bee** is a flying insect that makes honey.
beside, besides	Was the spoon **beside** the knife? (***Beside*** means "by the side of.") **Besides** the fastball, he needed a curve. (***Besides*** means "in addition to.")

blew, blue	**The wind blew the fog away.** (*Blew* is the past tense of the verb *blow*.) **The sun shone in the clear blue sky.** (*Blue* is a color.)
board, bored	**The school board posted its agenda on a bulletin board.** (A *board* is a group of people in charge; a *board* is also a piece of wood or cork.) **When Rashad got bored, he bored holes in the wood.** (*Bored* means "tired of something" or "to have drilled into something.")
borrow, lend	**I asked Mom, "Can I borrow $15 for a CD?"** (*Borrow* means "to *receive* for temporary use.") **She said, "I can lend you $15 until next Friday."** (*Lend* means "to *give* for temporary use.")
brake, break	**The parking brake held the car in place.** (A *brake* is used to slow or stop something.) **Someone tried to break my windshield.** (*Break* means "to split or crack.")
bring, take	**Please bring me a towel.** (*Bring* means "to move something toward the speaker.") **Take plenty of water when you go hiking.** (*Take* means "to carry along" or "to move something away from the speaker.")
by, bye, buy	**Have you walked by the Ribs Shack lately?** (*By* is a preposition meaning "near.") **"Bye," she said. "See you later."** (*Bye* is short for "good-bye.") **I can buy that much cheaper down the street.** (*Buy* is a verb meaning "to purchase.")
can, may	**Can you touch your nose with your tongue?** (*Can* suggests ability to do something.) **May I go to a movie tonight?** (*May* asks for permission to do something.)

capital, capitol	The **capital** of South Dakota is Pierre.
	(The noun *capital* refers to a city or to money.)
	Pierre begins with a **capital** letter.
	The mayor's opinion is of **capital** importance.
	(The adjective *capital* means "major or important.")
	The **capitol** in Madison, Wisconsin, is only three inches shorter than the one in Washington, D.C.
	(A *capitol* is a building in which government jobs are carried out.)
cell, sell	Plants and animals are made up of **cells**.
	Life in a jail **cell** is hard.
	(A *cell* is a small unit of life or a small room.)
	Camille hopes to **sell** her bicycle.
	(*Sell* is a verb meaning "to give up for a price.")
cent, scent, sent	The flower seeds cost 95 **cents** per packet.
	(A *cent* is a coin, also called a penny.)
	Julia loves the **scent** of roses.
	(*Scent* is a smell.)
	Sam's mom **sent** him to the store for some flowers.
	(*Sent* is the past tense of the verb *send*.)
choose, chose	Why did you **choose** that one?
	(*Choose* [chüz] is a verb meaning "to select or pick.")
	I **chose** that shirt because it's red.
	(*Chose* [chōz] is the past tense of the verb *choose*.)
clothes, close	Melva put the wet **clothes** in the dryer.
	(*Clothes* are items you wear.)
	She had to **close** the door before the machine would start.
	(*Close* means "to shut.")
coarse, course	The unsanded wood felt **coarse**.
	(*Coarse* means "rough or crude.")
	He hoped he would learn a lot in the shop **course**.
	(A *course* is a class; a *course* is also a path or direction taken.)

compliment, complement	**Aunt Oprah gave Shanika a compliment on her layer cake.** (***Compliment*** is an expression of praise.) **The cake was a perfect complement to Uncle John's birthday cake.** (***Complement*** refers to something that completes.)
council, counsel	**The city council approved a plan for a new skating rink.** (***Council*** refers to a group that advises.) **They received counsel from a local developer.** (***Counsel*** is a noun that means "advice"; ***counsel*** is also a verb that means "to advise.")
creak, creek	**Can you hear the floorboards creak?** (A ***creak*** is a squeaking sound.) **The creek dries up in the summer.** (A ***creek*** is a stream, a tiny river.)
dear, deer	**My uncle is dear to my heart.** (***Dear*** means "loved or valued"; it is a greeting used at the beginning of a letter.) **Most deer live in the country; some live in the suburbs.** (***Deer*** are animals.)
desert, dessert	**The barrel cactus grows in the desert.** (***Desert*** [deź-ert] is barren wilderness.) **Who would desert her best friend?** (The verb ***desert*** [di-zert´] means "to leave or abandon.") **My brother's favorite food is dessert.** (***Dessert*** [di-zert´] is a sweet served at the end of a meal.)
dew, do, due	**My shoes are wet from the morning dew on the grass.** (***Dew*** is moisture.) **Felipe will do his report today.** (***Do*** is a verb meaning "to make or carry out.") **It's not due until next week.** (***Due*** means "owed.")
die, dye	**Most plants will die without sunlight.** (***Die*** means "to stop living.") **Josie's brother dyed his hair orange.** (***Dye*** means "to change the color of something.")

doesn't, don't	Seiko **doesn't** know the address. (***doesn't*** = does not) Jane and Karl **don't** want to go. (***don't*** = do not)
farther, further	North Carolina is **farther** south than South Dakota. (***Farther*** refers to distance.) For **further** information, see an almanac. (***Further*** does not refer to distance, but it does mean "more or additional.")
fewer, less	Jake carries **fewer** books than Hank. (***Fewer*** refers to something you can count.) Mona has **less** homework than Tamika. (***Less*** refers to a general amount that you cannot count.)
find, fined	**Find** that overdue library book. (***Find*** means "to locate or discover.") The school library **fined** him for the overdue book. (***Fined*** means "charged a penalty.")
flower, flour	Cherry trees **flower** in early spring. (As a noun, ***flower*** refers to a blossoming plant. As a verb, ***flower*** refers to the act of blossoming.) Sam sprinkled **flour** on the piecrust. (***Flour*** is finely ground grain.)
for, four	Five candidates applied **for** the job. (***For*** is a preposition meaning "because of" or "directed to.") The panel asked each candidate **four** questions. (***Four*** is the number 4.)
good, well	Aaron is a **good** instructor. (***Good*** is an adjective describing the noun *instructor*.) Dillon ran **well** in the third race. (***Well*** is an adverb modifying the verb *ran*.)
hair, hare	Samantha wears her **hair** in braids. (***Hair*** refers to the growth covering our heads and bodies.) The **hare** has long ears for good hearing. (A ***hare*** is an animal similar to a rabbit.)

heal, heel	**Shallow cuts heal quickly.** (***Heal*** means "to return to health.") **The door bruised his heel.** (The ***heel*** is the back of the foot.)
hear, here	**Let's hear what he has to say.** (***Hear*** means "to listen.") **Will you put the desk here?** (***Here*** means "the area nearby," the opposite of *there*.)
heard, herd	**Delton heard the news yesterday.** (***Heard*** is the past tense of the verb *hear*.) **A herd of sheep is less dangerous than a herd of cattle.** (***Herd*** refers to a large group of animals.)
heir, air	**Few people die without at least one heir.** (An ***heir*** is a person who inherits or has the right to something.) **Fortunately the building had air conditioning.** (***Air*** is what we breathe.)
hi, high	**She says hi to everyone.** (***Hi*** is a brief greeting.) **The wall is almost 10 feet high.** (***High*** is an adjective meaning "tall.")
hole, whole	**The pen made a hole in the paper.** (***Hole*** refers to an opening.) **I had to recopy the whole paper.** (***Whole*** means "entire or complete.")
hour, our	**Some people try to fit more than 60 minutes into an hour.** (***Hour*** refers to time.) **We have a view of the sunset from our house.** (***Our*** is a pronoun showing possession.)
immigrate, emigrate	**Vladimir immigrated to this country in 1987.** (***Immigrate*** means "to come into a new country or area.") **He was 22 years old when he emigrated from Russia.** (***Emigrate*** means "to leave your country for another place.")

its, it's	**The pigeon ruffled its feathers.** (*Its* shows possession.) **It's easy to lose your way.** (*It's* is the contraction for "it is.")
knew, new	**Lupe knew her family planned to move.** (*Knew* is the past tense of the verb *know*.) **She would be going to a new school.** (*New* means "recent or different.")
knight, night	**A knight was similar to a soldier.** (*Knight* refers to an old military rank.) **They seldom fought during the night.** (*Night* refers to the time between sunset and sunrise.)
knot, not	**The boater tied a special knot.** (*Knot* refers to a lump of intertwined material.) **I do not know how to tie one.** (*Not* means "negative.")
know, no	**I know the best pizza place.** (*Know* means "to understand.") **No, I don't like pineapple on pizza.** (*No* is the opposite of yes.)
knows, nose	**Ben knows he has to study tonight.** (*Knows* means "understands.") **His nose will be inside a book!** (The *nose* is part of your face.)
lay, lie	**Please lay the books down on the table.** **I laid them down yesterday. I have laid them down before.** (*Lay* means "to place." *Lay* is a transitive verb, which means it needs a word to complete the meaning. In the sentence above, *books* and *them* complete the meaning by answering the question "what." *Laid* is the past tense and past participle of *lay*.) **Byron lies on the floor to study.** **He lay on the floor last night. He has lain there before.** (*Lie* means "to recline." *Lie* is an intransitive verb, so it does not need a word to complete the meaning. *Lay* is the past tense of *lie*; *lain* is the past participle.)

lead, led	**I will lead the way.** (***Lead*** [lēd] is a present-tense verb meaning "to guide.") **Curtis led the team to the championship.** (***Led*** [lĕd] is the past tense of *lead*.) **Lead is a heavy metal.** (***Lead*** [lĕd] refers to a metal or to graphite in a pencil.)
learn, teach	**The teacher wants everyone to learn two new formulas.** (***Learn*** means "to get information.") **Who will teach me the second one?** (***Teach*** means "to give information.")
leave, let	**Leave your glove on the bench.** (***Leave*** means "to allow something to remain behind.") **Will you let Greg use it?** (***Let*** means "to permit.")
like, as	**Juan looks like a rock star.** (***Like*** is a preposition meaning "similar to." It usually introduces a word or a phrase.) **Dave likes to sing as he runs.** (***As*** is a conjunction meaning "while" or "to the same degree." It usually introduces a clause.)
loose, lose, loss	**The door hinge was too loose.** (***Loose*** [lüs] means "free or untied.") **Did you lose one of the screws?** (***Lose*** [lüz] means "to misplace or fail to win.") **A loss like this makes it hard to continue.** (***Loss*** means "something lost.")
made, maid	**Elwan made two bookshelves for his mother.** (***Made*** is the past tense of the verb *make*.) **Charlene worked as a maid for three months.** (A ***maid*** is a woman who does domestic work.)
mail, male	**My dad hates junk mail.** (***Mail*** refers to letters and other messages that are sent.) **Male birds are generally more colorful than females.** (***Male*** refers to the masculine sex.)

main, Maine, mane	**Educating students is a school's main task.** (***Main*** means "the most important.") **Maine can experience very cold winters.** (***Maine*** is a state in the northeast United States.) **A lion's mane can be impressive.** (***Mane*** refers to the long hair on an animal's neck.)
meat, meet	**Which meat do you prefer—beef or pork?** (***Meat*** is food or flesh.) **Let's meet at the park.** (***Meet*** means "to come together.")
metal, medal	**Plastic has replaced some metal parts on cars.** (***Metal*** is an element like iron or gold.) **He proudly placed his gold medal on his desk.** (A ***medal*** is an award.)
miner, minor	**Underground coal miners have dangerous jobs.** (A ***miner*** takes valuable materials from the earth.) **Many nightclubs do not admit minors.** (A ***minor*** is an individual who is not legally an adult.) **There is just one minor problem with that.** (The adjective ***minor*** means "small, of lesser importance.")
moral, morale	**Was that moral behavior?** (***Moral*** [mor´-al] refers to what is right or wrong.) **Class morale dropped when Mr. Robinson left.** (***Morale*** [mo-ral´] refers to someone's emotional condition.)
morning, mourning	**I heard about Yvonne's dog Monday morning.** (***Morning*** refers to the part of the day before noon.) **She is still mourning about her loss.** (***Mourning*** means "showing sorrow.")
oar, or, ore	**You need two oars to row a boat.** (An ***oar*** is a stick with a wide end used to row a boat.) **Would you rather ride your bike or walk?** (***Or*** is a connecting word showing a choice.) **The ships carried iron ore.** (***Ore*** refers to a mineral that contains a valuable material.)

one, won	Roy bought **one** ticket for the concert. (***One*** is a number.) Renae **won** a pass to go backstage after the concert. (***Won*** refers to victory.)
pain, pane	Serena's broken ankle gave her a lot of **pain**. (***Pain*** is the feeling of being hurt.) William installed a new **pane** in his garage door. (A ***pane*** is a framed piece of glass.)
pair, pare, pear	Loren liked his new **pair** of gloves. (A ***pair*** is a couple, or two of something.) Peter will **pare** the potatoes later. (***Pare*** means "to peel.") It's not easy to find a good **pear** to eat. (A ***pear*** is a fruit.)
past, passed	The **past** cannot be changed. (noun) Don't let **past** mistakes stop you. (adjective) He could see the cat walk **past** the gate. (preposition) (***Past*** can be a noun, an adjective, or a preposition.) He **passed** the courthouse. (***Passed*** is the past tense of the verb *pass*, meaning "to move away or beyond.")
peace, piece	Are you at **peace** with your decision? (***Peace*** means "tranquillity or freedom from conflict.") May I have a **piece** of your cake? (A ***piece*** is a part of something.)
personal, personnel	Ahmal sent me a **personal** message. (***Personal*** [pér-son-al] means "private.") **Personnel** within one department must get along. (***Personnel*** [per-son-él] are people working at a job.)
plain, plane	The Serengeti **Plain** is a large area of land in Tanzania. (***Plain*** means "level area," "undecorated," or "clearly seen.") The carpenter used a **plane** to finish the tabletop. (***Plane*** means "flat and even" or "the tool used to smooth wood." It is also the short form of the word *airplane*.)

pore, pour, poor	**Humans sweat through their pores.** (***Pores*** [pōrz] are tiny openings in the skin.) **Please pour me a glass of milk.** (***Pour*** [pōr] means "to cause to flow.") **What a poor excuse for a party!** (***Poor*** [poȯr] means "low or needy quality.")
principal, principle	**Our principal came from New Jersey.** (The noun ***principal*** is a school administrator or a sum of money.) **One of his principal goals is to help each student become a good citizen.** (The adjective ***principal*** means "most important.") **Here's a good principle: "The only way to have a friend is to be one."** (The noun ***principle*** means "an idea or a belief.")
quiet, quit, quite	**A city can be quiet late at night.** (***Quiet*** [kwī'-et] is the opposite of noisy.) **After dark, the boys quit playing baseball.** (***Quit*** [kwĭt] means "to stop.") **The full moon last night was quite bright.** (***Quite*** [kwīt] means "completely or rather.")
quote, quotation	**You may quote me on that.** (***Quote*** is a verb.) **I used a quotation by Abraham Lincoln.** (***Quotation*** is a noun.)
raise, rays, raze	**Anne raised the window shades.** (***Raise*** means "to lift or elevate.") **The sun rays brightened the kitchen.** (***Rays*** are thin lines or beams.) **Our neighbors plan to raze the old shed.** (***Raze*** means "to tear down completely.")
read, red	**Phil, have you read the chapter about stars?** (***Read*** [rĕd] is the past tense of the verb *read* [rēd].) **Some stars are called red giants.** (***Red*** is a color.)

real, very, really	**Is that a real diamond?** (The adjective ***real*** means "genuine.") **We really enjoyed the very funny play.** (***Really*** means "truly"; ***very*** means "extremely." Do not use ***real*** in place of either of these adverbs.)
right, write, rite	**Which one is the right line?** (***Right*** means "correct or proper.") **Will you write me a postcard?** (***Write*** means "to record in print.") **The child was ready for the rite of christening.** (A ***rite*** is a ritual or ceremony.)
road, rode, rowed	**There's a dead opossum in the middle of the road.** (A ***road*** is a street or highway.) **I rode across town on the subway.** (***Rode*** is the past tense of the verb *ride*.) **They rowed their boats under the bridge.** (***Rowed*** means "to move a boat with oars.")
scene, seen	**Last night's sunset created a beautiful scene.** (***Scene*** refers to the place something happens.) **Ross has never seen such colors.** (***Seen*** is a form of the verb *see*.)
sea, see	**The Sargasso Sea is part of the Atlantic Ocean.** (A ***sea*** is a body of salt water, smaller than an ocean.) **Do you see what I mean?** (***See*** means "to detect with the eye or to understand.")
seam, seem	**One of the seams on my backpack is ripped.** (A ***seam*** is a line made by joining two pieces of material.) **We seem to be lost.** (***Seem*** means "to appear to exist.")
set, sit	**Spencer's sister set the table every night.** (The transitive verb ***set*** means "to place.") **Sit down and make yourself at home.** (The intransitive verb ***sit*** means "to put the body in a seated position.")

sew, so, sow	Chantel knows how to **sew** a dress. (**Sew** is a verb meaning "to stitch.") The high humidity drained us, **so** we had to rest a lot. (**So** is a connecting word.) Gardeners **sow** radish seeds early in the spring. (**Sow** means "to plant.")
sight, cite, site	He lost **sight** of the hills as the rain fell harder. (**Sight** is the ability to see.) Make sure you properly **cite** your sources in your report. (**Cite** means "to quote or refer to.") That's the **site** of the new stadium. (**Site** means "location or position.")
some, sum	Do you have **some** money? (**Some** means "an uncertain amount or part.") What's the **sum** of all your tips? (**Sum** means "the whole amount.")
son, sun	That man's **son** looks just like him. (A **son** is a male child.) Dark spots on the **sun** can affect our weather. (The **sun** is the center of Earth's solar system.)
sore, soar	Barry's arms were **sore** after his workout. (**Sore** means "painful.") The kite **soared** over the park. (**Soar** means "to fly or rise high into the air.")
stationery, stationary	I wrote a letter on my dad's business **stationery**. (**Stationery** is paper and envelopes for letters.) A **stationary** bike lets you pedal fast but go nowhere. (**Stationary** means "not movable or not moving.")
steal, steel	Did someone **steal** your hat? (**Steal** means "to take something without permission.") **Steel** beams form the skeletons of tall buildings. (**Steel** is a very strong metal.)

tail, tale	**I stepped on our cat's tail.** (*Tail* refers to the rear part.) **Stanley made up a wild tale to explain his late arrival.** (*Tale* refers to a story.)
than, then	**Today is colder than yesterday.** (*Than* is used in a comparison.) **I put on a thick ski jacket; then I was ready to walk to school.** (*Then* tells when.)
their, they're, there	**Have you seen their car?** (*Their* shows ownership.) **They're not parking it in the street.** (*They're* is a contraction for "they are.") **There it is—by the tree.** (*There* tells where.)
threw, through	**Tania threw the papers on the table.** (*Threw* is the past tense of the verb *throw*.) **She then rushed through the doorway.** (*Through* means "passing from one side to the other.")
to, too, two	**Patrice tossed the ball to Lamar.** (*To* is a preposition that can mean "in the direction of.") **He tried to score.** (*To* is also used to form an infinitive.) **However, his shot was too hard. Michelle missed, too.** (*Too* is an adverb meaning "very" or "also.") **They lost by two points.** (*Two* is a number.)
vain, vane, vein	**Wanting to look good doesn't necessarily mean you're vain.** (*Vain* means "thinking too highly of one's appearance or accomplishments." It can also mean "worthless.") **The weather vane was shaped like a horse.** (A *vane* is a flat piece of material set up to show which way the wind is blowing.) **The blood clot in his leg vein was painful.** **Mining the copper vein was costly.** (*Vein* refers to a blood vessel or to a mineral deposit.)

very, vary	Carmella's story was the **very** opposite of Marta's. (**Very** can be an adjective meaning "complete.") It was **very** funny. (**Very** can be an adverb meaning "extremely.") The details would **vary** each time they told their stories. (**Vary** is a verb meaning "to change.")
waist, waste	My dad has a 36-inch **waist**. (The **waist** is the part of the body just above the hips.) A mind is a terrible thing to **waste**. (The verb **waste** means "to wear away, decay" or "to spend or use carelessly"; the noun **waste** refers to useless material.)
wait, weight	Please **wait** for me. (**Wait** means "to stay somewhere expecting something.") Her **weight** varies from month to month. Sometimes she lifts **weights**. (**Weight** refers to a degree or unit of heaviness, or to a heavy object.)
ware, wear, where	She doesn't trust **wares** sold on TV infomercials. (**Ware** refers to a product that is sold.) Why do our teams **wear** such ugly uniforms? (**Wear** means "to have on or to carry on one's body.") I know **where** that is. (**Where** asks the question "in what place or situation?")
way, weigh	Do you know the **way** to the gym? (**Way** means "path or route.") That must **weigh** a ton. (**Weigh** means "to measure weight" or "to have a certain heaviness.")
weak, week	The bridge is too **weak** for the truck. (**Weak** means "not strong.") The bridge has been closed for a **week**. (A **week** is a period of seven days.)

weather, whether	**Do you like winter weather?** (***Weather*** refers to the condition of the atmosphere.) **They will go whether it rains or snows.** (***Whether*** refers to a possibility.)
which, witch	**Which book should I read next?** (***Which*** means "what one or ones out of a group.") **Not all witches ride broomsticks.** (A ***witch*** is someone using supernatural powers.)
who, which, that	**The man who called is a neighbor.** (***Who*** refers to people.) **The house, which no one wants to buy, is finally going to be torn down.** (***Which*** refers to nonliving objects or animals.) **The opossums that live in the attic will have to move.** (***That*** may refer to animals, people, or nonliving objects.)
who, whom	**Who called you last night?** (***Who*** is used as the subject in a sentence.) **To whom did you give the money?** (***Whom*** is used as the object of a preposition or as a direct object.)
who's, whose	**Who's going to the movie?** (***Who's*** is the contraction for "who is.") **Whose backpack is this?** (***Whose*** shows or asks about possession.)
wood, would	**A wood floor is hard to keep clean.** (***Wood*** is the material that trees are made of.) **Would you give me that map?** (***Would*** is a form of the verb *will*.)
your, you're	**Your essay is very funny, Cecily.** (***Your*** shows possession.) **You're writing with a lot of emotion.** (***You're*** is the contraction for "you are.")

Understanding Idioms

Idioms are phrases that are used in a special way. You can't understand an idiom just by knowing the meaning of each word in the phrase. You must learn it as a whole. For example, the idiom *bury the hatchet* means "to settle an argument," even though the individual words in the phrase mean something much different. This chapter will help you learn some of the common idioms in American English.

apple of his eye	Crown Ranch is the apple of his eye. (something he likes very much)
as plain as day	The mistake in the ad was as plain as day. (very clear)
as the crow flies	New London is 200 miles from here as the crow flies. (in a straight line)
at a snail's pace	My last hour at work passes at a snail's pace. (very, very slowly)
axe to grind	The manager has an axe to grind with that umpire. (disagreement to settle)
bad apple	There are no bad apples in this class. (a bad influence)
beat around the bush	Don't beat around the bush; answer the question. (avoid getting to the point)
benefit of the doubt	Everyone has been given the benefit of the doubt at least once. (another chance)
beyond the shadow of a doubt	Beyond the shadow of a doubt, this is my best science project. (for certain)
blew my top	When I saw the broken statue, I blew my top. (showed great anger)
bone to pick	Alison had a bone to pick with the student who copied her paper. (problem to settle)
brain drain	Brain drain is a serious problem in Bulgaria. (the best students moving elsewhere)

break the ice	The nervous ninth graders were afraid to break the ice. (start a conversation)
burn the midnight oil	Devon had to burn the midnight oil to finish his report. (work late into the night)
bury the hatchet	My sisters were told to bury the hatchet immediately. (settle an argument)
by the skin of her teeth	Anna avoided an accident by the skin of her teeth. (just barely)
champing at the bit	The skiers were champing at the bit to get on the slopes. (eager, excited)
chicken feed	The prize was chicken feed to some people. (not worth much money)
chip off the old block	Frank's just like his father. He's a chip off the old block. (just like someone else)
clean as a whistle	My boss told me to make sure the place was as clean as a whistle before I left. (very clean)
cold shoulder	I wanted to fit in with that group, but they gave me the cold shoulder. (ignored me)
crack of dawn	Ali delivers his papers at the crack of dawn. (first light of day, early morning)
cry wolf	If you cry wolf too often, no one will believe you. (say you are in trouble when you aren't)
dead of night	Hearing a loud noise in the dead of night frightened Bill. (middle of the night)
dirt cheap	A lot of clothes at that store are dirt cheap. (inexpensive, costing very little money)
doesn't hold a candle to	That award doesn't hold a candle to a gold medal. (is not as good as)
drop in the bucket	The contributions were a drop in the bucket. (a small amount compared to what's needed)

everything from A to Z	That catalog lists everything from A to Z. (a lot of different things)
face the music	Todd had to face the music when he broke the window. (deal with the punishment)
fish out of water	He felt like a fish out of water in the new math class. (someone in an unfamiliar place)
fit for a king	The food at the athletic banquet was fit for a king. (very special)
flew off the handle	Bill flew off the handle when he saw a reckless driver near the school. (became very angry)
floating on air	Celine was floating on air at the prom. (feeling very happy)
food for thought	The boys' foolish and dangerous prank gave us food for thought. (something to think about)
get down to business	After sharing several jokes, Mr. Sell said we should get down to business. (start working)
get the upper hand	The wrestler moved quickly on his opponent in order to get the upper hand. (gain the advantage)
give their all	Student volunteers give their all to help others. (work as hard as they can)
go fly a kite	Charlene stared at her nosy brother and said, "Go fly a kite." (go away)
has a green thumb	Talk to Mrs. Smith about your sick plant. She has a green thumb. (is good at growing plants)
has a heart of gold	Joe has a heart of gold. (is very kind and generous)
hit a home run	Rhonda hit a home run with her speech. (succeeded, or did well)
hit the ceiling	When my parents saw my grades, they hit the ceiling. (were very angry)

hit the hay	Exhausted from the hike, Jamal **hit the hay** without eating supper. (went to bed)
in a nutshell	Can you, **in a nutshell**, tell us your goals for this year? (in summary)
in one ear and out the other	Sharl, concerned about her pet, let the lecture go **in one ear and out the other**. (without really listening)
in the black	My aunt's gift shop is finally **in the black**. (making money)
in the nick of time	Janelle caught the falling vase **in the nick of time**. (just in time)
in the red	Many businesses start out **in the red**. (in debt)
in the same boat	The new tax bill meant everyone would be **in the same boat**. (in a similar situation)
iron out	Joe will meet with the work crew to **iron out** their complaints. (solve, work out)
it goes without saying	**It goes without saying** that saving money is a good idea. (it is clear)
it stands to reason	**It stands to reason** that your stamina will increase if you run every day. (it makes sense)
keep a stiff upper lip	**Keep a stiff upper lip** when you visit the doctor. (be brave)
keep it under your hat	**Keep it under your hat** about the pop quiz. (don't tell anyone)
knock on wood	My uncle **knocked on wood** after he said he had never had the flu. (did something for good luck)
knuckle down	After wasting half the day, we were told to **knuckle down**. (work hard)
learn the ropes	It takes every new employee a few months to **learn the ropes**. (get to know how things are done)

leave no stone unturned	The police plan to **leave no stone unturned** at the crime scene. (check everything)
lend someone a hand	You will feel good if you **lend someone a hand**. (help someone)
let's face it	**Let's face it.** You don't like rap. (let's admit it)
let the cat out of the bag	Tom **let the cat out of the bag** during lunch. (told a secret)
look high and low	We **looked high and low** for Jan's dog. (looked everywhere)
lose face	In some cultures, it is very distasteful to **lose face**. (be embarrassed)
needle in a haystack	Trying to find a person in New York is like trying to find a **needle in a haystack**. (something impossible to find)
nose to the grindstone	With all of these assignments, I have to keep my **nose to the grindstone**. (working hard)
on cloud nine	After talking to my girlfriend, I was **on cloud nine**. (feeling very happy)
on pins and needles	Nancy was **on pins and needles** during the championship game. (feeling nervous)
out the window	Once the rain started, our plans were **out the window**. (ruined)
over and above	**Over and above** the required work, Will cleaned up the lab. (in addition to)
pain in the neck	Franklin knew the report would be a **pain in the neck**. (very annoying)
pull your leg	Cary was only **pulling your leg**. (telling you a little lie as a joke)
put his foot in his mouth	Lane **put his foot in his mouth** when he answered the question. (said something embarrassing)

put the cart before the horse	Tonya put the cart before the horse when she sealed the envelope before inserting the letter. (did something in the wrong order)
put your best foot forward	When applying for a job, you should put your best foot forward. (do the best that you can do)
red-letter day	Sheila had a red-letter day because she did so well on her math test. (very good day)
rock the boat	I was told to keep quiet and not rock the boat. (cause trouble)
rude awakening	Jake will have a rude awakening when he sees the bill for his computer. (sudden, unpleasant surprise)
save face	His gift was clearly an attempt to save face. (fix an embarrassing situation)
see eye to eye	We see eye to eye about the need for a new school. (are in agreement)
shake a leg	I told Mako to shake a leg so that we wouldn't be late. (hurry)
shift into high gear	Greg had to shift into high gear to finish the test in time. (speed up, hurry)
sight for sore eyes	My grandmother's smiling face was a sight for sore eyes. (good to see)
sight unseen	Liz bought the coat sight unseen. (without seeing it first)
sink or swim	Whether you sink or swim in school depends on your study habits. (fail or succeed)
spilled the beans	Suddenly, Jose realized that he had spilled the beans. (revealed a secret)
spring chicken	Although Mr. Gordon isn't a spring chicken, he sure knows how to talk to kids. (young person)
stick to your guns	Know what you believe, and stick to your guns. (don't change your mind)

sweet tooth	Chocolate is often the candy of choice for those with a **sweet tooth**. (a love for sweets, like candy and cake)
take a dim view	My sister will **take a dim view** of that movie. (disapprove)
take it with a grain of salt	When you read that advertisement, **take it with a grain of salt**. (don't believe everything)
take the bull by the horns	It's time to **take the bull by the horns** so the project gets done on time. (take control)
through thick and thin	Those two girls have remained friends **through thick and thin**. (in good times and in bad times)
time flies	**Time flies** as you grow older. (time passes quickly)
time to kill	Grace had **time to kill**, so she read a book. (extra time)
to go overboard	The class was told not **to go overboard**. A $50.00 donation was fine. (to do too much)
toe the line	The new teacher made everyone **toe the line**. (follow the rules)
tongue-tied	He can talk easily with friends, but in class he is usually **tongue-tied**. (not knowing what to say)
turn over a new leaf	He decided to **turn over a new leaf** in school. (make a new start)
two peas in a pod	Ever since kindergarten, Lil and Eve have been like **two peas in a pod**. (very much alike)
under the weather	Guy was feeling **under the weather** this morning. (sick)
wallflower	Joan knew the other girls thought she was a **wallflower**. (a shy person)
word of mouth	Joseph learns a lot about his favorite team by **word of mouth**. (talking with other people)

Understanding Sentences

A **sentence** is made up of one or more words that express a complete thought. A sentence begins with a capital letter, and it ends with a period, a question mark, or an exclamation point.

> **My report is five pages long.**
>
> **What were you doing?**
>
> **Come here immediately!**

✳ For more information, turn to "Writing Basic Sentences," pages 83-90.

PARTS OF A SENTENCE

Subject and Predicate	A sentence must have both a subject and a predicate. The subject is the part of a sentence about which something is said. The predicate—which contains the verb—is the part of the sentence that says something about the subject. **The new Web site looks great.** (In this sentence, *The new Web site* is the subject, and *looks great* is the predicate.)
Understood Subject and Predicate	The subject, the predicate, or both may be "missing" from a sentence, but they must be clearly understood. **Put this over there.** (The subject, *you,* is unstated or understood.) **Who likes ice cream? Everyone.** (In the second sentence, *everyone* is the subject, but the predicate is unstated. *Does* is the understood predicate.) **What do I like about track meets? The relays.** (In the second sentence, both the subject and the verb are unstated. *I* is the understood subject, and *like* is the understood verb.)
Delayed Subject	In sentences that begin with *there* followed by a form of the "be" verb, the subject comes after the verb. The subject is also often delayed in questions. **There was a strange coat in my locker.** (The subject is *coat*; the verb is *was.*) **Where are my gloves?** (The subject is *gloves*; the verb is *are.*)

Subject

A **subject** is the part of a sentence that does something or is talked about. The subject can be a noun, a pronoun, or an infinitive phrase. A clause may also function as a noun.

Wolves howl. (noun)

They howl for different reasons. (pronoun)

To establish their turf may be one reason. (infinitive phrase)

That wolves and dogs are similar is obvious. (noun clause)

Simple Subject

The simple subject is the subject without the words that describe or modify it.

The best years of his life were spent in college.

Complete Subject

The complete subject is the simple subject and all the words that describe it.

The best years of his life were spent in college.

Compound Subject

A compound subject has two or more simple subjects.

Bernie Mac and Cedric are my two favorite comedians.

Predicate

A **predicate**, which contains the verb, is the part of the sentence that shows action or talks about the subject.

Musicians should practice regularly.

Simple Predicate

The simple predicate is the verb without the words that modify or complete it.

Mr. Jefferson understood the problem.

Complete Predicate

The complete predicate is the simple predicate with all the words that modify or complete it.

Mr. Jefferson understood the problem.

Compound Predicate

A compound predicate has two or more simple predicates, or verbs.

Alex looked at me and then turned away.

Modifiers

A **modifier** is a word or a group of words that describes another word.

> The flashing **lights distracted** some **people.**
> (*The* and *flashing* modify *lights*, and *some* modifies *people*.)

> **People cheered** wildly **after** the final **song.**
> (*Wildly* modifies *cheered*, and *the* and *final* modify *song*.)

Clauses

A **clause** is a group of words that has a subject and a predicate.

> **the referees discussed the play**
> (*Referees* is the subject, and *discussed* is the simple predicate in this clause.)

> **before they counted the basket**
> (*They* is the subject, and *counted* is the simple predicate in this clause.)

Independent Clauses

An independent clause expresses a complete thought and can stand alone as a sentence.

> **The referees discussed the play.**

Dependent Clauses

A dependent clause does not express a complete thought and cannot stand alone as a sentence. Dependent clauses usually begin with a subordinating conjunction like *before*. (See page 471.)

> **before they counted the basket**

 Some dependent clauses begin with relative pronouns like *who* or *that*. (See page 454.)

> **that won the game**

 An **independent clause** plus a **dependent clause** forms a complex sentence:

> **The referees discussed the play before they counted the basket.**

Phrases

A **phrase** is a group of related words that, unlike a clause, does not have a subject and a predicate. Phrases do not express complete thoughts, so they are not sentences.

> **the wet, heavy snow** (This is a noun phrase.)
>
> **has been falling** (This is a verb phrase.)
>
> **for three hours** (This is a prepositional phrase. See page 470.)

✳ If you put these phrases together, they would form a complete sentence:

> **The wet, heavy snow has been falling for three hours.**

BASIC PHRASES

Phrases are named by how they are used in a sentence.

Noun Phrase: the Olympics

Verb Phrase: began 3,000 years ago

Prepositional Phrase: in Greece

Verbal Phrases

A verbal phrase is a group of words introduced by a *verbal* (a verb used as another part of speech). There are three types of verbals: *gerunds, participles,* and *infinitives*. (See page 463.)

> **Finding the earring was not easy.**
> (*Finding the earring* is a gerund phrase, and it serves as the subject of the sentence.)

> **Looking at the bus schedule, we realized we would be late.**
> (*Looking at the bus schedule* is a participial phrase modifying the pronoun *we*.)

> **Please listen carefully to hear the chord change.**
> (*To hear the chord change* is an infinitive phrase, and it serves as an adverb modifying *listen*.)

TYPES OF SENTENCES

Simple Sentences	A simple sentence includes only one independent clause (and states only one complete thought). The subject may be simple or compound. The predicate may also be simple or compound.

> **My back aches**.
> (simple subject, simple predicate)
>
> **Boxing and wrestling are my least favorite sports**.
> (compound subject, simple predicate)
>
> **The pass receiver caught the ball and scored a touchdown**.
> (simple subject, compound predicate)

Compound Sentences	A compound sentence is made up of two or more simple sentences (also called independent clauses). The two sentences must be joined by a coordinating conjunction, punctuation, or both. (Coordinating conjunctions include words like *and, but,* and *or*. See page 471.)

> **Gerard has a job at the supermarket, and his brother works at a restaurant**.
> (A comma plus the conjunction *and* connects the two independent clauses in this compound sentence.)
>
> **Reney wanted to talk to her advisor, but he was not in his office**.
> (The comma plus the conjunction *but* connects the two independent clauses in this compound sentence.)

Complex Sentences	A complex sentence contains one independent clause (in **boldface**) and one or more dependent clauses (in red). Dependent clauses begin with a subordinating conjunction like *when* or a relative pronoun like *who* or *that*.

> **Chanel never seems embarrassed when she makes a mistake**.

KINDS OF SENTENCES

Declarative Sentences	Declarative sentences make statements. They tell something about a person, a place, a thing, or an idea. **January is usually the warmest month in the Southern Hemisphere.**
Interrogative Sentences	Interrogative sentences ask questions. **Why is there air?**
Tag Questions	Tag questions are questions that are tagged, or added, to the end of statements. The main verb in the statement is either positive (for example, *was*) or negative (*wasn't*). The verb in the "tag" is usually the opposite of the main verb. Tag question: **That was a great concert, wasn't it?** Answer: **Yes, it was.** (or) **No, it wasn't.** Tag question: **That last basket didn't count, did it?** Answer: **Yes, it did.** (or) **No, it didn't.**
Imperative Sentences	Imperative sentences give commands. They often contain an understood subject (*you*). **Think about all of the good times we've had.** **Check out this CD.**
Exclamatory Sentences	Exclamatory sentences communicate strong emotion or surprise. **It would be great to see you again!** **I won a gold medal!**

The Parts of Speech

In the English language there are eight parts of speech. They help you understand words and how to use them in sentences. Every word in every sentence is a part of speech—a noun, a verb, an adjective, and so forth. The chart below lists the **eight parts of speech**.

Nouns	Words that name people, places, things, or ideas **Jackie Robinson Peru locker freedom**
Pronouns	Words used in place of nouns **she me it they you everyone who**
Verbs	Words that show action or link a subject to another word in the sentence **scream pull find is were**
Adjectives	Words that describe nouns or pronouns **red heavy snowy warm beautiful**
Adverbs	Words that describe verbs, adjectives, and other adverbs **badly yesterday then quickly brightly**
Interjections	Words (set off by commas or exclamation points) that show strong emotions **Wait!** **Hurry,** give me the bandages!
Prepositions	Words that show position or direction and introduce prepositional phrases **of from for among into down**
Conjunctions	Words that connect other words or groups of words **but and nor yet unless**

NOUNS

A **noun** is a word that names a person, a place, a thing, or an idea.

PERSON:	Denzel Washington	actor
PLACE:	Arizona	state
THING:	peregrine falcon	bird
IDEA:	Veteran's Day	holiday

❋ An article—*a, an,* or *the*—oft en comes before a noun.

a sofa   an eye   the car

❋ A possessive pronoun can also come before a noun.

your paper   their shoes

Kinds of Nouns

Common Nouns	A common noun is any noun that does not name a specific person, place, thing, or idea. Common nouns are not capitalized. **woman card thought lake**
Proper Nouns	A proper noun names a specific person, place, thing, or idea. Proper nouns are capitalized. **Geraldo Jamaica Nintendo Christianity**
Concrete Nouns	A concrete noun names a thing that can be seen or touched. Concrete nouns are either common or proper. **street city building** **Fifth Avenue Portland White House**
Abstract Nouns	An abstract noun names something that you can think about but cannot see or touch. Abstract nouns can be either common or proper. **hope February confusion** **happiness Tuesday religion**

Number of Nouns

Singular or Plural	The number of a noun tells you whether the noun refers to one thing *(singular)* or more than one thing *(plural)*.
Singular Nouns	A singular noun names one person, place, thing, or idea. **room bully apple child**
Plural Nouns	A plural noun names more than one person, place, thing, or idea. **rooms bullies apples children** ✳ (See page 403 for the spelling of irregular plurals like *children*.)

Special Types of Nouns

Compound Nouns	A compound noun is made up of two or more words. **gearshift** (written as one word) **mug shot** (written as two words) **baby-sitter** (written as a hyphenated word)
Collective Nouns	A collective noun names a collection of persons, animals, places, or things. **PERSONS** **club tribe choir platoon family** **ANIMALS** **herd flock litter pack school** **PLACES** **Rocky Mountains United States** **THINGS** **cluster set mass**
Specific Nouns	Specific nouns make your writing come alive. ✳ See page 132 in "Writing with Style."

Count and Noncount Nouns

Count Nouns	Count nouns are nouns that can have *a, an,* or a number (*one, two, three,* and so forth) in front of them.

SINGULAR

a boot   an exercise   one minister

To make the plural of most count nouns, add *s* or *es* to the noun.

PLURAL

two boots   a few exercises   some ministers

Noncount Nouns	Noncount nouns can have neither *a, an,* or *one* nor a number word (*one, two, three,* and so forth) in front of them. They have no plural form.

luggage   flour   weather   clothes

✳ Some nouns can be count or noncount.

hair   light   paper   chicken

Noncount Weather Nouns	Many weather terms are noncount nouns.

rain   sleet   hail
snow   dew   lightning

Noncount Abstract Nouns	Many abstract nouns are noncount nouns. (Abstract nouns, name ideas rather than people, places, or things.

health   fun   laughter   coverage

Incorrect: I have a lot of funs.
Correct: I have a lot of fun.

Noncount Collective Nouns	The name of a whole category or group may be a noncount noun. But the parts of the category may be count nouns.

CATEGORY	PARTS		
furniture	bed	dresser	mirror
money	nickel	dime	

Gender of Nouns

Nouns can be categorized according to gender: feminine *(female)*, masculine *(male)*, neuter *(neither male nor female)*, or indefinite *(male or female)*.

<u>FEMININE</u> (female)

doe   mare   sister   niece   girl

<u>MASCULINE</u> (male)

buck   stallion   brother   nephew   boy

<u>NEUTER</u> (neither male nor female)

stick   dust   window

<u>INDEFINITE</u> (male or female)

student   teacher   doctor   cousin

Uses of Nouns

Subject Nouns

A noun may be the subject of a sentence. The subject is the part of the sentence that does something or is being talked about.

Jayleen **loves softball.**

Predicate Nouns

A predicate noun—also called a *predicate nominative*—follows a form of the *be* verb (*is, are, was, were*) and renames the subject.

Jayleen is a good player.

(*Player* is a predicate noun because it renames *Jayleen.*)

Possessive Nouns

A possessive noun shows ownership. An apostrophe is used with possessive nouns.

Jayleen's glove is expensive.

Object Nouns

An object noun is used as a direct object, an indirect object, or the object of a preposition.

Jayleen throws the ball **to the** catcher.

(*Ball* is the direct object; *catcher* is the object of the preposition *to.*)

PRONOUNS

A **pronoun** is a word that is used in place of a noun.

Victor lived with his grandmother.

(The pronoun *his* is used in place of the noun *Victor's.*)

Antecedents

An antecedent is the noun that a pronoun refers to or replaces. All pronouns have antecedents.

Jamal went to the store for his mother. Unfortunately, he forgot the list. (*Jamal* is the antecedent of the pronouns *his* and *he.*)

 Pronouns must *agree* with their antecedents. When the antecedent is singular, the pronoun that refers to it must also be singular. When the antecedent is plural, the pronoun that refers to it must be plural. (See page 89.)

Personal Pronouns

Personal pronouns are the most common pronouns. Here are some common personal pronouns: (Also see page 452.)

   I you he she it we they me him her

Number of Pronouns

Singular or Plural

Pronouns can be either singular or plural.

SINGULAR

Mike and I went to the game.

   I me you he she him her it

PLURAL

Mr. Edge put us into groups.

   we us you they them

 The pronouns *you, your,* and *yours* may be singular or plural.

Person of Pronouns

First Person	A first-person pronoun is used in place of the speaker. **I** bought pizza for my friends. **We** ate the pizza during the game.
Second Person	A second-person pronoun is used to name the person or thing spoken to. Gomez, did **you** feel the earthquake? Do **you** know who I am?
Third Person	A third-person pronoun is used to name the person or thing spoken about. **She** won't do that anymore. **It** was a very cold day. Sue bought **them** candy.

Personal Pronouns

SINGULAR PRONOUNS

	Subject Pronouns	Possessive Pronouns	Object Pronouns
First Person	I	my, mine	me
Second Person	you	your, yours	you
Third Person	he, she, it	his, her, hers, its	him, her, it

PLURAL PRONOUNS

	Subject Pronouns	Possessive Pronouns	Object Pronouns
First Person	we	our, ours	us
Second Person	you	your, yours	you
Third Person	they	their, theirs	them

 My, your, our, its, and *their* come before nouns and function as possessive adjectives. Other pronouns such as *his* or *her* may or may not come before nouns.

Uses of Pronouns

Subject Pronouns

A subject pronoun is used as the subject of a sentence.

He was only four years old.

(The pronoun *he* is the subject of this sentence.)

A subject pronoun is also used after a form of the *be* verb (*am, is, are, was, were,* and so forth). A subject pronoun in this position is called a predicate nominative.

I am he.

(The pronoun *he* is a predicate nominative in this sentence.)

Possessive Pronouns

A possessive pronoun shows ownership. (See page 452.) An apostrophe is not used with a possessive pronoun.

Where are your gloves?

Their main concern was safety.

The car is missing its spare tire.

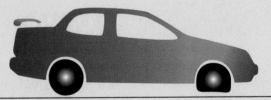

Object Pronouns

An object pronoun is used after an action verb or in a prepositional phrase.

Professional wrestling interests me.

(The pronoun *me* is a direct object.)

Why did you do that to them?

(The pronoun *them* is the object of the preposition *to.*)

Please give her some help.

(*Her* is an indirect object because it names the person *to whom* help will be given.)

Other Types of Pronouns

Relative Pronouns	A relative pronoun connects a dependent clause to the independent clause. (See page 442.) **Kail Johnson, who was our class president, moved to Brazil.**
Reflexive Pronouns	A reflexive pronoun refers back to the subject of a sentence. **George Washington Carver devoted himself to studying the peanut.**
Interrogative Pronouns	An interrogative pronoun asks a question. **Who has a date for the dance?**
Demonstrative Pronouns	A demonstrative pronoun points out a noun without naming the noun. **That is a long hallway.**
Indefinite Pronouns	An indefinite pronoun refers to people or things that are not named or known. **Someone painted the gym.**

TYPES OF PRONOUNS

Relative
who, whose, which, what, that, whoever, whatever, whichever

Reflexive
myself, himself, herself, itself, yourself, themselves, ourselves

Interrogative
who, whose, whom, which, what

Demonstrative
this, that, these, those

Indefinite

all	both	everything	nobody	several
another	each	few	none	some
any	each one	many	no one	somebody
anybody	either	most	nothing	someone
anyone	everybody	much	one	something
anything	everyone	neither	other	such

VERBS

A **verb** shows action or links the subject to another word in the sentence. The verb is always the main word in the predicate part of the sentence.

Booker T. Washington worked in a salt mine.
(*Worked* is an action verb.)

He was an African American.
(*Was* is a linking verb.)

Types of Verbs

Action Verbs

An action verb tells what the subject is doing.

Booker attended school.

Linking Verbs

A linking verb links a subject to a noun or an adjective in the predicate part of the sentence.

Booker became a teacher.
(The verb *became* links the noun *teacher* to the subject *Booker.*)

LINKING VERBS

**is are was were am been being smell
look taste feel appear seem become**

Helping Verbs

Helping verbs (also called auxiliary verbs) include *has, had,* and *have; do, does,* and *did;* and forms of the verb *be* (*is, are, was, were*). See the chart below.

Washington had worked so he could learn.
(The verb *had* helps state a past action: *had worked.*)

BE VERBS					
Present		Past		Future	
singular	plural	singular	plural	singular	plural
I am	we are	I was	we were	I will be	we will be
you are	you are	you were	you were	you will be	you will be
he, she, it is	they are	he, she, it was	they were	he, she, it will be	they will be

Modal Verbs	Modal verbs help the main verb express meaning. (See the chart below.) **Booker T. Washington could live simply.** (The modal *could* helps express the meaning of the main verb *live*.) Modal verbs are sometimes grouped with helping verbs as in the chart below.

COMMON MODAL VERBS

Modal	Expresses	Sample Sentence
can	*ability*	I **can** carry that easily.
could	*ability* *possibility*	He **could** baby-sit Tuesday. Bernice **could** be sick.
might	*possibility*	They **might** be early.
may	*possibility* *request*	She **may** sleep late Saturday. **May** I be excused?
must	*strong need*	You **must** study more.
have to	*strong need*	I **have to** exercise.
have got to	*strong need*	You **have got to** be home for supper.
ought to	*feeling of duty*	Lucius **ought to** see a dentist.
will	*intent*	I **will** finish that after supper.
would	*desire*	Rafael **would** like to take the train.
would + you	*polite request*	**Would you** help me?
could + you	*polite request*	**Could you** hand me that?
will + you	*polite request*	**Will you** give me a ride?
can + you	*polite request*	**Can you** make supper tonight?

Tenses of Verbs

The time of a verb is called its **tense.** Tense is shown by endings *(talked)*, by helping verbs *(did talk)*, or by both *(have talked)*.

Present Tense	The present tense of a verb states an action that is happening now or that happens regularly. **Today, we** honor **Booker's work.** **He** serves **as an inspiration for all of us.**
Past Tense	The past tense of a verb states an action that happened at a specific time in the past. **Booker** founded **Tuskegee Institute in Alabama.** **He** died **at age 59.**
Future Tense	The future tense of a verb states an action that will take place in the future. **I** will write **my report on Saturday.**

Perfect Tenses

Present Perfect Tense	The present perfect tense states an action that *is still going on.* Add *has* or *have* before the past form of the main verb. (The past participle is the part of the verb used with *has, have,* or *had.* See pages 460-461) **I** have **always** enjoyed **action movies.**
Past Perfect Tense	The past perfect tense states an action that *began and was completed* in the past. To use this tense, add *had* before the past participle form of the main verb. **He** had worked **on Saturday.**
Future Perfect Tense	The future perfect tense states an action that *will begin in the future and end at a specific time in the future.* Add *will have* before the past participle form of the main verb. **Rosa** will have practiced **for three hours.**

Continuous Tenses

Present Continuous Tense	The present continuous tense states an action that *is not finished at the time of stating it.* Here's how you form this tense:

the helping verb + the *ing* form
am, is, or *are*   of the main verb

am   **learning**

I am learning about the U.S. Constitution.

Past Continuous Tense	The past continuous tense states an action that *was happening at a certain time in the past.* It can also refer to an event that took place for a limited time. Here's how you form this tense:

the helping verb + the *ing* form
was or *were*   of the main verb

was   **learning**

I was learning about the Articles of Confederation last week.

Future Continuous Tense	The future continuous tense states an action that *will take place at a specific time in the future.* Here's how you form this tense:

will + the helping verb + the *ing* form
be   of the main verb

will   **be**   **studying**

Next week, I will be studying more about our country.

OR

phrase noting + the helping verb + the *ing* form
the future   *be*   of the main verb

am going to   **be**   **learning**

I am going to be learning about making laws.

Forms of Verbs

Singular and Plural Verbs	A singular verb is used when the subject in a sentence is singular. **The Constitution interests many people.** (The subject *Constitution* and the verb *interests* are both singular.) A plural verb is used when the subject is plural. **Citizens want a good economy.** (The subject *citizens* and the verb *want* are both plural.)
Active and Passive Voice	A verb is active if the subject is doing the action. **Congress made laws to protect us.** (The verb *made* is active because the subject *Congress* is doing the action.) A verb is passive if the subject is not doing the action. **Laws were made by Congress.** (The verb *were made* is passive because the subject *laws* is not doing the action.)
Regular Verbs	Most verbs in the English language are regular. You add *ed* to regular verbs when you state a past action or use *has, have,* or *had* with the verb. **REGULAR VERBS** **She jumps. Earlier she jumped. She has jumped.** **I laugh. Earlier I laughed. I have laughed.**
Irregular Verbs	Some verbs in the English language are irregular. (Their spelling is different in each tense.) Usually you do not add *ed* to an irregular verb when you state a past action or use *has, have,* or *had* with the verb. Instead of adding *ed*, the word changes. (See the chart on pages 460-461.) **IRREGULAR VERBS** **I write. Earlier I wrote. I have written.** **She sees. Earlier she saw. She has seen.**

COMMON IRREGULAR VERBS

The **principal parts** of the common irregular verbs are listed below. The part used with *has, have,* or *had* is called the **past participle.**

PRESENT TENSE	I draw.
PAST TENSE	Earlier I drew.
PAST PARTICIPLE	I have drawn.
PRESENT TENSE	She eats.
PAST TENSE	Earlier she ate.
PAST PARTICIPLE	She has eaten.

Present Tense	Past Tense	Past Participle	Present Tense	Past Tense	Past Participle
be (am, is, are)	was, were	been	eat	ate	eaten
begin	began	begun	fall	fell	fallen
bite	bit	bitten	feel	felt	felt
blow	blew	blown	fight	fought	fought
break	broke	broken	find	found	found
bring	brought	brought	flee	fled	fled
build	built	built	fly	flew	flown
burst	burst	burst	freeze	froze	frozen
buy	bought	bought	get	got	got, gotten
catch	caught	caught	give	gave	given
choose	chose	chosen	go	went	gone
come	came	come	grow	grew	grown
cost	cost	cost	hang (execute)	hanged	hanged
cut	cut	cut	hang (suspend)	hung	hung
dive	dove, dived	dived	hide	hid	hidden
do	did	done	hit	hit	hit
draw	drew	drawn	hold	held	held
drink	drank	drunk	hurt	hurt	hurt
drive	drove	driven			

COMMON IRREGULAR VERBS

Present Tense	Past Tense	Past Participle	Present Tense	Past Tense	Past Participle
keep	kept	kept	shrink	shrank	shrunk
know	knew	known	sing	sang	sung
lay (place)	laid	laid	sink	sank	sunk
lead	led	led	sit	sat	sat
leave	left	left	speak	spoke	spoken
lend	lent	lent	spend	spent	spent
let	let	let	spin	spun	spun
lie (deceive)	lied	lied	spread	spread	spread
lie (recline)	lay	lain	spring	sprang	sprung
lose	lost	lost	stand	stood	stood
make	made	made	steal	stole	stolen
meet	met	met	swear	swore	sworn
pay	paid	paid	swim	swam	swum
put	put	put	swing	swung	swung
raise	raised	raised	take	took	taken
read	read	read	teach	taught	taught
ride	rode	ridden	tear	tore	torn
ring	rang	rung	tell	told	told
rise	rose	risen	think	thought	thought
run	ran	run	throw	threw	thrown
say	said	said	wake	woke, waked	woken, waked
see	saw	seen			
sell	sold	sold	wear	wore	worn
send	sent	sent	weave	wove	woven
set	set	set	win	won	won
shake	shook	shaken	write	wrote	written
shine (light)	shone	shone			
show	showed	shown			

Uses of Action Verbs

Transitive Verbs	A verb is transitive if it is followed by an object (*noun* or *pronoun*). The object makes the meaning of the verb complete.
	Joe Sullivan raised money for schools. (Without the object *money*, the meaning of the transitive verb *raised* would be incomplete.)
	He also started a food pantry for the poor. (Without the object *pantry*, the meaning of the transitive verb *started* would be incomplete.)
Followed by a Direct Object	A direct object receives the action of a transitive verb. The direct object answers the question *what?* or *whom?* after the verb.
	Bianca helped many children. (The noun *children* is a direct object. It answers the question *helped whom?*)
	The class read the book. (The noun *book* is a direct object. It answers the question *read what?*)
Followed by an Indirect Object	An indirect object receives the action of a transitive verb, indirectly. An indirect object names the object or person *to whom* or *for whom* something is done.
	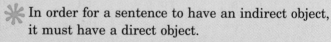 In order for a sentence to have an indirect object, it must have a direct object.
	Our teacher gave Thomas four reports. (*Thomas* is an indirect object because *Thomas* names the person *to whom* the reports were given. *Reports* is the direct object in the sentence.)
	Thomas sent his cousin the reports. (*Cousin* is an indirect object because *cousin* names the person *to whom* the reports were sent. *Reports* is the direct object in the sentence.)

More Uses of Action Verbs

Intransitive Verbs	An intransitive verb does not need an object to make its meaning complete. **World War I began in 1914.** (*Began* is intransitive because there is no direct object following it. The date *1914* is the object of the preposition *in*.)
Special Verbs	Some verbs can be transitive or intransitive. **We do math problems in class.** (The direct object *problems* receives the action of the transitive verb *do*.) **Nick does well in math.** (There is no direct object in this sentence, so the verb *does* is intransitive.)

Verbals

	Verbals are words that are made from verbs but are used as other parts of speech.
Gerund	A gerund is a verb form that ends in *ing* and is used as a noun. **Sleeping in class is not wise.** (The gerund *sleeping* serves as the subject in this sentence.)
Participle	A participle is a verb form that ends in *ing* or *ed*. A participle is used as an adjective. **Sleeping students usually don't hear well.** (The participle *sleeping* modifies the noun *students*.)
Infinitive	An infinitive is a verb form introduced by the word *to*. It is used as a noun, an adjective, or an adverb. **Do you want to sleep on the sofa?** (The infinitive *to sleep* is used as a noun and serves as a direct object.)

COMMON TWO-WORD VERBS

This chart lists verbs in which two words work together to express a specific action.

break down	to take apart or fall apart
call off	cancel
call up	make a phone call
clear out	leave a place quickly
cross out	draw a line through
figure out	find a solution
fill in/out	complete a form or an application
fill up	fill a container or tank
find out	discover
get in	enter a vehicle
get out of	leave a car, a house, or a situation
get over	recover from a sickness or a problem
give back	return something
give in/up	surrender or quit
hand in	give homework to a teacher
hand out	give someone something
hang up	put down a phone receiver
leave out	omit or don't use
let in/out	allow someone or something to enter or leave
look up	find information
pay back	return money or a favor
pick out	choose
point out	call attention to
put away	return something to its proper place
put down	place something on a table, the floor, etc.
put off	delay doing something
shut off	turn off a machine or light
take part	participate
talk over	discuss
think over	consider carefully
try on	put on clothing to see if it fits
turn down	lower the volume
turn up	raise the volume
write down	write on a piece of paper

✳ It is best not to divide a two-word verb in a sentence. For example, write "I *handed out* the papers," not "I *handed* the papers *out*."

ADJECTIVES

Adjectives are words that modify nouns or pronouns.

brilliant **musician**   full **moon**

- Adjectives tell what kind, how many, or which one.

  vast **universe**   six **continents**   this **one**

- In English, adjectives usually come *before* the words they describe.

  narrow **streets**   fast **cars**

- In English, adjectives are never plural—even when the nouns they describe are plural.

  blue **diamonds**   small **feet**   strong **hands**

Articles

A, an, and *the* are special adjectives called articles. The article *the* can come before singular or plural words.

the **hydrant**   the **windows**   the **fourth planet**

The article *a* comes before singular words that begin with consonant sounds or before singular words that begin with the long *u* sound.

a **green beret**

a **historic event**

a **unique combination**

The article *an* comes before singular words that begin with vowel sounds, except for the long *u* sound.

an **ear**   an **unusual hair color**   an **egg**

Proper Adjectives

Proper adjectives are formed from proper nouns. Proper adjectives are usually capitalized.

The African continent is the second largest in the world.

Common Adjectives

Common adjectives are any adjectives that are not proper. They are usually not capitalized.

Carol won four medals in local meets.

Special Kinds of Adjectives

Compound Adjectives	Compound adjectives are made up of more than one word. Some compound adjectives are spelled as one word; others are hyphenated. **His car has a low-powered engine.** **This model enjoys worldwide popularity.**
Demonstrative Adjectives	Demonstrative adjectives point out specific nouns. For example, *this* and *these* point out nouns that are nearby, and *that* and *those* point out nouns that are distant. **This desk is neater than that desk.** **Those windows are cleaner than these windows.** ✳ When *this, that, these,* and *those* do not come before nouns, they are pronouns, *not* adjectives.
Indefinite Adjectives	Indefinite adjectives tell *approximately* (not exactly) how many or how much. **Most people keep their cars for a few years. Some individuals drive the same car for many years. Few people can afford a new car every year.**
Predicate Adjectives	Predicate adjectives follow linking verbs and describe subjects. **This school is huge.** (*Huge* describes the subject *school. Huge* follows the linking verb *is.*) **It looks square from a distance.** (*Square* describes the subject *it. Square* follows the linking verb *looks.*) **The warehouse appears tiny and empty next to the school.** (*Tiny* and *empty* describe the subject *warehouse.* These two adjectives follow the linking verb *appears.*)

Forms of Adjectives

Positive Adjectives	The positive or base form of an adjective describes a noun without comparing it to another noun. **The Empire State Building is tall.** **The video was helpful.**
Comparative Adjectives	The comparative form of an adjective compares two people, places, things, or ideas. **The Sears Tower is taller than the Empire State Building.** (The ending *er* is added to one-syllable adjectives.) **The demonstration was more helpful than the video.** (The word *more* is usually added before adjectives with two or more syllables.)
Superlative Adjectives	The superlative form of an adjective compares three or more people, places, things, or ideas. **Asia is the largest continent on earth.** (The ending *est* is added to one-syllable adjectives.) **Ramon is the most interesting person I know.** (The word *most* is usually added before adjectives with two or more syllables.)
Two-Syllable Adjectives	Some adjectives that are two syllables long show comparisons either by their *er/est* endings or by using the words *more* and *most*. happy happier happiest happy more happy most happy

SPECIAL FORMS OF ADJECTIVES

Positive	Comparative	Superlative
good	better	best
bad	worse	worst
many	more	most
little	less	least

✳ Do not use *more* or *most* with forms of *good* and *bad*.

ADVERBS

Adverbs are words that modify verbs, adjectives, or other adverbs.

> **Michael sneezed loudly.**
> (*Loudly* modifies the verb *sneezed.*)
>
> **It was intensely cold.**
> (*Intensely* modifies the adjective *cold.*)
>
> **We walked rather quickly.**
> (*Rather* modifies the adverb *quickly.*)

✳ In English, adverbs can come before or after the words they modify.

> **The new student speaks slowly.**
> (*Slowly* modifies the verb *speaks.*)
>
> **The coach loudly called my name.**
> (*Loudly* modifies the verb *called.*)

Types of Adverbs

Adverbs of Time	Adverbs of time tell *when, how often,* or *how long.* **I knew I would never attend another concert, even though I often had the opportunity.**
Adverbs of Place	Adverbs of place tell *where, to where,* or *from where.* **After walking outside, he turned left.**
Adverbs of Manner	Adverbs of manner tell *how* something is done. **How precisely do you need this cut? You played that piece well.**
Adverbs of Degree	Adverbs of degree tell *how much* or *how little.* **Was she partly at fault?**

Forms of Adverbs

Positive Adverbs	In the positive or base form, an adverb does not make a comparison. My brother talks fast. Your bicycle rides smoothly.
Comparative Adverbs	The comparative is formed by adding *er* to one-syllable adverbs or the word *more* or *less* before longer adverbs. My brother talks faster than my sister. Your bike rides more smoothly than mine.
Superlative Adverbs	The superlative is formed by adding *est* to one-syllable adverbs or the word *most* or *least* before longer adverbs. My brother talks fastest when he's excited. Your bike runs most smoothly when it's tuned up.

SPECIAL FORMS OF ADVERBS

Positive	Comparative	Superlative
well	better	best
badly	worse	worst
quickly	more quickly	most quickly
fairly	less fairly	least fairly

 Do not confuse *well* and *good*. (See page 421.)

INTERJECTIONS

Interjections are words or phrases that express strong emotions. Commas or exclamation marks separate interjections from the rest of the sentence.

Oh, no! The TV broke.

Wow, that's a bright shirt!

PREPOSITIONS

Prepositions are words that show position or direction and introduce prepositional phrases.

Let's all go to the concert. (The preposition *to* shows direction and introduces the prepositional phrase *to the concert.*)

Prepositional Phrases

A prepositional phrase includes a preposition, the object of the preposition (a noun or a pronoun), and any words that modify the object.

Jimmy slid underneath the ancient truck.
(*Underneath* is a preposition; *truck* is the object of the preposition; *the* and *ancient* modify the object.)

 Prepositional phrases are used as adjectives or adverbs.

Most people run away from trouble.
(The prepositional phrase *away from trouble* is used as an adverb modifying the verb *run.*)

The top of the spine supports the skull.
(The prepositional phrase *of the spine* is used as an adjective modifying the noun *top.*)

COMMON PREPOSITIONS

aboard	away from	except	near	through
about	because of	except for	of	throughout
above	before	for	off	till
according to	behind	from	on	to
across	below	from between	on top of	together
across from	beneath	from under	onto	toward
after	beside	in	opposite	under
against	besides	in addition to	out	underneath
along	between	in back of	out of	until
along with	beyond	in place of	outside	up
alongside	but	in regard to	outside of	up to
alongside of	by	in spite of	over	upon
among	concerning	inside	over to	with
apart from	considering	inside of	past	within
around	despite	instead of	prior to	without
aside from	down	into	regarding	
at	during	like	since	

CONJUNCTIONS

Conjunctions connect individual words or groups of words. (See the chart below.)

My aunt and uncle live in Cleveland.

Do you want this one or that one?

Kinds of Conjunctions

Coordinating Conjunctions

A coordinating conjunction connects equal parts: two or more words, phrases, or clauses.

Toya wanted to be first in line, but she overslept.

(The conjunction *but* connects two independent clauses to make a compound sentence.)

Correlative Conjunctions

Correlative conjunctions are used in pairs.

Neither the rain nor the darkness depressed him. (*Neither* and *nor* work as a pair in this sentence to connect two words.)

Subordinating Conjunctions

A subordinating conjunction introduces the dependent clause in a complex sentence. (See page 444.)

The desert climate is considered harsh because it is so hot and dry.

COMMON CONJUNCTIONS

Coordinating   and, but, or, nor, for, so, yet

Correlative   either/or, neither/nor, not only/but also, both/and, whether/or, as/so

Subordinating   after, although, as, as if, as long as, as though, because, before, if, in order that, since, so, so that, though, unless, until, when, where, whereas, while

 Relative pronouns can also connect clauses. (See page 454.)

Student
Almanac

Language

Science

Mathematics

Computers

Geography

Government

History

Language

The language lists in this section of your handbook should be both interesting and helpful. You can look through this section when you want to work on your handwriting, study traffic signs, or send a "signed" message across a noisy room.

Manual Alphabet (Sign Language)

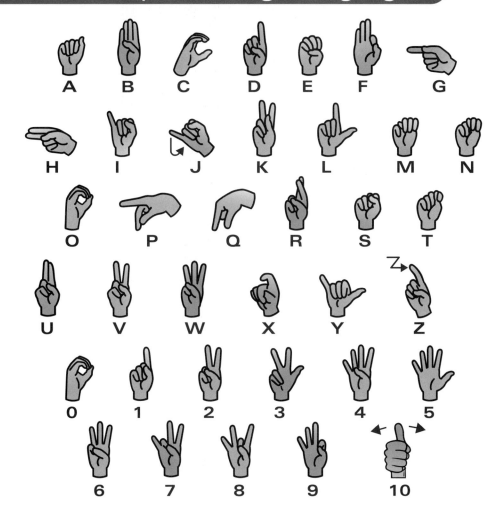

Language Families

Language families are groups of languages. Languages within a specific group are related because they all developed from the same language. English belongs to the **Indo-European** language family, as do many other languages. (See the chart below.)

The map shows all of the major language families plus the main languages in each family. (See the key on the next page.)

The Indo-European Family Today

Albanian

Armenian

Balto-Slavic
- Bulgarian
- Czech
- Latvian
- Lithuanian
- Polish
- Russian
- Serbo-Croatian
- Slovak
- Slovenian
- Ukrainian

Celtic
- Breton
- Irish (Celtic)
- Scots (Celtic)
- Welsh

Germanic
- Dutch
- English
- German
- Scandinavian
  - Danish
  - Icelandic
  - Norwegian
  - Swedish

Greek

Indo-Iranian
- Bengali
- Farsi
- Hindi
- Pashto
- Urdu

Romance
- French
- Italian
- Portuguese
- Romanian
- Spanish

Major Language Families

Indo-European

Sino-Tibetan

Afro-Asian

Uralic and Altaic

Japanese and Korean

Dravidian

Malayo-Polynesian

Mon-Khmer

Niger-Kordofanian

Nilo-Saharan

Khoisan

All others

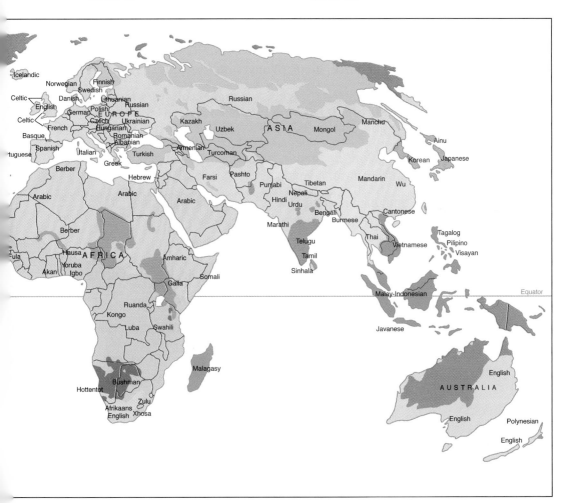

English from Around the World

Words from many languages have been added to English. This chart shows you some of these words. Use a dictionary to discover the origin of other words.

Native American	caribou, caucus, husky, moccasin, raccoon, sequoia, skunk, squash, terrapin
Egyptian	ammonia, barge, bark, gum, paper, sack
German	blitz, clock, clown, luck, poodle, rocket, sling, snorkel, stroll
Greek	academy, alphabet, cemetery, crocodile, dinosaur, idea, marathon, panic, sheriff, skeleton, tyrant
Gaelic	bother, brisk, dune, phony, slob, swap, twig, whiskey
Arabic	admiral, alcohol, algebra, average, coffee, harem, hazard, giraffe, mattress, monkey, safari, sherbet, soda
India	bungalow, bandanna, jumble, jute, shampoo, sugar, tank, tom-tom, yoga
French	ambulance, arson, bar, basin, bribe, hurt, peg, plug, rock, umpire, valet, zest
Spanish	capsize, rodeo, tornado, tune, vanilla
Scandinavian	boulder, dangle, drip, fjord, fog, smile, walrus, wicker
Chinese	gung ho, ketchup, kung fu, tea, typhoon, wok
Dutch	ahoy, ballast, block, grumble, heckle, pamper, roster, snoop, spa, stove, yacht
Latin	album, animal, autumn, doctor, inch, motor, ounce, street, victor
African	aardvark, bongo, canary, commando, gorilla, slim, trek, zebra
Farsi (Iran, Afghanistan)	bazaar, caravan, scarlet, shawl, tiger

Cursive Alphabet

Aa Bb Cc Dd
Ee Ff Gg Hh
Ii Jj Kk Ll
Mm Nn Oo
Pp Qq Rr Ss
Tt Uu Vv
Ww Xx Yy Zz

Braille Alphabet

1	2	3	4	5	6	7	8	9	0
a	b	c	d	e	f	g	h	i	j	k	l	m	n	o

| p | q | r | s | t | u | v | w | x | y | z | CAPITAL SIGN | NUMERAL SIGN |

Traffic Signs

RED Regulatory Signs

These signs are red to get your attention: they tell you to do (or not do) something. The red circle and slash tells you NO.

BLACK AND WHITE Informational Signs

Informational signs are black and white and are either square or rectangular. They provide basic information for pedestrians and drivers.

YELLOW Warning Signs

Yellow in color, these signs warn of a possible danger. Many warning signs are diamond shaped.

GREEN Directional or Guide Signs

These green signs give traffic directions or provide information on trail and bike routes.

BLUE Service Signs

These blue signs mean there are services nearby.

Science

The science facts that follow are both interesting and helpful to have at your fingertips. From "Animal Facts" to the "Periodic Table of the Elements," you will find useful information for quick reference.

Animal Facts

Animal	Male	Female	Young	Group	Gestation (days)	Longevity (years)
Bear	He-bear	She-bear	Cub	Sleuth	180-240	18-20 (34)*
Cat	Tom	Queen	Kitten	Clutter/Clowder	52-65	10-17 (30)
Cattle	Bull	Cow	Calf	Drove/Herd	280	9-12 (25)
Chicken	Rooster	Hen	Chick	Brood/Flock	21	7-8 (14)
Deer	Buck	Doe	Fawn	Herd	180-250	10-15 (26)
Dog	Dog	Bitch	Pup	Pack/Kennel	55-70	10-12 (24)
Donkey	Jack	Jenny	Foal	Herd/Pace	340-385	18-20 (63)
Duck	Drake	Duck	Duckling	Brace/Herd	21-35	10 (15)
Elephant	Bull	Cow	Calf	Herd	515-760	30-60 (98)
Fox	Dog	Vixen	Cub/Kit	Skulk	51-60	8-10 (14)
Goat	Billy	Nanny	Kid	Tribe/Herd	135-163	12 (17)
Goose	Gander	Goose	Gosling	Flock/Gaggle	30	25-30
Horse	Stallion	Mare	Filly/Colt	Herd	304-419	20-30 (50+)
Lion	Lion	Lioness	Cub	Pride	105-111	10 (29)
Monkey	Male	Female	Boy/Girl	Band/Troop	149-179	12-15 (29)
Rabbit	Buck	Doe	Bunny	Nest/Warren	27-36	6-8 (15)
Sheep	Ram	Ewe	Lamb	Flock/Drove	121-180	10-15 (16)
Swan	Cob	Pen	Cygnet	Bevy/Flock	30	45-50
Swine	Boar	Sow	Piglet	Litter/Herd	101-130	10 (15)
Tiger	Tiger	Tigress	Cub		105	19
Whale	Bull	Cow	Calf	Gam/Pod/Herd	276-365	37
Wolf	Dog	Bitch	Pup	Pack	63	10-12 (16)

* ( ) Record for oldest animal of this type

Classification of Animals

Animals are grouped, or classified, according to their similarities. Each classification gets more specific. Scientists use Latin as a common language to make sure they are talking about the same thing. Below is the classification for a white-tailed deer.

Classification	White-Tailed Deer	Explanation
Kingdom	Animalia	It is an animal.
Phylum	Chordata	It has a backbone.
Class	Mammalia	It is warm-blooded and covered with hair.
Order	Artiodactyla	It is an even-toed animal.
Family	Cervidae	It is a deerlike animal.
Genus	Odocoileus	It is a deer in North America.
Species	Odocoileus virginianus	It is in the eastern United States.

Branches of Science

PHYSICAL Studies of matter and energy

Physics ■ Study of matter and energy
Chemistry ■ Study of structure and the properties of matter
Astronomy ■ Study of matter in outer space

EARTH Studies of the earth and the atmosphere

Geology ■ Study of the land
Paleontology ■ Study of prehistoric life
Meteorology ■ Study of the atmosphere

LIFE Studies of living things

Biology ■ Study of life
Botany ■ Study of plant life
Zoology ■ Study of animal life

The Metric System

Even though the metric system is not the official system of measurement in the United States, it is used in science, medicine, and some other fields.

The metric system is based on the decimal system (units of 10), so there are no fractions. The table below lists the basic measurements in the metric system.

● LINEAR MEASURE (LENGTH OR DISTANCE)

1 centimeter	= 10 millimeters	= 0.3937 inch
1 decimeter	= 10 centimeters	= 3.937 inches
1 meter	= 10 decimeters	= 39.37 inches or 3.28 feet
1 dekameter	= 10 meters	= 393.7 inches
1 kilometer	= 1,000 meters	= 0.621 mile

● SQUARE MEASURE (AREA)

1 square centimeter	= 100 square millimeters	= 0.155 square inch
1 square decimeter	= 100 square centimeters	= 15.5 square inches
1 square meter	= 100 square decimeters	= 1,549.9 sq. inches or 1.196 sq. yards
1 square dekameter	= 100 square meters	= 119.6 square yards
1 square kilometer	= 100 square hectometers	= 0.386 square mile

● CAPACITY MEASURE

1 centiliter	= 10 milliliters	= 0.338 fluid ounce
1 deciliter	= 10 centiliters	= 3.38 fluid ounces
1 liter	= 10 deciliters	= 1.057 liquid qts. or 0.908 dry qt.
1 kiloliter	= 1,000 liters	= 264.18 gallons or 35.315 cubic feet

● LAND MEASURE

1 centare	= 1 square meter	= 1,549.9 square inches
1 hectare	= 100 ares	= 2.471 acres
1 square kilometer	= 100 hectares	= 0.386 square mile

● VOLUME MEASURE

1 cubic centimeter	= 1,000 cubic millimeters	= 0.061 cubic inch
1 cubic decimeter	= 1,000 cubic centimeters	= 61.023 cubic inches
1 cubic meter	= 1,000 cubic decimeters	= 35.314 cubic feet

● WEIGHTS

1 centigram	= 10 milligrams	= 0.1543 grain
1 decigram	= 10 centigrams	= 1.5432 grains
1 gram	= 10 decigrams	= 15.432 grains
1 dekagram	= 10 grams	= 0.3527 ounce
1 kilogram	= 1,000 grams	= 2.2046 pounds

American to Metric Table

The following table shows you what the most common measurements are in the American system and the metric system. You probably already know that 1 inch equals 2.54 centimeters, but did you know that 1 gallon equals 3.7853 liters?

● LINEAR MEASURE (LENGTH OR DISTANCE)

1 inch		= 2.54 centimeters
1 foot	= 12 inches	= 0.3048 meter
1 yard	= 3 feet	= 0.9144 meter
1 mile	= 1,760 yards or 5,280 feet	= 1,609.3 meters

● SQUARE MEASURE (AREA)

1 square inch		= 6.452 square centimeters
1 square foot	= 144 square inches	= 929 square centimeters
1 square yard	= 9 square feet	= 0.8361 square meter
1 acre	= 4,840 sq. yards	= 0.4047 hectare
1 square mile	= 640 acres	= 259 hectares or 2.59 sq. kilometers

● CUBIC MEASURE

1 cubic inch		= 16.387 cubic centimeters
1 cubic foot	= 1,728 cubic inches	= 0.0283 cubic meter
1 cubic yard	= 27 cubic feet	= 0.7646 cubic meter
1 cord	= 8 cord feet	= 3.625 cubic meters

● DRY MEASURE

1 pint		= 0.5505 liter
1 quart	= 2 pints	= 1.1012 liters
1 peck	= 8 quarts	= 8.8096 liters
1 bushel	= 4 pecks	= 35.2383 liters

● LIQUID MEASURE

4 fluid ounces	= 1 gill	= 0.1183 liter
1 pint	= 4 gills	= 0.4732 liter
1 quart	= 2 pints	= 0.9463 liter
1 gallon	= 4 quarts	= 3.7853 liters

Some Ways to Measure When You Don't Have a Ruler

1. A standard sheet of paper is 8-1/2 inches by 11 inches.
2. A quarter is approximately 1 inch wide.
3. A penny is approximately 3/4 inch wide.
4. U.S. paper currency is 6-1/8 inches long by 2-5/8 inches wide.

Conversion Table

To change metric measurements into American measurements, multiply by the numbers listed below. To change American to metric, divide by those numbers.

To Change	to	Multiply By
acres	square miles	0.001562
Celsius	Fahrenheit	*1.8

*(Multiply Celsius by 1.8; then add 32.)

To Change	to	Multiply By
cubic meters	cubic yards	1.3079
cubic yards	cubic meters	0.7646
Fahrenheit	Celsius	*0.556

*(Multiply Fahrenheit by .556 after subtracting 32.)

To Change	to	Multiply By
feet	meters	0.3048
feet	miles	0.0001894
feet/sec.	miles/hr.	0.6818
grams	ounces	0.0353
grams	pounds	0.002205
hours	days	0.04167
inches	centimeters	2.5400
liters	gallons (U.S.)	0.2642
liters	pints (dry)	1.8162
liters	pints (liquid)	2.1134
liters	quarts (dry)	0.9081
liters	quarts (liquid)	1.0567
meters	miles	0.0006214
meters	yards	1.0936
metric tons	tons	1.1023
miles	kilometers	1.6093
miles	feet	5,280
miles/hr.	feet/min.	88
millimeters	inches	0.0394
ounces	grams	28.3495
ounces	pounds	0.0625
pounds	kilograms	0.4536
pounds	ounces	16
quarts (dry)	liters	1.1012
square feet	square meters	0.0929
square kilometers	square miles	0.3861
square meters	square feet	10.7639
square miles	square kilometers	2.5900
square yards	square meters	0.8361
tons	metric tons	0.9072
tons	pounds	2,000
yards	meters	0.9144
yards	miles	0.0005682

Sun

Mercury

Venus

Earth

Mars

Jupiter

Saturn

Uranus

Neptune

Pluto

Our Solar System

The nine planets in our solar system orbit (revolve around) the sun.

Mercury has the shortest year. It is 88 days long.

Venus spins the slowest. It takes 243 days to spin around once.

Earth supports life for plants, animals, and people.

Mars has less gravity than Earth. A 50-pound person would weigh about 19 pounds on Mars.

Jupiter is the largest planet. It is 318 times more massive than Earth.

Saturn has seven rings. It also has 30 moons.

Uranus has the most rings—15.

Neptune is three times as cold as Earth.

Pluto is the smallest planet and the farthest from the sun.

	Sun	Moon	Mercury	Venus	Earth	Mars	Jupiter	Saturn	Uranus	Neptune	Pluto
Orbital Speed (in miles per second)		0.6	29.8	21.8	18.5	15.0	8.1	6.0	4.2	3.4	3.0
Rotation on Axis	24 days 16 hrs. 48 min.	27 days 7 hrs. 43 min.	59 days	243 days	23 hrs. 56 min.	24 hrs. 37 min.	9 hrs. 55 min.	10 hrs. 39 min.	17 hrs. 8 min.	16 hrs. 7 min.	6 days
Mean Surface Gravity (Earth = 1.00)		0.16	0.39	0.9	1.00	0.38	2.53	1.07	0.91	1.14	0.07
Density (times that of water)	100 (core)	3.3	5.4	5.3	5.5	3.9	1.3	0.7	1.27	1.6	2.03
Mass (times that of Earth)	333,000	0.012	0.056	0.82	6×10^{21} metric tons	0.10	318	95	14.5	17.2	0.0026
Approx. Weight of a 150-Pound Human		24	59	135	150	57	380	161	137	171	11
Number of Moons	9 planets	0	0	0	1	2	58	30	21	11	1
Mean Distance to Sun (in millions of miles)		93.0	36.0	67.24	92.96	141.7	483.8	887.1	1,783.9	2,796.4	3,666
Revolution Around Sun		365.25 days	88.0 days	224.7 days	365.25 days	687 days	11.86 years	29.46 years	84.0 years	165 years	248 years
Approximate Surface Temperature (degrees Fahrenheit)	10,000° (surface) 27,000,000° (center)	lighted side 260° dark side -280°	-346° to 950°	850°	-126.9° to 136°	-191° to -24°	-236°	-203°	-344°	-360°	-342° to -369°
Diameter (in miles)	865,400	2,155	3,032	7,519	7,926	4,194	88,736	74,978	32,193	30,775	1,423

Periodic Table of the Elements

Key / Legend:

- Alkali metals
- Alkaline earth metals
- Transition metals
- Lanthanide series
- Actinide series
- Other metals
- Nonmetals
- Noble gases

Atomic Number ———
Symbol ———
Atomic Weight (or Mass Number of most stable isotope if in parentheses) ———

2
He
Helium
4.00260

(Of elements 110-121, some are still unknown, and some are recently claimed but unnamed. They have temporary systematic names.)

1a	2a	3b	4b	5b	6b	7b	8	8	8	1b	2b	3a	4a	5a	6a	7a	0
1 **H** Hydrogen 1.00797																	2 **He** Helium 4.00260
3 **Li** Lithium 6.941	4 **Be** Beryllium 9.0128											5 **B** Boron 10.811	6 **C** Carbon 12.01115	7 **N** Nitrogen 14.0067	8 **O** Oxygen 15.9994	9 **F** Fluorine 18.9984	10 **Ne** Neon 20.179
11 **Na** Sodium 22.9898	12 **Mg** Magnesium 24.305											13 **Al** Aluminum 26.9815	14 **Si** Silicon 28.0855	15 **P** Phosphorus 30.9738	16 **S** Sulfur 32.064	17 **Cl** Chlorine 35.453	18 **Ar** Argon 39.948
19 **K** Potassium 39.0983	20 **Ca** Calcium 40.08	21 **Sc** Scandium 44.9559	22 **Ti** Titanium 47.88	23 **V** Vanadium 50.94	24 **Cr** Chromium 51.996	25 **Mn** Manganese 54.9380	26 **Fe** Iron 55.847	27 **Co** Cobalt 58.9332	28 **Ni** Nickel 58.69	29 **Cu** Copper 63.546	30 **Zn** Zinc 65.39	31 **Ga** Gallium 69.72	32 **Ge** Germanium 72.59	33 **As** Arsenic 74.9216	34 **Se** Selenium 78.96	35 **Br** Bromine 79.904	36 **Kr** Krypton 83.80
37 **Rb** Rubidium 85.4678	38 **Sr** Strontium 87.62	39 **Y** Yttrium 88.905	40 **Zr** Zirconium 91.224	41 **Nb** Niobium 92.906	42 **Mo** Molybdenum 95.94	43 **Tc** Technetium (98)	44 **Ru** Ruthenium 101.07	45 **Rh** Rhodium 102.906	46 **Pd** Palladium 106.42	47 **Ag** Silver 107.868	48 **Cd** Cadmium 112.41	49 **In** Indium 114.82	50 **Sn** Tin 118.71	51 **Sb** Antimony 121.75	52 **Te** Tellurium 127.60	53 **I** Iodine 126.905	54 **Xe** Xenon 131.29
55 **Cs** Cesium 132.905	56 **Ba** Barium 137.33	57-71* Lanthanides	72 **Hf** Hafnium 178.49	73 **Ta** Tantalum 180.948	74 **W** Tungsten 183.85	75 **Re** Rhenium 186.207	76 **Os** Osmium 190.2	77 **Ir** Iridium 192.22	78 **Pt** Platinum 195.08	79 **Au** Gold 196.967	80 **Hg** Mercury 200.59	81 **Tl** Thallium 204.383	82 **Pb** Lead 207.19	83 **Bi** Bismuth 208.980	84 **Po** Polonium (209)	85 **At** Astatine (210)	86 **Rn** Radon (222)
87 **Fr** Francium (223)	88 **Ra** Radium 226.025	89-103** Actinides	104 **Rf** Rutherfordium (261)	105 **Db** Dubnium (262)	106 **Sg** Seaborgium (263)	107 **Bh** Bohrium (262)	108 **Hs** Hassium (265)	109 **Mt** Meitnerium (266)	110 (269)	111 (272)							

***Lanthanides**

57 **La** Lanthanum 138.906	58 **Ce** Cerium 140.12	59 **Pr** Praseodymium 140.908	60 **Nd** Neodymium 144.24	61 **Pm** Promethium (145)	62 **Sm** Samarium 150.36	63 **Eu** Europium 151.96	64 **Gd** Gadolinium 157.25	65 **Tb** Terbium 158.925	66 **Dy** Dysprosium 162.50	67 **Ho** Holmium 164.930	68 **Er** Erbium 167.26	69 **Tm** Thulium 168.934	70 **Yb** Ytterbium 173.04	71 **Lu** Lutetium 174.967

****Actinides**

89 **Ac** Actinium 227.028	90 **Th** Thorium 232.038	91 **Pa** Protactinium 231.036	92 **U** Uranium 238.029	93 **Np** Neptunium 237.048	94 **Pu** Plutonium (244)	95 **Am** Americium (243)	96 **Cm** Curium (247)	97 **Bk** Berkelium (247)	98 **Cf** Californium (251)	99 **Es** Einsteinium (252)	100 **Fm** Fermium (257)	101 **Md** Mendelevium (258)	102 **No** Nobelium (259)	103 **Lr** Lawrencium (260)

Mathematics

This chapter is your guide to the language of mathematics. It lists and defines many of the common (and not so common) mathematical signs, symbols, shapes, and terms. The chapter also includes helpful math tables and easy-to-follow guidelines for solving word problems.

Common Math Symbols

+	plus (addition)
−	minus (subtraction)
×	multiplied by
÷	divided by
=	is equal to
>	is greater than
<	is less than
±	plus or minus
%	percent
¢	cents
$	dollars
°	degree

Advanced Math Symbols

´	minute (also foot)
´´	second (also inch)
:	is to (ratio)
π	pi (pi = 3.14)
√	square root
≠	is not equal to
≥	is greater than or equal to
≤	is less than or equal to
∠	angle
⊥	is perpendicular to
‖	is parallel to
∴	therefore

A Chart of Prime Numbers Less than 500

2	3	5	7	11	13	17	19	23	29
31	37	41	43	47	53	59	61	67	71
73	79	83	89	97	101	103	107	109	113
127	131	137	139	149	151	157	163	167	173
179	181	191	193	197	199	211	223	227	229
233	239	241	251	257	263	269	271	277	281
283	293	307	311	313	317	331	337	347	349
353	359	367	373	379	383	389	397	401	409
419	421	431	433	439	443	449	457	461	463
467	479	487	491	499					

Multiplication and Division Table

X	0	1	2	3	4	5	6	7	8	9	10
0	0	0	0	0	0	0	0	0	0	0	0
1	0	1	2	3	4	5	6	7	8	9	10
2	0	2	4	6	8	10	12	14	16	18	20
3	0	3	6	9	12	15	18	21	24	27	30
4	0	4	8	12	16	20	24	28	32	36	40
5	0	5	10	15	20	25	30	35	40	45	50
6	0	6	12	18	24	30	36	42	48	54	60
7	0	7	14	21	28	35	42	49	56	63	70
8	0	8	16	24	32	40	48	56	64	72	80
9	0	9	18	27	36	45	54	63	72	81	90
10	0	10	20	30	40	50	60	70	80	90	100

Decimal Equivalents of Common Fractions

1/2	.5000	1/32	.0313	3/11	.2727	6/11	.5455
1/3	.3333	1/64	.0156	4/5	.8000	7/8	.8750
1/4	.2500	2/3	.6667	4/7	.5714	7/9	.7778
1/5	.2000	2/5	.4000	4/9	.4444	7/10	.7000
1/6	.1667	2/7	.2857	4/11	.3636	7/11	.6364
1/7	.1429	2/9	.2222	5/6	.8333	7/12	.5833
1/8	.1250	2/11	.1818	5/7	.7143	8/9	.8889
1/9	.1111	3/4	.7500	5/8	.6250	8/11	.7273
1/10	.1000	3/5	.6000	5/9	.5556	9/10	.9000
1/11	.0909	3/7	.4286	5/11	.4545	9/11	.8182
1/12	.0833	3/8	.3750	5/12	.4167	10/11	.9091
1/16	.0625	3/10	.3000	6/7	.8571	11/12	.9167

Roman Numerals

I	1	VIII	8	LX	60	$\overline{V}$	5,000
II	2	IX	9	LXX	70	$\overline{X}$	10,000
III	3	X	10	LXXX	80	$\overline{L}$	50,000
IV	4	XX	20	XC	90	$\overline{C}$	100,000
V	5	XXX	30	C	100		
VI	6	XL	40	D	500	$\overline{D}$	500,000
VII	7	L	50	M	1,000	$\overline{M}$	1,000,000

Word Problems

Solving word problems requires careful reading, thinking, and planning. If you try to take shortcuts, you will probably not solve the problems correctly. The guidelines below give you the important steps to follow the next time you work on word problems.

Guidelines for Solving Word Problems

1. **Read the problem carefully.** It's important that you understand all the parts. Pay special attention to the key words and phrases—such as "in all" or "how many." Read the problem again to be sure you understand it well. (Draw a picture or diagram if that helps make the problem easier to figure out.)

2. **Collect the information.** Gather the information you need to solve the problem. First of all, find all the numbers in the problem. (Remember, some numbers may be written as words.) Also study any maps, charts, or graphs that go along with the problem. They often contain important information, too.

3. **Set up the problem.** Decide whether you need to add, subtract, multiply, or divide. Do this by looking for the key words and phrases in the problem.

   - The following words tell you to add or multiply: *altogether, in all, in total.*
   - The following phrases tell you to subtract: *how many more than, how many less than, find the difference, how many are left, how much younger than.*
   - Each of these phrases tells you to divide: *how much . . . each (or per), how many . . . each (or per).*

4. **Solve the problem.** Once the problem is set up, with all the steps in the right order, you're ready to solve it. Show your work so you can check it later.

5. **Check your answer.** Here are several ways to check your answer: Do the problem again, do it a different way, use a calculator, or start with your answer and work backward.

Sample Word Problem I

Problem: Ray Ann buys a wallet for $6.50, a T-shirt for $6.35, and socks for $3.50. The sales tax she pays is 5 percent. She gives the clerk $20.00. How much change will she get back?

STEP 1: Read the problem.	*Discussion:* As you read the problem, you'll find four main points: Ray Ann buys three items; she pays sales tax on the items; she gives the clerk $20; and she receives change.
STEP 2: Collect the information.	*Discussion:* The numbers you will need to solve the problem are $6.50, $6.35, $3.50, 5%, and $20.00.
STEP 3: Set up and solve the problem.	*Discussion:* You will need to do four calculations.

(a.) $ 6.50 wallet
      6.35 T-shirt
  + 3.50 socks
  $ 16.35 total

(a) Add the prices for the three items that were purchased.

(b.) $ 16.35 total
  ×   .05 tax
    .8175 total tax

(b) Multiply the sum by the sales tax. The total is rounded up to 82¢.

(c.) $ .82 sales tax
  + 16.35 purchases
  $ 17.17 total bill

(c) Add the sales tax to the total cost of the items.

(d.) $ 20.00 payment
  − 17.17 total bill
  $ 2.83 change

(d) Subtract this total from $20.00.

STEP 4: Check your answer.	*Discussion:* Check your answer by reviewing your work. Make sure you have added, multiplied, and subtracted accurately.

Answer: Ray Ann gets back $2.83 in change.

Sample Word Problem II

Problem: Twenty-four students went on a field trip to a science museum. Half of the group decided to tour an old submarine. The other half went to the "History of Flight" display. One-third of that group viewed the space exhibits, while two-thirds explored the propeller-driven planes. How many students toured the submarine, viewed the space exhibits, and explored the planes?

STEP 1: Read the problem carefully.	*Discussion:* The key words are "how many."
STEP 2: Collect the information.	*Discussion:* The numbers you need to solve this problem are 24, 1/2, 1/3, and 2/3.
STEP 3: Set up the problem. $24 \times 1/2 = X$ $X \times 1/3 = Y$ $X \times 2/3 = Z$	*Discussion:* To solve this problem, you will need to multiply and subtract. (Draw a diagram to guide your work.) 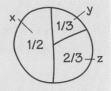
STEP 4: Solve the problem. $\dfrac{24}{1} \times \dfrac{1}{2} = \dfrac{24}{2} = 12$ $\dfrac{12}{1} \times \dfrac{1}{3} = \dfrac{12}{3} = 4$ $\dfrac{12}{1} \times \dfrac{2}{3} = \dfrac{24}{3} = 8$	*Discussion:* You will need to do three calculations. (1) To determine the number of students who viewed the submarines, multiply $24 \times 1/2$. (2) To determine the number of students who viewed the space exhibits, multiply $12 \times 1/3$. (3) To determine the number of students who explored the planes, multiply $12 \times 2/3$.
STEP 5: Check your answer.	*Discussion:* Review your work to be sure your answers are correct.

Answer: Twelve students toured the submarine, four viewed the space exhibits, and eight explored the planes.

Math Terms

Addition (+) is combining numbers to get a total, which is called a *sum*. The sum of 3 plus 5 is 8; $3 + 5 = 8$.

An **angle** is made when two rays share a common endpoint. An angle is measured in degrees. The three most common angles are *acute, obtuse,* and *right angles*.

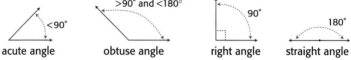

acute angle   obtuse angle   right angle   straight angle

Area is the total surface within a closed figure (circle, square). The area of a rectangle is figured by multiplying the length by the width. Area is measured in square units such as square inches or feet.

area

The **average** is found by adding a group of numbers together and then dividing that sum by the number of separate numbers. The average of 7, 8, and 9 is 8, because $7 + 8 + 9 = 24$, and $24 \div 3$ numbers $= 8$. This is also called the mathematical *mean*.

A **circle** is a round, closed figure. All the points on its circumference (edge) are the same distance from the center of the figure.

Circumference is the distance around the edge of a circle.

circumference

A **common denominator** is a multiple shared by the denominators of two or more fractions. For example, 6 is a common denominator of 1/2 (3/6) and 1/3 (2/6); 6 is a multiple of both 2 and 3. To add or subtract fractions, you must find a common denominator; $1/2 + 1/3 = 3/6 + 2/6 = 5/6$. The lowest common denominator is also called the *least common multiple* (LCM) of the denominators.

Congruent (≅) is the term for two figures, line segments, or angles that are the same size and shape.

congruent triangles

Data is a set of numbers collected to compare.

A **decimal** is a fraction written in the decimal number system. (*Decimal* means "based on the number 10.") Decimals are written using a decimal point and place values—tenths, hundredths, thousandths, and so on. The fraction 1/2 is .5, or 5/10.

A **degree** is a unit of measurement for angles and arcs. It is written as a small circle [°]. You can write 90° or 90 degrees. There are 360° in a circle.

The **denominator** is the bottom number of a fraction. In the fraction 1/3, the denominator is 3. It indicates the number of parts needed to make a whole unit.

A **diagonal** is a straight line from one vertex of a quadrilateral to the opposite vertex.

The **diameter** is the length of a straight line through the center of a circle.

diameter

A **dividend** is a number to be divided. In the equation $12 \div 2 = 6$, 12 is the dividend.

Division ($\div$) is a basic math operation used to determine how many times one quantity is contained in another. Division also tells you how many times you have to subtract a number to reach zero. For example, $10 \div 5 = 2$ because you subtract 5 two times to reach zero ($10 - \mathbf{5} = 5 - \mathbf{5} = 0$).

The **divisor** is the number that divides the dividend. In the statement $12 \div 2 = 6$, 2 is the divisor.

An **equation** is a statement that says two numbers or mathematical expressions are equal to each other ($2 + 10 = 12$ or $x + 4 = 9$). Equations use the equal sign (=).

An **estimate** is a reasonable guess at an answer. If you add 6.24 and 5.19, you can estimate the answer will be around 11, because $6 + 5 = 11$.

An **even number** is a number that can be divided by 2 without having a remainder (2, 4, 6, and so on). For example, $4 \div 2 = 2$.

An **exponent** is the small, raised number to the right of the base number that shows how many times the number is to be multiplied by itself. In the expression 2^3, 3 is the exponent (2 is the base). So, 2^3 means you need to multiply 2 three times ($2 \times 2 \times 2 = 8$).

A **factor** is a number that is being multiplied. In $4 \times 3 = 12$, the factors are 4 and 3.

A **fraction** is a number that expresses a part of a whole. In the fraction 3/4, 4 is the *denominator*—the number of equal parts that make up the whole. The number 3 is the *numerator*—the number of parts being talked about.

$= {}^3/_4$

fraction

Geometry is the study of two-dimensional shapes (circles, triangles), solids (spheres, cubes), and positions in space (points).

A **horizontal** is a line parallel to the earth's surface, or horizon, going across rather than up and down. A *vertical* is a line that is straight up and down and perpendicular to the horizon.

A **hypotenuse** of a right triangle is the side opposite the right angle.

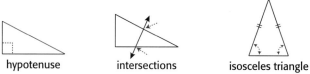

An **intersection** is the point where two figures in geometry cross each other.

An **isosceles triangle** is a triangle with two sides of equal length and two congruent angles. (See *triangle.*)

Length is the distance along a line from one point to another.

A **line** is all points formed by extending a line segment both directions, without end.

line

Lowest common denominator (See *common denominator.*)

Mean is another word for *average.* (See *average.*)

The **median** is the middle number when a group of numbers is arranged in order from the least to the greatest, or greatest to least. In 1, 4, 6, the median (middle number) is 4. In 1, 4, 6, 8, the median is 5, halfway between 4 and 6.

A **multiple** is a quantity into which another quantity can be divided, with zero as the remainder (both 6 and 9 are multiples of 3).

Multiplication (×) is like addition because you add the same number a certain number of times (2 × 4 = 4 + 4). When you multiply numbers, the answer is called the *product.* The product of 2 times 4 is 8 because 2 × 4 = 8. (A raised dot also means multiplication. 2 × 3 is the same as 2 • 3.)

The **numerator** is the top number of a fraction. In the fraction 5/6, the numerator is 5.

An **obtuse** angle is an angle greater than 90 degrees and less than 180 degrees. (See *angle.*)

An **odd number** is a number that cannot be divided evenly by 2. The numbers 1, 3, 5, 7, and so on, are odd numbers.

Opposite numbers are any two numbers whose sum is zero (–2 and +2 are opposite numbers).

Parallel refers to lines that never intersect.

Percent is a way of expressing a number as a fraction of 100. (Percent means "per hundred.") The percent symbol is %. So, 1/2 expressed as a percentage is 50/100, which is 50%.

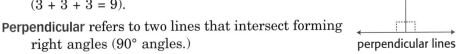

The **perimeter** is the distance around the edge of a multisided figure. If a triangle has three sides, each 3 feet long, its perimeter is 9 feet (3 + 3 + 3 = 9).

Perpendicular refers to two lines that intersect forming right angles (90° angles.)

Pi (π) is the ratio of the circumference of a circle to its diameter. Pi is approximately 3.14.

Place value is the value of the place of a digit depending on where it is in the number.

    3497 is 3—thousands, 4—hundreds, 9—tens, 7—ones

    .3497 is 3—tenths, 4—hundredths, 9—thousandths, 7—ten-thousandths

A **point** is an exact location on a plane.

A **positive number** is a number greater than 0.

A **prime number** is a number that cannot be divided evenly by any number except itself and 1. The number 6 is not a prime number because it can be divided by 1, 2, 3, and 6. The number 5 is a prime number because it can only be divided evenly (without a remainder) by 1 and 5.

The **product** is the number you get when you multiply two or more numbers. For example, 8 is the product of 2 times 4, because 2 × 4 = 8.

The **quotient** is the number you get when you divide one number by another number. If 8 is divided by 4, the quotient is 2, because 8 ÷ 4 = 2.

The **radius (r)** is the distance from the center of a circle to its circumference. (The radius is half the diameter.)

A **ratio** is a way of comparing two numbers by dividing one by the other. The ratio of 3 to 4 is 3/4. If there are 20 boys and 5 girls in your class, the ratio of boys to girls is 20/5 (4/1 in lowest terms), or 4 : 1.

A **rectangle** is a four-sided closed figure with four right angles and with opposite sides parallel and congruent.

A **right angle** is an angle that measures 90 degrees. A right angle is formed when two perpendicular lines meet. (See *angle*.)

Rounding is a way to figure an approximate number if you don't need an exact number. If 2,323 people attended a soccer game, you could say about 2,000 people were there (to the nearest 1,000). If 2,857 people attended, you could say 3,000. Round up if the number is greater than half (2,500 is halfway between 2,000 and 3,000). Round down if the number is less than half.

A **solid** is a three-dimensional figure in geometry, like a cube, a cone, a prism, or a sphere.

solid

A **square** is a rectangle that has four sides of equal length and four right angles. *Square* also refers to the product of a number multiplied by itself. The square of 4 is 16 ($4^2 = 16$; $4 \times 4 = 16$).

square

The **square root** of a number is a number that, when multiplied by itself, gives the original number as the product. The symbol for square root is $\sqrt{}$. The square root of 4 is 2, because $2 \times 2 = 4$ ($\sqrt{4} = 2$).

Subtraction (−) is the inverse (opposite) of addition. Instead of adding one number to another, you take one number away from another. When you subtract two numbers, you find the difference between them. So, $11 - 6 = 5$.

The **sum** is the number you get when you add numbers. For example, 7 is the sum of 4 plus 3, because $4 + 3 = 7$.

A **triangle** is a closed figure with three sides. The sum of the angles in every triangle is 180°. Triangles can be classified by *sides:* equilateral, scalene, or isosceles; or by *angles:* right, equiangular, acute, or obtuse.

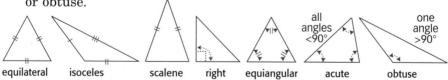

equilateral   isoceles   scalene   right   equiangular   acute   obtuse

A **vertex** is the point where two sides of a plane figure meet (corner). The plural of *vertex* is *vertices*.

vertex

Vertical (See *horizontal*.)

Computers

An Internet service provider (ISP) allows you to conduct research and communicate on-line. The provider gives you access, via a personal computer or a local-area network (LAN), to the World Wide Web, e-mail, and instant messages. (Study the chart below to see how the Net works.) An instant messenger is a program that alerts you when friends are on-line and provides "chat" service.

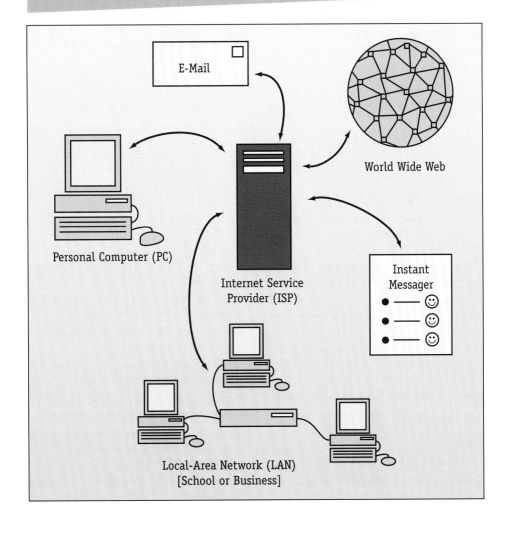

Computer Terms

Access To open and use a computer file.

ASCII (American Standard Code Information Interchange) A set of letters, numbers, and various symbols that computers use to store and work with data.

Audio file A computer document of sounds.

Backup A duplicate copy of a file or program, made in case the original is lost or destroyed.

Bit A unit of computer memory.

Boot To start up a computer system by loading a program into the memory. Also called *start up*.

BPS (Bits Per Second) A measure of how fast data is transmitted over a network.

Browser A computer program that allows a user to view information on the Internet.

Bug An error in a program.

Byte Eight bits of information acting as a single piece of data. Computer memory is measured in bytes.

CD (compact disk) A medium used for storing audio, text, and video data.

Character A letter or number used to display information on a computer screen or printer.

Chip A tiny piece of silicon with thousands of electrical elements. Also called an *integrated circuit*.

Circuit board A board inside every computer, used to hold and connect computer chips and electrical parts.

Command An instruction telling a computer to perform a certain task.

Compress To make a file smaller for easier storage or transmission.

Computer A machine that can accept data, process it, and then output the results.

Computer program Software that contains commands telling the computer to perform certain tasks.

Configuration A computer and all devices connected to it.

CPU (Central Processing Unit) The part that performs computations and controls other parts of the computer system.

CRT (Cathode Ray Tube) The type of electronic vacuum tube found in some computer monitors and TV screens.

Cursor A pointer on the monitor that shows where the next character typed on the keyboard will appear.

Cyberspace The imaginary world perceived by humans when using a computer network or a virtual reality program. (See *virtual reality*.)

Database A program and a collection of information organized in such a way that a computer can access a certain item or group of items.

Desktop The monitor screen as it appears when the computer is on but no programs are open.

Device A piece of computer hardware that performs a certain task.

Directory The table of contents for all files on a disk.

Disk drive The device that reads and writes information on a disk.

Download To copy a program or file from another computer to your own.

Drag To move items on the screen by pressing the mouse button while sliding the mouse.

DVD (Digital Video Disk) A CD with high-resolution audio and video.

Emoticon A set of characters that, when viewed sideways, resembles a face and adds emotion to messages. :)

Error message A message that is displayed by the computer and that tells you what type of error has occurred.

Exit To close or quit a program.

FAQ's (Frequently Asked Questions) A list of often asked questions and answers.

File A collection of information stored under a single title.

Floppy disk A magnetic storage device that records computer data.

Font A typeface (type style).

Footprint The space on a desk taken up by a computer.

Format To prepare (initialize) a blank disk for use.

Freeware Software in the public domain (can be used free of charge).

FTP (File Transfer Protocol) A system for uploading and downloading files on the Internet or on a network.

GB (Gigabyte) A measure of computer memory; 1,000 megabytes (MB).

Hard copy A printed copy.

Hard drive A device for long-term storage of files and programs.

Hardware The mechanical parts of a computer system.

Host A computer that serves other computers in a computer-to-computer link.

HTML (Hypertext Markup Language) The code used to format pages for viewing on a Web browser.

Hypertext or **hypermedia** A system of Web-like links among pages on the Internet or within a program.

Icon A picture or a symbol identifying computer folders, files, or functions.

Interactive A computer program that allows the user and computer to exchange information.

Interface The hardware and software that is used to link one computer or computer device to another. Also the way a program communicates to a user.

K (Kilobyte) A measure of computer memory; 1,024 bytes (about 170 words).

Keyboard An input device used to enter information on a computer by striking keys.

Laser printer A printer that uses a laser to make high-quality printouts.

Link A connection from one hypertext page to another.

Listserve A program sending e-mail messages to addresses organized around a topic, allowing its subscribers to conduct discussion by e-mail. Also called a *mailing list* or a *mail server*.

Load To move information from a storage device into a computer's memory.

Mainframe A large computer, with many terminals, with power enough to be used by many people at once. (See *terminal*.)

MB (Megabyte) 1,000 kilobytes (K).

Memory Chips in the computer that store data and programs.

Menu A list of program choices from which a user can select.

Modem (MOdulator DEModulator) A device that handles information or data over cable or phone lines.

Monitor A video screen that displays computer information.

Mouse A manual input device that controls the pointer on the screen.

MUD (Multi-User Domain) An imaginary world made up of "rooms" where users interact with the setting and other users.

Multimedia A program that can combine text, graphics, video, voice, music, and animation.

Newsgroup A bulletin-board style discussion on a timely topic.

On-line To be connected to a computer network.

On-line service A business that serves as a network, providing e-mail, chat rooms, and so on.

Open To load a program for use.

Operating system The software system that controls a computer (Windows, Mac OS, etc.).

Output Information that a computer sends out to a monitor, printer, modem, or other device.

Peripheral A device connected to a computer (a printer, a monitor).

Pixel One dot on the screen. There are usually 72 pixels per inch.

Printout A hard copy; a computer document printed on paper.

Program A set of instructions that tells a computer what to do.

Programmer A person who writes or produces a computer program.

Programming language A special language used when writing a computer program.

Prompt A question or an instruction on the screen that asks users to make a choice or give information.

Quit To close a program.

RAM (Random Access Memory) The part of a computer's memory that stores programs and documents while you are using them.

Resolution The number of dots per square inch (dpi) on a computer screen. Images on the screen are made up of tiny dots. The more dots there are, the higher the resolution and the clearer the picture.

ROM (Read-Only Memory) The part of a computer's memory that contains its permanent instructions. It cannot record new data.

Save To transfer a document for permanent storage.

Scanner A device used to read a printed image, picture, or text and save it as an electronic file.

Server The hosting computer of a network. (See *host*.)

Shareware Programs made as demonstrations for a test period, then paid for.

Software The program that tells a computer how to do a certain task.

Spam Bulk (junk) e-mail that is sent to many people at once.

Spreadsheet A computer program that displays numbers and text in a worksheet form.

Surfing Exploring the Internet, going from link to link.

System A collection of hardware and software working together to form a working computer.

Terminal A keyboard and monitor sharing a mainframe (computer) with other terminals.

Text file A computer document made up of ASCII characters only.

Upload To send a file from one computer to another computer.

Virtual reality A technology that puts users in a computer-created environment.

Virus A command (bug) that is put into a computer system to cause problems.

Window A box on a computer screen in which text or graphics is displayed.

Word processor A program that allows users to write, revise, edit, save, and print text documents.

Geography

To study geography, you need maps, including *political maps* like the ones provided in this chapter. Political maps show how the world is divided into countries and states. The chapter also includes guidelines for using maps, a special time-zone map, and much more.

Using Maps

Mapmakers use special marks and symbols to show direction (north, south, east, and west). On most maps, north is at the top. But you should always check the *directional finder* (compass rose) to make sure you know where north is. If there is no symbol, you can assume that north is at the top of the page.

The Legend

Other important marks and symbols are explained in a box printed on each map. This box is called the *legend,* or *key.* It is included to help you understand and use the map. This map legend, which goes with the United States map, also includes symbols for state capitals and state boundaries.

UNITED STATES		
✪ National Capital		——— International Boundaries
Austin ◉ State Capitals		——— State Boundaries
Dallas • Cities		**TEXAS** State Names
0 100 200 300 400 Miles		

The Map Scale

Legends also explain the map scale. The map scale shows you how far it really is between places. For example, a scale might show that one inch on the map equals 100 miles on the earth. If two cities are shown five inches apart, then they are really 500 miles apart. A ruler makes using a scale easy, but even an index card or a piece of paper will work. Here is the enlarged scale from the map of the United States.

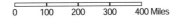

0   100   200   300   400 Miles

Latitude and Longitude

Latitude and *longitude* lines are another part of many maps and are very useful. These are imaginary lines, placed on a map by map-makers, and used to locate any point on the earth.

Latitude ● The imaginary lines that go from east to west around the earth are called lines of **latitude.** The line of latitude that goes around the earth exactly halfway between the North Pole and the South Pole is called the *equator.* Latitude is measured in degrees, with the equator being 0 degrees (0°).

Above the equator, the lines are called *north latitude* and measure from 0° to 90° north (the North Pole). Below the equator, the lines are called *south latitude* and measure from 0° to 90° south (the South Pole). On a map, latitude numbers are printed along the sides.

Longitude ● The lines on a map that run north and south from the North Pole to the South Pole are lines of **longitude.** Longitude is also measured in degrees, beginning with 0 degrees. The line of longitude located at 0° is called the *prime meridian* and passes through Greenwich, England.

Lines east of the prime meridian are called *east longitude.* Lines west of the prime meridian are called *west longitude.* On most maps, longitude numbers are printed at the top and bottom.

Coordinates ● The latitude and longitude numbers of a country or other place are called its **coordinates.** In each set of coordinates, latitude is given first, then longitude. To locate a place on a map using its coordinates, find the point where the two lines cross.

✳ On the map of the globe above, Guinea is located at 10° N, 10° W. Can you find it? If not, check the map on page 509.

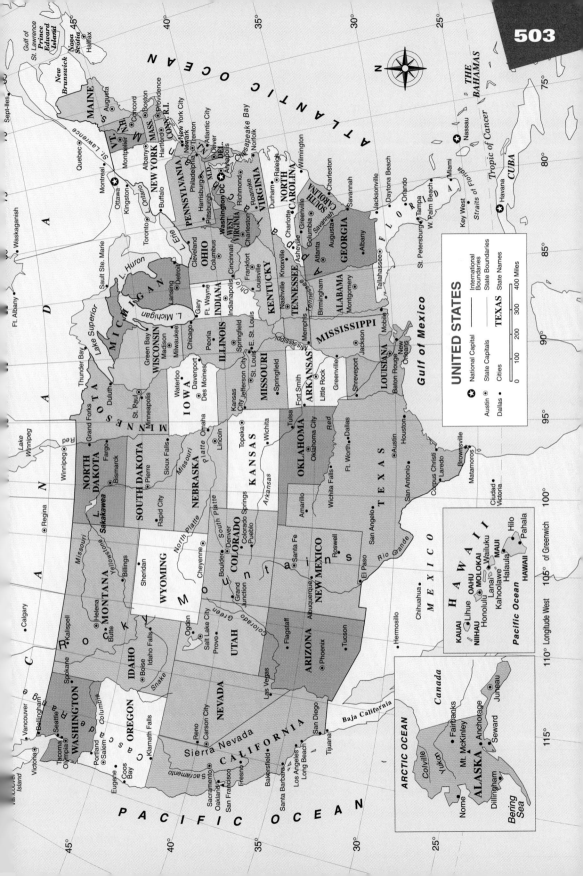

UNITED STATES

★ National Capital
⊛ State Capitals
• Cities

Austin
Dallas

International
Boundaries
State Boundaries
TEXAS State Names

0 100 200 300 400 Miles

ATLANTIC OCEAN

N

THE BAHAMAS

Tropic of Cancer

CUBA

Straits of Florida

Gulf of Mexico

PACIFIC OCEAN

MEXICO

105° Longitude West

110°

115°

H A W A I I

KAUAI
NIIHAU
OAHU
Lihue
Honolulu
MOLOKAI
Lanai
MAUI
Wailuku
Kahoolawe
Halaula
HAWAII
Hilo
Pahala

MAUI

Pacific Ocean

ARCTIC OCEAN

Canada

ALASKA

Fairbanks
Mt. McKinley
Nome
Colville
Yukon
Anchorage
Juneau
Seward
Dillingham

Bering Sea

Baja California

MAINE
VT.
N.H.
MASS.
CONN. R.I.
NEW YORK
PENNSYLVANIA
OHIO
INDIANA
MICHIGAN
WISCONSIN
ILLINOIS
MINNESOTA
IOWA
MISSOURI
KENTUCKY
TENNESSEE
WEST VIRGINIA
VIRGINIA
NORTH CAROLINA
SOUTH CAROLINA
GEORGIA
ALABAMA
MISSISSIPPI
ARKANSAS
LOUISIANA
FLORIDA
OKLAHOMA
TEXAS
KANSAS
NEBRASKA
SOUTH DAKOTA
NORTH DAKOTA
MONTANA
WYOMING
COLORADO
NEW MEXICO
ARIZONA
UTAH
NEVADA
IDAHO
OREGON
WASHINGTON
CALIFORNIA

Rocky Mountains
Sierra Nevada

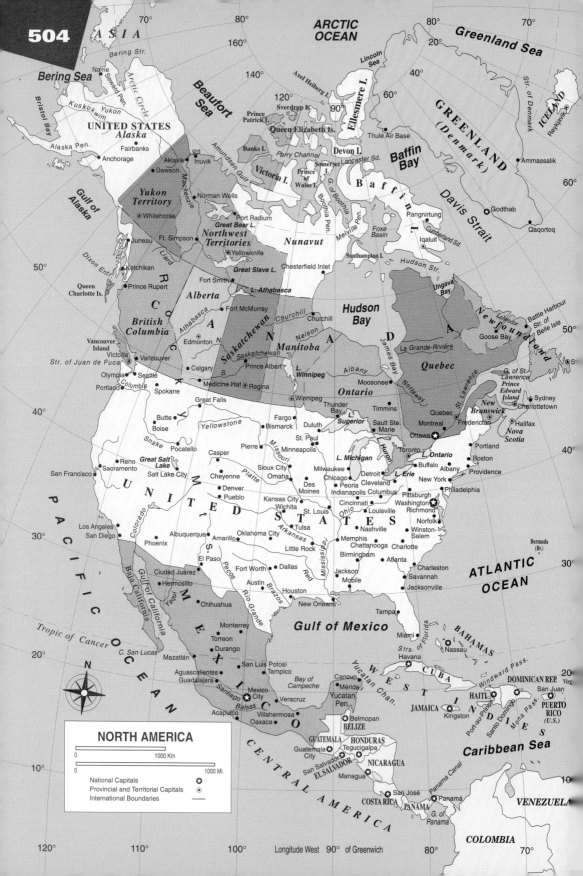

ASIA

70°   80°   160°   ARCTIC OCEAN   80°   20°   70°   Greenland Sea

Bering Sea

Nome   Seward Pen.   Bering Str.   140°   Axel Heiberg I.   40°   GREENLAND (Denmark)   ICELAND   Reykjavik

Bristol Bay   Arctic Circle   Yukon   Kuskokwim   Beaufort Sea   120°   Prince Patrick I.   Sverdrup Is.   90°   60°   Lincoln Sea   Thule Air Base   Str. of Denmark

UNITED STATES   *Alaska*   Banks I.   Queen Elizabeth Is.   Devon I.   Baffin Bay   Ammassalik

Fairbanks   Aklavik   Inuvik   Parry Channel   Somerset   Lancaster Sd.

Anchorage   Alaska Pen.   Dawson   Norman Wells   Victoria I.   Prince of Wales I.   G. of Boothia   Pangnirtung   Godthab

Gulf of Alaska   Yukon Territory   *Whitehorse*   Port Radium   Boothia Pen.   Melville Pen.   Foxe Basin   Cumberland Sd.   Qaqortoq

Juneau   Ft. Simpson   Northwest Territories   *Yellowknife*   Nunavut   Iqaluit

Dixon Entr.   Ketchikan   Great Bear L.   Great Slave L.   Chesterfield Inlet   Southampton I.   Hudson Str.   Davis Strait

Queen Charlotte Is.   Prince Rupert   Fort Smith   L. Athabasca   Ungava Bay

British Columbia   Alberta   Fort McMurray   Churchill   Churchill   Hudson Bay   Labrador   Battle Harbour   Str. of Belle Isle

Vancouver Island   Victoria   Vancouver   Edmonton   Saskatchewan   Nelson   Manitoba   James Bay   La Grande-Rivière   Goose Bay   Newfoundland

Str. of Juan de Fuca   Calgary   Saskatchewan   Prince Albert   L. Winnipeg   Albany   Quebec   G. of St. Lawrence   Prince Edward Island

Olympia   Seattle   Medicine Hat   Regina   Winnipeg   Ontario   Moosonee   St. Lawrence   New Brunswick   Sydney   Charlottetown

Portland   Spokane   Great Falls   Fargo   Thunder Bay   Timmins   Fredericton   Halifax   Nova Scotia

Butte   Boise   Yellowstone   Bismarck   Duluth   L. Superior   Sault Ste. Marie   Montreal   Portland

Reno   Sacramento   Snake   Pocatello   Pierre   Minneapolis   St. Paul   L. Huron   Ottawa   Toronto   L. Ontario   Boston

San Francisco   Great Salt Lake   Salt Lake City   Casper   Sioux City   Milwaukee   Chicago   Detroit   L. Erie   Buffalo   Albany   Providence

Cheyenne   Omaha   Des Moines   Peoria   Cleveland   New York   Philadelphia

Los Angeles   San Diego   Denver   Pueblo   Kansas City   St. Louis   Indianapolis   Columbus   Pittsburgh   Washington   Richmond

Phoenix   Albuquerque   Amarillo   Oklahoma City   Wichita   Cincinnati   Louisville   Norfolk   Winston-Salem

El Paso   Fort Worth   Dallas   Little Rock   Memphis   Nashville   Chattanooga   Charlotte   Charleston

Ciudad Juárez   Austin   Houston   Jackson   Mobile   Birmingham   Atlanta   Savannah   Bermuda (Br.)

Hermosillo   Chihuahua   New Orleans   Gulf of Mexico   Tampa   Jacksonville   ATLANTIC OCEAN

MEXICO   Monterrey   Torreon   Durango   Miami   BAHAMAS   Nassau

Mazatlán   San Luis Potosí   Tampico   Havana   CUBA   DOMINICAN REP.

Aguascalientes   Guadalajara   Mexico City   Veracruz   Cancún   Mérida   Yucatan Chan.   JAMAICA   Kingston   HAITI   PUERTO RICO (U.S.)

Acapulco   Oaxaca   Villahermosa   Yucatan Pen.   BELIZE   Belmopan   Caribbean Sea

GUATEMALA   HONDURAS   Tegucigalpa   WEST INDIES

Guatemala City   San Salvador   EL SALVADOR   NICARAGUA   Managua

San José   COSTA RICA   PANAMÁ   Panamá   Panama Canal   VENEZUELA

CENTRAL AMERICA   G. of Panamá   COLOMBIA

NORTH AMERICA

0	1000 Km
0	1000 Mi.

National Capitals   ⊛
Provincial and Territorial Capitals   ⊙
International Boundaries   —

Tropic of Cancer   Baja California   Gulf of California   C. San Lucas

PACIFIC OCEAN

120°   110°   100°   Longitude West   90°   of Greenwich   80°   70°

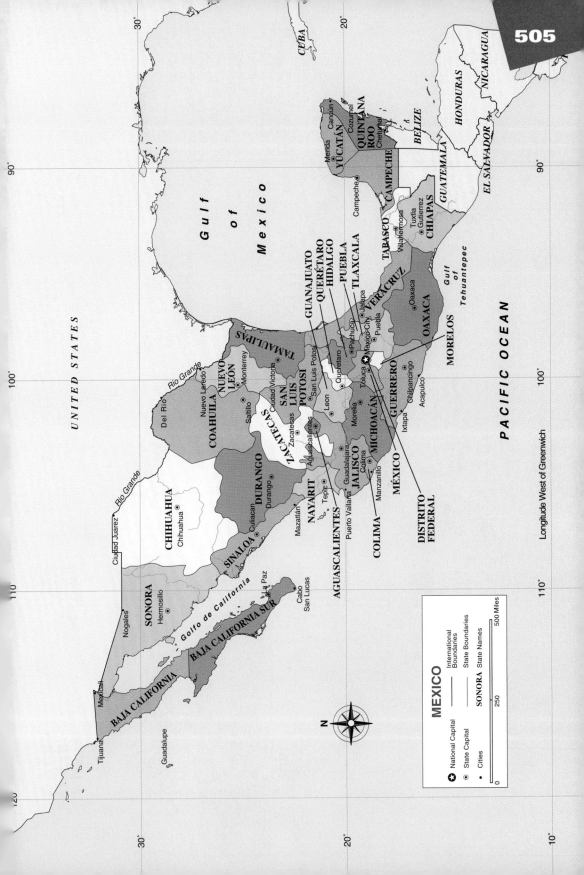

505

MEXICO

- ⊛ National Capital
- ◉ State Capital
- • Cities

— International Boundaries
— State Boundaries
SONORA State Names

0   250   500 Miles

UNITED STATES

Rio Grande

BAJA CALIFORNIA

Tijuana
Mexicali
Nogales
Guadalupe

SONORA
Hermosillo

BAJA CALIFORNIA SUR

Golfo de California

La Paz
Cabo San Lucas

CHIHUAHUA
Chihuahua
Ciudad Juarez
Rio Grande

SINALOA
Culiacan
Mazatlán

DURANGO
Durango

COAHUILA
Del Rio
Nuevo Laredo
Saltillo

NUEVO LEÓN
Monterrey

TAMAULIPAS
Ciudad Victoria

ZACATECAS
Zacatecas

SAN LUIS POTOSI
San Luis Potosi

AGUASCALIENTES
Aguascalientes

NAYARIT
Tepic

JALISCO
Guadalajara
Puerto Vallarta

COLIMA
Colima
Manzanillo

GUANAJUATO
Leon

QUERÉTARO
Queretaro

MICHOACÁN
Morelia

HIDALGO
Pachuca

MÉXICO
Toluca

DISTRITO FEDERAL
Mexico City

MORELOS

PUEBLA
Puebla

TLAXCALA

VERACRUZ
Jalapa

GUERRERO
Chilpancingo
Acapulco
Ixtapa

OAXACA
Oaxaca

TABASCO
Villahermosa

CHIAPAS
Tuxtla Gutierrez

CAMPECHE
Campeche

YUCATÁN
Merida
Cancún
Cozumel

QUINTANA ROO
Chetumal

Gulf of Mexico

Gulf of Tehuantepec

PACIFIC OCEAN

CUBA

BELIZE

GUATEMALA

HONDURAS

EL SALVADOR

NICARAGUA

Longitude West of Greenwich

N

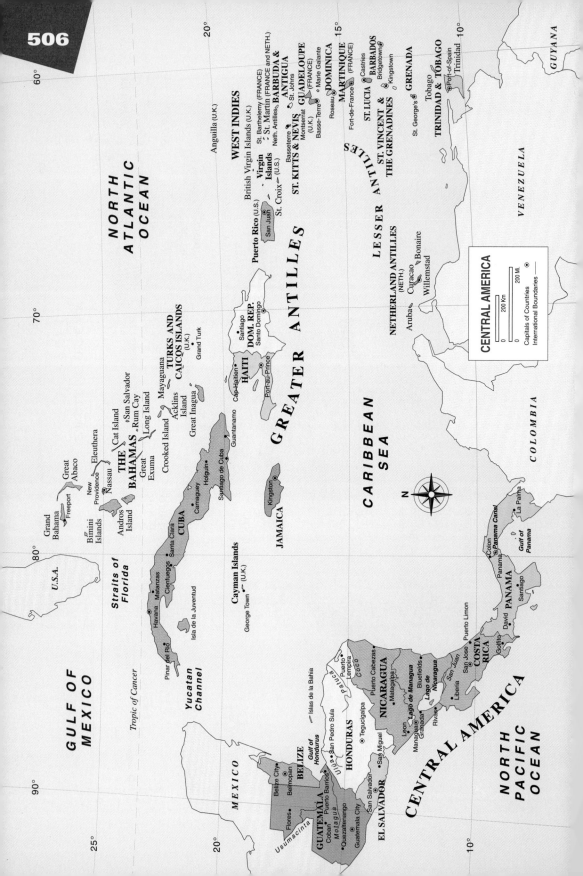

NORTH ATLANTIC OCEAN

GULF OF MEXICO

U.S.A.

Straits of Florida

Tropic of Cancer

Yucatan Channel

Grand Bahama
Great Abaco
Freeport
Bimini Islands
New Providence
Nassau
Andros Island
Eleuthera
Cat Island
San Salvador
Rum Cay
Long Island
THE BAHAMAS
Great Exuma
Crooked Island
Acklins Island
Great Inagua
Mayaguana

Anguilla (U.K.)

WEST INDIES

British Virgin Islands (U.K.)
Virgin Islands
St. Croix (U.S.)
Puerto Rico (U.S.)
San Juan

St. Barthelemy (FRANCE)
St. Martin (FRANCE and NETH.)
Neth. Antilles
Basseterre
ST. KITTS & NEVIS
Basse-Terre
Montserrat (U.K.)
BARBUDA & ANTIGUA
St. Johns
GUADELOUPE (FRANCE)
Marie Galante
Roseau
DOMINICA
Fort-de-France
MARTINIQUE (FRANCE)
Castries
ST. LUCIA
Kingstown
BARBADOS
Bridgetown
ST. VINCENT & THE GRENADINES
St. George's
GRENADA
Tobago
TRINIDAD & TOBAGO
Port-of-Spain
Trinidad

LESSER ANTILLES

TURKS AND CAICOS ISLANDS (U.K.)
Grand Turk

Santiago
DOM. REP.
Santo Domingo
Cap-Haïtien
HAITI
Port-au-Prince

GREATER ANTILLES

Pinar del Río
Havana
Matanzas
Cienfuegos
Santa Clara
CUBA
Camaguey
Holguín
Santiago de Cuba
Guantanamo
Isla de la Juventud

Cayman Islands (U.K.)
George Town

JAMAICA
Kingston

CARIBBEAN SEA

NETHERLAND ANTILLES (NETH.)
Aruba
Curaçao
Bonaire
Willemstad

VENEZUELA

COLOMBIA

N

La Palma
Panama Canal
Colon
Panama
Gulf of Panama
Santiago
PANAMA
David
Golfito
Puerto Limon
COSTA RICA
San José
San Juan
Liberia
Bluefields
Lago de Nicaragua
Rivas
Granada
Managua
León
Lago de Managua
Matagalpa
NICARAGUA
Puerto Cabezas
Coco
Patuca
Puerto Lempira
HONDURAS
San Pedro Sula
Tegucigalpa
San Miguel
Gulf of Honduras
Islas de la Bahia
Ulúa
BELIZE
Belize City
Belmopan
San Salvador
EL SALVADOR
San José
Guatemala City
GUATEMALA
Cobar
Puerto Barrios
Motagua
Quezaltenango
Flores
Usumacinta

M E X I C O

CENTRAL AMERICA

NORTH PACIFIC OCEAN

CENTRAL AMERICA
0   200 Km
0   200 Mi.
⊙ Capitals of Countries
— International Boundaries

GUYANA

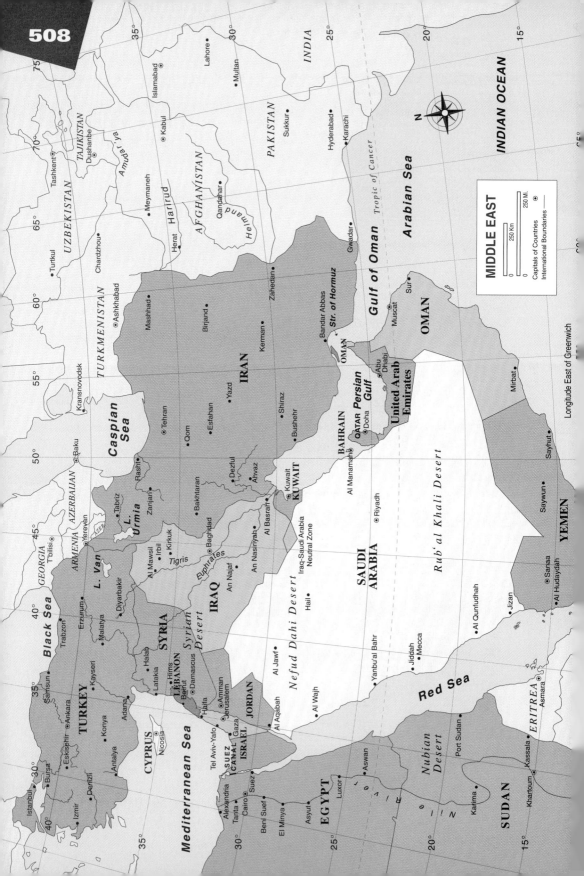

MIDDLE EAST

0   250 Km
0   250 Mi.

Capitals of Countries
International Boundaries

N

INDIAN OCEAN

Arabian Sea

Tropic of Cancer

Gulf of Oman

Str. of Hormuz

Longitude East of Greenwich

INDIA

Lahore
Multan

PAKISTAN

Sukkur

Hyderabad
Karachi

Gwadar

OMAN

Sur

Muscat

Mirbat

Sayhut

YEMEN

Sanaa
Al Hudaydah
Saywun

Jizan

Al Qunfudhah

Rub' al Khali Desert

United Arab
Emirates

Abu
Dhabi

OMAN

QATAR   Persian
Doha   Gulf

BAHRAIN

Al Manamah

Riyadh

SAUDI
ARABIA

Iraq-Saudi Arabia
Neutral Zone

KUWAIT

Kuwait

Mecca
Jiddah

Yanbu'al Bahr

Nefud Dahi Desert

Hail

Al Jawf

Al Wajh

Al Aqabah

Nubian
Desert

Port Sudan

Karima

Khartoum

Kassala

Asmara

ERITREA

SUDAN

Red Sea

Aswan

Luxor

Asyut

El Minya

Beni Suef

Cairo

Suez

SUEZ
CANAL

Alexandria

Tanta

EGYPT

Mediterranean Sea

CYPRUS

Nicosia

Tel Aviv-Yafo

Gaza

Jerusalem

ISRAEL

JORDAN

Amman

LEBANON

Beirut

Damascus

Hims

Latakia

Halab

SYRIA

Syrian
Desert

Adana

Konya

Antalya

Denizli

Izmir

Bursa

Istanbul

TURKEY

Samsun

Ankara

Eskisehir

Kayseri

Malatya

Erzurum

Trabzon

Diyarbakir

Black Sea

GEORGIA

T'bilisi

ARMENIA

Yerevan

AZERBAIJAN

Baku

L. Van

L.
Urmia

Tabriz

Zanjan

Rasht

Bakhtaran

Baghdad

Kirkuk

Irbil

Al Mawsil

Tigris

Euphrates

IRAQ

An Najaf

An Nasiriyah

Al Basrah

Dezful

Ahvaz

Bushehr

Shiraz

Estahan

Qom

Tehran

Yazd

Kerman

IRAN

Birjand

Mashhad

Zahedan

Bandar Abbas

Caspian
Sea

Kransnovodsk

Ashkhabad

TURKMENISTAN

Chardzhou

Turtkul

UZBEKISTAN

Tashkent

TAJIKISTAN

Dushanbe

Amu Dar'ya

Herat

Meymaneh

AFGHANISTAN

Qandahar

Helmand

Harirud

Kabul

Islamabad

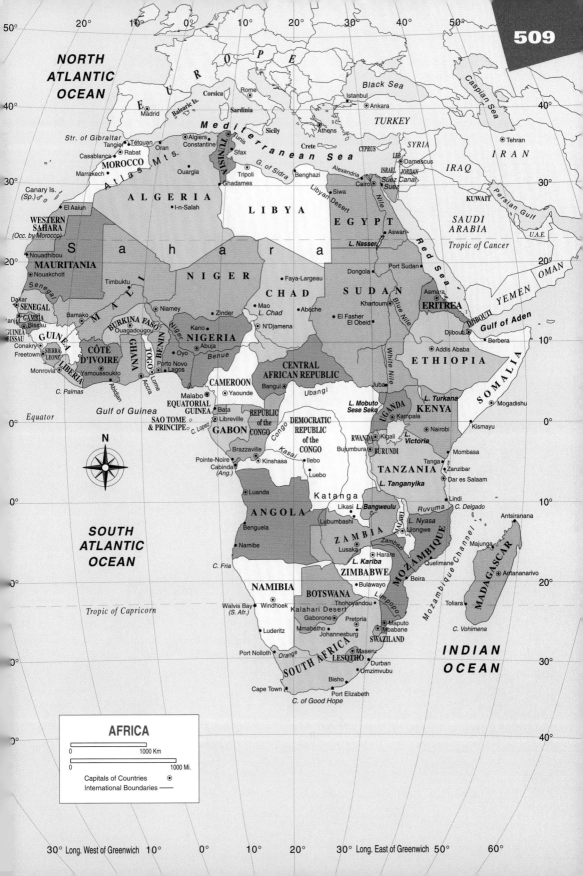

AFRICA

0   1000 Km

0   1000 Mi.

Capitals of Countries ⊙
International Boundaries ——

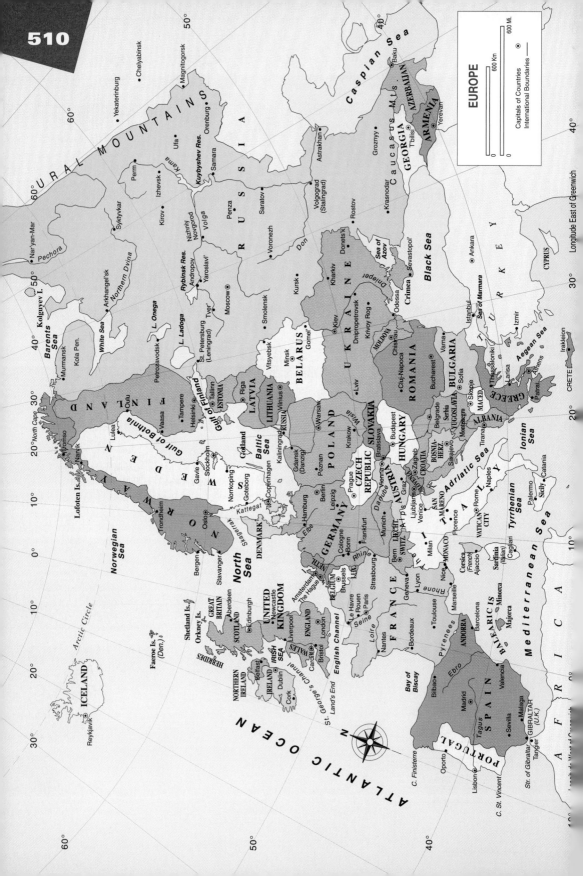

EUROPE

600 Km
600 Mi.

Capitals of Countries ⊙
International Boundaries ──

ATLANTIC OCEAN

ICELAND

Reykjavik •

Norwegian Sea

Lofoten Is.

Tromsø
Narvik

Faeroe Is.
(Den.)

Shetland Is.

Orkney Is.

HEBRIDES

GREAT BRITAIN

SCOTLAND
Aberdeen
Edinburgh

NORTHERN IRELAND
Belfast

IRELAND
Dublin •

Cork •

IRISH SEA

UNITED KINGDOM
Newcastle
Liverpool

WALES
Cardiff

ENGLAND
London

Bristol

St. George's Channel

Land's End

English Channel

North Sea

N O R W A Y

Bergen
Stavanger
Trondheim
Oslo •

Skagerrak

Kattegat

DENMARK
Copenhagen

S W E D E N
Göteborg
Norrköping
Stockholm •
Gävle

Gotland

Baltic Sea

Öland

Oulu

F I N L A N D
Vaasa
Tampere
Helsinki •
Gulf of Finland
Tallinn

ESTONIA

Riga
LATVIA

LITHUANIA
Vilnius

Kaliningrad (RUSSIA)

Gdansk (Danzig)

Poznań

Wisła

Warsaw •

P O L A N D

Kraków

Łódź

Berlin •
Leipzig
Hamburg
Elbe
Bremen
Hannover
Cologne
Bonn •
Frankfurt
G E R M A N Y
Munich
Danube

Luleå

Murmansk

Kola Pen.

White Sea

Barents Sea

Kolguyev I.

Nar'yan-Mar

Pechora

Northern Dvina

Arkhangel'sk

Syktyvkar

L. Onega

Petrozavodsk

L. Ladoga

St. Petersburg (Leningrad) •

Tver'

Moscow •

Smolensk

Vitsyebsk

Minsk •
BELARUS

Gomel

Kyiv •
U K R A I N E

Lviv

R U S S I A

Yekaterinburg •
Chelyabinsk •
Magnitogorsk •

Perm •
Izhevsk •
Kirov •

Ufa •
Kama
Kuybyshev Res.
Orenburg •
Samara •
Penza •
Volga
Saratov •

Rybinsk Res.
Nizhniy Novgorod •
Andropov •
Yaroslavl' •

Kursk •

Voronezh •

Don

Astrakhan' •

Volgograd (Stalingrad) •

Rostov •

Krasnodar •

Grozny' •

Caucasus Mts.

GEORGIA
Tbilisi •

ARMENIA
Yerevan •

AZERBAIJAN
Baku •

Caspian Sea

Kharkiv •
Dnipropetrovsk •
Donets'k •
Kryvy Rog •
Dnieper
MOLDOVA
Chişinău •
Odessa •
Crimea
Sevastopol'

Sea of Azov

Black Sea

ROMANIA
Cluj-Napoca •
Bucharest •

BULGARIA
Varna •
Sofia •

Belgrade •
YUGOSLAVIA
Serbia
Montenegro
Sarajevo •
BOSNIA-HERZ.

CROATIA
Zagreb •

SLOVENIA
Ljubljana

Budapest •
HUNGARY

Vienna •
Bratislava •
SLOVAKIA

CZECH REPUBLIC
Prague •

AUSTRIA
Graz

SWITZ.
LIECHT.
Bern •

Skopje •
MACED.

ALBANIA
Tiranë •

Adriatic Sea

Venice
Florence
Milan •
I T A L Y
Rome •
VATICAN CITY
SAN MARINO
Naples
Corsica (French)
Ajaccio
Sardinia (Italian)
Cagliari
Tyrrhenian Sea
Palermo
Sicily
Catania

MONACO
Nice
Genoa
Turin •
Po
Alps

Ionian Sea

GREECE
Thessaloníki •
Lárisa •
Athens •
Patrai •

CRETE

Aegean Sea

Sea of Marmara
Istanbul •
İzmir •

T U R K E Y
Ankara •

CYPRUS

İrakleíon

F R A N C E
Le Havre
Rouen
Paris •
Seine
Loire
Nantes
Bordeaux
Toulouse
Lyon •
Rhône
Marseille
Strasbourg
Geneva

NETH.
Amsterdam •
The Hague
BELGIUM
Brussels •
LUX.

Rhine

Bay of Biscay

Ebro

Bilbao
Barcelona
Madrid •
S P A I N
Valencia
Sevilla
Málaga

PORTUGAL
Oporto
Lisbon •
Tagus

ANDORRA

Pyrenees

BALEARIC IS.
Minorca
Majorca

Mediterranean Sea

GIBRALTAR (U.K.)
Str. of Gibraltar
Tangier

C. St. Vincent

C. Finisterre

A F R I C A

U R A L   M O U N T A I N S

Arctic Circle

N

Longitude East of Greenwich

40°
50°
60°
50°
40°
30°
20°
10°
0°
10°
20°
30°
40°
50°
60°

North Cape

ATLANTIC
OCEAN

GREENLAND

UNITED STATES
(Alaska)

ICELAND

ARCTIC
North Pole
OCEAN

BERING
SEA

ALEUTIAN IS.

BRITISH ISLES

Svalbard

BARENTS
SEA

EAST
SIBERIAN
SEA

Anadyr

Komandorskiye Is.

London
NORTH
SEA

Paris

Berlin

Warsaw

BALTIC SEA

St. Petersburg

Vienna

Moscow

Kiev

NOVAYA ZEMLYA

SEVERNAYA
ZEMLYA

KARA SEA

LAPTEV SEA

Nordvik

NEW
SIBERIAN IS.

Arctic Circle

Srednekolymsk

Kolyma

Magadan

Kamchatka Pen.

Petropavlovsk-
Kamchatskiy

EUROPE

Dudinka

Salekhard

Khanty-Mansiysk

R U S S I A

Lena

Yakutsk

Nikolayevsk

Sakhalin I.

SEA OF
OKHOTSK

KURIL IS.

Perm'
Yekaterinburg
Chelyabinsk
Magnitogorsk

Ob'

Tomsk
Novosibirsk
Barnaul

Krasnoyarsk

Kirensk

L. Baykal

Chita

Irkutsk

Ulan-Ude

Komsomol'sk

Skovorodino

Amur

Khabarovsk

Hokkaido

Hakodate

Vladivostok

Sendai

Honshu

40°

Omsk

Ural'sk

Gur'yev

Karaganda

Semipalatinsk

Hovd

Uliastay

Ulaanbaatar

Qiqihar
Changchun

Shenyang

N. KOREA

Dandong

Pyongyang

SEA
OF
JAPAN

Tokyo

Nagoya

BLACK SEA

Ankara

Istanbul

TURKEY

Adana

Erzurum

CASPIAN SEA

KAZAKHSTAN

ARAL SEA

L. Balkhash

Bishkek

Alma-Ata

Urumqi

SINKIANG

MONGOLIA

Gobi

INNER MONGOLIA

Beijing

Tianjin

GREAT WALL

Jinan

Seoul

S.
KOREA

Hiroshima

Shikoku

Kyushu

Nagasaki

YELLOW
SEA

GRAND CANAL

Huang

Tabriz

Krasnovodsk

TURKMENISTAN

Ashkhabad

Tashkent

UZBEK.

Syrdarya

Kokand

KYRGYZ.

Aksu

Shache

Hotan

C H I N A

Yumen

Jiuquan

Lanzhou

Xi'an

Kaifeng

Nanjing

Wuhan

Shanghai

EAST
CHINA
SEA

Tropic of Cancer

MED.
SEA

CYPRUS

LEBANON

Aleppo

Beirut

SYRIA

Jerusalem

Damascus

ISRAEL

Amman

IRAQ

Baghdad

Basra

I R A N

Tehran

Mashad

Amudarya

Herat

AFGHANISTAN

Kabul

Srinagar

Islamabad

Himalaya

TIBET

Lhasa

Thimphu

BHUTAN

Chongqing

Changsha

Fuzhou

Taipei

TAIWAN

PACIFIC
OCEAN

20°

KUWAIT

Shiraz

Quetta

NEPAL

Kathmandu

Chang (Yangtze)

Guangzhou

HONG KONG

BAHRAIN

QATAR

RED SEA

Mecca

Riyadh

U.N.-ARAB EMIR.

Persian G.

Bandar Abbas

PAKISTAN

Gwadar

G. of Oman

Muscat

Karachi

New Delhi

Kanpur

Indus

I N D I A

Brahmaputra

Myitkyina

Mandalay

MYANMAR

Hanoi

LAOS

Hainan

SOUTH
CHINA
SEA

Luzon

Manila

PHILIPPINES

Samar

Mindoro

Leyte

SAUDI
ARABIA

Sanaa

YEMEN

OMAN

Ahmadabad

Daman

Bombay

Hyderabad

Yanam

Vientiane

Rangoon

THAILAND

Bangkok

G. of Tonkin

Palawan

Negros

Davao

Mindanao

Aden

G. of Aden

Socotra

ARABIAN
SEA

Bangalore

Mahe

Madras

Karikal

Daman

CAMBODIA

Phnom Penh

VIETNAM

Ho Chi Minh City
(Saigon)

Kota Kinabalu

SABAH

Manado

CELEBES
SEA

SEYCHELLES

Madurai

SRI LANKA
(CEYLON)

Colombo

Kandy

G. of
Thailand

BRUNEI

SARAWAK

Kuching

Borneo

Celebes

BANDA
SEA

MADAGASCAR

MALDIVES

Male

George Town

Medan

Str. of Malacca

MALAYA

Kuala Lumpur

MALAYSIA

SINGAPORE

Banjarmasin

Makassar Str.

Ujung Pandang

East Timor

Timor

FLORES SEA

Flores

BAY OF
BENGAL

BANGLA-
DESH

Dhaka

Calcutta

Equator

Sumatra

INDONESIA

JAVA SEA

Palembang

Jakarta

JAVA

Surabaya

Sumbawa

TIMOR
SEA

AFRICA

S U N D A   I S.

N

INDIAN OCEAN

Broome

Tropic of Capricorn

AUSTRALIA

Perth

20°

ASIA

0   1200 Km

0   1200 Mi.

◉ Capitals of Countries

── International Boundaries

60° Longitude East of Greenwich 80°   100°   120°

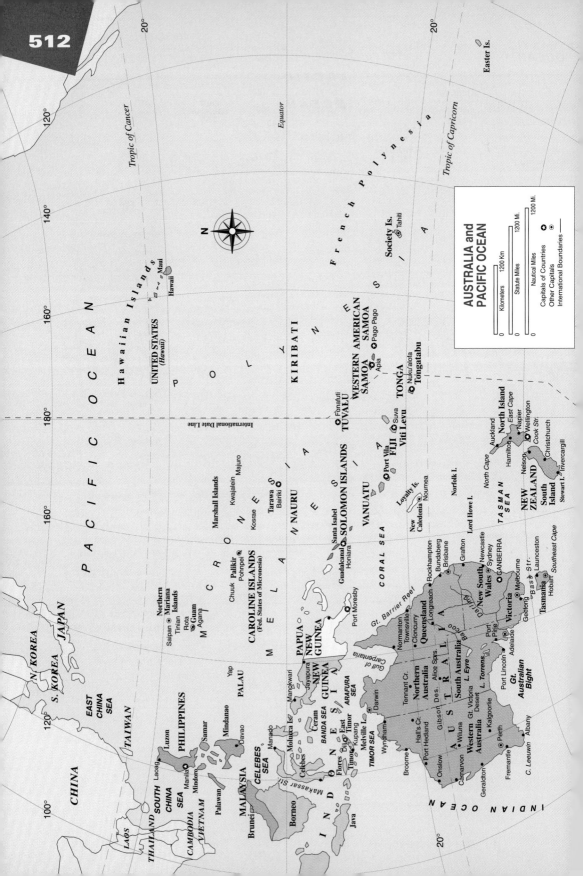

AUSTRALIA and
PACIFIC OCEAN

Kilometers   1200 Km
Statute Miles   1200 Mi.
Nautical Miles   1200 Mi.

✪ Capitals of Countries
⊛ Other Capitals
——— International Boundaries

PACIFIC OCEAN

Tropic of Cancer

Equator

Tropic of Capricorn

Easter Is.

CHINA

THAILAND
CAMBODIA
VIETNAM
LAOS

N. KOREA
S. KOREA
JAPAN
TAIWAN

EAST
CHINA
SEA

SOUTH
CHINA
SEA

PHILIPPINES
Laoag
Luzon
Manila
Mindoro
Samar
Palawan
Davao
Mindanao
Manado

MALAYSIA
Brunei
Borneo
Celebes
CELEBES
SEA
Makassar Str.

I N D O N E S I A
Java
Flores
Bali
Lombok
Sumbawa
Kupang
Timor
East
Timor
Ceram
Moluca Isl.
BANDA SEA
ARAFURA
SEA
TIMOR SEA
Melville I.

PALAU
Yap

Northern
Mariana
Islands
Saipan
Tinian
Rota
Guam
Agana

CAROLINE ISLANDS
(Fed. States of Micronesia)
Chuck Palikir
Pohnpei
Kosrae

M I C R O N E S I A

Marshall Islands
Kwajalein Majuro

Hawaiian Islands
Maui
Hawaii

UNITED STATES
(Hawaii)

International Date Line

P O L Y N E S I A

KIRIBATI

Tarawa
Bairiki

NAURU

TUVALU
Funafuti

Western
Samoa
Apia
American
Samoa
Pago Pago

TONGA
Nuku'alofa
Tongatabu

Society Is.
Tahiti

French Polynesia

FIJI
Suva
Viti Levu

VANUATU
Port Vila

SOLOMON ISLANDS
Honiara
Santa Isabel
Guadalcanal

M E L A N E S I A

PAPUA
NEW
GUINEA
Port Moresby
Jayapura
Mangkwari

Norfolk I.

New
Caledonia
Noumea
Loyalty Is.

Lord Howe I.

CORAL SEA

Gulf of
Carpentaria

Gt. Barrier Reef

A U S T R A L I A

Northern
Australia
Darwin
Wyndham
Halls Cr.
Tennant Cr.
Alice Sprs.
Gt. Sandy
Des.
Gibson Des.

Western
Australia
Broome
Port Hedland
Onslow
Carnarvon
Geraldton
Wiluna
Kalgoorlie
Perth
Fremantle
C. Leeuwin
Albany

Queensland
Normanton
Cloncurry
Townsville
Longreach
Rockhampton
Bundaberg
Brisbane
Grafton

South Australia
Gt. Victoria
Desert
L. Eyre
L. Torrens
Port
Pirie
Port Lincoln
Gt.
Australian
Bight
Adelaide

New South
Wales
Newcastle
Sydney
CANBERRA

Victoria
Melbourne
Geelong

Bass Str.
Tasmania
Launceston
Hobart
Southeast Cape

Darling

Murray

Barcoo

TASMAN
SEA

NEW
ZEALAND
North Cape
Auckland
Hamilton
North Island
East Cape
Napier
Wellington
Cook Str.
Nelson
South
Island
Christchurch
Invercargill
Stewart I.

INDIAN OCEAN

Index to World Maps

Country	Latitude	Longitude	Country	Latitude	Longitude
Afghanistan	33° N	65° E	Costa Rica	10° N	84° W
Albania	41° N	20° E	Côte d'Ivoire	8° N	5° W
Algeria	28° N	3° E	Croatia	45° N	16° E
Andorra	42° N	1° E	Cuba	21° N	80° W
Angola	12° S	18° E	Cyprus	35° N	33° E
Antigua and			Czech Republic	50° N	15° E
Barbuda	17° N	61° W	Denmark	56° N	10° E
Argentina	34° S	64° W	Djibouti	11° N	43° E
Armenia	41° N	45° E	Dominica	15° N	61° W
Australia	25° S	135° E	Dominican Rep.	19° N	70° W
Austria	47° N	13° E	East Timor	10° S	125° E
Azerbaijan	41° N	47° E	Ecuador	2° S	77° W
Bahamas	24° N	76° W	Egypt	27° N	30° E
Bahrain	26° N	50° E	El Salvador	14° N	89° W
Bangladesh	24° N	90° E	Equatorial Guinea	2° N	9° E
Barbados	13° N	59° W	Eritrea	17° N	38° E
Belarus	54° N	25° E	Estonia	59° N	26° E
Belgium	50° N	4° E	Ethiopia	8° N	38° E
Belize	17° N	88° W	Fiji	19° S	174° E
Benin	9° N	2° E	Finland	64° N	26° E
Bhutan	27° N	90° E	France	46° N	2° E
Bolivia	17° S	65° W	Gabon	1° S	11° E
Bosnia-			The Gambia	13° N	16° W
Herzegovina	44° N	18° E	Georgia	43° N	45° E
Botswana	22° S	24° E	Germany	51° N	10° E
Brazil	10° S	55° W	Ghana	8° N	2° W
Brunei Darussalam	4° N	114° E	Greece	39° N	22° E
Bulgaria	43° N	25° E	Greenland	70° N	40° W
Burkina Faso	13° N	2° W	Grenada	12° N	61° W
Burundi	3° S	30° E	Guatemala	15° N	90° W
Cambodia	13° N	105° E	Guinea	11° N	10° W
Cameroon	6° N	12° E	Guinea-Bissau	12° N	15° W
Canada	60° N	95° W	Guyana	5° N	59° W
Cape Verde	16° N	24° W	Haiti	19° N	72° W
Central African			Honduras	15° N	86° W
Republic	7° N	21° E	Hungary	47° N	20° E
Chad	15° N	19° E	Iceland	65° N	18° W
Chile	30° S	71° W	India	20° N	77° E
China	35° N	105° E	Indonesia	5° S	120° E
Colombia	4° N	72° W	Iran	32° N	53° E
Comoros	12° S	44° E	Iraq	33° N	44° E
Congo,			Ireland	53° N	8° W
Dem. Rep. of the	4° S	25° E	Israel	31° N	35° E
Congo,			Italy	42° N	12° E
Republic of the	1° S	15° E	Jamaica	18° N	77° W

Country	Latitude	Longitude	Country	Latitude	Longitude
Japan	36° N	138° E	Oman	22° N	58° E
Jordan	31° N	36° E	Pakistan	30° N	70° E
Kazakhstan	45° N	70° E	Palau	8° N	138° E
Kenya	1° N	38° E	Panama	9° N	80° W
Kiribati	0° N	175° E	Papua New Guinea	6° S	147° E
North Korea	40° N	127° E	Paraguay	23° S	58° W
South Korea	36° N	128° E	Peru	10° S	76° W
Kuwait	29° N	47° E	The Philippines	13° N	122° E
Kyrgyzstan	42° N	75° E	Poland	52° N	19° E
Laos	18° N	105° E	Portugal	39° N	8° W
Latvia	57° N	25° E	Qatar	25° N	51° E
Lebanon	34° N	36° E	Romania	46° N	25° E
Lesotho	29° S	28° E	Russia	60° N	80° E
Liberia	6° N	10° W	Rwanda	2° S	30° E
Libya	27° N	17° E	St. Kitts & Nevis	17° N	62° W
Liechtenstein	47° N	9° E	Saint Lucia	14° N	61° W
Lithuania	56° N	24° E	Saint Vincent and		
Luxembourg	49° N	6° E	the Grenadines	13° N	61° W
Macedonia	43° N	22° E	San Marino	44° N	12° E
Madagascar	19° S	46° E	São Tomé and		
Malawi	13° S	34° E	Príncipe	1° N	7° E
Malaysia	2° N	112° E	Saudi Arabia	25° N	45° E
Maldives	2° N	70° E	Scotland	57° N	5° W
Mali	17° N	4° W	Senegal	14° N	14° W
Malta	36° N	14° E	Serbia	45° N	21° E
Marshall Islands	7° N	172° E	Seychelles	5° S	55° E
Mauritania	20° N	12° W	Sierra Leone	8° N	11° W
Mauritius	20° S	57° E	Singapore	1° N	103° E
Mexico	23° N	102° W	Slovakia	49° N	19° E
Micronesia	5° N	150° E	Slovenia	46° N	15° E
Moldova	47° N	28° E	Solomon Islands	8° S	159° E
Monaco	43° N	7° E	Somalia	10° N	49° E
Mongolia	46° N	105° E	South Africa	30° S	26° E
Montenegro	43° N	19° E	Spain	40° N	4° W
Morocco	32° N	5° W	Sri Lanka	7° N	81° E
Mozambique	18° S	35° E	Sudan	15° N	30° E
Myanmar	25° N	95° E	Suriname	4° N	56° W
Namibia	22° S	17° E	Swaziland	26° S	31° E
Nauru	1° S	166° E	Sweden	62° N	15° E
Nepal	28° N	84° E	Switzerland	47° N	8° E
The Netherlands	52° N	5° E	Syria	35° N	38° E
New Zealand	41° S	174° E	Taiwan	23° N	121° E
Nicaragua	13° N	85° W	Tajikistan	39° N	71° E
Niger	16° N	8° E	Tanzania	6° S	35° E
Nigeria	10° N	8° E	Thailand	15° N	100° E
Northern Ireland	55° N	7° W	Togo	8° N	1° E
Norway	62° N	10° E	Tonga	20° S	173° W

Country	Latitude	Longitude	Country	Latitude	Longitude
Trinidad & Tobago	11° N	61° W	Uruguay	33° S	56° W
Tunisia	34° N	9° E	Uzbekistan	40° N	68° E
Turkey	39° N	35° E	Vanuatu	17° S	170° E
Turkmenistan	40° N	55° E	Venezuela	8° N	66° W
Tuvalu	8° S	179° E	Vietnam	17° N	106° E
Uganda	1° N	32° E	Wales	53° N	3° W
Ukraine	50° N	30° E	Western Samoa	10° S	173° W
United Arab			Yemen	15° N	44° E
Emirates	24° N	54° E	Yugoslavia	44° N	19° E
United Kingdom	54° N	2° W	Zambia	15° S	30° E
United States	38° N	97° W	Zimbabwe	20° S	30° E

Geographic Facts

THE CONTINENTS

	Area (Sq Km)	Percent of Earth's Land
Asia	44,026,000	29.7
Africa	30,271,000	20.4
North America	24,258,000	16.3
South America	17,823,000	12.0
Antarctica	13,209,000	8.9
Europe	10,404,000	7.0
Australia	7,682,000	5.2

LONGEST RIVERS

	Length (Km)
Nile, *Africa*	6,671
Amazon, *South America*	6,437
Chang Jiang (Yangtze), *Asia*	6,380
Mississippi-Missouri, *North America*	5,971
Ob-Irtysk, *Asia*	5,410
Huang (Yellow), *Asia*	4,672
Congo, *Africa*	4,667
Amur, *Asia*	4,416
Lena, *Asia*	4,400
Mackenzie-Peace, *North America*	4,241

MAJOR ISLANDS

	Area (Sq Km)
Greenland	2,175,600
New Guinea	792,500
Borneo	725,500
Madagascar	587,000
Baffin	507,500
Sumatra	427,300
Honshu	227,400
Great Britain	218,100
Victoria	217,300
Ellesmere	196,200
Celebes	178,700
South (New Zealand)	151,000
Java	126,700

THE OCEANS

	Area (Sq Km)	Percent of Earth's Water Area
Pacific	166,241,000	46.0
Atlantic	86,557,000	23.9
Indian	73,427,000	20.3
Arctic	9,485,000	2.6

World Time Zones

The world's 24 time zones start at the prime meridian. When going west, travelers must set their watches back one hour for each time zone they cross. Going east, they must set their watches forward one hour for each zone.

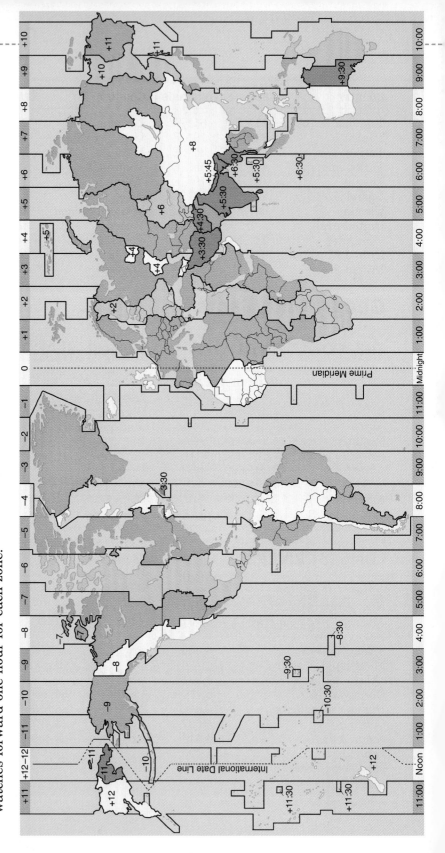

Government

Every country in the world has a government. The purpose of the government is to make and enforce laws and to protect the rights of its citizens. Every major country in the world also has a constitution, a basic set of laws by which the people are governed.

The U.S. Constitution establishes the form of the United States government and explains the rights and responsibilities of its citizens. This section of your handbook takes a closer look at those rights and responsibilities, and how the government is organized. We hope you find it interesting and useful.

Branches of Government

Legislative Branch	Executive Branch	Judicial Branch

Duties/Responsibilities

Makes Laws	Enforces Laws Makes Policy	Interprets Laws

Components

Congress	President	Supreme Court
Senate / House of Representatives	Vice President	Circuit Courts
President of the Senate / Speaker of the House	Cabinet	District Courts
		Special Courts

President's Cabinet

The Cabinet is a group of advisors appointed by the president to help set policies and make decisions. The Cabinet usually meets weekly with the president.

Department of State

Department of Education

Department of Health and Human Services

Department of Defense

Department of Commerce

Department of the Treasury

Department of Veterans Affairs

Department of Housing and Urban Development

Department of the Interior

Department of Energy

Department of Agriculture

Attorney General

Department of Labor

Department of Homeland Security

Department of Transportation

Individual Rights & Responsibilities

Individual Rights

Freedom of Assembly

Freedom to hold meetings. Meetings must be peaceful.

Freedom of Speech

Freedom to express ideas and opinions. No one may say untrue things about other citizens.

Freedom of Petition

Freedom to ask the government to pass laws.

Freedom of the Press

Freedom to print books, newspapers, and magazines. No one may print things that hurt American citizens.

Freedom of Religion

Freedom to practice the religion of your choice.

Freedom of Equal Justice

All persons accused of a crime must receive fair and equal treatment under the law.

Freedom and Security of Citizens

No one may search someone's home. People have the right to bear arms to protect themselves.

Duties of Citizenship

- American citizens must serve as jury members when called upon.
- American citizens must pay taxes to fund the government.
- American citizens must attend school.
- American citizens must testify in court.
- American citizens must obey the law.
- American citizens must help to defend the nation.

U.S. Presidents & Vice Presidents

1	George Washington	April 30, 1789 – March 3, 1797	John Adams	1
2	John Adams	March 4, 1797 – March 3, 1801	Thomas Jefferson	2
3	Thomas Jefferson	March 4, 1801 – March 3, 1805	Aaron Burr	3
	Thomas Jefferson	March 4, 1805 – March 3, 1809	George Clinton	4
4	James Madison	March 4, 1809 – March 3, 1813	George Clinton	
	James Madison	March 4, 1813 – March 3, 1817	Elbridge Gerry	5
5	James Monroe	March 4, 1817 – March 3, 1821	Daniel D. Tompkins	6
	James Monroe	March 4, 1821 – March 3, 1825		
6	John Quincy Adams	March 4, 1825 – March 3, 1829	John C. Calhoun	7
7	Andrew Jackson	March 4, 1829 – March 3, 1833	John C. Calhoun	
	Andrew Jackson	March 4, 1833 – March 3, 1837	Martin Van Buren	8
8	Martin Van Buren	March 4, 1837 – March 3, 1841	Richard M. Johnson	9
9	William Henry Harrison*	March 4, 1841 – April 4, 1841	John Tyler	10
10	John Tyler	April 6, 1841 – March 3, 1845		
11	James K. Polk	March 4, 1845 – March 3, 1849	George M. Dallas	11
12	Zachary Taylor*	March 5, 1849 – July 9, 1850	Millard Fillmore	12
13	Millard Fillmore	July 10, 1850 – March 3, 1853		
14	Franklin Pierce	March 4, 1853 – March 3, 1857	William R. King	13
15	James Buchanan	March 4, 1857 – March 3, 1861	John C. Breckinridge	14
16	Abraham Lincoln	March 4, 1861 – March 3, 1865	Hannibal Hamlin	15
	Abraham Lincoln*	March 4, 1865 – April 15, 1865	Andrew Johnson	16
17	Andrew Johnson	April 15, 1865 – March 3, 1869		
18	Ulysses S. Grant	March 4, 1869 – March 3, 1873	Schuyler Colfax	17
	Ulysses S. Grant	March 4, 1873 – March 3, 1877	Henry Wilson	18
19	Rutherford B. Hayes	March 4, 1877 – March 3, 1881	William A. Wheeler	19
20	James A. Garfield*	March 4, 1881 – Sept. 19, 1881	Chester A. Arthur	20
21	Chester A. Arthur	Sept. 20, 1881 – March 3, 1885		
22	Grover Cleveland	March 4, 1885 – March 3, 1889	Thomas A. Hendricks	21
23	Benjamin Harrison	March 4, 1889 – March 3, 1893	Levi P. Morton	22
24	Grover Cleveland	March 4, 1893 – March 3, 1897	Adlai E. Stevenson	23
25	William McKinley	March 4, 1897 – March 3, 1901	Garret A. Hobart	24
	William McKinley*	March 4, 1901 – Sept. 14, 1901	Theodore Roosevelt	25
26	Theodore Roosevelt	Sept. 14, 1901 – March 3, 1905		
	Theodore Roosevelt	March 4, 1905 – March 3, 1909	Charles W. Fairbanks	26
27	William H. Taft	March 4, 1909 – March 3, 1913	James S. Sherman	27
28	Woodrow Wilson	March 4, 1913 – March 3, 1917	Thomas R. Marshall	28
	Woodrow Wilson	March 4, 1917 – March 3, 1921		
29	Warren G. Harding*	March 4, 1921 – Aug. 2, 1923	Calvin Coolidge	29
30	Calvin Coolidge	Aug. 3, 1923 – March 3, 1925		
	Calvin Coolidge	March 4, 1925 – March 3, 1929	Charles G. Dawes	30
31	Herbert C. Hoover	March 4, 1929 – March 3, 1933	Charles Curtis	31

32 Franklin D. Roosevelt ...... March 4, 1933 – Jan. 20, 1937 ....John N. Garner 32

    Franklin D. Roosevelt .... Jan. 20, 1937 – Jan. 20, 1941 ....John N. Garner

    Franklin D. Roosevelt .... Jan. 20, 1941 – Jan. 20, 1945 ....Henry A. Wallace 33

    Franklin D. Roosevelt* ...... Jan. 20, 1945 – April 12, 1945 ....Harry S. Truman 34

33 Harry S. Truman .... April 12, 1945 – Jan. 20, 1949

    Harry S. Truman............... Jan. 20, 1949 – Jan. 20, 1953 ....Alben W. Barkley 35

34 Dwight D. Eisenhower .... Jan. 20, 1953 – Jan. 20, 1957 ....Richard M. Nixon 36

    Dwight D. Eisenhower .... Jan. 20, 1957 – Jan. 20, 1961 ....Richard M. Nixon

35 John F. Kennedy* .... Jan. 20, 1961 – Nov. 22, 1963 ....Lyndon B. Johnson 37

36 Lyndon B. Johnson............. Nov. 22, 1963 – Jan. 20, 1965

    Lyndon B. Johnson............. Jan. 20, 1965 – Jan. 20, 1969 .....Hubert H. Humphrey 38

37 Richard M. Nixon............... Jan. 20, 1969 – Jan. 20, 1973 ....Spiro T. Agnew 39

    Richard M. Nixon* .... Jan. 20, 1973 – Aug. 9, 1974..................Gerald R. Ford 40

38 Gerald R. Ford .... Aug. 9, 1974 – Jan. 20, 1977 .....Nelson A. Rockefeller 41

39 James E. Carter .... Jan. 20, 1977 – Jan. 20, 1981 ....Walter Mondale 42

40 Ronald W. Reagan .... Jan. 20, 1981 – Jan. 20, 1985 ....George H. W. Bush 43

    Ronald W. Reagan .... Jan. 20, 1985 – Jan. 20, 1989 ....George H. W. Bush

41 George H. W. Bush............. Jan. 20, 1989 – Jan. 20, 1993 ....J. Danforth Quayle 44

42 William J. Clinton .... Jan. 20, 1993 – Jan. 20, 1997 ....Albert Gore, Jr. 45

    William J. Clinton .... Jan. 20, 1997 – Jan. 20, 2001 ....Albert Gore, Jr.

43 George W. Bush .... Jan. 20, 2001 – ....Richard B. Cheney 46

(*Did not finish term)

Order of Presidential Succession

1. Vice president
2. Speaker of the House
3. President pro tempore of the Senate
4. Secretary of state
5. Secretary of the treasury
6. Secretary of defense
7. Attorney general
8. Secretary of the interior
9. Secretary of agriculture
10. Secretary of commerce
11. Secretary of labor
12. Secretary of health and human services
13. Secretary of housing and urban development
14. Secretary of transportation
15. Secretary of energy
16. Secretary of education
17. Secretary of veterans affairs
18. Secretary of homeland security

The U.S. Constitution

The Constitution is made up of three main parts: a **preamble,** 7 **articles,** and 27 **amendments.** The *preamble* states the purpose of the Constitution, the *articles* explain how the government works, and the 10 original *amendments* list the basic rights guaranteed to all American citizens. Together, these parts contain the laws and guidelines necessary to set up and run a successful national government.

Besides giving power to the national government, the U.S. Constitution gives some power to the states and some to the people. Remember this when you study the Constitution.

The Preamble

We the people of the United States, in order to form a more perfect Union, establish justice, insure domestic tranquility, provide for the common defense, promote the general welfare, and secure the blessings of liberty to ourselves and our posterity, do ordain and establish this Constitution for the United States of America.

The Articles of the Constitution

The articles of the Constitution explain how each branch of government works and what each can and cannot do. The articles also explain how the federal and state governments must work together, and how the Constitution can be amended or changed.

ARTICLE 1 explains the legislative branch, how laws are made, and how Congress works.

ARTICLE 2 explains the executive branch, the offices of the President and Vice President, and the powers of the executive branch.

ARTICLE 3 explains the judicial branch, the Supreme Court and other courts, and warns people about trying to overthrow the government.

ARTICLE 4 describes how the United States federal government and the individual state governments work together.

ARTICLE 5 tells how the Constitution can be amended, or changed.

ARTICLE 6 states that the United States federal government and the Constitution are the law of the land.

ARTICLE 7 outlines how the Constitution must be adopted to become official.

The Bill of Rights

To get the necessary votes to approve the Constitution, a number of changes (amendments) had to be made. These 10 original amendments are called the Bill of Rights. They guarantee all Americans some very basic rights, including the right to worship and speak freely and the right to have a jury trial.

AMENDMENT 1 People have the right to worship, to speak freely, to gather together, and to question the government.

AMENDMENT 2 People have the right to bear arms.

AMENDMENT 3 The government cannot have soldiers stay in people's houses without their permission.

AMENDMENT 4 People and their property cannot be searched without the written permission of a judge.

AMENDMENT 5 People cannot be tried for a serious crime without a jury. They cannot be tried twice for the same crime or be forced to testify against themselves. Also, they cannot have property taken away while they are on trial. Any property taken for public use must receive a fair price.

AMENDMENT 6 In criminal cases, people have a right to a trial, to be told what they are accused of, to hear witnesses against them, to get witnesses in their favor, and to have a lawyer.

AMENDMENT 7 In cases involving more than $20, people have the right to a jury trial.

AMENDMENT 8 People have a right to fair bail (money given as a promise the person will return for trial) and to fair fines and punishments.

AMENDMENT 9 People have rights that are not listed in the Constitution.

AMENDMENT 10 Powers not given to the federal government are given to the states or to the people.

The Other Amendments

The Constitution and the Bill of Rights were ratified in 1791. Since that time, more than 7,000 amendments to the Constitution have been proposed. Because three-fourths of the states must approve an amendment before it becomes law, just 27 amendments have been passed. The first 10 are listed under the Bill of Rights; the other 17 are listed below. (The date each amendment became law is given in parentheses.)

AMENDMENT 11 A person cannot sue a state in federal court. (1795)

AMENDMENT 12 President and Vice President are elected separately. (1804)

AMENDMENT 13 Slavery is abolished, done away with. (1865)

AMENDMENT 14 All persons born in the United States or those who have become citizens enjoy full citizenship rights. (1868)

AMENDMENT 15 Voting rights are given to all citizens regardless of race, creed, or color. (1870)

AMENDMENT 16 Congress has the power to collect income taxes. (1913)

AMENDMENT 17 United States Senators are elected directly by the people. (1913)

AMENDMENT 18 Making, buying, and selling alcoholic beverages is no longer allowed. (1919)

AMENDMENT 19 Women gain the right to vote. (1920)

AMENDMENT 20 The President's term begins January 20; Senators' and Representatives' terms begin January 3. (1933)

AMENDMENT 21 (Repeals Amendment 18) Alcoholic beverages can be made, bought, and sold again. (1933)

AMENDMENT 22 The President is limited to two elected terms. (1951)

AMENDMENT 23 District of Columbia residents gain the right to vote. (1961)

AMENDMENT 24 All voter poll taxes are forbidden. (1964)

AMENDMENT 25 If the Presidency is vacant, the Vice President takes over. If the Vice Presidency is vacant, the President names someone and the Congress votes on the choice. (1967)

AMENDMENT 26 Citizens 18 years old gain the right to vote. (1971)

AMENDMENT 27 No law changing the pay for members of Congress will take effect until after an election of Representatives. (1992)

History

A famous American author, Oliver Wendell Holmes, once said, "When I want to understand what is happening today or try to decide what will happen tomorrow, I look back." In other words, we can learn a lot about the world around us by looking at what has happened in the past—by studying history.

Historical Time Line

The historical time line on the next 11 pages covers the period from 1500 to the present. The time line is divided into three main parts: U.S. and World History, Science and Inventions, and Literature and Life. You'll discover many interesting pieces of information in this section.

Thousands of years before this time, people migrated across a land bridge from Asia to North America. These people were the ancestors of the Native Americans, who eventually formed different tribal cultures based on the climate, the animals and plants, and the landforms in each particular region. As you'll see on the map below, the tribes lived in one of eight major regions. American history really begins with the Native Americans.

Pacific Northwest

Great Plateau

California

Great Basin

Plains

Northeast Woodland

Desert Southwest

Southeast Woodland

Native American Regions

1500	1520	1540	1560	1580

U.S. and World History

1492
Columbus lands in the West Indies.

1519
Magellan begins three-year voyage around the world.

1565
Spain settles St. Augustine, Florida, the first permanent European colony.

1513
Ponce de León explores Florida; Balboa reaches Pacific.

1570
League of Iroquois Nations is formed.

1519
Aztec empire dominates Mexico.

1588
England defeats the Spanish Armada and rules the seas.

Science and Inventions

1507
Book on surgery is developed.

1545
French painter Garamond sets first type.

1585
Dutch mathematicians introduce decimals.

1530
Bottle corks are invented.

1531
Halley's comet appears and causes panic.

1558
The magnetic compass is invented by John Dee.

1509
Watches are invented.

1596
The thermometer is invented.

Literature and Life

1580
The first water closet is designed in Bath, England.

1500
The game of bingo is developed.

1536
The first songbook is used in Spain.

1507
Glass mirrors are greatly improved.

1564
The first horse-drawn coach is used in England.

1599
Copper coins are first made.

U.S. POPULATION: (Native American)
approximately 1,100,000

(Spanish)
1,021

1600   1620   1640   1660   1680   1700

1607
The first English settlement is established at Jamestown, Virginia.

1629
The charter for Massachusetts Bay Colony is established.

1619
First African slaves are brought to Virginia.

1620
Plymouth Colony is founded by Pilgrims.

1673
Marquette and Joliet explore the Mississippi River for France.

1682
William Penn founds Pennsylvania.

1608
The telescope is invented.

1629
Human temperature is measured by a physician in Italy.

1682
Halley's comet is studied by Edmund Halley and named for him.

1641
First cotton factories open in England.

1671
The first calculation machine is invented.

1609
Galileo makes the first observations with a telescope.

1643
Torricelli invents the barometer.

1687
Newton describes gravity.

1600
Shakespeare's plays are performed at Globe Theatre in London.

1630
Popcorn is introduced to the Pilgrims by Native Americans.

1658
The first illustrated book for children, *World of Invisible Objects*, is written by John Comenius.

1622
The year begins on January 1, instead of March 25.

1653
The first postage stamps are used in Paris.

1666
A great fire destroys most of London.

1685
The first drinking fountain is used in England.

1605
The first modern novel, *Don Quixote de la Mancha*, is written by Miguel de Cervantes.

1697
Charles Perrault writes *Tales of Mother Goose*.

(English)
350   2,302   26,634   75,058   151,507

1700	1710	1720	1730	1740

U.S. and World History

1700
France builds forts at Mackinac and Detroit to control fur trade.

1712
Carolina is divided into North and South Carolina.

1733
The British Molasses Act places taxes on sugar and molasses.

1718
New Orleans is founded by France.

1707
England (English) and Scotland (Scots) become Great Britain (British).

1747
The Ohio Company is formed to settle the Ohio River Valley.

Science and Inventions

1701
Seed drill that plants seeds in a row is invented by Jethro Tull.

1728
The first dental drill is used by Pierre Fauchard.

1735
Rubber is found in South America.

1709
The pianoforte (first piano) is invented by Christofori Bartolommeo.

1742
Benjamin Franklin invents the efficient Franklin stove.

Literature and Life

1700
The Selling of Joseph by Samuel Sewall is the first book against slavery of Africans.

1718
First hot-water home heating system is developed.

1726
Jonathan Swift writes *Gulliver's Travels*.

1731
Benjamin Franklin begins the first public library.

1704
The *Boston News-Letter* is the first successful newspaper in the American colonies.

1737
An earthquake in Calcutta, India, kills 300,000 people.

U.S. POPULATION: (English Colonies)

250,888	331,711	466,185	629,445	905,563

1750	1760	1770	1780	1790	1800

1750
Flatbed boats and Conestoga wagons begin moving settlers west.

1763
Britain wins the French and Indian War.

1765
The Stamp Act tax is imposed on the colonies by Britain.

1775
The first battles of the Revolutionary War are fought.

1776
The Declaration of Independence is signed on July 4.

1781
The British surrender October 19.

1787
The U.S. Constitution is signed.

1789
The French Revolution begins.

1789
George Washington becomes the first U.S. president.

1752
Benjamin Franklin discovers that lightning is a form of electricity.

1764
"Spinning jenny," a machine for spinning cotton, is invented.

1770
The first steam carriage is invented.

1783
The first hot-air balloon is flown.

1793
Eli Whitney invents the cotton gin to remove the seeds from cotton.

1796
The smallpox vaccine is developed.

1752
The first American hospital is established in Philadelphia.

1757
Streetlights are installed in Philadelphia.

1755
The U.S. Postal Service is established.

1764
Mozart writes his first symphony.

1773
Phillis Wheatley publishes a book of poetry.

1782
The American bald eagle is first used as a symbol of the United States.

1786
The first ice-cream company in America begins production.

1790
The U.S. government takes its first official census.

1791
Benjamin Bannekar surveys the new capital, Washington, D.C.

1,170,760	1,593,625	2,148,076	2,780,369	3,929,157

1800	1810	1820	1830	1840

U.S. and World History

1800
Washington, D.C., becomes the U.S. capital.

1803
The Louisiana Purchase doubles the size of the U.S.

1804
Lewis and Clark explore the Louisiana Territory and the Northwest.

1814
U.S. defeats Britain in the War of 1812.

1819
The U.S. acquires Florida from Spain.

1823
The Monroe Doctrine warns Europe not to interfere in the Western Hemisphere.

1830
Native Americans are forced west by the Indian Removal Act.

1836
Texans defend the Alamo.

1838
The Cherokee Nation is forced west on the "Trail of Tears."

1848
Gold is discovered in California.

Science and Inventions

1800
The battery is invented by Count Volta.

1802
Robert Fulton builds the first steamboat.

1816
The stethoscope is invented.

1816
Joseph Niépce takes the first photograph.

1836
Samuel Morse invents the telegraph.

1839
Kirkpatrick Macmillan invents the bicycle.

1846
Elias Howe invents the sewing machine.

1849
The safety pin is invented.

Literature and Life

1804
The first book of children's poems is published.

1812
Uncle Sam becomes a symbol of the U.S.

1814
Francis Scott Key writes "The Star-Spangled Banner."

1828
The first *Webster's Dictionary* is published.

1834
Louis Braille perfects a writing system for the blind.

1846
Harriet Tubman conducts the Underground Railroad.

1848
Sojourner Truth writes about being a woman.

U.S. POPULATION:

5,308,080	7,240,102	9,638,453	12,860,702	17,063,353

1850	1860	1870	1880	1890	1900

1865
The Civil War ends, and the 13th Amendment to the Constitution ends slavery.

1860
Abraham Lincoln is elected president.

1892
An immigration station is opened at Ellis Island, N.Y.

1869
Immigrant workers complete the coast-to-coast railroad in Utah.

1898
The U.S. defeats Spain in the Spanish-American War.

1876
Custer and the 7th Cavalry are defeated at Little Big Horn.

1861
The Civil War begins.

1870
The 15th Amendment gives African Americans the right to vote.

1851
Isaac Singer produces a sewing machine.

1876
Alexander Graham Bell invents the telephone.

1893
Charles and Frank Duryea build the first successful U.S. gasoline-powered automobile.

1860
Jean Lenoir builds an internal combustion engine.

1879
Thomas Edison invents the lightbulb.

1896
Marconi invents the wireless radio.

1850
Levi Strauss makes the first blue jeans.

1864
The Red Cross is established.

1871
The great Chicago fire destroys the downtown area.

1892
The "Pledge of Allegiance" is written by F. Bellamy.

1886
The Statue of Liberty is erected in New York Harbor to welcome immigrants.

1896
The first movie is shown in the U.S.

1852
Harriet Beecher Stowe's novel *Uncle Tom's Cabin* strengthens the anti-slavery movement.

1869
Chewing gum is patented.

1876
The National Baseball League is established.

1896
The Nobel Prizes for peace, science, and literature are created.

23,191,876	31,443,321	38,558,371	50,189,209	62,979,766

1900	1905	1910	1915	1920

U.S. and World History

1900
Women compete in the Olympics for the first time.

1909
National Association for the Advancement of Colored People (NAACP) is founded.

1917
The U.S. enters World War I.

1917
Puerto Rico becomes a commonwealth of the U.S.

1918
World War I ends in Europe.

1918
The Russian Revolution begins.

1904
One million immigrants arrive in the U.S., mostly from Europe.

1914
The Panama Canal opens.

1920
Women are given the right to vote.

Science and Inventions

1901
Walter Reed discovers yellow fever is carried by mosquitoes.

1903
Orville and Wilbur Wright fly the first successful airplane.

1904
New York City develops a subway system.

1911
Marie Curie wins the Nobel Prize in chemistry.

1912
Garrett Morgan invents automatic traffic light.

1913
Henry Ford establishes the assembly line for making automobiles.

1915
A coast-to-coast telephone system is established.

1921
The tuberculosis vaccine is discovered.

1922
The electron scanner for television is developed.

Literature and Life

1900
The hot dog is created in New York City.

1900
American Baseball League is established.

1903
The first World Series is played.

1905
First nickelodeon movie theater is established in Pittsburgh.

1906
San Francisco suffers a massive earthquake.

1913
Boys Life magazine is published by Boy Scouts.

1912
The *Titanic* strikes an iceberg and sinks.

1913
Arthur Wynne invents the crossword puzzle.

1918
More than 20 million people die in a worldwide flu epidemic.

1923
Bessie Smith, "Empress of the Blues," records her first record.

1920
The first radio station, KDKA, is founded in Pittsburgh.

U.S. POPULATION:
76,212,168   92,228,496   106,021,537

1925	1930	1935	1940	1945	1950

1927
Charles Lindbergh is the first to fly solo across the Atlantic.

1933
Franklin Roosevelt becomes president and enacts the New Deal to end the Depression.

1941
The U.S. enters World War II on Dec. 7.

1945
The United States joins the United Nations.

1925
Nellie Ross is the first woman to be elected governor (Wyoming).

1933
Amelia Earhart is the first woman to fly solo across the Atlantic.

1947
The Marshall Plan is approved to help rebuild war-torn Europe.

1929
Wall Street stock market crashes.

1935
Dennis Chavez becomes the first Hispanic U.S. senator.

1945
World War II ends.

1929
Alexander Fleming develops penicillin.

1938
Modern-type ballpoint pens are developed.

1926
John Baird introduces his television system.

1935
Radar is invented.

1938
The photocopy machine is produced.

1931
The Empire State Building (102 stories, 1,250 feet) is completed as the tallest in the world.

1939
Dr. Charles Drew sets up first blood bank.

1940
Enrico Fermi develops the nuclear reactor.

1925
Potato chips are produced in New York City.

1933
Albert Einstein immigrates to the U.S.

1947
Jackie Robinson becomes the first African American major-league baseball player.

1927
Wings wins the first Academy Award for motion pictures.

1931
"The Star-Spangled Banner" becomes the U.S. national anthem.

1936
Jesse Owens is first person to win four Olympic medals.

1947
Anne Frank's *Diary of a Young Girl* is published.

1938
Superman "Action Comics" are created.

123,202,624   132,164,569

1950	1955	1960	1965	1970

U.S. and World History

1950
The United States enters the Korean War.

1955
The Civil Rights movement begins when Rosa Parks refuses to move to the back of the bus.

1959
Alaska and Hawaii become states.

1965
U.S. troops are sent to Vietnam.

1969
Neil Armstrong and Buzz Aldrin are the first men on the moon.

1954
The Supreme Court bans racial segregation in pubic schools.

1962
Cesar Chavez starts the National Farm Workers Association.

1968
Martin Luther King, Jr., is assassinated.

1954
The Korean War ends.

1963
President John F. Kennedy is assassinated.

Science and Inventions

1954
Jonas Salk develops the polio vaccine.

1960
First laser invented by Theodor Maiman.

1971
The space probe *Mariner* maps the surface of Mars.

1963
Cassette tapes are developed.

1951
Fluoridated water is discovered to prevent tooth decay.

1957
Russia launches the first satellite, *Sputnik I*.

1974
First public application of the Internet.

1958
Stereo long-playing records are produced.

Literature and Life

1950
New York City is the world's largest city, with 8 million people.

1957
Elvis Presley is the most popular rock 'n' roll musician in the U.S.

1964
The Beatles appear on *The Ed Sullivan Show*.

1973
Dr. Martin Cooper makes first call on a cell phone.

1951
Fifteen million American homes have televisions.

1963
Martin Luther King, Jr., delivers "I Have a Dream" speech.

1970
The first Earth Day focuses on protecting the environment.

1955
Disneyland opens.

U.S. POPULATION:
151,325,798

179,323,175

203,302,031

| 1975 | 1980 | 1985 | 1990 | 1995 | 2000 |

1975
The Vietnam War ends.

1981
U.S. hostages are returned from Iran after 444 days.

1989
The Berlin Wall in Germany is torn down.

1995
More than 23 million people living in the U.S. were born in other countries.

1981
Sandra Day O'Connor becomes the first woman Supreme Court Justice.

1991
The Soviet Union becomes a commonwealth of 10 independent nations.

1979
Iran seizes U.S. hostages.

1983
Sally Ride becomes the first U.S. woman in space.

1991
Persian Gulf War "Operation Desert Storm" begins.

1976
The Concorde is the first supersonic passenger jet.

1984
Compact discs (CD's) are developed.

1991
Scientists report a growing danger of a hole in the earth's ozone layer.

1977
Apple Computer produces first personal computer.

1997
First DVD player introduced in U.S.

1981
Scientists identify AIDS.

1987
Dr. Ben Carson is first doctor to separate Siamese twins joined at the head.

1999
Scientists map the first chromosome.

1976
An earthquake in Tangshan, China, kills 240,000 people.

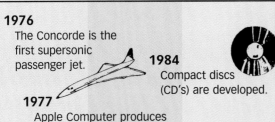

1986
Martin Luther King, Jr., Day is proclaimed a national holiday.

1993
In the New York City school district, more than 100 languages are spoken.

1976
The U.S. celebrates 200 years as a nation.

1994
Walk Two Moons wins the Newbery Award.

1987
The Whipping Boy wins the Newbery Award.

1994
Zlata's Diary: A Child's Life in Sarajevo, by a Bosnian teenager, is a bestseller in the U.S.

1979
Yellow ribbons symbolize support for return of U.S. hostages in Iran.

226,542,203   248,709,873

2000

U.S. and World History

2001
George W. Bush becomes first son of a president to take office since John Quincy Adams in 1825.

2003
The U.S. invades Iraq.

2001
U.S. forces invade Afghanistan and remove the Taliban regime from power.

2003
The space shuttle *Columbia* breaks apart during reentry.

2001
Terrorist-flown planes destroy the World Trade Center in NYC and hit the Pentagon in Washington, D.C.

Science and Inventions

2000
The U.S. Food and Drug Administration approves a new glucose (blood sugar) monitor.

2001
President Bush allows limited funding for stem-cell research.

Literature and Life

2000
The U.S. population reaches 285 million.

2002
Former president Jimmy Carter wins the Nobel Peace Prize.

2000
Wildfire burns over 7,000,000 acres of land in the western United States.

2002
Winter Olympics held at Salt Lake City, Utah.

U.S. POPULATION:
287,109,706

Credits

Page 21 Excerpt from *Catfish and Mandala*, by Andrew X. Pham. Copyright © 1999 by Andrew X. Pham. Reprinted with permission of Farrar, Straus and Giroux, LLC.

Page 21 Passage from *The Short Sweet Dream of Eduardo Gutiérrez* by Jimmy Breslin. Published by Random House, Inc.

Page 22 Excerpt from *Newsweek,* December 27, 1982, "What's Wrong with Black English?" by Rachel L. Jones. Reprinted by permission of Tribune Media Services.

Page 22 Reprinted with permission of Simon & Schuster Adult Publishing Group from *A Beautiful Mind:* A Biography of John Forbes Nash, Jr., by Sylvia Nasar. Copyright © 1998 by Sylvia Nasar.

Page 23 Excerpt from *An American Story* by Debra J. Dickerson. Published by Random House, Inc.

Page 23 Reprinted with the permission of The Free Press, A Division of Simon & Schuster Adult Publishing Group, from *A Personal Odyssey* by Thomas Sowell. Copyright © 2000 by Thomas Sowell.

Page 34 An excerpt from *Starting with "I"* by Youth Communications. Copyright © 1997 by Youth Communications. Reprinted by permission of Persea Books, Inc. (New York)

Page 34 An excerpt from novelist Robert Cormier from the book titled *How Writers Write* by Pamela Lloyd. Copyright © 1987 by Pamela Lloyd. Reproduced courtesy of Thomson Learning Australia.

Page 131 From *Always Running—La Vida Loca, Gang Days in L.A.* by Luis J. Rodriguez. (Curbstone Press, 1993) Reprinted with permission of Curbstone Press.

Page 216 Selection from "Truth Surfaces About a Nazi Submarine" by Cliff Tarpy. Reprinted with permission of National Geographic Society.

Pages 268 From *The World Book Encyclopedia*. Copyright 1997 by World Book, Inc. Reprinted with permission of the publisher.

Page 318 From *The New Roget's Thesaurus in Dictionary Form,* edited by Norman Lewis. Reprinted with permission of Penguin Putnam Inc.

Page 320 Copyright © 2000 by Houghton Mifflin Company. Reproduced by permission from *The American Heritage College Dictionary, Third Edition.*

Pages 474-475 From *The World Book Encyclopedia*. Copyright 1997 by World Book, Inc. Reprinted by permission of the publisher.

The publishers have made every effort to locate the owners of all copyrighted works and to obtain permission to reprint them. Any errors or omissions are unintentional and corrections will be made in future printings if necessary.

Index

The **index** will help you find specific information in the handbook. Entries in italics are words from the "Commonly Misused Words" section.